Contributions to Management Science

The series *Contributions to Management Science* contains research publications in all fields of business and management science. These publications are primarily monographs and multiple author works containing new research results, and also feature selected conference-based publications are also considered. The focus of the series lies in presenting the development of latest theoretical and empirical research across different viewpoints.

This book series is indexed in Scopus.

Florinda Matos • Carmine Basile
Ludo Pyis • Leif Edvinsson • Göran Roos
Editors

Intellectual Capital in a Global Business Landscape

Unlocking Strategic Opportunities and Driving Growth

Springer

Editors
Florinda Matos
DINÂMIA'CET-IUL – ISCTE – University Institute of Lisbon
Lisbon, Portugal

Carmine Basile
The AREOPA Group
Brussels, Belgium

Ludo Pyis
The AREOPA Group
Brussels, Belgium

Leif Edvinsson
Lund University
Stockholm, Sweden

Göran Roos
Intellectual Capital Services Limited
Buckingham, UK

ISSN 1431-1941 ISSN 2197-716X (electronic)
Contributions to Management Science
ISBN 978-3-031-86361-5 ISBN 978-3-031-86362-2 (eBook)
https://doi.org/10.1007/978-3-031-86362-2

This Springer imprint is published by the registered company Springer Nature Switzerland AG
The registered company address is: Gewerbestrasse 11, 6330 Cham, Switzerland

Preface

According to Professor Nicklas Lundblad (from Google DeepMind), a crucial factor is the speed of questioning, which is closely linked to the ancient skill of *Quizzics*—the art and science of asking questions. Inspired by this key idea from Professor Lundblad, this book will introduce you to some thought-provoking aspects of the landscape of Intellectual Capital (IC).

IC can be associated with what Leonardo da Vinci referred to as *Saper Vedere* ("knowing how to see"), and it can also be integrated with a new form of Artificial Intelligence, which, beyond simply being artificial intelligence, also represents Apple intelligence.

This dimension of Apple Intelligence is particularly fascinating. It may trace back to Steve Jobs' ideas on ergonomics and the design philosophy behind Apple and Macintosh. What we are moving towards is a new form of artful design for the unknown, much like the works of Victor Vasarely and digital art. And this is, perhaps, more user friendly. As a result, we are witnessing the rapid growth of AI today. We also observe that companies like Apple have been overtaken in value by Nvidia and others. It has become a kind of "Formula One" race among AI companies, each competing to reduce the "not knowing" at the highest speed.

This also leads to the need for future centres and the navigation of futurized knowledge. This is an area I have been working on for a long time. This book is primarily about the intellectual capital of futurizing, offering a kaleidoscope of different perspectives.

Now, enjoy the reading! It presents a global landscape of IC aspects. With that, I wish you happy reading, happy discovery, and, most importantly, a swift embrace of the future.

Lund University
Stockholm, Sweden

Leif Edvinsson

About the Book

Why publish a book with the title *Intellectual Capital in a Global Business Landscape—Unlocking Strategic Opportunities and Driving Growth*?

The global landscape faces unprecedented complexity in the coming years. Whilst companies remain the primary drivers of economic growth, they confront mounting challenges alongside broader societal concerns.

In today's rapidly evolving business environment, organisational success increasingly hinges upon adaptability and swift response to change. The strategic management of intellectual capital has emerged as a crucial lever for enhancing digital competitiveness whilst advancing the United Nations' sustainability agenda.

Corporate longevity and expansion now fundamentally depend upon foresight and future-readiness, necessitating resilient strategies that enable continuous adaptation. This volume, drawing upon insights from distinguished business leaders and academics, offers guidance on intellectual capital management best practices whilst helping organisations anticipate forthcoming challenges.

The conclusions presented herein represent merely an initial exploration of this vast subject. Indeed, each chapter raises questions warranting further scholarly examination, suggesting numerous avenues for future research and discourse.

The Editors

Contents

About the Editors

Florinda Matos is a Professor of General Management at Iscte Business School, Iscte—University Institute of Lisbon, and an associate research fellow at DINÂMIA'CET—IUL—Centre for Socioeconomic and Territorial Studies, where she leads several international projects. She is an expert in knowledge management and intellectual capital management. Additionally, she is the founder and president of the Intellectual Capital Association (ICAA) and she is an ambassador for Portugal in The New Club of Paris.

Carmine Basile heads the Institute of Innovation & Intellectual Capital at the AREOPA Group. He holds an MSc in Knowledge Management for Innovation and a PhD in Strategy & Leadership, both from Cranfield University. He has taught Strategic Marketing, Market Understanding and Team Behaviour to EMBAs, Master Students and Executives, and led the Cranfield Customer Management focus, a club of organisations from a wide range of sectors working together to drive forward best practice in customer management.

Ludo Pyis started his own company in the early 1990s, the AREOPA Group. Today, the AREOPA Group is the global leader in the field of knowledge management and intellectual capital. He is a respected keynote speaker on topics of intellectual accounting systems and heads two research and development centres for the creation of new applications in the field of intellectual capital.

Leif Edvinsson is a key pioneering contributor to Intellectual Capital (IC) theory and practice. He was the world's first Director of IC in 1991. He was responsible for prototyping in 1996 the Skandia Future Centre as a Lab for Organisational design. In 1998, he was awarded the Brain Trust "Brain of the Year" award, UK. He is listed in "Who's Who in the World", he's an earlier associate member of the Club of Rome and the co-founder and founding chairman of the New Club of Paris. In 2013, he was awarded the Thought Leader Award by the European Commission, Intel and the Peter Drucker Association. In 2015, he was appointed to the Advisory Board of JIN, the Japan Innovation Network, and, in 2016, to the Advisory Board of Norway

Open Innovation Forum. Together with the UN, he was awarded the KM Award 2017, in Geneva Palais des Nations, by km-a.net. He is a regular guest speaker at international events and organisations, including the BBC, CIO, INSEAD, and the American Productivity and Quality Centre.

Göran Roos is managing director of Intellectual Capital Services Limited, Adjunct Professor at the Institute for Sustainability, Energy and Resources (ISER), The University of Adelaide and Part-Time Visiting Professor in Business Performance and Intangible Asset Management, Centre for Business Performance, Cranfield School of Management, Cranfield University. He is a CSIRO Affiliate as well as a fellow of the Australian Academy of Technological Sciences and Engineering (ATSE) and of the Royal Swedish Academy of Engineering Sciences (IVA).

Introduction

Florinda Matos and Göran Roos

The evolution of business value creation has fundamentally shifted towards balancing profit generation with societal well-being, establishing sustainability as a cornerstone of contemporary business models. This transformation necessitates significant changes in organisational management approaches, particularly in how organisations leverage their intangible assets—commonly referred to as intellectual capital.

Research has demonstrated that organisations that centre their business models on effective intellectual capital management create sustainable value while improving their environmental and social impact. A notable framework proposed by Matos et al. (2019) introduced the 'IC 5P for the future' concept, aligning intellectual capital management with United Nations principles of People, Planet, Prosperity, Peace, and Partnership. However, despite this framework's potential, progress in business

F. Matos (✉)
DINÂMIA'CET-IUL – ISCTE – University Institute of Lisbon, Lisbon, Portugal

ICLab – ICAA – Intellectual Capital Association, Santarém, Portugal

The New Club of Paris, Vienna, Austria
e-mail: florinda.matos@iscte-iul.pt

G. Roos
Intellectual Capital Services Limited, Buckingham, UK

Institute for Sustainability, Energy and Resources (ISER), The University of Adelaide, Adelaide, Australia

School of Communication, Leadership and Marketing, Kristiania University College—Ernst G Mortensen Foundation, Oslo, Norway

Centre for Business Performance, Cranfield School of Management, Cranfield University, Bedford, UK
e-mail: goran@roos.org.uk

F. Matos et al. (eds.), *Intellectual Capital in a Global Business Landscape*, Contributions to Management Science, https://doi.org/10.1007/978-3-031-86362-2_1

model transformation and value creation has been limited and, in some instances, regressed.

Multiple factors have contributed to this stagnation. Global challenges including the COVID-19 pandemic, geopolitical conflicts such as the Ukrainian War, the rapid advancement of artificial intelligence, escalating climate disasters, and increasing social unrest have created a complex operating environment for organisations. These challenges have highlighted both the significance and complexity of sustainable business transformation.

Numerous organisations remain hesitant to prioritise long-term sustainability over immediate profitability. Similarly, consumer behaviour continues to be primarily driven by short-term considerations such as price and trends, rather than accounting for broader social and environmental impacts. This misalignment between current practices and sustainable imperatives presents significant risks to both human welfare and planetary health.

This volume examines how intellectual capital management can accelerate the transition towards sustainable business practices. Through its chapters, it provides a comprehensive analysis of how organisations can leverage their intellectual assets to create lasting value while meeting contemporary sustainability challenges. This introductory chapter specifically focuses on tracing the evolution of value creation through the lens of intellectual capital management, establishing a foundation for the detailed discussions that follow.

1 Setting the Stage: The Transformation of Business Value

1.1 The Shifting Paradigm of Value Creation

Historical Perspective on Business Value Creation

The conceptualisation of business value creation has evolved significantly throughout the economic history. During the Industrial Revolution, scholars focused primarily on physical capital and labour as value creators (Mokyr, 2018), as reflected in Smith's (1776) work on wealth creation through labour specialisation and capital accumulation.

A significant shift occurred in the early twentieth century with Taylor's scientific management principles, though still emphasising tangible assets (Nelson, 1974). Penrose's (1959) post-war research introduced firm-specific resources as crucial value creation determinants. The 1980s brought theoretical advancement through the resource-based view (Wernerfelt, 1984; Barney, 1991), coinciding with growing market-to-book ratios suggesting increased importance of intangible assets (Lev, 2000).

The knowledge economy's emergence transformed value creation understanding further, with Stewart's (1997) work on intellectual capital establishing knowledge assets as primary value drivers. Blair and Wallman (2000) demonstrated that by the century's end, intangible assets comprised up to 85% of corporate market value in leading economies. Contemporary perspectives now encompass stakeholder theory (Freeman et al., 2010) and digital value creation through platform economics (Parker et al., 2016), challenging traditional value chain models.

The Rise of Intangible Assets as Primary Value Drivers

The emergence of intangible assets as primary value drivers marks a fundamental shift in business economics since the 1980s, evidenced by growing disparities between book values and market capitalisations (Lev, 2000). Hall (2001) demonstrated this through market value per employee significantly exceeding tangible asset replacement costs. Nakamura's (2001) research revealed US businesses were investing $1 trillion annually in intangible assets, matching traditional capital investment levels. Corrado et al. (2009) confirmed intangible assets as crucial growth drivers in advanced economies.

Information technology and digitalisation have accelerated this trend and, in turn, created new forms of intangible value while diminishing physical assets' importance (Haskel & Westlake, 2018). Platform-based business models exemplify value generation with minimal tangible assets (Brynjolfsson & McAfee, 2014). Haskel and Westlake (2018) identified four key properties of intangible assets, i.e. scalability, sunkness, spillovers, and synergies, significantly impacting business strategy and competition.

Recent analysis by Ocean Tomo (2020), updating Elsten and Hill (2017), showed intangible assets comprising 90% of S&P 500 companies' market value in 2020, compared to 17% in 1975, necessitating new approaches to business valuation and management (Lev & Gu, 2016).

Current Statistics on Intangible vs. Tangible Assets in Modern Economies

World Intellectual Property Organization (WIPO) World Intellectual Property Report (2022) indicates intangible assets comprise one-third of global value chain production value (USD 5.9 trillion in 2014), with investment growing threefold compared to tangible assets, reaching USD 4.7 trillion in 2023. In the United States, Corrado et al. (2022) report intangible investment reached 18.6% of gross domestic product (GDP) in 2019, exceeding tangible investment, which was only at 13.4%.

European markets show similar trends, with Brand Finance (2022) reporting intangible assets representing 74% of total enterprise value for listed companies. Haskel and Westlake (2022) note UK businesses invest £169 billion annually in intangible assets versus £118 billion in tangible assets.

Sectoral analysis reveals technology and healthcare sectors leading in intangible intensity (Peters & Taylor, 2017). Brand Finance (2022) reports sector-specific intangible asset proportions: technology (90%), healthcare (87%), financial services (79%), industrial manufacturing (67%), and utilities (43%).

Cross-country comparisons show geographical variations, with the US, UK, and Nordic countries leading in intangible asset intensity (OECD, 2021). China's industrial sector invested 14% of value added in intangible assets by 2013 (Hao & Wu, 2021), comparable to the United Kingdom and approximately 70% of US levels.

2 Understanding Intellectual Capital in Contemporary Business

2.1 Conceptual Framework of Intellectual Capital

Defining Intellectual Capital in the Modern Context

Edvinsson and Malone (1997) define intellectual capital as the possession of knowledge, applied experience, organisational technology, customer relationships, and professional skills providing competitive advantage. Dean and Kretschmer (2007) critique the term 'capital' as inconsistently applied within this domain.

Two principal taxonomic approaches emerge: Martín-de-Castro et al. (2011), following Edvinsson and Malone (1997), propose human, structural, and relational capital. Alternatively, Roos et al. (2005) present monetary, physical, relational, organisational, and human resources. Dumay (2016) emphasises intellectual capital's dynamic nature as a system enabling sustainable value creation, while Ballow et al. (2004a, b, c) distinguish between intangible assets and intellectual capital. This asset is 'understood as an intangible, a renewable and a manageable asset, available at micro-level (individuals and organisations) and at a macro level (cities, regions and countries), that can be managed to create sustainable wealth' (Matos et al., 2019, p. 4).

The digital era introduced new elements, with Cuozzo et al. (2017) identifying components like big data analytics, digital platform orchestration, and ecosystem positioning. Giuliani (2015) advocates for context-dependent assessment approaches, supported by Inkinen's (2015) research demonstrating synergistic interaction between different dimensions. Roos (2019) further contributes by identifying distinct characteristics for each resource category, including ownership, economic behaviour, and strategic logic, though measurement challenges persist due to nonadditive nature and context-dependent value creation (Roos et al., 2005).

Key Components: Human, Structural, and Relational Capital

The tripartite framework of intellectual capital has evolved considerably since Edvinsson and Malone (1997). Initially categorised into structural and human capital by early practitioners (Edvinsson & Sullivan, 1996), the framework expanded to include relational capital (Roos & Roos, 1997).

Human capital comprises competencies and capabilities within the workforce, defined as 'useful resources embodied in people' (Roos et al., 2005). Ployhart and Moliterno (2011), Bloom and Van Reenen (2007, 2010), and Bloom et al. (2012) demonstrate how human capital emerges through aggregation of individual capabilities. Organisational capital (formerly structural capital) represents company-owned assets including processes, systems, and intellectual property, enabling knowledge retention (Kianto et al., 2013).

Relational capital encompasses organisational relationships characterised by co-controlled nature and network behaviour (Roos, 2019). Building on Nahapiet and Ghoshal's (1998) work, empirical research by Cabrita and Bontis (2008) and Kotabe et al. (2003) demonstrates these resources' significance in value creation. This modern framework provides theoretical grounding while maintaining practical applicability (Pike et al., 2005; Kraaijenbrink et al., 2010).

Research by Matos et al. (2022) demonstrates that organisations with substantial relational capital exhibit enhanced capacity to navigate periods of turbulence and crisis, while simultaneously strengthening their organisational resilience. The development of relational capital and subsequent improvement in adaptive capabilities are fundamentally supported by key factors in stakeholder relationships, including inter-organisational cooperation, collaborative practices, established trust networks, and effective communication channels. These elements collectively contribute to an organisation's capacity to respond to environmental changes and maintain operational continuity during periods of uncertainty.

Evolution of Intellectual Capital Theory and Practice

The theoretical development of intellectual capital has evolved through distinct phases since its origins in resource-based accounting (Robinson, 1933; Chamberlin, 1933). The term was first used by Galbraith in 1969 (Hudson, 1993), though early development was primarily practitioner-led (Kaufmann & Schneider, 2004).

Key development stages include Initial Formation (1980s–1996), marked by resource-based theory emergence and Scandinavian practitioner influence (Edvinsson & Sullivan, 1996); Academic Development (1997–2004), focusing on classification systems and dynamic perspectives (Marr & Chatzkel, 2004); and Critical Examination (2004–present), emphasising measurement frameworks and practical application (Guthrie et al., 2012; Dumay & Garanina, 2013).

Recent developments reflect sophisticated understanding of knowledge assets, including systems theory integration (Cosenz & Noto, 2016), management tool development (Roos, 2014a), and business model innovation (O'Connor & Roos, 2018). Measurement approaches have evolved to incorporate multiple stakeholder perspectives (Pike & Roos, 2004, 2007), suggesting continued integration with strategic management practice (Kraaijenbrink et al., 2010).

2.2 *The Interconnection with Business Model Innovation*

Impact of Intellectual Capital on Business Model Transformation

The relationship between intellectual capital and business model transformation interlinks fundamentally with competitive advantage (Teece, 2018). Zott and Amit (2010) identify three mechanisms, i.e. value creation architecture, capture mechanisms, and network organisation, encompassing resource configuration, revenue development, and ecosystem orchestration.

Beattie and Smith (2013) demonstrate how effective intellectual capital deployment enables innovative value propositions and sustainable revenue streams. In digital contexts, Bharadwaj et al. (2013) show intellectual capital enabling platform development and service transformation through algorithm-based value creation and knowledge-intensive services.

Schiuma (2010) emphasises successful transformation requires orchestrating human capital for innovation, structural capital for efficiency, and relational capital for ecosystem engagement.

Role of Intellectual Capital in Sustainable Business Models

Intellectual capital fundamentally enables sustainable business models through specific mechanisms (Boons & Lüdeke-Freund, 2013). Bocken et al. (2014) identify key areas including knowledge-based innovation for sustainable design and circular economy expertise, alongside organisational learning for sustainability competence (Roos, 2014).

Evans et al. (2017) outline intellectual capital components supporting sustainability: human capital (environmental expertise, stakeholder management), structural capital (sustainable processes, measurement systems), and relational capital (sustainability partnerships, industrial symbiosis) (Agarwal & Strachan, 2008). Geissdoerfer et al. (2018) identify three mechanisms: resource optimisation through circular management (Ayres, 1994), stakeholder integration (Frosch & Gallopoulos, 1989), and innovation capability for sustainable solutions (Roos, 2011).

The circular economy implementation requires specific intellectual capital configurations maximising multiple profit pools (Roos, 2014) while addressing social dilemmas through waste hierarchy approaches (European Union, 2008).

3 The Digital Transformation Imperative

3.1 Digital Technologies as Intellectual Capital Enablers

Key Digital Technologies Affecting Intellectual Capital Management

Digital technologies have transformed organisational intellectual capital management (Bharadwaj et al., 2013). George et al. (2014) demonstrate artificial intelligence (AI)'s enhancement of knowledge discovery through pattern recognition and decision support via algorithm-based analysis. Cloud technologies enable scalable knowledge storage and collaboration (Wang et al., 2016), while big data analytics facilitate customer behaviour analysis and predictive modelling (McAfee et al., 2012).

Porter and Heppelmann (2014) identify Internet of Things (IoT)'s contribution through real-time data collection and operational intelligence. Blockchain technology impacts intellectual capital management via knowledge authentication and trust management through smart contracts (Risius & Spohrer, 2017).

Data as a New Form of Intellectual Capital

Data has evolved into a core strategic asset beyond traditional operational by-products (Mayer-Schönberger & Cukier, 2013). Alharthi et al. (2017) identify distinct characteristics including non-rivalrous consumption, increasing returns, and network effects, alongside management requirements for accumulation, quality, and security.

Günther et al. (2017) outline three value creation mechanisms: direct (product innovation, process optimisation), indirect (ecosystem orchestration, platform development), and transformative (business model innovation, market creation). Abbasi et al. (2016) emphasise critical management components through governance structures (ownership frameworks, quality control) and technical infrastructure (storage, analytics platforms).

Matos et al. (2020b) proposed a data-driven Intellectual Capital Management Scoring System to be used in the auditing of the IC management of organisations. The authors demonstrate that the use of data collection and statistical treatment can support a reliable system to audit intellectual capital management.

Digital Platforms and Ecosystem Thinking

Digital platforms fundamentally transform organisational value creation through networked interactions (Gawer & Cusumano, 2014). Parker et al. (2016) identify core elements: technical architecture (interaction enablement, boundary resources), governance structure (participation rules, value appropriation), and economic properties (network effects, market coordination).

Jacobides et al. (2018) outline value creation through complementarity management and ecosystem orchestration, while Tiwana (2013) emphasises architecture design and governance mechanisms. Platforms represent sophisticated resource deployment systems combining organisational and relational resources (Fernström et al., 2004, Roos et al., 2005), guided by value network and shop logic (Roos, 2018). The IC Navigator approach demonstrates how platforms orchestrate resource transformations for competitive advantage through network effects (Roos, 2014a, 2017, 2018).

3.2 *Challenges and Opportunities in the Digital Age*

Digital Transformation of Intellectual Capital Management

The digital transformation of intellectual capital represents a fundamental organisational shift (Vial, 2021). Key dimensions include knowledge creation and capture, where organisations leverage advanced technologies for systematic accumulation (Sambamurthy et al., 2003), enhanced by real-time data collection (George et al., 2014). AI systems enable novel insight generation through pattern recognition (Brynjolfsson & McAfee, 2017) and facilitate collaborative knowledge creation (Faraj et al., 2011).

Knowledge storage has evolved through cloud-based repositories (Leonardi, 2014) and semantic networks (Kane et al., 2015). Von Krogh (2018) identifies how AI systems transform traditional knowledge management through natural language processing and content generation. Frey and Osborne (2017) demonstrate AI's role in knowledge synthesis, augmentation, and scaling, while Haenlein and Kaplan (2019) emphasise balancing AI insights with human expertise.

Successful transformation requires structural and process adaptations (Kane et al., 2019). Structurally, organisations must develop digital capabilities (Yeow et al., 2018), enable cross-functional integration (Leonardi, 2017), and adopt agile methodologies (Rigby et al., 2020). Process transformations include workflow digitisation (Baptista et al., 2020), knowledge automation (Leonardi & Vaast, 2017), and digital value creation (Hess et al., 2016).

Key challenges span technical domains—legacy integration (Gregory et al., 2015), data quality (Wang & Strong, 1996), security (Dhillon et al., 2016)—and organisational aspects, i.e. skill development (Kane et al., 2016), change management (Besson & Rowe, 2012), and cultural transformation (Hartl & Hess, 2017). Leadership and digital upskilling alignment remains crucial for addressing these challenges (Sia et al., 2016; Matos et al., 2020a, b).

Digital Capabilities as Competitive Advantages

Digital capabilities provide sustainable competitive advantage through operational efficiency and innovation (Bharadwaj et al., 2013). From an intellectual capital perspective, this involves transforming human and organisational resources into relational and monetary resources under value network logic (Fernström et al., 2004; Roos et al., 2005; Roos, 2019).

Teece (2018) demonstrates how digital capabilities function as dynamic capabilities across technology exploitation, innovation, analytics, and ecosystem orchestration. Karimi and Walter (2015) show organisations with superior digital capabilities achieve enhanced efficiency and customer relationships, illustrating the interaction between organisational and human resources in resource deployment systems (Roos et al., 2005).

Successful development requires structured approaches including strategic planning, architecture development, and talent acquisition (Hess et al., 2016), alongside dynamic capabilities development (Mrkwicka & Schögel, 2016). The IC Navigator approach reveals how digital capabilities emerge from organisational and human resource interaction, typically evolving from value shop to network logic (Fernström et al., 2004; Roos, 2014a, 2017, 2018).

4 Sustainability as a Strategic Driver

4.1 The Sustainability–Intellectual Capital Nexus

Integration of Sustainability into Intellectual Capital Management

The integration of sustainability into intellectual capital management represents a fundamental organisational shift (Boons & Lüdeke-Freund, 2013; Matos et al., 2019). Eccles et al. (2014) demonstrate how high-sustainability organisations develop distinct approaches to managing intellectual capital. Key pathways include capturing sustainability practices (Hart & Dowell, 2011), developing sustainable innovation capabilities (Adams et al., 2016), and integrating stakeholder perspectives (Sharma & Henriques, 2005).

Chen (2008) introduces green intellectual capital comprising human, structural, and relational elements, while Kianto et al. (2014) emphasise renewal capital through research partnerships and innovation programmes. Melville (2010) examines the technology's role in supporting environmental initiatives, and Baba et al. (2009) document cross-sector collaboration importance.

This transformation spans human resources (environmental expertise), organisational resources (knowledge repositories), and relational resources (stakeholder engagement), requiring distinct renewal capabilities (Kianto et al., 2014) and sophisticated measurement mechanisms (Maas et al., 2016). The effectiveness bridges environmental, social, and economic value creation (Boons & Lüdeke-Freund, 2013).

Environmental and Social Aspects of Intellectual Capital

Environmental and social dimensions of intellectual capital have become critical for organisational management (Hart & Dowell, 2011). Building on Chen's (2008) green intellectual capital framework, research has expanded across multiple dimensions.

Environmental human capital encompasses expertise, innovation capabilities and sustainability competencies (Chen, 2008), with Renwick et al. (2013) emphasising green HR practices. Environmental structural capital integrates sustainability into the core processes (Eccles et al., 2014), incorporating analytics and artificial intelligence (Melville, 2010; Nishant et al., 2020) and circular economy principles (Geissdoerfer et al., 2017).

Environmental relational capital extends to multi-stakeholder initiatives (Gray & Stites, 2013) and community engagement (Boiral et al., 2020). Albertini (2019) introduces 'green dynamic capabilities' for addressing evolving environmental challenges. Friede et al. (2015) demonstrate positive relationships between environmental, social, and governance (ESG) criteria and financial performance, highlighting environmental intellectual capital's strategic importance.

4.2 *Creating Sustainable Value Through Intellectual Capital*

Sustainable Innovation and Intellectual Capital

The relationship between sustainable innovation and intellectual capital remains crucial in organisational management, building on Adams et al. (2016). Bocken et al. (2014) identify key mechanisms including sustainability-oriented research and development (R&D) and eco-innovation capabilities. Inigo and Albareda (2019) emphasise sustainability-oriented absorptive capacity for eco-innovation.

Pieroni et al. (2019) propose a framework for sustainable business model innovation, while Chen (2008) introduces 'green intellectual capital', contributing to environmental performance (Yusliza et al., 2020) and competitive advantage (Astuti & Datrini, 2021). Mady et al. (2023) explore synergies between knowledge management and sustainability practices.

Geissdoerfer et al. (2018) develop frameworks for sustainable circular business models, emphasising collaborative networks and transformative solutions. Parida and Wincent (2019) investigate digitalisation's role in sustainable business model innovation, particularly in circular economy contexts.

5 Future Perspectives and Research Agenda

5.1 Emerging Trends and Challenges

The landscape of intellectual capital (IC) management is undergoing significant transformation, influenced by globalisation, sustainability imperatives, digitalisation, and increasing interconnectivity. Contemporary developments in the digital economy, distributed work arrangements, and open innovation frameworks are fundamentally altering the mechanisms through which organisations create, maintain, and disseminate knowledge within their IC management structures.

The emergence of the knowledge economy has precipitated a departure from conventional employment paradigms, compelling organisations to reconceptualise their approaches to talent acquisition, development, and retention. Traditional human capital management methodologies are being critically examined, necessitating the development of novel strategies for workforce integration, professional development, and knowledge preservation.

The COVID-19 pandemic has accelerated the adoption and legitimisation of remote work practices, introducing multifaceted challenges in the management of human, structural, and particularly relational capital. Organisations face complex imperatives in maintaining workforce engagement, facilitating knowledge transfer, protecting intellectual property, ensuring operational reliability, and managing stakeholder relationships in virtual environments. This shift has elevated the strategic importance of technological infrastructure as a critical component of structural capital.

The efficacy of remote operations necessitates sophisticated technological systems that facilitate collaborative work, secure information exchange, and performance evaluation while fostering cohesion and shared purpose among geographically dispersed teams. These systems must integrate seamlessly with existing organisational processes while supporting new modes of work.

The open innovation paradigm, which promotes external collaboration to catalyse internal innovation, presents significant opportunities for knowledge leverage. However, this approach introduces substantial risks regarding data security and intellectual property protection. Successfully navigating this complex landscape requires organisations to implement robust governance frameworks and strengthen relational capital through the development of trust mechanisms, communication protocols, and shared operational norms.

Additional challenges emerge from the need to address cultural and institutional variations in global markets while safeguarding intellectual property and maintaining ethical standards. Responding effectively to these trends and challenges requires organisations to adopt adaptive and innovative approaches aligned with Sustainable Development Goals, implementing human-centred technological solutions that balance economic imperatives with broader societal considerations.

5.2 *Future Scenarios for Intellectual Capital Management*

The future landscape of intellectual capital (IC) management is likely to undergo substantial transformation, driven by technological advancement—particularly artificial intelligence—and the imperative to address climate-related challenges through social and economic adaptation. Several key scenarios merit examination.

Expansion of Relational Capital

Organisational success will increasingly depend upon the cultivation of global partnerships and networks to access critical knowledge and resources. These collaborative networks will prove essential for research, development, and innovation activities, facilitating the growth of open innovation practices. The rapid development of COVID-19 vaccines exemplifies how such networks can accelerate innovation through collaborative effort. Organisations must consequently develop sophisticated frameworks and methodologies to effectively manage and evaluate these complex relationships.

Evolution of Green Intellectual Capital

Sustainability considerations are becoming increasingly central to IC strategy development. The transition towards circular economy models necessitates the development of 'circular intellectual capital'—a framework that enables environmentally conscious management across all aspects of the value chain. As organisations face mounting pressure to align with global sustainability objectives, IC management becomes crucial for developing sustainability competencies and implementing effective environmental management practices. Key areas of focus are as follows:

- Human capital development in sustainability, renewable energy, critical thinking, and artificial intelligence
- Structural capital enhancement through sophisticated knowledge repositories and data management systems
- Relational capital cultivation through expanded global sustainability networks

Advancement in Personalisation of Intellectual Capital Management

The emergence of sophisticated artificial intelligence technologies, particularly generative AI, is enabling increasingly personalised approaches to IC management. These technologies facilitate:

- Customised knowledge acquisition
- Predictive analysis of emerging competencies
- Enhanced stakeholder engagement through personalised interactions
- Proactive strategy development based on trend analysis

This technological capability suggests a shift towards predictive IC management frameworks that enable organisations to anticipate emerging trends and implement proactive strategies to mitigate potential operational disruptions.

5.3 *Impact of Emerging Technologies*

Emerging technologies, including artificial intelligence, blockchain, augmented reality, and quantum computing, are fundamentally transforming intellectual capital (IC) management, reshaping organisational approaches to knowledge creation, management, protection, and application. These technologies present both opportunities and challenges for contemporary organisations.

Artificial Intelligence Applications

Artificial intelligence technologies enhance organisational decision-making processes through real-time data management and task automation. When effectively implemented, AI systems enable human capital to shift focus from routine operations to higher-value activities, including creative endeavours and strategic planning initiatives. This reallocation of human resources potentially enhances organisational innovation capacity and strategic effectiveness.

Blockchain Infrastructure

Blockchain technology provides robust solutions for secure and transparent knowledge sharing, particularly within collaborative networks. This technology strengthens both structural and relational capital through:

- Systematic documentation of key organisational processes
- Enhanced supply chain transparency
- Secure intellectual property protection mechanisms
- Improved trust in inter-organisational relationships

Augmented Reality Implementation

Augmented reality technology contributes to multiple aspects of IC development:

- Human capital enhancement through immersive training, particularly in high-risk operational environments
- Structural capital optimisation via process simulation and refinement
- Relational capital development through enhanced customer engagement, including personalised product demonstrations and innovative marketing approaches

Quantum Computing Potential

Quantum computing presents significant opportunities for IC development through its capacity to address complex optimisation challenges. Its enhanced data processing capabilities support:

- Advanced innovation processes
- Sophisticated financial management systems
- Enhanced cybersecurity protocols
- Complex pattern recognition and analysis

Implementation Challenges

Despite their transformative potential, these technological advances present significant challenges as follows:

- Cybersecurity risk management
- Ethical data utilisation
- Workforce adaptation and skills development
- Integration with existing systems and processes

The deployment of these technologies requires careful consideration of both their potential benefits and associated risks, necessitating comprehensive strategic planning and robust governance frameworks.

5.4 Evolution of Business Models and Value Creation

Contemporary business models are experiencing a fundamental shift from traditional frameworks towards value network-based structures, positioning intellectual capital management as a critical component of organisational strategy. This transformation represents a significant departure from conventional management paradigms, with organisations increasingly adopting customer-centric and service-oriented approaches in place of product-centric models.

In this evolving landscape, the role of customers has transformed from passive consumers to active co-creators, often referred to as 'prosumers'. Knowledge has emerged as a crucial competitive differentiator, with competitive advantage increasingly determined by both the speed of knowledge acquisition and its qualitative aspects. Relational capital has become particularly significant in this context, facilitating:

- Enhanced customer interactions
- Personalised experience creation
- Development of loyalty frameworks
- Establishment of trust-based relationships

Value creation in contemporary organisations is increasingly dependent upon the quality of stakeholder interactions, both internal and external, with traditional product attributes becoming secondary considerations. This shift emphasises the importance of retained organisational knowledge in process optimisation, contributing to more agile and robust structural capital development.

The effectiveness of value creation within these emerging business ecosystems relies heavily on the management of various intangible assets as follows:

- Brand reputation development
- Employees experience enhancement
- Collaborative network cultivation
- Knowledge management systems

As organisations increasingly embrace circular economy principles and sustainability imperatives, intellectual capital strategies must evolve to incorporate environmentally conscious practices and frameworks. This adaptation requires the integration of sustainable practices across all aspects of intellectual capital management, from human capital development to structural and relational capital enhancement.

Traditional business models are changing to new models based on value networks. Therefore, intellectual capital management becomes fundamental, which implies a change in the conventional management paradigm. Organisations are transitioning from product-centric models to customer- and service-oriented models. The customer becomes a co-creator (prosumer), and knowledge becomes the key competitive differentiator—power becomes the possession of whoever has first access to knowledge and the quality of that knowledge. As we have already highlighted, relational capital is increasingly seen as a key factor of competitive advantage, as it allows interactions with customers, creates personalised experiences and generates loyalty and trust. The value created depends on the quality of interactions with customers (internal or external) and the experiences they remember, placing aspects such as product attributes in the background. The retained knowledge allows for improving organisational processes, thus contributing to strengthening and making structural capital more agile. Creating value in these ecosystems, therefore, depends on the effective management of intangible assets, such as brand reputation, employee experience and collaborative networks. Furthermore, as companies adopt circular economy principles and become more sustainable, CI strategies will have to adapt while also being greener.

5.5 Key Research Questions and Gaps

The field of intellectual capital (IC) research has expanded significantly over the past two decades. However, several fundamental questions remain inadequately addressed, with limited consensus among academics and practitioners. Analysis of the current literature reveals several critical areas requiring further investigation:

1. *Standardisation of Measurement Frameworks*. A significant challenge lies in developing standardised IC definition and measurement frameworks applicable across diverse industries. The absence of universally accepted metrics impedes:
   (a) Comparative analysis of IC performance across organisations
   (b) Evaluation of IC effectiveness within specific sectors
   (c) Assessment of IC's strategic impact on organisational outcomes
   (d) Development of industry benchmarks
2. *Resilience and Crisis Adaptation*. The relationship between IC and organisational resilience during global crises requires deeper examination. Investigation of IC's role during pandemics, climate emergencies, geopolitical conflicts, and economic disruptions could enhance understanding of:
   (a) Adaptive capacity development
   (b) Crisis response mechanisms
   (c) Long-term sustainability strategies
   (d) Organisational resilience frameworks
3. *Technological Impact Assessment*. The long-term implications of emerging technologies on IC composition and management remain inadequately understood. Priority research areas include:
   (a) The influence of AI on IC dynamics
   (b) Blockchain applications in IC management
   (c) Ethical considerations in technological implementation
   (d) Social implications of IC technological transformation
4. *Sustainability Integration*. Further research is needed to elucidate the relationship between IC management and sustainability principles. Key areas for investigation include:
   (a) Integration of sustainability metrics into IC frameworks
   (b) Development of sustainable IC management practices
   (c) Alignment of IC strategies with environmental objectives
   (d) Measurement of IC's contribution to sustainable outcomes

These research gaps represent significant opportunities for advancing understanding of IC's role in contemporary organisational management and sustainable development.

In the last two decades, many researchers have focused on the topic of intellectual capital. However, some of the main questions on the topic remain little studied or with a lack of consensus among the scientific community and practitioners. The following issues mainly stand out:

1. How can IC definition and measurement frameworks be standardised across industries? The lack of universally accepted metrics hinders the ability to compare and evaluate the performance of ICs, limiting their strategic potential.
2. How does IC contribute to resilience and adaptability during global crises, such as pandemics, climate emergencies, wars or economic crises? Understanding this relationship can help organisations build more robust CI strategies that support long-term sustainability.
3. What are the long-term impacts of emerging technologies on IC composition and management? Research is needed to explore how AI, blockchain and other innovations are reshaping the dynamics of IC, with a focus on ethical implications and social impact.
4. How can IC management leverage sustainability? It is necessary to demonstrate to organisations how the management of intellectual capital can be the basis of management, complying with the principles of sustainability.

5.6 *Methodological Challenges and Opportunities*

Research in intellectual capital (IC) management presents significant methodological challenges while simultaneously offering opportunities for advancing understanding in this field. These challenges and opportunities warrant systematic examination.

Key Methodological Challenges

The complexity of IC research stems from multiple factors as follows:

- Capturing the dynamic and contextual nature of IC management
- Integrating qualitative and quantitative methodological approaches
- Reconciling diverse disciplinary perspectives from economics, management, and technology
- Measuring intangible contributions to innovation and competitiveness
- Addressing cultural variations in IC conceptualisation and implementation
- Developing consistent measurement frameworks across different organisational contexts

The assessment of IC's contribution to organisational performance presents particular difficulties, requiring consideration of both tangible metrics (such as registered patents and documented processes) and intangible factors (including employee creativity and organisational culture). This complexity is further amplified by the need to account for cultural differences across global markets, necessitating more sophisticated macroeconomic analytical approaches.

Emerging Opportunities

Contemporary technological developments offer promising opportunities for addressing these methodological challenges through:

- Big data analytics applications
- Machine learning implementations
- Longitudinal study frameworks
- Pattern recognition methodologies
- Cross-cultural comparative analyses

These tools enable more sophisticated investigation of relationships within IC structures and their impact on organisational outcomes.

Extended temporal studies offer particular value in:

- Tracking IC evolution over time
- Identifying drivers of sustainable growth
- Understanding innovation dynamics
- Assessing competitive advantage development
- Evaluating long-term value creation

The integration of diverse analytical approaches presents opportunities for:

- Creating more robust evaluation models
- Developing credible value measurement frameworks
- Establishing financial metrics for IC management
- Enhancing cross-organisational comparability
- Improving strategic decision-making capabilities

With regard to methodological challenges and opportunities, IC research faces several challenges, including capturing the dynamic and contextual nature of intellectual capital management, the integration of qualitative data with quantitative models and the interdisciplinary approach that combines economic, managerial and technological perspectives. For example, measuring the contribution of intellectual capital management to innovation and competitiveness is complex, as it involves tangible metrics (e.g. registered patents) and intangible factors (e.g. employee creativity). Furthermore, cultural differences also increase complexity, requiring more macroeconomic approaches. The opportunities appear to lie in the use of advanced analytical tools, such as big data analysis, machine learning and longitudinal studies, to discover patterns and differentiated relationships within the IC.

These analyses can allow us to develop more robust and convincing models of the business community. Longitudinal studies can provide information on the evolution of IC over time, allowing us to identify the factors that drive sustainable growth, innovation and competitiveness. The use of these different metrics also makes it possible to find credible formulas that allow measuring the added value, in financial terms, of intellectual capital management.

5.7 *Implications for Practice and Policy*

The evolution of intellectual capital (IC) management presents significant implications for both organisational practice and policy development. These implications warrant careful consideration across multiple domains.

Organisational Development Initiatives

Contemporary IC management necessitates comprehensive training programmes addressing:

- Artificial intelligence implementation and governance
- Ethical considerations in knowledge management
- Sustainability integration
- Digital transformation competencies
- Cross-cultural collaboration capabilities

Policy Framework Enhancement

Policy mechanisms should be developed to encourage IC investment and knowledge asset protection, including:

- Tax incentives for research and development activities
- Financial support for IC management initiatives
- Protection frameworks for intellectual property
- Regulatory structures supporting knowledge-based innovation
- Incentives for sustainable practice adoption

Collaborative Framework Development

The advancement of IC management requires structured approaches to collaboration, encompassing:

- Public–private partnership development

- International research consortium formation
- Cross-sector knowledge transfer mechanisms
- Interdisciplinary research initiatives
- Global innovation networks

These collaborative structures can accelerate knowledge creation and transfer while addressing complex global challenges facing contemporary organisations.

Implementation Considerations

Successful execution of these implications requires:

- Systematic policy development
- Stakeholder engagement
- Resource allocation
- Performance measurement
- Regular evaluation and adjustment

Practical implications for future CI research include but are not limited to the following:

- Develop training and learning programs adapted to the emerging needs of IC management, such as skills in AI, ethics, and sustainability.
- Promote policies that encourage investments in IC and protect knowledge assets in an equitable way. For example, tax incentives favour companies that invest in R&D and better manage intellectual capital.
- Promote collaborative initiatives, such as public–private partnerships and national international research consortia, accelerating the processes of knowledge creation and transfer. This interdisciplinary collaboration agenda can enable you to address global challenges and opportunities that affect companies and businesses.

6 Chapter Structure and Contributions

This book follows a simple structure, starting with some conceptional ideas, followed by the presentation of specific methods to manage IC.

Chapter 1

This chapter introduces intellectual capital (IC) as a strategic asset in the global business landscape, focusing on its key dimensions: human, structural, and relational. It highlights the importance of IC in navigating modern economic and technological challenges.

Chapter 2
This chapter examines companies' readiness for digital transformation, emphasising human, structural, and relational capital. Findings from a global survey reveal structural capital as the most prepared, while relational capital presents opportunities for improvement.

Chapter 3
This chapter presents a taxonomy for measuring intellectual capital in the green economy to promote sustainability and growth. The framework emphasises balancing economic objectives with environmental stewardship to drive value creation and competitive advantage.

Chapter 4
This chapter discusses how intellectual capital (IC) drives economic growth and improves organisational performance in the digital era. It introduces technologies and mechanisms that enhance IC visibility, validated through case studies.

Chapter 5
This chapter integrates intangible metrics into the ESG framework using a novel value theory combining non-linearity and fuzzy logic. It introduces an adaptive decision support system to improve the evaluation and prediction of ESG-related intangibles.

Chapter 6
This chapter links spirituality and leadership to the development of intellectual capital (IC), fostering economic and social transformation. It presents an interdisciplinary framework connecting spirituality to IC's human, social, and renewal dimensions.

Chapter 7
This chapter analyses how national factors, such as skilled labour and appropriation systems, influence intellectual capital (IC) and innovation. Relational capital emerges as a consistent driver of innovation across diverse environments.

Chapter 8
This chapter explores how Industry 4.0 technologies and servitisation foster value co-creation within manufacturing networks. A case study highlights how collaboration generates intangible assets like relational capital for competitive advantage.

Chapter 9
This chapter examines the dynamic relationship between knowledge gains and losses to sustain intellectual capital (IC). Proactive IC management strategies are proposed to mitigate risks and enhance organisational adaptability.

Chapter 10
This chapter investigates the relationship between intellectual capital (IC) and regional sustainability using a dynamic monitoring model. A Portuguese case study illustrates the challenges and opportunities in aligning IC with sustainability goals.

Chapter 11

This chapter reviews the historical development of intellectual capital (IC) theory, its applications across levels, and critiques of its frameworks. It highlights IC's role in driving innovation and competitiveness while identifying future research directions.

Chapter 12

This chapter emphasises structured onboarding and digital solutions to enhance IC and long-term organisational performance. Organisational socialisation is presented as a key factor in developing and retaining intellectual capital (IC).

Chapter 13

This chapter explores assigning monetary value to ESG metrics using innovative valuation models. A case study demonstrates the integration of sustainability reporting with financial metrics and highlights future research possibilities.

Chapter 14

This chapter emphasises renewal capital (RC) as essential for fostering innovation within intellectual capital (IC). It links human resource management (HRM) practices to RC development, highlighting their impact on organisational renewal and competitive advantage.

We hope you find enjoyment in the next chapters and that they help enhance intellectual capital as the primary asset for creating value within organisations in the digital era.

References

Abbasi, A., Sarker, S., & Chiang, R. H. (2016). Big data research in information systems: Toward an inclusive research agenda. *Journal of the Association for Information Systems, 17*(2), 1–32.

Adams, R., Jeanrenaud, S., Bessant, J., Denyer, D., & Overy, P. (2016). Sustainability-oriented innovation: A systematic review. *International Journal of Management Reviews, 18*(2), 180–205.

Agarwal, A., & Strachan, P. (2008). Is industrial symbiosis only a concept for developed countries. *The Journal for Waste & Resource Management Professionals*, 42–43.

Albertini, E. (2019). The contribution of management control systems to environmental capabilities. *Journal of Business Ethics, 159*(4), 1163–1180.

Alharthi, A., Krotov, V., & Bowman, M. (2017). Addressing barriers to big data. *Business Horizons, 60*(3), 285–292.

Astuti, P. D. & Datrini, L. (2021). Green competitive advantage: Examining the role of environmental consciousness and green intellectual capital. *Management Science Letters*. 1141–1152. https://doi.org/10.5267/j.msl.2020.11.025.

Ayres, R. U. (1994). Industrial metabolism: Theory and policy. In R. U. Ayres & U. E. Simonis (Eds.), *Industrial metabolism: Restructuring for sustainable development* (pp. 3–20). United Nations University Press.

Baba, Y., Shichijo, N., & Sedita, S. R. (2009). How do collaborations with universities affect firms' innovative performance? The role of "Pasteur scientists" in the advanced materials field. *Research Policy, 38*(5), 756–764.

Ballow, J., Burgman, R., Roos, G., & Molnar, M. (2004b). *A new paradigm for managing shareholder value*. Accenture Institute for High Performance Business.

Ballow, J. J., Thomas, R. J., & Roos, G. (2004a). Future value: The $7 trillion challenge. *Journal of Applied Corporate Finance, 16*(1), 71–76.

Ballow, J. J., Thomas, R. J., & Roos, G. (2004c). Future value: The $7 trillion challenge. *Outlook, 1*, 28–37.

Baptista, J., Stein, M. K., Klein, S., Watson-Manheim, M. B., & Lee, J. (2020). Digital work and organisational transformation: Emergent Digital/Human work configurations in modern organisations. *The Journal of Strategic Information Systems, 29*(2), 101618.

Barney, J. (1991). Firm resources and sustained competitive advantage. *Journal of Management, 17*(1), 99–120.

Beattie, V., & Smith, S. J. (2013). Value creation and business models: Refocusing the intellectual capital debate. *The British Accounting Review, 45*(4), 243–254.

Besson, P., & Rowe, F. (2012). Strategising information systems-enabled organisational transformation: A transdisciplinary review and new directions. *The Journal of Strategic Information Systems, 21*(2), 103–124.

Bharadwaj, A., El Sawy, O. A., Pavlou, P. A., & Venkatraman, N. (2013). Digital business strategy: Toward a next generation of insights. *MIS Quarterly, 37*(2), 471–482.

Blair, M. M., & Wallman, S. H. (Eds.). (2000). *Unseen wealth: Report of the Brookings task force on intangibles*. Rowman & Littlefield.

Bloom, N., Genakos, C., Sadun, R., & Van Reenen, J. (2012). Management practices across firms and countries. *The Academy of Management Perspectives, 26*(1), 12–33.

Bloom, N., & Van Reenen, J. (2007). Measuring and explaining management practices across firms and countries. *The Quarterly Journal of Economics, 122*(4), 1351–1408.

Bloom, N., & Van Reenen, J. (2010). Why do management practices differ across firms and countries? *The Journal of Economic Perspectives, 24*(1), 203–224.

Bocken, N. M. P., Short, S. W., Rana, P., & Evans, S. (2014). A literature and practice review to develop sustainable business model archetypes. *Journal of Cleaner Production, 65*, 42–56.

Boiral, O., Heras-Saizarbitoria, I., & Brotherton, M. C. (2020). Improving environmental management through indigenous peoples' involvement. *Environmental Science & Policy, 103*, 10–20.

Boons, F., & Lüdeke-Freund, F. (2013). Business models for sustainable innovation: State-of-the--art and steps towards a research agenda. *Journal of Cleaner Production, 45*, 9–19.

Brand Finance. (2022). *Global intangible finance tracker (GIFT™) 2022: An annual review of the world's intangible value*. Brand Finance plc.

Brynjolfsson, E., & McAfee, A. (2014). *The second machine age: Work, progress, and prosperity in a time of brilliant technologies*. WW Norton & Company.

Brynjolfsson, E., & McAfee, A. (2017). The business of artificial intelligence. *Harvard Business Review, 95*(4), 3–11.

Cabrita, M. D. R., & Bontis, N. (2008). Intellectual capital and business performance in the Portuguese banking industry. *International Journal of Technology Management, 43*(1–3), 212–237.

Chamberlin, E. H. (1933). *The theory of monopolistic competition*. Harvard University Press.

Chen, Y. S. (2008). The positive effect of green intellectual capital on competitive advantages of firms. *Journal of Business Ethics, 77*(3), 271–286.

Corrado, C., Haskel, J., Jona-Lasinio, C., & Iommi, M. (2022). Intangible capital and modern economies. *Journal of Economic Perspectives, 36*(3), 3–28.

Corrado, C., Hulten, C., & Sichel, D. (2009). Intangible capital and US economic growth. *Review of Income and Wealth, 55*(3), 661–685.

Cosenz, F., & Noto, G. (2016). Applying system dynamics modelling to strategic management: A literature review. *Systems Research and Behavioral Science, 33*(6), 703–741.

Cuozzo, B., Dumay, J., Palmaccio, M., & Lombardi, R. (2017). Intellectual capital disclosure: A structured literature review. *Journal of Intellectual Capital, 18*(1), 9–28.

Dean, A., & Kretschmer, M. (2007). Can ideas be capital? Factors of production in the postindustrial economy: A review and critique. *Academy of Management Review, 32*(2), 573–594.

Dhillon, G., Syed, R., & Pedron, C. (2016). Interpreting information security culture: An organisational transformation case study. *Computers & Security, 56*, 63–69.

Dumay, J. (2016). A critical reflection on the future of intellectual capital: From reporting to disclosure. *Journal of Intellectual Capital, 17*(1), 168–184.

Dumay, J., & Garanina, T. (2013). Intellectual capital research: A critical examination of the third stage. *Journal of Intellectual Capital, 14*(1), 10–25.

Eccles, R. G., Ioannou, I., & Serafeim, G. (2014). The impact of corporate sustainability on organisational processes and performance. *Management Science, 60*(11), 2835–2857.

Edvinsson, L., & Malone, M. S. (1997). *Intellectual capital: Realising your company's true value by finding its hidden brainpower*. Harper Business.

Edvinsson, L., & Sullivan, P. (1996). Developing a model for managing intellectual capital. *European Management Journal, 14*(4), 356–364.

Elsten, C., & Hill, N. (2017). Intangible asset market value study? *les Nouvelles-Journal of the Licensing Executives Society, 52*(4), 245–247.

European Union. (2008). Directive 2008/98/EC on waste (Waste Framework Directive). *Official Journal of the European Union*.

Evans, S., Vladimirova, D., Holgado, M., Van Fossen, K., Yang, M., Silva, E. A., & Barlow, C. Y. (2017). Business model innovation for sustainability: Towards a unified perspective for creation of sustainable business models. *Business Strategy and the Environment, 26*(5), 597–608.

Faraj, S., Jarvenpaa, S. L., & Majchrzak, A. (2011). Knowledge collaboration in online communities. *Organisation Science, 22*(5), 1224–1239.

Fernström, L., Pike, S., & Roos, G. (2004). Understanding the truly value creating resources–the case of a pharmaceutical company. *International Journal of Learning and Intellectual Capital, 1*(1), 105–120.

Freeman, R. E., Harrison, J. S., Wicks, A. C., Parmar, B. L., & De Colle, S. (2010). *Stakeholder theory: The state of the art*. Cambridge University Press.

Frey, C. B., & Osborne, M. A. (2017). The future of employment: How susceptible are jobs to computerisation? *Technological Forecasting and Social Change, 114*, 254–280.

Friede, G., Busch, T., & Bassen, A. (2015). ESG and financial performance: Aggregated evidence from more than 2000 empirical studies. *Journal of Sustainable Finance & Investment, 5*(4), 210–233.

Frosch, R. A., & Gallopoulos, N. E. (1989). Strategies for manufacturing. *Scientific American, 261*(3), 144–153.

Gawer, A., & Cusumano, M. A. (2014). Industry platforms and ecosystem innovation. *Journal of Product Innovation Management, 31*(3), 417–433.

Geissdoerfer, M., Savaget, P., Bocken, N. M., & Hultink, E. J. (2017). The circular economy – A new sustainability paradigm? *Journal of Cleaner Production, 143*, 757–768.

Geissdoerfer, M., Vladimirova, D., & Evans, S. (2018). Sustainable business model innovation: A review. *Journal of Cleaner Production, 198*, 401–416.

George, G., Haas, M. R., & Pentland, A. (2014). Big data and management. *Academy of Management Journal, 57*(2), 321–326.

Giuliani, M. (2015). Rome wasn't built in a day… reflecting on time, intellectual capital and intellectual liabilities. *Journal of Intellectual Capital, 16*(1), 2–19.

Gray, B., & Stites, J. P. (2013). Sustainability through partnerships: Capitalising on collaboration. *Network for Business Sustainability*. Accessed November 13, 2024, from https://nbs.net/sustainability-through-partnerships-a-systematic-review/

Gregory, R. W., Keil, M., Muntermann, J., & Mähring, M. (2015). Paradoxes and the nature of ambidexterity in IT transformation programs. *Information Systems Research, 26*(1), 57–80.

Günther, W. A., Mehrizi, M. H. R., Huysman, M., & Feldberg, F. (2017). Debating big data: A literature review on realising value from big data. *The Journal of Strategic Information Systems, 26*(3), 191–209.
Guthrie, J., Ricceri, F., & Dumay, J. (2012). Reflections and projections: A decade of intellectual capital accounting research. *The British Accounting Review, 44*(2), 68–82.
Haenlein, M., & Kaplan, A. (2019). A brief history of artificial intelligence: On the past, present, and future of artificial intelligence. *California Management Review, 61*(4), 5–14.
Hall, R. E. (2001). The stock market and capital accumulation. *American Economic Review, 91*(5), 1185–1202.
Hao, J. X., & Wu, H. X. (2021). *China's investment in intangible assets by industry: A preliminary estimation in an extended sources-of-growth framework.* RIETI discussion paper series 21-E-029. The Research Institute of Economy, Trade and Industry.
Hart, S. L., & Dowell, G. (2011). A natural-resource-based view of the firm: Fifteen years after. *Journal of Management, 37*(5), 1464–1479.
Hartl, E., & Hess, T. (2017). The role of cultural values for digital transformation: Insights from a Delphi study. *Americas Conference on Information Systems (AMCIS).*
Haskel, J., & Westlake, S. (2018). *Capitalism without capital: The rise of the intangible economy.* Princeton University Press.
Haskel, J., & Westlake, S. (2022). *Restarting the future: How to fix the intangible economy.* Princeton University Press.
Hess, T., Matt, C., Benlian, A., & Wiesböck, F. (2016). Options for formulating a digital transformation strategy. *MIS Quarterly Executive, 15*(2), 123–139.
Hudson, W. J. (1993). *Intellectual capital: How to build it, enhance it, use it.* Wiley.
Inigo, E. A., & Albareda, L. (2019). Sustainability oriented innovation dynamics: Levels of dynamic capabilities and their path-dependent and self-reinforcing logics. *Technological Forecasting and Social Change, 139*, 334–351.
Inkinen, H. (2015). Review of empirical research on intellectual capital and firm performance. *Journal of Intellectual Capital, 16*(3), 518–565.
Jacobides, M. G., Cennamo, C., & Gawer, A. (2018). Towards a theory of ecosystems. *Strategic Management Journal, 39*(8), 2255–2276.
Kane, G. C., Palmer, D., Phillips, A. N., & Kiron, D. (2015). Is your business ready for a digital future? *MIT Sloan Management Review, 56*(4), 37–44.
Kane, G. C., Palmer, D., Phillips, A. N., Kiron, D., & Buckley, N. (2016). Aligning the organisation for its digital future. *MIT Sloan Management Review, 58*(1), 1–27.
Kane, G. C., Phillips, A. N., Copulsky, J., & Andrus, G. (2019). How digital leadership is (n't) different. *MIT Sloan Management Review, 60*(3), 34–39.
Karimi, J., & Walter, Z. (2015). The role of dynamic capabilities in responding to digital disruption: A factor-based study of the newspaper industry. *Journal of Management Information Systems, 32*(1), 39–81.
Kaufmann, L., & Schneider, Y. (2004). Intangibles: A synthesis of current research. *Journal of Intellectual Capital, 5*(3), 366–388.
Kianto, A., Andreeva, T., & Pavlov, Y. (2013). The impact of intellectual capital management on company competitiveness and financial performance. *Knowledge Management Research and Practice, 11*(2), 112–122.
Kianto, A., Ritala, P., Spender, J. C., & Vanhala, M. (2014). The interaction of intellectual capital assets and knowledge management practices in organisational value creation. *Journal of Intellectual Capital, 15*(3), 362–375.
Kotabe, M., Martin, X., & Domoto, H. (2003). Gaining from vertical partnerships: Knowledge transfer, relationship duration, and supplier performance improvement in the US and Japanese automotive industries. *Strategic Management Journal, 24*(4), 293–316.
Kraaijenbrink, J., Spender, J. C., & Groen, A. J. (2010). The resource-based view: A review and assessment of its critiques. *Journal of Management, 36*(1), 349–372.

Leonardi, P. M. (2014). Social media, knowledge sharing, and innovation: Toward a theory of communication visibility. *Information Systems Research, 25*(4), 796–816.
Leonardi, P. M. (2017). The social media revolution: Sharing and learning in the age of leaky knowledge. *Information and Organization, 27*(1), 47–59.
Leonardi, P. M., & Vaast, E. (2017). Social media and their affordances for organising: A review and agenda for research. *Academy of Management Annals, 11*(1), 150–188.
Lev, B. (2000). *Intangibles: Management, measurement, and reporting*. Rowman & Littlefield.
Lev, B., & Gu, F. (2016). *The end of accounting and the path forward for investors and managers*. John Wiley & Sons.
Maas, K., Schaltegger, S., & Crutzen, N. (2016). Integrating corporate sustainability assessment, management accounting, control, and reporting. *Journal of Cleaner Production, 136*, 237–248.
Mady, K., Battour, M., Aboelmaged, M., & Abdelkareem, R. S. (2023). Linking internal environmental capabilities to sustainable competitive advantage in manufacturing SMEs: The mediating role of eco-innovation. *Journal of Cleaner Production, 417*, 137928.
Marr, B., & Chatzkel, J. (2004). Intellectual capital at the crossroads: Managing, measuring, and reporting of IC. *Journal of Intellectual Capital, 5*(2), 224–229.
Martín-de-Castro, G., Delgado-Verde, M., López-Sáez, P., & Navas-López, J. E. (2011). Towards 'an intellectual capital-based view of the firm': Origins and nature. *Journal of Business Ethics, 98*, 649–662.
Matos, F., Selig, P. M., & Henriqson, E. (Eds.). (2022). *Resilience in a digital age. Global challenges in organisations and society*. Springer. https://doi.org/10.1007/978-3-030-85954-1
Matos, F., Vairinhos, V., & Godina, R. (2020b). Reporting of intellectual capital management using a scoring model. *Sustainability, 12*(19), 8086. https://doi.org/10.3390/su12198086
Matos, F., Vairinhos, V., Salavisa, I., Edvinsson, L., & Massaro, M. (Eds.). (2020a). *Knowledge, people, and digital transformation. Contributions to management science*. Springer. https://doi.org/10.1007/978-3-030-40390-4
Matos, F., Vairinhos, V., Selig, P., & Edvinsson, L. (Eds.). (2019). *Intellectual capital management as a driver of sustainability perspectives for organizations and society*. Springer. https://doi.org/10.1007/978-3-319-79051-0
Mayer-Schönberger, V., & Cukier, K. (2013). *Big data: A revolution that will transform how we live, work, and think*. Houghton Mifflin Harcourt.
McAfee, A., Brynjolfsson, E., Davenport, T. H., Patil, D. J., & Barton, D. (2012). Big data: The management revolution. *Harvard Business Review, 90*(10), 60–68.
Melville, N. P. (2010). Information systems innovation for environmental sustainability. *MIS Quarterly, 34*(1), 1–21.
Mokyr, J. (2018). *The British industrial revolution: An economic perspective*. Routledge.
Mrkwicka, K., & Schögel, M. (2016, February). *Managing digital interactions: Distinctive capabilities and the influence of the organizational model*. American Marketing Association.
Nahapiet, J., & Ghoshal, S. (1998). Social capital, intellectual capital, and the organisational advantage. *Academy of Management Review, 23*(2), 242–266.
Nakamura, L. (2001). *What is the U.S. gross investment in intangibles? (At least) one trillion dollars a year!* Federal Reserve Bank of Philadelphia Working paper no. 01-15.
Nelson, D. (1974). Scientific management, systematic management, and labor, 1880–1915. *The Business History Review, 48*(4), 479–500.
Nishant, R., Kennedy M., & Corbett J. (2020). Artificial intelligence for sustainability: Challenges, opportunities, and a research agenda. *International Journal of Information Management, 53*, 102104, ISSN 0268–4012. https://doi.org/10.1016/j.ijinfomgt.2020.102104.
O'Connor, A., & Roos, G. (2018). Visualising intellectual capital transformations for strategic design of entrepreneurial business models. In S. Griffith, K. Carruthers, & M. Bliemel (Eds.), *Visual tools for developing cross-disciplinary collaboration, innovation and entrepreneurship capacity* (pp. 243–260). Common Ground Research Networks.
Ocean Tomo. (2020). *Intangible asset market value study*. Ocean Tomo, LLC.

OECD. (2021). *OECD science, technology and innovation outlook 2021: Times of crisis and opportunity*. OECD Publishing.

Parida, V., & Wincent, J. (2019). Why and how to compete through sustainability: A review and outline of trends influencing firm and network-level transformation. *International Entrepreneurship and Management Journal, 15*, 1–19.

Parker, G. G., Van Alstyne, M. W., & Choudary, S. P. (2016). *Platform revolution: How networked markets are transforming the economy and how to make them work for you*. W. W. Norton & Company.

Penrose, E. T. (1959). *The theory of the growth of the firm*. Oxford University Press.

Peters, R. H., & Taylor, L. A. (2017). Intangible capital and the investment-q relation. *Journal of Financial Economics, 123*(2), 251–272.

Pieroni, M. P., McAloone, T. C., & Pigosso, D. C. (2019). Business model innovation for circular economy and sustainability: A review of approaches. *Journal of Cleaner Production, 215*, 198–216.

Pike, S., Fernström, L., & Roos, G. (2005). Intellectual capital: Management approach in ICS Ltd. *Journal of Intellectual Capital, 6*(4), 489–509.

Pike, S., & Roos, G. (2004). Mathematics and modern business management. *Journal of Intellectual Capital, 5*(2), 243–256.

Pike, S., & Roos, G. (2007). The validity of measurement frameworks: Measurement theory. In A. Neely (Ed.), *Business performance measurement: Unifying theory and integrating practice* (pp. 218–236). Cambridge University Press.

Ployhart, R. E., & Moliterno, T. P. (2011). Emergence of the human capital resource: A multilevel model. *Academy of Management Review, 36*(1), 127–150.

Porter, M. E., & Heppelmann, J. E. (2014). How smart, connected products are transforming competition. *Harvard Business Review, 92*(11), 64–88.

Renwick, D. W., Redman, T., & Maguire, S. (2013). Green human resource management: A review and research agenda. *International Journal of Management Reviews, 15*(1), 1–14.

Rigby, D., Elk, S., & Berez, S. (2020). *Doing agile right: Transformation without chaos*. Harvard Business Press.

Risius, M., & Spohrer, K. (2017). A blockchain research framework: What we (don't) know, where we go from here, and how we will get there. *Business & Information Systems Engineering, 59*, 385–409.

Robinson, J. (1933). *Economics of imperfect competition*. Macmillan.

Roos, G. (2011). How to get paid twice for everything you do, Part 2: Value– Appropriating innovations. *Ericsson Business Review, 3*, 56–61.

Roos, G. (2014). Business model innovation to create and capture resource value in future circular material chains. *Resources, 3*(1), 248–274.

Roos, G. (2014a). The intellectual capital navigator as a strategic tool. In P. Ordóñez de Pablos (Ed.), *International business strategy and entrepreneurship: An information technology perspective* (pp. 1–22). IGI Global.

Roos, G. (2017). *Technology-driven productivity improvements and the future of work: Emerging research and opportunities*. IGI Global.

Roos, G. (2018). Resource deployment system implications of migrating the firm into a digital value creation paradigm. *Knowledge Management Research and Practice, 16*(3), 281–291.

Roos, G. (2019). *Optimising resource deployment within the firm: Overcoming theoretical problems with a practical application*. Doctoral dissertation, University of South Australia.

Roos, G., Pike, S., & Fernström, L. (2005). *Managing intellectual capital in practice*. Butterworth-Heinemann.

Roos, G., & Roos, J. (1997). Measuring your company's intellectual performance. *Long Range Planning, 30*(3), 413–426.

Sambamurthy, V., Bharadwaj, A., & Grover, V. (2003). Shaping agility through digital options: Reconceptualising the role of information technology in contemporary firms. *MIS Quarterly, 27*(2), 237–263.

Schiuma, G. (Ed.). (2010). *Managing knowledge assets and business value creation in organisations: Measures and dynamics: measures and dynamics*. IGI Global.
Sharma, S., & Henriques, I. (2005). Stakeholder influences on sustainability practices in the Canadian forest products industry. *Strategic Management Journal, 26*(2), 159–180.
Sia, S. K., Soh, C., & Weill, P. (2016). How DBS Bank pursued a digital business strategy. *MIS Quarterly Executive, 15*(2), 105–121.
Smith, A. (1776). *An inquiry into the nature and causes of the wealth of nations*. W. Strahan and T. Cadell.
Stewart, T. A. (1997). *Intellectual capital: The new wealth of organisations*. Doubleday.
Teece, D. J. (2018). Business models and dynamic capabilities. *Long Range Planning, 51*(1), 40–49.
Tiwana, A. (2013). *Platform ecosystems: Aligning architecture, governance, and strategy*. Morgan Kaufmann.
Vial, G. (2021). Understanding digital transformation: A review and a research agenda. In A. Hinterhuber, T. Vescovi, & F. Checchinato (Eds.), *Managing digital transformation* (pp. 13–66). Taylor & Francis.
Von Krogh, G. (2018). Artificial intelligence in organisations: New opportunities for phenomenon-based theorising. *Academy of Management Discoveries, 4*(4), 404–409.
Wang, N., Liang, H., Jia, Y., Ge, S., Xue, Y., & Wang, Z. (2016). Cloud computing research in the IS discipline: A citation/co-citation analysis. *Decision Support Systems, 86*, 35–47.
Wang, R. Y., & Strong, D. M. (1996). Beyond accuracy: What data quality means to data consumers. *Journal of Management Information Systems, 12*(4), 5–33.
Wernerfelt, B. (1984). A resource-based view of the firm. *Strategic Management Journal, 5*(2), 171–180.
World Intellectual Property Organization. (2022). *World intellectual property report 2022: The direction of innovation*. WIPO.
Yeow, A., Soh, C., & Hansen, R. (2018). Aligning with new digital strategy: A dynamic capabilities approach. *The Journal of Strategic Information Systems, 27*(1), 43–58.
Yusliza, M. Y., Yong, J. Y., Tanveer, M. I., Ramayah, T., Faezah, J. N., & Muhammad, Z. (2020). A structural model of the impact of green intellectual capital on sustainable performance. *Journal of Cleaner Production, 249*, 119334.
Zott, C., & Amit, R. (2010). Business model design: An activity system perspective. *Long Range Planning, 43*(2–3), 216–226.

Assessing Digital Readiness of Intellectual Capital: A Global Study of Human, Structural, and Relational Dimensions

Ronald Orth, Markus Will, Felix Budde, Florian Kidschun, and Alida Soar Gomes

Abstract This study investigates the readiness of companies' intellectual capital (IC) for digital transformation in a global business context. The research focuses on the three dimensions of IC: human capital, structural capital, and relational capital. By linking the concepts of IC and digital transformation, the study aims to assess the status quo of companies' intangible resources in supporting the ongoing digitalization process. The methodology involves a global survey using the "Digital Transformation Assessment" tool developed by Fraunhofer IPK, which captures and assesses the essential value creation elements of companies in the context of digital transformation. The survey results, based on responses from 948 companies across various industry sectors and regions, reveal that structural capital shows the highest readiness for digitalization, followed by human capital. Relational capital, particularly in terms of integrating external stakeholders like customers and suppliers into digital process chains, presents the greatest potential for improvement. The study also conducts an international comparison, highlighting regional differences in the IC dimensions. The findings provide valuable insights into the strengths and weaknesses of companies' IC in the context of digital transformation, offering implications for business strategies and practices to navigate the challenges of digitalization successfully.

1 Introduction

In today's global corporate environment, an increasingly knowledge-based business context, intellectual capital (IC) continues to be the key source of strategic differentiation and competitive advantage. As a representation of the intangible resource

R. Orth (✉) · M. Will · F. Budde · F. Kidschun · A. S. Gomes
Fraunhofer Institute for Production Systems and Design Technology IPK, Berlin, Germany
e-mail: ronald.orth@ipk.fraunhofer.de; markus.will@ipk.fraunhofer.de; felix.budde@ipk.fraunhofer.de; florian.kidschun@ipk.fraunhofer.de; alida.soar.gomes@ipk.fraunhofer.de

F. Matos et al. (eds.), *Intellectual Capital in a Global Business Landscape*, Contributions to Management Science, https://doi.org/10.1007/978-3-031-86362-2_2

base of an organization, it comprises the necessary knowledge and competencies (human capital), internal structures for efficient collaboration (structural capital), and external relations to the market (relational capital) that are needed to drive business processes, which produce the necessary output and respective value for the customer.

Against this background, the fast-advancing digital transformation is affecting many different aspects of the companies' value creation and therewith presents new requirements to its resources, which are crucial to drive increasingly digitalized business processes. Therefore, organizations must systematically evaluate their IC in order to react to new requirements and consequently derive effective measures for improvement to reach sustainable business success. In recent years, several authors investigated the impact of IC and its components on digital transformation performance and competitive advantage. The results show that intellectual capital serves as a foundation for successful digital transformation, enabling organizations to innovate, adapt, compete, collaborate, and manage risks effectively in the rapidly evolving digital landscape (Grineva et al., 2023; Zhang et al., 2023; Nedoluzhko, 2022; Rusdi, 2023; Roos 2018).

By interlinking the two topics "intellectual capital" and "digital transformation", this chapter aims at investigating the following research questions:

- How ready is the companies' human capital for digital transformation? Do the employees have the necessary abilities and skills as well as the right competences to cope with this ongoing change process?
- How ready is the companies' structural capital for digital transformation? Do the organizational structures and processes meet the necessary requirements for digitalization, and is the corporate culture supporting the respective transformation of the business?
- How ready is the companies' relational capital for digital transformation? Are the supply chains and channels to the customers already incorporating the potential of digital solutions to be more efficient, agile, and service-oriented?

In essence, digital transformation is the incorporation of digital technologies to metamorphose business processes and services, transmuting them from the analog to the digital world. Digital transformation, however, is a multilayered topic that goes far beyond pure automation or the implementation of modern technologies. Value creation structures are rapidly evolving due to the impetus of digital transformation, catalyzed significantly by the COVID-19 pandemic, which expedited digitalization globally in 2020 (Robertson et al., 2022; Gavrila & Ancillo, 2021; Penco et al., 2022). Other drivers include a shifting consumer demand and the need to remain competitive in the market. A 2020 survey by the International Data Corporation (IDC) found that customer demand was the main driver of digital transformation (DT) for an organization, according to 26% of respondents. Other popular factors motivating DT included the need to keep up with the competition. Overall, the incorporation of technologies for digital transformation gives organizations unparalleled agility to respond to market changes and intensifies innovation. Companies are therefore required to put previous business practices and strategies as well as their own processes, structures, and products to the test. In the 2022 scenario, projections point to an estimated investment of 1.85 trillion US dollars in business digitalization. Looking ahead, by 2026, this global trend of investment in digital transformation is expected to almost double, reaching 3.4 trillion US dollars (Statista, 2023).

In this context, researchers at Fraunhofer IPK are conducting a global study in which companies can determine the status quo of their individual digital journey. In particular, the intangible value drivers (e.g., organization, culture, leadership, competencies, internal collaboration, external relationships) are at the center of the analysis. The purpose of this article is therefore to investigate the interaction between intellectual capital and digital transformation in more detail.

Success factors and barriers will be examined, and implications for the business perspective will be derived. For this purpose, the "intellectual capital statement" method is presented in the second section. It provides a reference model that, on the one hand, explains the underlying conceptual understanding of IC and, on the other hand, can be used for structuring, analyzing, and designing IC on company level. Section 3 provides background on the approach, the tools, and the database that was evaluated to analyze the state of digital transformations in different countries and industry sectors. In the fourth and fifth sections, both perspectives are brought together, and selected results on the status quo of IC in the context of digital transformations are discussed.

2 Intellectual Capital Statement: Made in Germany

The methodology and procedure to deliver an intellectual capital statement (ICS), based on the methodology "Wissensbilanz—Made in Germany" (ICS m.i.G.), is described in detail in several sources (BMWi, 2004, 2013a; Bornemann & Alwert, 2007; Edvinsson & Kivikas, 2007; Will, 2015); thus, only a short introduction should be sufficient here.

An intellectual capital statement is a strategic management instrument for assessing and developing the intellectual capital (IC) of an organization. It shows how intellectual capital is linked to corporate goals, business processes, and the business success of an organization using indicators to measure these elements.

The structural model describes the main elements of the ICS as well as their interrelations (Fig. 1).

The organization is embedded in the business environment. Regularly, a vision of the founders and owners serves as general guiding principle for major decisions and strategic positioning. Depending on the business strategy, managerial decisions

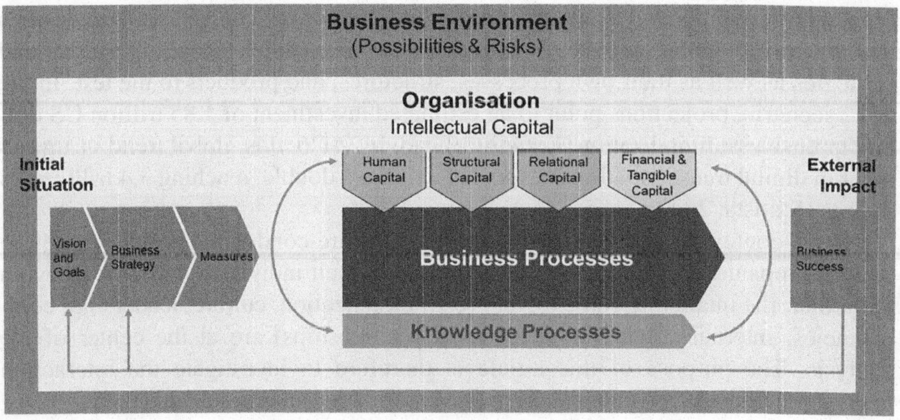

Fig. 1 Structural model of intellectual capital statement

lead to operational measures. These measures serve to improve business processes and the utilization of intellectual capital in those processes.

Intellectual capital (IC) is divided into three categories: human capital (HC), structural capital (SC), and relational capital (RC). It describes the intangible resources of an organization:

- Human capital (HC) is defined as "what the single employee brings into the value-adding processes."
- Structural capital (SC) is defined as "what happens between people, how people are connected within the company, and what remains when the employee leaves the company."
- Relational capital (RC) is defined as "the relations of the company to external stakeholders."

Business processes (BP) are chains of activities within an organization and their network-like contexts that produce outputs and therewith valuable outcomes for consumers. They describe the interaction of people, resources, knowledge, and information in cohesive steps.

Business success (BS) is the operating result, which is achieved through the employment of corporate (intangible) resources in the business processes. Business success comprises tangible (e.g., growth, revenue) and intangible (e.g., image, customer loyalty) business results.

In order to develop an intellectual capital statement, the company goes through an assessment process which involves collecting data and information on each of the three dimensions. After collecting the data, the company analyzes it in a workshop-based process to identify the strengths and weaknesses of its intellectual capital. This analysis is used to develop an intellectual capital management plan, which aims to improve the company's performance.

The target group of an intellectual capital statement can be all interest groups and persons who are of importance to the organization. They can be divided into internal and external target groups. The internal groups include, in addition to management, above all employees and organizational units, while the intellectual capital statement for external purposes largely addresses investors, potential employees, customers, and partners (BMWi, 2004, p. 12).

Based on the results of the German pilot project, 15 standard IC factors have been extracted "bottom–up" from the actual ICSs of 50 pilot SMEs. This set of harmonized IC factors has been used and continuously reviewed during the later stages of the German project and during the European project. The results from practice proved that approx. 80–90% of individual IC elements could be harmonized on an aggregated level, whereas the remaining 10–20% are completely individual (Mertins & Will, 2008). Within the European Guideline for Intellectual Capital Statements (European Commission, 2008), these harmonized IC factors were agreed upon as a basic standard set of factors which were relevant to the major part of companies when assessing and analyzing IC. On the basis of a firm's assessment of a set of standardized IC factors, strengths and weaknesses of IC can be compared between different companies, e.g., the respective industrial sector, different branches, size, regions, etc., and can reveal the very specific IC strategy of a sector, branch, region, or any other group of companies. The 15 standard IC factors are as follows:

Human Capital
- Professional competence
- Social competence
- Employee motivation
- Leadership ability

Structural Capital
- Internal cooperation and knowledge transfer
- Management instruments
- IT and explicit knowledge
- Product innovation
- Process optimization and innovation
- Corporate culture

Relational Capital
- Customer relationships
- Supplier relationships
- Public relationships
- Investor relationships
- Relationships to cooperation partners

The method ICS m.i.G. has achieved a comparatively high level of dissemination in the German-speaking area but also internationally (Bornemann et al., 2021). By 2011, it was implemented by trained ICS moderators in over 1,000 companies in Germany and Europe, using a software created for this purpose, the "ICS Toolbox," developed by Fraunhofer IPK. The guidelines (BMWi, 2004, 2013a), the ICS Toolbox (BMWi, 2013b), and information brochures have been accessed more than 100,000 times. The findings from the project have been integrated into the teaching of several public and private universities, and more than 400 consultants and users have been trained as certified "ICS moderators" through a specially designed training program at Fraunhofer Academy.

3 Digital Transformation Assessment

Digitalization fundamentally transforms the value creation processes of businesses across industries, influencing new business models, product/service development, and relationships with consumers, partners, and suppliers. This shift has a substantial influence on internal processes and skills of employees, requiring businesses to adjust quickly. Assessment models for digital transformation have evolved into critical instruments for helping firms through this complicated journey. These models serve as a basis for roadmaps, which analyze existing digital maturity and outline paths to greater efficiency and effectiveness. They usually include technology, infrastructure, worker capabilities, customer experience, and operational processes.

While they can offer valuable insights and guidance for organizations undergoing digital transformation, Digital Transformation Assessment models pose limitations. They can be rigid and prescriptive, leading organizations to focus too narrowly on specific aspects of digital transformation. This can limit innovation and creativity, as companies may feel compelled to conform to a predefined set of guidelines rather than adapting to their unique circumstances. In this context, many assessment models place a strong emphasis on technology adoption and infrastructure. While technology is a crucial component of digital transformation, an isolated focus on it can neglect other critical aspects, such as strategy, organizational culture, and competence development (Bellantuono et al., 2021; Aghamiri et al., 2022; Hajoary, 2020).

To structure the multilayered topic of digital transformation in companies, a reference framework was developed at Fraunhofer IPK that captures the essential value creation elements of a company in the context of digital transformation. Based on this framework, an assessment tool, the "Digital Transformation Assessment" (DTA), was created, aiming to survey the current state of digital transformation of companies worldwide (Kidschun et al., 2021).

The development of the DTA followed a multistep approach. First, relevant models from the areas of digital transformation were identified and analyzed by means of a systematic literature review. Although the main subjects of this research work were digital transformation models, Industry 4.0 and organizational development models have also been investigated to ensure a holistic view of the phenomenon of digital transformation as well as to consider and connect different facets. Based on the analyzed models, a holistic framework was developed that embodies an organization in digital transformation. The framework consists of seven dimensions that contribute to the fundamental and holistic understanding of a company, considering its whole value chain, represented by the dimensions of corporate strategy, leadership and corporate culture, organization and processes, employees and competences, technology, products and services, supply chain and networks, and their development in the context of digital transformation.

Subsequently, the related DTA questionnaire (LimeSurvey) based on the 7 dimensions of digital transformation was developed, which contains 33 assessment items. For their assessment, close-scaled questions formulated as statements are used. In the first part of the questionnaire, the participants are asked to weigh their agreement or disagreement to given statements on a given 5-point Likert scale, where level 1 describes a complete lack of attributes supporting the concepts of digital transformation and level 5 represents the state-of-the-art of required attributes.

The second part of the questionnaire determines the current and future relevance of the dimensions from the company's current perspective. This involves identifying how important the participant considers the listed dimensions for successfully shaping the digital transformation today and how the relevance of the respective dimension will change in the next 5 years against the backdrop of ongoing digitization.

After the assessment, demographic data is collected that allows for in-depth comparisons with relevant peer groups, enabling companies to determine their position on their individual digital transformation path and therewith uncovering specific digitalization gaps and improvement potential. The following demographic data is collected in a database:

(1) Company data: (a) location (by country), (b) industry sector (by NACE code), (c) annual turnover, (d) number of employees, (e) age of the organization, (f) type of products, and (g) main target markets
(2) Respondent data: (a) position, (b) department/function, and (c) age of the person

The total processing time of the questionnaire with its 33 assessment items is about 15 minutes. After completion, participants immediately receive their initial company-specific online evaluation report. The results are presented in a top–down approach, starting with their aggregated form using the average scores in the seven dimensions and consecutively breaking them down to their individual item assessment scores. The report includes a wide range of easy-to-interpret visualizations such as radar charts and provides a summary and initial recommendation for each dimension. In addition, great importance is attached to data security. Therefore, the survey complies with the data protection regulations of Art. 4 EU-GDPR, and the evaluations are only carried out based on anonymized data. The DTA questionnaire is available in five languages (English, German, Portuguese, Hungarian, Chinese).

The participants were reached by an open-call approach, allowing a wide range of international businesses, professionals, and organizations to participate in the survey. The outreach of the survey was expanded through the implementation of

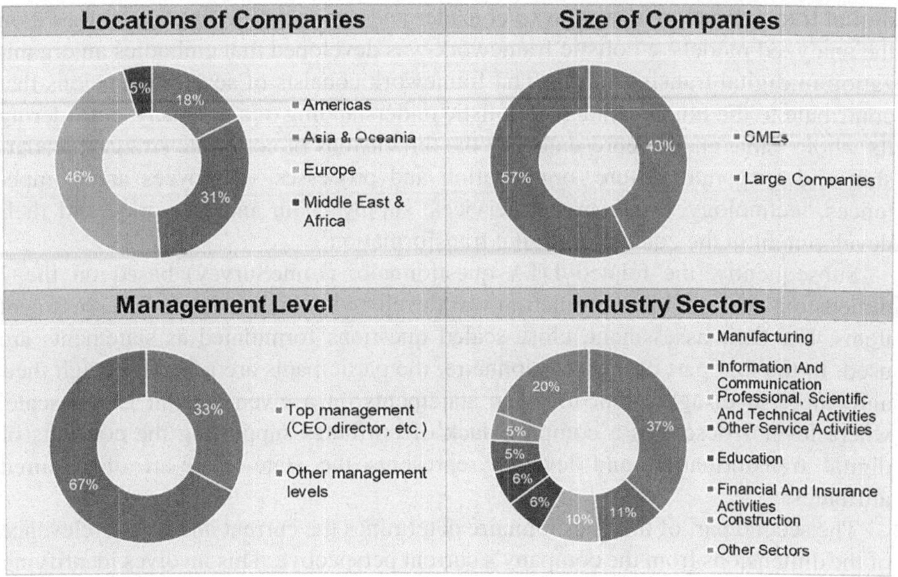

Fig. 2 Digital Transformation Assessment (DTA): database

various strategies, including the use of social media, professional networks, placement on relevant websites, newsletters, journals, magazines, and collaborations with industry partners. The survey was also presented at specific workshops and conferences.

The results cover a total period of 33 months, from June 2020 to August 2023, with a total of 948 responses. Although data collection was limited due to the possible scope of the survey, the sample size appears to be substantial and appropriate for the objectives of the study. The responses can be companies active in several industry sectors (Fig. 2). There is a near-even distribution of participating SMEs (43%) and large companies (57%). The organizations are mainly originating from Europe (46%), Asia and Oceania (31%), and the Americas (18%) and are active in a broad range of industry sectors, with a strong representation of manufacturing (37%), followed by ICT (11%) and professional, scientific, and technical activities (10%).

4 IC and Digitalization Analysis

Therefore, based on the two approaches described earlier, the intellectual capital statement (ICS) (Sect. 2) and the Digital Transformation Assessment (DTA) (Sect. 3), this section merges these two perspectives in order to answer the guiding questions, as laid out in the Introduction (Sect. 1).

When analyzing the DTA entries, only complete answers were considered, i.e., those from respondents who completed all the pages of the questionnaire. During data processing, entries that seemed to contradict this format, such as those identical to the previous one, with the same selections in all items, or completely blank, were excluded.

Secondly, for each point, the share of agreement was calculated based on the 5-point Likert scale. Subsequently, the data was categorized into groups of agreement, which would be utilized in the examination of the digital transformation status quo. The categories were, then, identified as "Strong" for responses of "Strongly agree" and "Rather agree"; "Moderate" for responses of "Partly agree"; and "Weak" for instances of combined disagreements ("Rather disagree" and "Strongly disagree"). The category of "Moderate" was treated distinctly (not grouped) due to its representation of a neutral standpoint, lacking a clear inclination toward agreement or disagreement. This methodology enabled the extraction of valuable insights and facilitated the formulation of decisions guided by data analysis.

With regard to the limitations of the survey, as mentioned earlier (Sect. 3), the aim was to reach a sample of approximately 1000 entries, after they had been completed and filtered, as explained at the beginning of this section. Furthermore, it is important to emphasize that the survey was carried out by means of self-assessment. This can introduce bias into the answers; therefore, the results are interpreted qualitatively here.

Taking the assessment items of the DTA and the respective responses from the surveyed companies into account, the following aspects of the intangible resource base's readiness for digital transformation in the global business context are investigated.[1]

Inside the **human capital** dimension, the employees' personal and social competences to cope with the requirements of an increasingly digitalized business context as well as their skills regarding the use of concrete digital technologies as part of their daily work routine are analyzed on the one hand. On the other hand, the leadership aspect covers the managers' commitment regarding the company's digitalization as well as the systematic development of the staff's competences and skills for the digital requirements. The employees' and managers' competences and mindset represent the most important prerequisite for any digitalization process, as any use of digital tools, technologies, or infrastructure can only be successful if the necessary competence base is established. The respective findings and assessment results are summarized in Sect. 4.1.

The IC dimension of **structural capital** comprises a wide range of digitalization aspects, from "hard facts" like digital technologies, data usage, and IT infrastructure to "soft facts" such as cultural aspects to cope with the accompanying change process of digital transformation, as well as internal procedures and structures for efficient collaboration. Moreover, the systematic development and innovation of

[1] A detailed overview regarding the matching of IC factors and digitalization items can be found in Appendix I.

digitalized products and processes as well as adequate corporate strategies for digitalization are assessed in this dimension. Taking the basic definition of structural capital into account (cf. Sect. 2), this dimension represents the actual organizational ability and readiness for digitalization, independent from the staff's competence base, including the company's products and services, its organization and processes, as well as the technologies in use. The respective results are discussed in Sect. 4.2.

Within the third IC dimension, the **relational capital**, specific aspects of digitally enabled interfaces and interaction with the customers as well as the digital integration of the supply chain and partner network are being investigated. Only here, the full potential of digital technologies can be brought into effect, considering the broad productivity gains from digitally integrated supply chains and value creation networks as well as the increased customer benefit and satisfaction through new customization opportunities, additional product features, or a faster and more convenient interaction with the customer. These aspects are analyzed and discussed in Sect. 4.3.

The assessment of readiness for digital transformation in the three IC dimensions is shown in Fig. 3. In general, it can be noted that all dimensions are well scored, but, at the same time, still have potential for improvement. The dimension structural capital shows the highest assessment regarding the digitalization aspects as summarized above, i.e., the internal structures and processes are already relatively well prepared for the companies' digital transformation journey. Also, human capital seems to be relatively well developed regarding the readiness for digitalization in general terms, i.e., the existing competencies and abilities already meet a good share of the requirements for the digital transformation. At the same time, the relational capital shows the highest potential for improvement in comparison to the other two

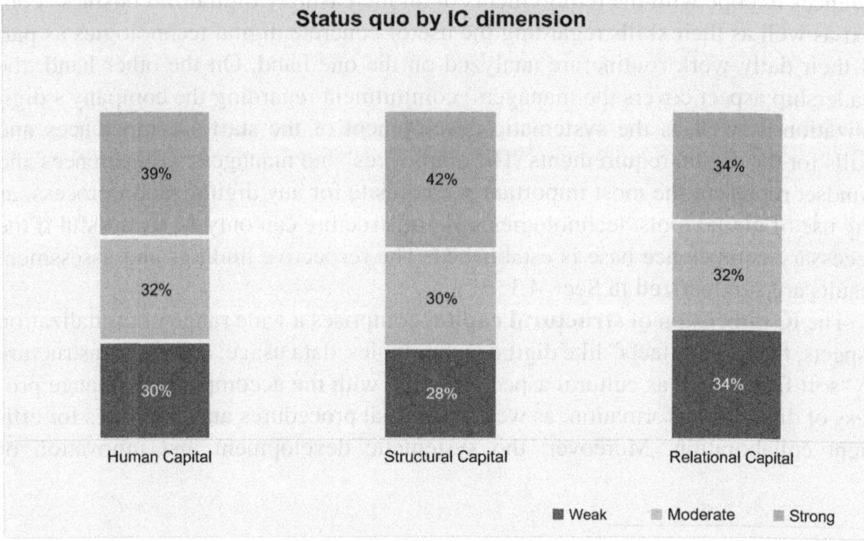

Fig. 3 Assessment of readiness for digital transformation in the three IC categories

categories of IC, which may illustrate the more complex challenge to integrate external stakeholders, like customers and suppliers, into the digital process chains.

These overall insights will be detailed in the following sections, investigating the single items of the Digital Transformation Assessment in the perspective of intellectual capital.

4.1 Human Capital

The ongoing digitalization is changing job profiles and placing new demands on employees' skills. According to a study by the World Economic Forum, almost half of all employees will need new or different professional skills in the next 4 years (World Economic Forum, 2020) to cope with new tasks. In addition to technical skills, these also include social, communicative, and personal competencies. Since these skills are subject to rapid change, companies must systematically track and evaluate them. On the basis of identified gaps, employees must be prepared for changes in their working environment through training, education measures, or coaching in order to exploit the potential of digitalization. The use of digital technologies in human resource management can help to systematize all HR processes (Schumacher et al., 2016; KPMG, 2015; Matt et al., 2015), but also enable new forms and ways of learning and acquiring skills.

How far these requirements on the human capital are met and how far these new opportunities to develop the human capital are used are investigated in this section, analyzing the following items of the Digital Transformation Assessment (Fig. 4):

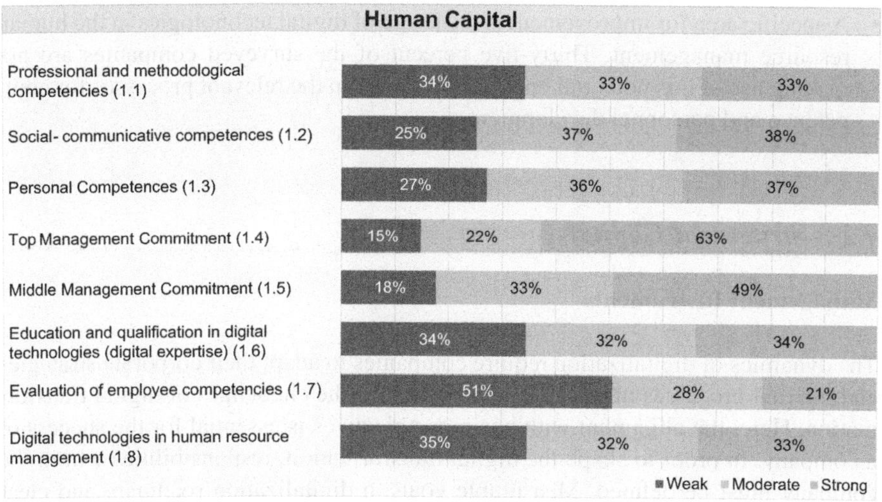

Fig. 4 Assessment of digitalization items in human capital ($n = 948$)

As a first conclusion from the survey results, the following findings in relation to digitalization and human capital can be derived:

- The employees' personal (1.3) and social-communicative competences (1.2) represent relative strengths within the human capital dimension when it comes to supporting the digital transformation of the surveyed companies.
- In comparison to these "soft skills," the professional and methodological competences (1.1) and the education and qualification in digital technologies (digital expertise) (1.6) show a considerable weaker status quo, with more than one-third of the surveyed companies assessing these factors as insufficiently developed. Hence, these basic "hard skills" for the successful incorporation and use of digital technologies in the employees' daily work represent an important field of improvement for many companies.
- When linking this finding to the weakest factor in human capital—the evaluation of employee competences (1.7)—it becomes apparent that one important prerequisite for a systematic development of the employees' digital competences is missing in more than half of the surveyed companies. A systematic evaluation of necessary competences by means of digital technologies could be a good starting point and an important driver to trigger improvements in the well-targeted competence development to support successful digital transformation.
- The management commitment for digitalization initiatives in the surveyed companies shows the best assessment within the human capital dimension. Both leadership levels, the top management and middle management, seem to actively support the strategic route toward digitalization inside their companies, which is an important success factor for any change process. However, especially the commitment of middle managers toward digitalization shows some room for improvement, as roughly half of the respondents are only partly or not completely satisfied with the support by middle management.
- A specific area for improvement is the usage of digital technologies in the human resource management. Thirty-five percent of the surveyed companies are not making use of this potential boost of efficiency in the relevant processes for competence and personnel development.

4.2 *Structural Capital*

Management Instruments

The dynamics of digitalization require companies to adapt their corporate strategies and internal processes in order to be prepared for the challenges of digital transformation. Here, the alignment with business objectives is essential for the success of a company. In order to shape the digital transformation, responsibilities within the company must be defined. Measurable goals, a digitalization roadmap, and clear control points help to keep a constant eye on the success of implementation. Such

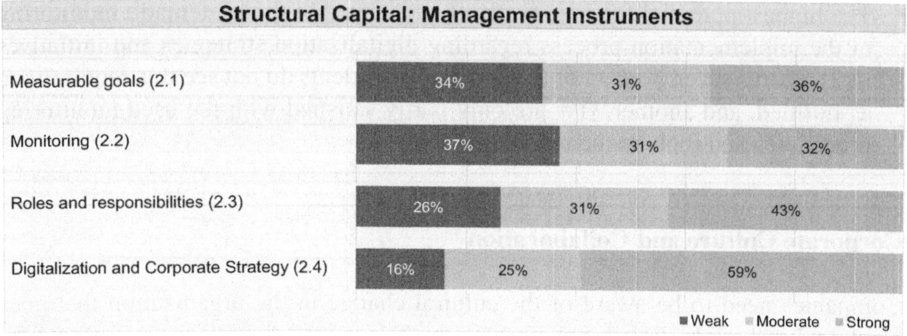

Fig. 5 Assessment of digitalization items in structural capital: management instruments ($n = 948$)

monitoring also makes it possible to dynamically adapt strategic initiatives if changes in the framework conditions make this necessary (Agca et al., 2017; Appelfeller & Feldmann, 2018; Back & Berghaus, 2015; Kinkel et al., 2016). These kinds of management instruments will support the leadership team and therefore have an impact on the way how decisions are made and what information paths are incorporated in the decision-making process.

With regard to the use of management instruments to shape and drive the digital transformation, the survey results are summarized in Fig. 5 based on selected items and the response distribution.

As a first conclusion from the survey results, the following findings in relation to digitalization and structural capital, focusing on the management instruments in use, can be derived:

- The strongest factor is the integration of digitalization strategies with the corporate strategies (item 2.4) of the surveyed companies. Almost 60% of the respondents are satisfied, and another 25% are at least partly satisfied with this important prerequisite for successful digitalization initiatives. Only if the company can link concrete business results and benefits to certain digitalization projects, the company as a whole can successfully plan and execute a well-targeted roadmap, answering the important questions first: "Why should we incorporate digital technologies and solutions, and what for? What is the benefit for us and for the client?"
- When it comes to implementing these integrated digitalization strategies, one of the decisive next steps is the clear assignment of the necessary roles and responsibilities for digitalization initiatives (2.3). This requirement is also met in the majority of the surveyed companies, with 74% of the respondents being at least partly satisfied.
- Another important success factor for strategy implementation is breaking down the strategic objectives into measurable goals (2.1) in order to make this process manageable on the operational level. Here, the responses show a heterogeneous assessment, with more than one-third of the respondents not being satisfied yet with the definition of measurable goals.

- The highest potential for improvement is detected in the systematic monitoring of the implementation process regarding digitalization strategies and initiatives (2.2). Thirty-seven percent of the survey respondents do not see this requirement as fulfilled, and another 31% are only partly satisfied with the used monitoring procedures and tools in their company.

Corporate Culture and Collaboration

Companies need to be aware of the cultural change in the organization that goes hand in hand with digital transformation. The cultural realignment affects all employees in the company and must be supported by the management team. The management team needs to recognize the threats posed by the digital transformation and its challenges and involve the employees in the transformation process (Matt et al., 2015; Gill & VanBoskirk, 2016; KPMG, 2015). In this context, a balanced internal corporate communication must show clear reasons why and for what digital transformation is important and which obstacles have to be overcome together.

For far-reaching change processes such as digital transformation, a positive culture of error is essential to be able to try things pragmatically and to learn quickly from the experiences made. Only when the digital transformation has arrived in the minds of the employees and, thus, in the culture of the organization, the potential of digitization can be exploited. Therefore, any organizational culture needs to accommodate external changes, foster innovation, and involve employees in change processes (participatory culture), while delivering enough space to try new ideas (Appelfeller & Feldmann, 2018; Back & Berghaus, 2015; Deloitte, 2018; Kinkel et al., 2016).

Some initial findings of the survey, as illustrated in Fig. 6, show that:

- Innovative forms of work using digital technologies (2.8) are already adopted by the majority of the companies surveyed and thus represent the biggest strength

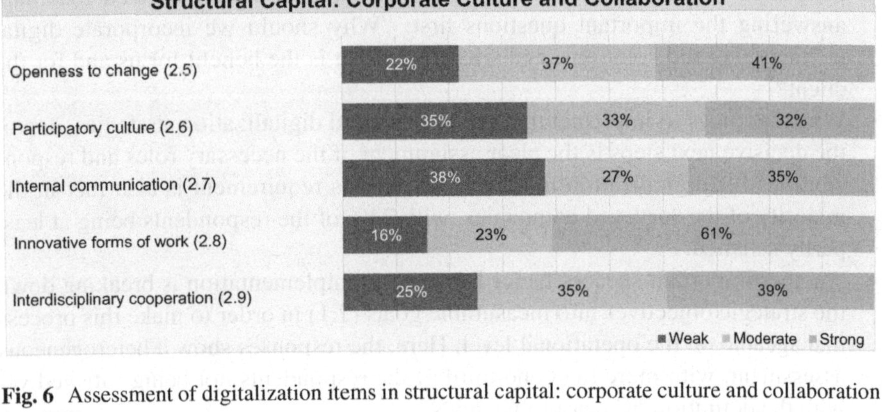

Fig. 6 Assessment of digitalization items in structural capital: corporate culture and collaboration ($n = 948$)

within this part of structural capital. The flexibility gained by the new forms of work, including the possibility for remote work based on digital collaboration tools, is already a reality for 61% of the respondents; another 23% are at least partly satisfied with the existing forms of new work.

- Looking at general characteristics of the corporate culture, the openness to change, i.e., a positive attitude of the employees toward the changes brought about by digitalization (2.5), is also assessed as a relative strength, whereas the participatory culture (2.6) is somewhat lacking behind, with 35% of the respondents not being satisfied with the active involvement of the employees in the transformation process and in shaping the company's digitalization path.
- While the necessary interdisciplinary cooperation to drive and execute digitalization initiatives inside the company (2.9) is assessed on an intermediate level, the well-targeted internal communication of activities for the digital transformation (2.7) appears as the biggest weakness within the corporate culture, with 38% of the respondents not being satisfied with this success factor.

In the overall, this part of the survey results shows that corporate culture is generally supporting the incorporation of changes, with new forms of work already being adopted in most of the surveyed companies, which may reflect the boost of these technologies during the coronavirus pandemic in 2020.

On the other end, internal communication needs to be improved significantly, including participative approaches to involve the employees in the ongoing initiatives of digital transformation in their companies. As research in the field of change management and knowledge management has shown, involvement is the most effective way of creating motivation and a willingness to change the own behavior among employees in the context of a change process (Finke & Will, 2003). Therefore, internal communication activities should include participative elements from the beginning when initializing fundamental change processes such as the digital transformation.

Linking this finding to the strategic management instruments discussed above, it becomes apparent that companies should pay attention to managing the whole change process in an integrated way. This includes developing integrated corporate and digitalization strategies, deriving measurable goals, assigning roles and responsibilities, and regularly monitoring the implementation progress, while continuously communicating these activities and intermediate results to the staff, providing adequate channels for feedback and opportunities to engage actively in the process, which can range from quick internal surveys to discussion forums, workshops, and dedicated working groups for specific sub-topics of the respective digitalization project. This holistic approach to change management seems to be one important success factor for the companies' digitalization initiatives in practice. Not only should the single elements be improved according to their improvement potential as shown above, but also the close integration of these elements is an important challenge to be tackled by companies engaging in digitalization programs.

Innovation: Products and Processes

Digitalization not only opens up huge potential to improve existing products or processes through the use of data-based services, but also to develop completely new business models. This also includes new ways of collecting data and evaluating its innovation and market potential (Sánchez & Zuntini, 2018). Successful companies constantly learn from the way their customers use their products and services. Products are continuously changed and adapted, and new and existing target groups are addressed differently. Companies are increasingly involving their customers (and other partners) actively in product development. For example, companies can expand their existing product portfolio with digital solutions in order to offer (existing) customers added value.

On the other hand, digital solutions provide options for making (internal) processes more efficient. Process innovation optimizes procedures in companies according to certain aspects. This can take place either noticeably for the company's customers or even directly aimed at them or is not noticed by them at all in the case of internal process innovations. By using digital tools and technologies to redesign business processes, improved ways of working can be achieved (e.g., time and resource savings).

Both dimensions of digital innovation—products and processes—were examined in the survey on the basis of different items by their response distribution (Fig. 7).

The following findings can be derived for the digitalization aspects in structural capital with a focus on the innovation of products (including services) and processes:

- The systematic monitoring and analysis of market potential arising from new digital technologies (2.10) is already an ongoing process in the majority of the surveyed companies. Forty-four percent of the respondents are satisfied with the use of this source for constantly developing their business models, which represents the strongest factor in this category of systematic innovation.

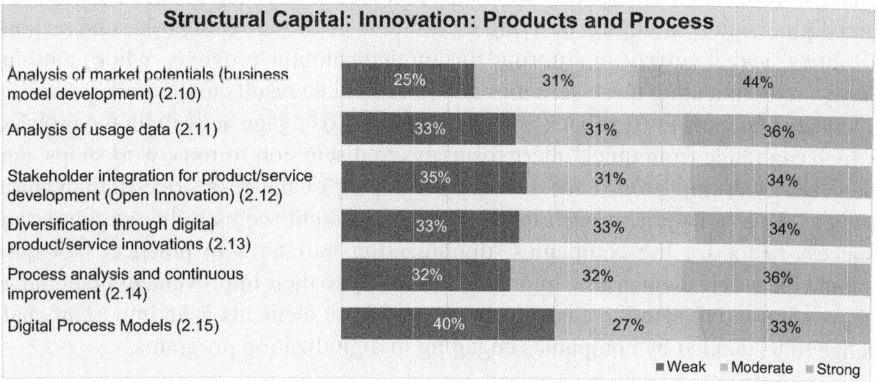

Fig. 7 Assessment of digitalization items in structural capital: innovation—products and processes ($n = 948$)

- Also, the analysis of usage data (2.11), i.e., data generated from the users of the companies' products, is a regular source for deriving improvements and further developments of the products and services for 36% of the responding companies, and at least partly used in another 31%.
- A very similar distribution of the assessment can be found for the regular analysis of internal processes and procedures with regard to potential improvements by implementing digital technologies (2.14).
- A somewhat higher potential for improvement is shown in the integration of customers and other external stakeholders in the development of digital products and services in an open innovation approach (2.12), as well as in the usage of digital technologies for new products or supplements (2.13) as a way to diversify their own product portfolio from competition.
- The weakest assessment in this category was given to the option of digital process models (2.15) as a means to continuously plan, design, and monitor the internal business processes, with 40% of the respondents not being satisfied, and another 27% only partly satisfied. This more comprehensive way of digitally managing processes internally can be seen as a next stage, based on, but at the same time expanding and partly automating the existing regular analysis and improvements of internal process performance (see item 2.14).

A prerequisite for unlocking the potential of digitalization to optimize processes is to systematically analyze the company's business processes (e.g., by establishing process working groups that regularly review and adapt the business processes of the company to the need for change due to new technologies). While the basic stage of analyzing the processes (manually) to determine the potential for improvement and development by implementing digital technologies is already a relatively widespread reality in the surveyed companies, the more complex stage of implementing and using digital process models shows room for advancements. Under the label "digital twin" or "digital shadow," digital models are becoming increasingly important. A digital twin is the virtual image of an object or system from the real world. In addition to individual objects and products, it can also be used to represent processes, services, and entire plants or factories in the digital world. Such virtual models can help to integrate data (in real time) and thus increase process efficiency. But less complex solutions such as computer-aided design (CAD), computer-aided manufacturing (CAM), or workflow management systems also fall into this category of digital process models.

In a similar logic, the continuous innovation of products and services is already relying on data-based market analysis and on data-based analysis of product usage in the majority of companies, whereas the full integration of customers and partners into the product development process by using digital technologies in an open innovation approach shows a larger potential for improvement and for unlocking the full potential of digitalization.

Information and Communication Technology (ICT)

Thoughtful digitalization based on modern software solutions and architectures forms the basis for digital services, innovations, and a modern process organization. Investments in a powerful IT infrastructure are therefore an important prerequisite for successful digital transformation (Matt et al., 2015; Appelfeller & Feldmann, 2018). Moreover, digital innovations often thrive on the evaluation of data in large quantities. The integration and analysis of these data volumes can lead to completely new insights in the company. However, many companies are not yet aware of the value of data and its analysis. In this context, IT security is becoming increasingly more important. Companies must be aware of potential risks and establish appropriate rules and standards to ward off dangers (Schuh et al., 2017; Schumacher et al., 2016; Lichtblau et al., 2015).

These aspects of digitalization of the structural capital in the area of information and communication technologies are analyzed based on five selected items (Fig. 8). The main findings to be derived from this analysis include:

- In general, the ICT-related items show the best assessment by the surveyed companies within the structural capital dimension.
- The biggest strength lies in the IT security (2.18), with 66% of the respondents being satisfied with the standards and regulations in place. This is good news in terms of the risks which come along with the digitalization efforts, being mitigated on a technical level.
- Also, the investments (2.16) and regular updating of the IT infrastructure (2.17) are satisfactory to almost half of the respondents.
- Very similarly, the collaboration technologies in use (2.20) are meeting the requirements of around half of the surveyed companies, and at least partly for another 28%.
- The biggest potential for improvement lies in the integration of data (2.19). Here, 32% are not satisfied yet with the IT and data architecture and the ways to collect, consolidate, aggregate, and evaluate data from various sources and in real time.

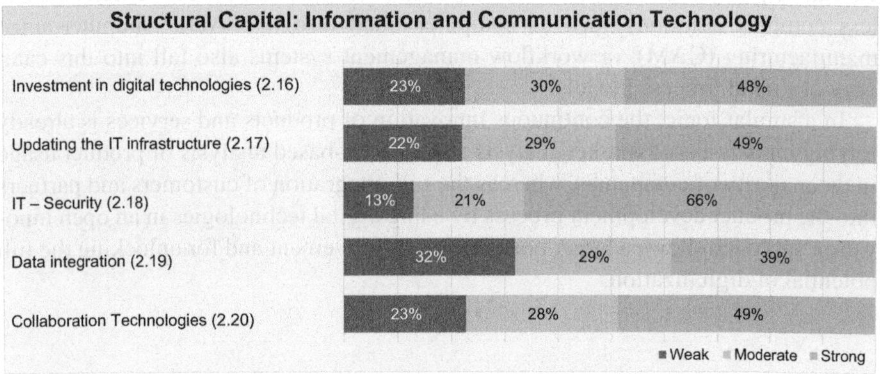

Fig. 8 Assessment of digitalization items in structural capital: ICT ($n = 948$)

4.3 Relational Capital

The digital transformation has changed customer behavior and expectations enormously in recent years. In the digital space, users expect support via different channels, with correspondingly fast and competent customer service. Points of contact between companies and customers are increasing due to digitalization, and companies need to build these touchpoints in a targeted manner.

An automated and seamless exchange of information between companies and their value creation partners enables a more dynamic collaboration and creates more transparency. This will form the basis to take advantage of common market conditions and to exploit synergies. It therefore makes sense to reach agreements with partners on which data should be exchanged. Digital interfaces must be coordinated considering technical, organizational, and legal aspects (Appelfeller & Feldmann, 2018).

One of the biggest challenges in the digital transformation does lie in developing an integrated supply chain approach that connects with suppliers and customers. Achieving full digital collaboration and then using it effectively throughout the supply chain require all stakeholders involved to develop processes, capabilities, and systems to support them. Culturally, they must develop the responsibility and trust to openly share accurate information in a timely manner. For many organizations, this requires a maturity far beyond that exhibited in their traditional supplier, partner, and customer relationships (Agca et al., 2017).

These aspects of digitalization within the relational capital dimension are assessed by the following items of the Digital Transformation Assessment (Fig. 9):

Key findings in the relational capital dimension are the following:

- The surveyed companies assess the IT- and data-based customer management (3.1) as the strongest factor regarding digitalization within the relational capital, with 42% of the respondents being satisfied with the used technologies to ana-

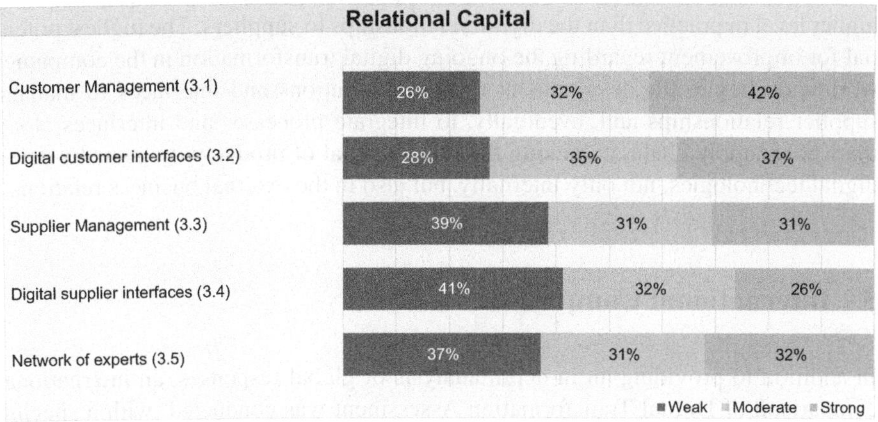

Fig. 9 Assessment of digitalization items in relational capital ($n = 948$)

lyze and process customer data for the purposes of improving sales, after-sales services, and complaint management. However, 26% are still not satisfied with the utilization of these basic technologies to manage the relationship to customers.

- The next stage of digitalization of customer relationships is to (more) digital interfaces for the customers (3.2), like online shops, chatbots, digital offers for direct download, interaction on social media, etc. These more advanced digital solutions for a better customer experience are already a reality for 37% of the responding companies, lacking behind the more basic technologies described above, and showing a higher potential for improvement, with 28% not being satisfied with the technologies in use in their company.
- When it comes to the supplier side of the value chain, the survey clearly shows the biggest potential for improvement in the digital transformation journeys of companies worldwide. Even the more basic management of suppliers (3.3), like data-based evaluation of suppliers and supplier risks or an automated order management, shows significant room for improvement, with 39% of the respondents not being satisfied.
- This gap is even bigger regarding the more advanced integration of digital supplier interfaces (3.4) with fully digital supplier communication and data exchange to digital delivery planning and real-time monitoring of order status and inventories. Forty-one percent are not satisfied with the installed solutions or do not have any solutions yet, and the satisfaction rate drops to the minimum of 26%.
- Using the knowledge and expertise of external experts and networks (3.5) to advance in the digital transformation is a reality for only 32% of the respondents, with another 31% only partly using this opportunity for improving the company's digitalization in the overall. Hence, this aspect of the relational capital, including networking with scientists and specialists as well as projects or working groups with cooperation partners, also shows a great potential to be explored by the companies when engaging in the further development of digital solutions for their business model.

In a nutshell, the digital relationships to customers are already on a significantly higher level in practice than the digital relationships to suppliers. The highest potential for improvement regarding the ongoing digital transformation in the companies worldwide lies in the development of digital solutions and interfaces to manage supplier relationships and, eventually, to integrate processes and interfaces along the whole supply chain, unlocking the full potential of productivity gains by using digital technologies, not only internally, but also in the external business relations.

5 International Comparison

In addition to providing an in-depth analysis of global responses, an international comparison of Digital Transformation Assessment was conducted, with a specific focus on intellectual capital. This comprehensive examination delves into continental disparities in the three dimensions of intellectual capital: human capital, structural capital, and relational capital.

5.1 *Human Capital*

The analysis of the IC dimension human capital reveals interesting geographical trends. Overall, enterprises from different global regions show a mostly moderate status quo of their digital transformation. While companies from Europe and Asia show a higher digital readiness, American companies from both North and South America seem to be slightly less developed (Fig. 10).

A deeper look at the detailed assessment items of human capital allows an analysis of specific regional differences.

Europe demonstrates a strong commitment from top to middle management (1.4 and 1.5), with over half of the participants strongly agreeing with this strength in management. However, challenges arise in the evaluation of employee competencies (1.7) and integrating digital technologies into human resource management (1.8). This could be attributed to a conservative approach to performance evaluation and a slower adoption of advanced digital tools, influenced by the desire to balance technological advances with established competencies.

In **Asia and Oceania**, the trend of leadership commitment is similar, which is shown in their efforts to cultivate a highly qualified workforce and create a culture of strong leadership that facilitate digital initiatives. Asia and Oceania are performing best of all regions in top management commitment (1.4), with around 69% of

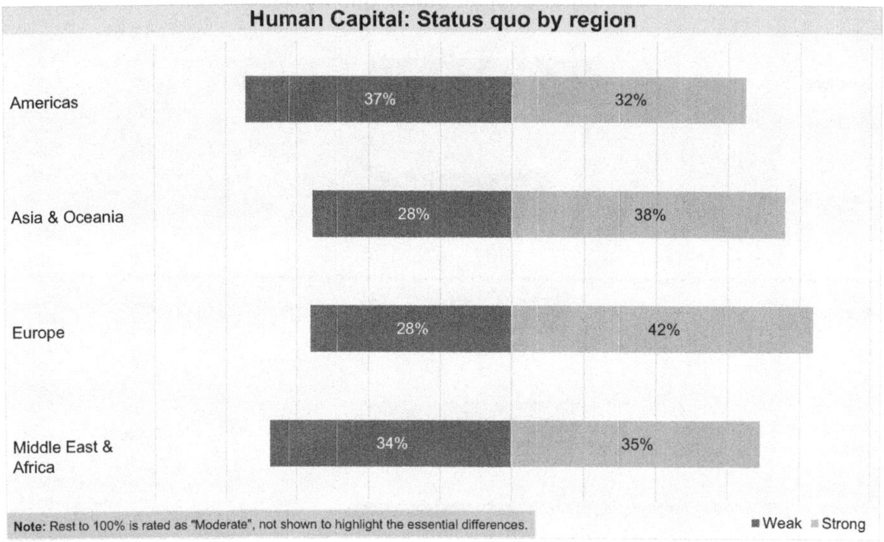

Fig. 10 Comparison of global regions in the assessment of human capital

respondents considering this item to be strong, followed by middle management commitment (1.5). The region faces challenges in two key human capital areas, namely, the education and qualification in digital technologies (1.6) and the evaluation of employee competencies (1.7).

The **Middle East and Africa and the Americas** also show a tendency toward strong leadership, albeit with comparatively lower scores. In the Middle East and Africa, the level of personal competences in the digital environment (1.3) is rated as an area for improvement, followed by the evaluation of employee competences (1.7). Finally, in the case of the Americas, the region faces the same challenge as the others in the evaluation of employee competencies (1.7), but American companies show the lowest average item performance (2.3 out of 5, while the overall average is 2.6), where more than 60% of respondents considered this item to be weak. Professional and methodological digital skills (1.1) are also rated with room for improvement.

5.2 *Structural Capital*

Comparing the status quo of structural capital at a global level, the overall picture is more positive than for human capital. Europe and Asia and Oceania scored best in terms of the status quo of digital transformation. Companies from the Americas as well as the Middle East and Africa appear to be lagging slightly behind in the comparison (Fig. 11).

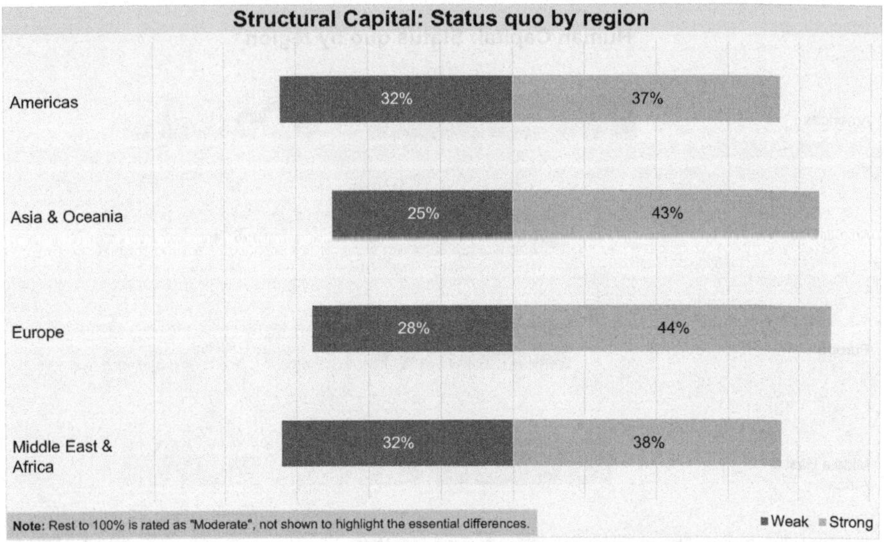

Fig. 11 Comparison of global regions in the assessment of structural capital

The detailed analysis shows that the participants from all the four regions rated the IT security (2.18) as the strongest dimension, which reflects awareness of digital challenges. The other ratings vary.

In addition to their performance in IT security (2.18), Asia and Oceania is also consistently strong in digitalization and corporate strategy (2.4). Compared to other regions, Asia and Oceania seems to be even better positioned to adapt and seize the opportunities offered by the digital age due to their strategic agility. Challenges are found in digital process models (2.15) and stakeholder integration for product and service development (2.12).

In **Europe**, besides IT security (2.18), the assessment of innovative forms of work (2.8) stands out. This significance can be attributed to significant investments in technology infrastructure and a corporate culture that encourages innovation and teamwork. The region is notable not just for its data protection laws, such as General Data Protection Regulation (GDPR), but also for fostering innovation in the workplace, supporting collaboration techniques. These same characteristics, however, can also be attributed to the region's challenges in monitoring (2.2) and digital process models (2.15).

In the **Americas**, while demonstrating strengths in IT security (2.18) and innovative forms of work (2.8), companies face significant challenges in monitoring (2.2) and participatory culture (2.6).

Middle East and Africa exhibited outstanding performance in two items: IT security (2.18) and collaboration technologies (2.20). This achievement can be linked to the quick adoption of collaborative technologies, as well as the increased emphasis on investing in cybersecurity solutions. Nevertheless, in spite of these improvements, the region's total performance was still behind that of the other regions. This can be attributed mostly because of the difficulties observed in digital process models (2.15). The largest problem, however, is found in monitoring (2.2).

5.3 *Relational Capital*

Exploring relational capital, regional variations in customer and digital supplier interfaces can be observed. While European enterprises are leading in the dimension of relational capital, the rest of the world lacks behind just slightly (Fig. 12).

Europe, Asia and Oceania, and the Americas exhibit consistency in customer management (3.1) and digital customer interfaces (3.2), showcasing a collective commitment to customer-centric strategies in a digital landscape. Digital supplier interfaces (3.3) and supplier management (3.4), on the other hand, are seen as obstacles. These might be related to difficulties in the integration of digital systems with suppliers, resulting in obstacles in communication and external collaboration.

The **Middle East and Africa** excels in the implementation of digital customer interfaces (3.2) as well as customer management (3.1). The region also faces the

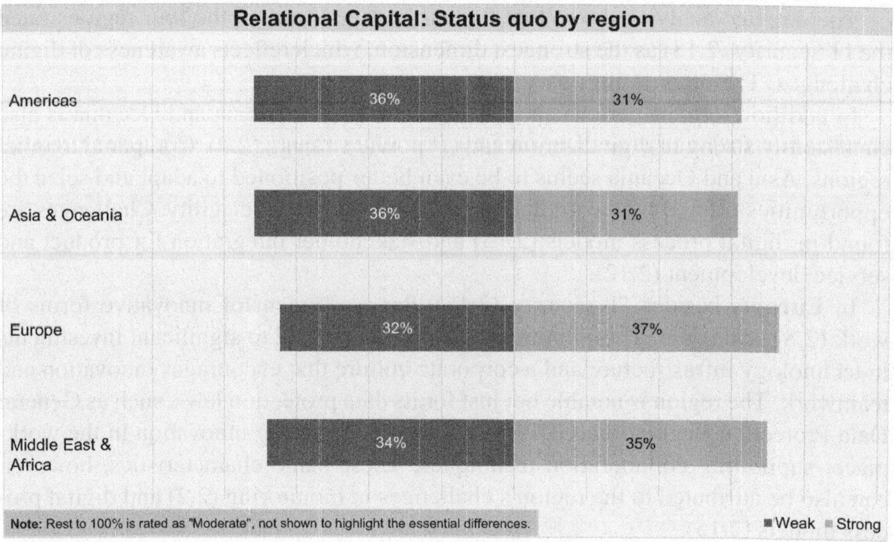

Fig. 12 Comparison of global regions in the assessment of relational capital

biggest challenges with its digital supplier interfaces (3.4). But also, their network of experts (3.5) shows challenges in establishing a strong community of outside for organizational development and innovation.

5.4 Comparison by Regional Profiles

The following tables summarize the results from the perspective of the different regions. A distinction is made between human capital, structural capital, and relational capital. For each type of IC, the two factors with the best rating and the two factors with the greatest potential for improvement are listed here.

Asia and Oceania

Table 1 summarizes the assessment results for the region Asia and Oceania on the strengths and weaknesses in the three dimensions of intellectual capital in the context of digital transformation.

Americas

Table 2 summarizes the assessment results for the Americas regarding strengths and weaknesses in the three dimensions of intellectual capital in the context of digital transformation.

Table 1 Strengths and weaknesses of Asia and Oceania in terms of intellectual capital

	Human capital	Structural capital	Relational capital
Best-rated factors	Top management commitment (1.4) Middle management commitment (1.5)	IT security (2.18) Digitalization and corporate strategy (2.4)	Customer management (3.1) Digital customer interfaces (3.2)
Highest potential for improvement	Education and qualification in digital technologies (1.6) Evaluation of employee competencies (1.7)	Digital process models (2.15) Stakeholder integration for product and service development (2.12)	Digital supplier interfaces (3.3) Supplier management (3.4)

Table 2 Strengths and weaknesses of the Americas in terms of intellectual capital

	Human capital	Structural capital	Relational capital
Best-rated factors	Top management commitment (1.4) Middle management commitment (1.5)	IT security (2.18) Innovative forms of work (2.8)	Customer management (3.1) Digital customer interfaces (3.2)
Highest potential for improvement	Evaluation of employee competencies (1.7) Professional and methodological digital skills (1.1)	Monitoring (2.2) Participatory culture (2.6)	Digital supplier interfaces (3.3) Supplier management (3.4)

Table 3 Strengths and weaknesses of Europe in terms of intellectual capital

	Human capital	Structural capital	Relational capital
Best-rated factors	Top management commitment (1.4) Middle management commitment (1.5)	IT security (2.18) Innovative forms of work (2.8)	Customer management (3.1) Digital customer interfaces (3.2)
Highest potential for improvement	Evaluation of employee competencies (1.7) Integrating digital technologies into HRM (1.8)	Monitoring (2.2) Digital process models (2.15)	Digital supplier interfaces (3.3) Supplier management (3.4)

Europe

Table 3 summarizes the assessment results for Europe on the strengths and weaknesses in the three dimensions of intellectual capital in the context of digital transformation.

Table 4 Strengths and weaknesses of Middle East and Africa in terms of intellectual capital

	Human capital	Structural capital	Relational capital
Best-rated factors	Top management commitment (1.4) Middle management commitment (1.5)	IT security (2.18) Collaboration technologies (2.20)	Customer management (3.1) Digital customer interfaces (3.2)
Highest potential for improvement	Personal competences in the digital environment (1.3) Evaluation of employee competencies (1.7)	Monitoring (2.2) Digital process models (2.15)	Digital supplier interfaces (3.3) Network of experts (3.5)

Middle East and Africa

Table 4 summarizes the assessment results for the region Middle East and Africa regarding strengths and weaknesses in the three dimensions of intellectual capital in the context of digital transformation.

6 Summary

The discussion on digital transformation emphasizes its complexity, which goes beyond mere automation and reshapes the entire value creation structures. Companies worldwide are being called upon to redesign their practices, strategies, processes, and products. In a global study of around 1,000 companies, researchers at Fraunhofer IPK have determined the maturity level of digital transformation. The focus here is on intangible value drivers, the intellectual capital of organizations.

The results show that at a global level, structural capital and human capital are already well developed in general. In contrast, relational capital shows the greatest potential for improvement and highlights the challenge of integrating external stakeholders into digital value chains. Even though there are geographical differences, similarities were identified between the regions.

In the area of human capital, it has become clear that, regardless of the region, top and middle management have recognized the relevance of digital transformation and are actively fostering its implementation in the company. However, there is a great need for action in all regions, especially when it comes to assessing the digital skills of employees. The right tools do not yet appear to be in place for this purpose. However, such an assessment is important in order to be able to systematically implement programs to develop digital skills of the employees that are critical to success.

The already established standards and mechanisms for IT security are a strength in the structural capital dimension of all regions. The need for improvement at a global level is seen particularly in the use of suitable management tools to monitor the digital transformation progress in the company. Such monitoring systems are important so that the current status can always be kept in view and, if necessary, measures can be taken to adapt to it.

With regard to relational capital, there are also similarities across all regions: the use of digital media and formats to manage customer relationships is already quite well developed. However, all regions see potential for improvement in better digitalizing the interfaces between companies and their suppliers. In the age of global, closely interlinked value chains, this appears to be an important field of action for the future.

While the study provides valuable insights into the subject matter, it is essential to acknowledge its limitations. Self-assessment methods inherently introduce the potential for bias, influenced by factors such as participants' management level, industry sector, age, and other demographic variables. These biases as well as the specific sample of companies could affect the accuracy and generalizability of the findings. Therefore, caution should be exercised when interpreting the results, and future research may benefit from conducting follow-up interviews or case studies with a subset of companies to gain deeper insights into their experiences and challenges in developing capital for digital transformation. This addition of qualitative data could complement the quantitative findings as well as mitigate the abovementioned limitations and provide a more comprehensive understanding of the phenomenon under study.

References

Agca, O., Gibson, J., Godsell, J., Ignatius, J., Davies, C. W., & Xu. (2017). *An Industry 4 readiness assessment tool*. Crimson & Co, University of Warwick.

Aghamiri, S., Karima, J., & Cavus, N. (2022). Advantages of digital transformation models and frameworks for business: A systematic literature review. *International Journal of Advanced Computer Science and Applications, 13*(12).

Appelfeller, W., & Feldmann, C. (2018). *Die digitale Transformation des Unternehmens. Systematischer Leitfaden mit zehn Elementen zur Strukturierung und Reifegradmessung*. Springer Gabler. https://doi.org/10.1007/978-3-662-54061-9

Back, A., & Berghaus, S. (2015). *Digital Maturity & Transformation Studie*. Hg. v. Universität St. Gallen Institut für Wirtschaftsinformatik.

Bellantuono, N., Nuzzi, A., Pontrandolfo, P., & Scozzi, B. (2021). Digital transformation models for the I4. 0 transition: Lessons from the change management literature. *Sustainability, 13*(23), 12941.

BMWi. (2004). *Intellectual capital statement – Made in Germany*. Guideline 1.0. Ger-man Ministry for Economics and Technology (BMWi) Berlin. http://akwissensbilanz.org/en/ics-guidelines/

BMWi. (2013a). *Wissensbilanz – Made in Germany*. Leitfaden 2.0. Dritte überarbeitete Auflage. Bundesministerium für Wirtschaft und Technologie (BMWi). http://akwissensbilanz.org/leitfaeden-und-mehr/

BMWi. (2013b). *Wissensbilanz toolbox 2.0*. Software zur Erstellung einer Wissensbilanz. Dritte überarbeitete Auflage. Bundesministerium für Wirtschaft und Technologie. http://akwissensbilanz.org/en/german-ic-toolbox/

Bornemann, M., & Alwert, K. (2007). The German guideline for intellectual capital statements – Method and experiences. *Journal for Intellectual Capital, 8*(4), 563–576. Emerald Group Publishing Limited ISSN 1469–1930.

Bornemann, M., Alwert, K., & Will, M. (2021). Lessons learned in intellectual capital management in Germany between 2000 and 2020 – History, applications, outlook. *Journal of Intellectual Capital, 22*(3), 560–586. https://doi.org/10.1108/JIC-03-2020-0085

Deloitte. (2018). *Digital maturity model*. Achieving digital maturity to drive growth.

Edvinsson, L., & Kivikas, M. (2007). Intellectual capital (IC) or Wissensbilanz process: Some German experiences. *Journal of Intellectual Capital, 8*(3), 376–385. https://doi.org/10.1108/14691930710774821

European Commission. (2008). *InCaS: Intellectual capital statement – Made in Europe*. European ICS Guideline [online]. www.incas-europe.org

Finke, I., & Will, M. (2003). Motivation for knowledge management. In K. Mertins, P. Heisig, & J. Vorbeck (Eds.), *Knowledge management. Concepts and best practices* (pp. 66–91). Springer-Verlag.

Gavrila, S., & de Lucas Ancillo, A. (2021). COVID-19 as an entrepreneurship, innovation, digitization and digitalization accelerator: Spanish Internet domains registration analysis. *British Food Journal, 123*(10), 3358–3390.

Gill, M., & VanBoskirk, S. (2016). *The digital maturity model 4.0. Benchmarks: Digital business transformation playbook*. Hg. v. Forrester.com

Grineva, N., Mikhailova, S., & Kontsevaya, N. (2023, September). Econometric modeling of the company's intellectual capital in the context of digitalization. In *2023 16th international conference management of large-scale system development (MLSD)* (pp. 1–5). IEEE.

Hajoary, P. K. (2020). Industry 4.0 maturity and readiness models: A systematic literature review and future framework. *International Journal of Innovation and Technology Management, 17*(07), 2030005.

Kidschun, F., Hecklau, F., Orth, R., & Kohl, H. (2021). Digital transformation assessment: A systematic approach to evaluate and shape the digital organization. In *Presentation at TAKE 2021 theory and applications in the knowledge economy, July 7th–9th, virtual conference*.

Kinkel, S., Rahn, J., & Rieder, B. (2016). *IMPULS. Digital-Vernetztes Denken in der Produktion. Stiftung für den Maschinenbau, den Anlagenbau und die Informationstechnik*. Hg. v. Fraunhofer ISI, ILIN und VDMA IMPULS-Stiftung.

KPMG (Hg.). (2015). *Information technology services. Are you ready for digital trans-formation? Measuring your digital business aptitude*.

Lichtblau, K., Stich, V., Bertenrath, R., Blum, M., Bleider, M., Millack, A. et al. (2015). *Industrie 4.0 readiness*. Hg. v. VDMA.

Matt, C., Hess, T., & Benlian, A. (2015). Digital transformation strategies. *Business & Information Systems Engineering, 57*(5), 339–343. https://doi.org/10.1007/s12599-015-0401-5

Mertins, K., & Will, M. (2008). InCaS: Intellectual capital statement – Made in Europe; strategic relevance of intellectual capital in European SMEs and sectoral differences. In *Proceedings of the 9th European conference on knowledge management*.

Nedoluzhko, O. V. (2022). *Assessment of intellectual capital of organization in conditions of digitalization* (Series: Eco-nomics) (Vol. 3, pp. 46–54). Vestnik of Astrakhan State Technical University.

Penco, L., Profumo, G., Serravalle, F., & Viassone, M. (2022). Has COVID-19 pushed digitalisation in SMEs? The role of entrepreneurial orientation. *Journal of Small Business and Enterprise Development*.

Robertson, J., Botha, E., Walker, B., Wordsworth, R., & Balzarova, M. (2022). Fortune favours the digitally mature: The impact of digital maturity on the organisational resilience of SME retailers during COVID-19. *International Journal of Retail & Distribution Management, 50*(8/9), 1182–1204.

Roos, G. (2018). Resource deployment system implications of migrating the firm into a digital value creation paradigm. *Knowledge Management Research and Practice, 16*(3), 281–291.

Rusdi, M. (2023). The moderatoring role of digital transformation strategy on the relationship between intellectual capital and competitive advantage in private universities in South Sumatra, Indonesia. *Asian Journal of Economics, Business and Accounting, 23*(19), 36–54.

Sánchez, M. A., & Zuntini, J. I. (2018). Organizational readiness for the digital transformation: A case study research. *Revista Gestão & Tecnologia, 18*, 70–99.

Schuh, G., Ander, R., Gausemeier, J., ten Hompel, M., & Wahlster, W. (Eds.). (2017). *Industrie 4.0 Maturity Index. Managing the Digital Transformation of Companies (acatech STUDY)*. Herbert Utz Verlag. https://www.acatech.de/wp-content/uploads/2018/03/acatech_STUDIE_Maturity_Index_eng_WEB-1.pdf

Schumacher, A., Erol, S., & Sihn, W. (2016). A maturity model for assessing industry 4.0 readiness and maturity of manufacturing enterprises. *Procedia CIRP, 52*, 161–166. https://doi.org/10.1016/j.procir.2016.07.040

Statista. (2023). Retrieved August 29, 2023, from https://www.statista.com/study/74997/dossier-digital-transformation/

Will, M. (2015). Intellectual capital statement as a strategic management tool – The European approach. In P. Ordoñez de Pablos & L. Edvinsson (Eds.), *Intellectual capital in organizations. Non-financial reports and accounts (= Routledge advances in organizational learning and knowledge management)* (pp. 93–108). Routledge Chapman & Hall.

World Economic Forum (Eds.). (2020). *The future of jobs report 2020*. Accessed August 2, 2023, from https://www.weforum.org/reports/the-future-ofjobs-report-2020

Zhang, Y., Li, H., & Yao, Z. (2023). Intellectual capital, digital transformation and firm performance: Evidence based on listed companies in the Chinese construction industry. *Engineering Construction and Architectural Management*.

An Intellectual Capital Resource Taxonomy and Measurement System for the Green Economy

Göran Roos

Abstract This chapter introduces a pioneering intellectual capital taxonomy and measurement system for the green economy, aimed at facilitating strategic management of intellectual resources to achieve sustainable development and economic growth. It provides a structured framework for classifying and measuring intellectual capital, such as human knowledge, organisational processes, and technological assets, to promote environmental sustainability and economic prosperity. The taxonomy enhances strategic decision-making through effective communication, benchmarking, and identification of value creation opportunities. Developed from a 'bottom–up' approach for precision and clarity, it integrates various resources into a holistic view, supporting future research and application in the green economy. The chapter underscores the taxonomy's role in strategic management within the green economy, highlighting its potential to balance economic goals with environmental stewardship and to drive sustainable development and competitive advantage.

This chapter draws heavily on Roos (2019). Optimising resource deployment within the firm: overcoming theoretical problems with a practical application (Doctoral Dissertation, University of South Australia).

G. Roos (✉)
Intellectual Capital Services Limited, Buckingham, UK

Institute for Sustainability, Energy and Resources (ISER), The University of Adelaide, Adelaide, Australia

School of Communication, Leadership and Marketing, Kristiania University College—Ernst G Mortensen Foundation, Oslo, Norway

Centre for Business Performance, Cranfield School of Management, Cranfield University, Bedford, UK
e-mail: goran@roos.org.uk

F. Matos et al. (eds.), *Intellectual Capital in a Global Business Landscape*, Contributions to Management Science, https://doi.org/10.1007/978-3-031-86362-2_3

1 An Intellectual Capital Taxonomy

The dynamic sphere of the green economy has underscored the critical importance of intellectual capital (IC) management as a cornerstone for achieving organisational success. Within this context, organisations are increasingly required to chart a course through the intricacies of sustainable development, compelling them to devise methodologies for the effective delineation and quantification of their intellectual assets. Intellectual capital, an aggregation of human knowledge, organisational processes, customer relations, and technological assets, presents a multifaceted challenge. Its inherent diversity not only complicates management efforts but also impedes organisations' capabilities to harness these assets towards fostering environmental sustainability alongside economic expansion. The evolution of intellectual capital research has seen a shift from reporting to disclosure, as critically examined by Dumay (2016), highlighting the need for more dynamic and context-specific approaches, to intellectual capital management.

In response to these exigencies, the present manuscript proffers an intellectual capital taxonomy and measurement framework, specifically tailored for entities operating within the green economy. This framework endeavours to equip organisations with a lucid and definitive mechanism for the classification of intellectual resources. Such a mechanism is instrumental in engendering a profound comprehension of the resources' distinct attributes, behaviours, and the interplay among them. Moreover, by instituting a uniform lexicon and structuring resources into coherent categories, the taxonomy facilitates seamless communication among stakeholders, enables the benchmarking of intellectual capital across diverse scenarios, and, crucially, underpins the systematic measurement of intellectual capital. This measurement is indispensable for the identification of avenues for value generation, the enhancement of performance metrics, and the formulation of strategic directives that harmonise economic aims with sustainability imperatives. Secundo et al. (2020) provide a structured literature review that underscores the interconnections between sustainable development, intellectual capital, and technology policies, further emphasising the relevance of this taxonomy in the green economy context.

The taxonomy is conceptualised from foundational principles, ensuring a meticulous categorisation of resources predicated on their intrinsic characteristics to guarantee both comprehensiveness and uniqueness. This methodical approach mitigates the prevalent ambiguities and inaccuracies that often beleaguer the management of intellectual capital. Additionally, the taxonomy is congruent with the tenets of the resource-based view, integrating an array of resources—monetary, physical, relational, organisational, and human—into a holistic perspective. This endeavour seeks to propel forward the discourse on intellectual capital within the green economy, laying down a robust groundwork for subsequent research initiatives and pragmatic applications in this pivotal domain.

A taxonomy within the intellectual capital sphere serves multiple pivotal functions. It offers a systematic schema for classifying a broad spectrum of resources, thereby elucidating their distinct characteristics and the dynamics between them. The establishment of a standardised terminology is crucial for ensuring unambiguous communication among the intellectual capital community, thereby averting potential misunderstandings. Such clarity and organisation are essential for fostering effective knowledge exchange and collaboration among researchers and practitioners alike. The taxonomy thus acts as a scaffold that organises resources into logical groupings, revealing their influence on organisational performance and facilitating a more nuanced analysis and evaluation. Furthermore, a well-defined taxonomy permits the comparative analysis of intellectual capital across different entities and sectors, thereby enabling the identification of exemplary practices, optimising performance, and guiding the strategic allocation of resources within the domain of intellectual capital.

This proposed taxonomy is designed to categorise resources in a manner that aligns seamlessly with existing literature, establishing clear definitions that facilitate the accurate assignment of resources within this framework. Alcaniz et al. (2011) offer various theoretical perspectives on intellectual capital, which provide additional support for the resource-based view adopted in this taxonomy. The development of the taxonomy, as elucidated in subsequent sections, adopts a 'bottom–up' approach by identifying specific attributes and aggregating them in such a way that ensures no attribute is overlooked or redundantly categorised. This strategy significantly diminishes the categorisation confusion prevalent within the intellectual capital field, thereby enhancing the precision of resource-based view categorisations and their associated strategic domains. The theoretical foundation for these categorisations is meticulously detailed, setting the stage for a comprehensive understanding of intellectual capital's role in advancing the green economy.

To link with the language of the resource-based view and for the reasons summarised by Dean and Kretschmer (2007),[1] the label 'resource' was given to the categories of firm assets that contributed to its IC. This was a break with the origins of the IC domain, which labelled these same attributes as 'capital'—and still does in a majority of the publications in the field.

To identify the categories within an intellectual capital perspective, the first step was to adopt the overarching categories used in accounting: a firm's monetary and physical resources. This was then followed by investigating the different resources (or capitals) identified in the literature through a measurement theoretical lens applied to resource attributes. The aim was to identify attribute combinations under which resources could be categorised that fulfilled the two first measurement theoretical requirements of completeness (meaning that no resource should be able to be

[1] Dean and Kretschmer (2007) critique the use of the term 'capital' within the domain of intellectual capital and point out that this central concept is neither well nor consistently defined and, as used it generally, does not adhere to the characteristics of the term capital in the general academic literature (this is one of the reasons why the author uses the term resource rather than the term capital). They also point out that there is a common use where intellectual capital is taken as synonymous with intangible assets (see Ballow et al., 2004a, b, c for a clear distinction between these two terms), and this use is erroneous as we will see later in the chapter.

found that would not fit under one of the identified categories) and distinctness (meaning that no resource should be able to be fitted simultaneously under two separate categories). In addition, the aim was to find an agreeable number of categories. Given the aim is to discover value creation occurring within firms, the starting point was to identify what 'resource attributes' could be identified for the resources (or capitals) found in the literature. Resource attributes are defined as that dimension of a resource that captures its characteristics at a given point in time or how it behaves over time when interacting with other resources. These behaviours were identified as follows: decreasing marginal return, increasing marginal return, and network economic behaviour; additive and nonadditive; rivalrous and non-rivalrous; known conversion rate to monetary value and unknown conversion rate to monetary, owned by the firm and not owned by the firm; high information asymmetry and low information asymmetry; and whether full, partial, or no excludability exists. Based on these behaviours, five resource categories can be identified:

Monetary: All resources of a monetary or monetarily equivalent nature are captured by this category, for example, cash, bonds, shares, unused borrowing capacity, etc.

Physical: In this category are all resources that hold a physical form and mass, for example, machines, bricks, tools, etc. or, in simple terms, anything that you can touch and any inseparable attribute of these, for example, location. This domain also includes energy in different forms, e.g., electricity.

Relational: This category includes all relationships that individuals hold on behalf of the organisation or that the organisation holds independent of individuals through organisational resources like, for example, contracts. These relationships can be with customers, consumers, intermediaries, representatives, suppliers, partners, owners, lenders, or any other stakeholder. These relationships are all held with parties outside the object under observation (e.g., outside the firm if the firm is the object under observation).

Organisational: The intuitive definition of this category was first articulated by Leif Edvinsson (in Edvinsson & Malone, 1997, pp. 19 & 46) as: 'all those things that remained behind when the staff went home for the night but that you cannot find on the balance sheet'. The author has modified this to: 'The results of human endeavours that are owned by the company and that remain in the organisation when the employees have left the building and are not classified as monetary or physical'. This includes resources such as brands, intellectual property, processes, systems, organisational structures, information (on paper or in databases), and all other results of human endeavour that takes non-monetary or non-physical form.

Human: The final category covers all the attributes that relate to individuals as resources for the company with the additional requirement that they cannot be replaced by machines or written down on a piece of paper. This includes resources such as competence, attitude, skill, tacit knowledge, personal networks, etc.

This categorisation aligns with but also expands upon the work of Cricelli et al. (2014), who proposed an overall index of intellectual capital based on similar resource distinctions.

Some characteristics of the above-discussed resources are summarised in Table 1.

There is a further distinction worth noting: that between resource type and whether a resource is tangible or intangible. This reflects the debate about the recognisability of the resource. The argument about whether a resource is a traditional economic resource (monetary or physical) or an intellectual capital resource (relational, organisational, or human) represents a debate about the form, and ultimately the economic behaviour, of the resource. This is not a semantic distinction. The argument that intangibles and intellectual capital resources are not the same thing is

Table 1 Resource characteristics

			Intellectual capital category		
	Monetary resources	Physical resources	Relational resources	Organisational resources	Human resources
Description	Financial resources that take the form of cash assets (such as marketable securities) that can easily be converted to pure cash	Anything that can be touched, for example, has a physical presence (that is what you would normally find under the heading of plant and equipment in the balance sheet)	The relationships held by individuals on behalf of the firm or that are embodied in the form of contracts with the firm as one party. The outcome of desires to hold explicit or implicit relationships with the firm by external parties	The result of human endeavours developed internally in the firm or acquired externally by the firm that is now owned by the firm and that are not physical or monetary in nature	All useful resources that are embodied in people
Owned and controlled by	Firm	Firm	Nobody owns, and the resource is co-controlled	Firm	Individual
Economic behaviour	Decreasing marginal return	Decreasing marginal return	Network economic behaviour	Network economic behaviour	Increasing marginal return
Known conversion rate to monetary value	Yes	No	No	No	No
Additive	Yes	Yes	No	No	No
Information asymmetry	Low	Low	High	High	High
Rivalry resource	Yes	Yes	No	No	No

(continued)

Table 1 (continued)

	Intellectual capital category				
	Monetary resources	Physical resources	Relational resources	Organisational resources	Human resources
Excludability	Yes	Yes	No	Partial	No
Examples of appropriation mechanisms ('Value appropriation mechanisms do not create new value but instead determine the relative share of relational rents that the focal firm can appropriate' (Lavie, 2007, p. 1191).)	Financing structure and cost of capital	IP (patents, trademarks, copyrights, and design rights) Firm-specific assets Lead time Secrecy	First mover advantage Network size Reputation Bargaining power Customer retention Long-term contracts Exclusive agreements	IP (patents, trademarks, copyrights, and design rights) Causal ambiguity Contracts Agreement stability Imperfect mobility Brand Lead time Secrecy	Shared Values/ Goals Innovativeness Absorptive capacity
Drives towards a strategic logic (in the meaning of Stabell & Fjeldstad, 1998) of:	Value chain	Value chain	Value network Although can drive towards a value shop logic in the very early stages of the resource lifecycle and towards value chain in the very late stages of the resource lifecycle	Value network Although can drive towards a value shop logic in the very early stages of the resource lifecycle and towards value chain in the very late stages of the resource lifecycle	Value Shop

self-evident. There are many intellectual capital resources that have a tangible expression. Likewise, there are many traditional economic resources that have intangible expressions. Table 2 separates resource type from the issue of accounting recognisability with some illustrative examples.

A helpful way to visualise the organisation's resource portfolio is to express the portfolio in the form of a resource distinction tree (RDT). This helps the organisation to identify, prioritise, and evaluate the most important resources necessary for the organisation's value creation efforts. An RDT is a hierarchical structure that, in a stepwise way, breaks down overarching resources into constituent resources until a suitable level of granularity is achieved. There are four criteria for identifying a resource on each level of a hierarchy:

Table 2 Separation of resource type from accounting recognisability (with examples)

		Intellectual capital category				
		Monetary resources	Physical resources	Relational resources	Organisational resources	Human resources
Accounting recognisability	Tangible	Cash	Building	Repeat order	Employee contract	Physical presence
	Intangible	Borrowing capacity	Building location	Preferred supplier status	Organisational culture	Problem-solving ability

1. Each resource must be distinct, meaning that the definition of a resource must be clear and separate from the definitions of all other resources at that level.
2. Each resource level must be complete, meaning that there must be no relevant resources missing from a given level of the RDT.
3. Each resource must be independent from other resources, meaning that if one of the resources changes, there must be no automatic and instantaneous change in any of the other resources on that level.
4. Finally, the RDT must be agreeable, meaning that it must be broken down to a level that is suitable for the purpose for which it is intended.

If these requirements are adhered to, the RDT will, in a structured and easily accessible way, show all resources broken down to a suitable[2] level of granularity, which the organisation can access for value-creating purposes. The two highest levels of the resource distinction tree are shown in Fig. 1.

The labels given to the resources on level 3 and higher in the RDT can be organisational specific, and the actual labels themselves are irrelevant as long as the definitions adhere to the criteria listed above. There are limitations to this approach: First, the need to break down a resource into its constituent parts (which is done using the organisational- and context-specific language and using management's subjective lens) so that the resulting resources adhere to the requirements 1–4 above may require the breakup of what management and the organisational- and context-specific language considers intuitive resources into non-intuitive resources that adhere to the classification characteristics outlined in Table 1. This is a challenge that is not easy to overcome for individuals unused to doing this. Second, there may be strong interactions between the resulting 'sub'-resources that are implicitly taken for granted in the originating resource since they may not be visible from the outside and they may be lost in the subdivision.

This section has outlined the taxonomy for resources, with a definition of the requirements that a given resource will have to fulfil in order to be classified as a specific resource category.

[2] Suitable here refers to the minimum number of resources necessary for being able to draw conclusions that are meaningful and actionable given the problem that is to be addressed. Commonly, this would be on level 3 in the RDT—that is one level finer distinctions than those shown in Fig. 1.

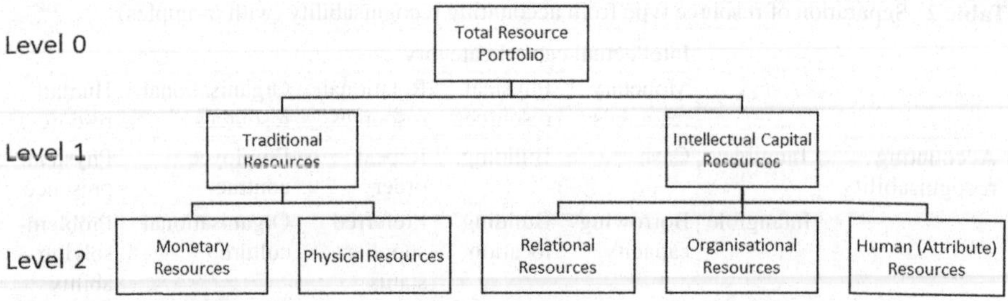

Fig. 1 The generic beginning of a resource distinction tree

2 A Measurement System

Measurement is the process of assigning numbers to things in such a way that the relationships of the numbers reflect the relationships of the attributes of the things being measured. The construction of a measurement system requires the application of measurement theory, a branch of applied mathematics. The fundamental idea of measurement theory is that a measurement is not the same as the object being measured but is, instead, a representation of it. This means that if conclusions are to be drawn about the object, it is necessary to consider the nature of the correspondence between the attribute and the measurement. Proper use of measurement theory significantly reduces the risk of making meaningless statements.

The modern theory of measurement dates only from the nineteenth-century work of Helmholtz (1887), which laid the basis for one-dimensional extensive relational measurement theory. The formalisation of measurement theory was motivated by the need to understand what it means to measure things in the social sciences. The key contributor to the development and application of measurement theory in this domain is generally accepted to be Stevens (1946) although it was not until the 1970s that measurement was fully axiomatised (Scott & Suppes, 1958; Suppes & Zines, 1963; Krantz et al., 1971; Narens, 1985; Suppes et al., 1989; Luce et al., 1990).

In measurement theory, it was shown that numerical representations of values and laws are only numerical codes of algebraic structures representing the real properties of these values and laws. Thus, hierarchical structures are primary representations of values and laws. When applying measurement systems in accordance with measurement theory for the measurement of the value of something, four important outcomes from the independence of value definition must be considered:

1. Both the object to be measured or valued and the context in which the object exists must be precisely defined.
2. The definitions used are inclusive (at every hierarchical level) of all opinions and requirements from all stakeholders.
3. All stakeholders are initially assigned equal importance.
4. Every stakeholder is accountable for the veracity of their opinion.

When dealing with complex objects, the principles of axiology must be extended to include the use of multi-attribute value theory (MAVT). MAVT is often considered to be similar to multi-attribute utility theory (MAUT) but with no uncertainties about the consequences of the alternatives, whereas MAUT explicitly recognises uncertainties (Keeney & Raiffa, 1976). It is worth noting that economic value has been demonstrated to be compliant with axiology by Zúñiga (2000).

This is in line with the discussion in Menger (1883), who distinguishes between first-order goods (which have immediate value) and higher-order goods (which are enablers). Both Menger (1883) and Zúñiga (2000) consider the issue of independence of view and argue that while value and valuations may be personal, all observers may be wrong in their valuations since there is an ultimate ex post arbiter of value, which is the market.

MAVT allows the representation of complex entities using a hierarchical structure in which the elements of value are contained in a complete set of mutually independent attributes. Such value measurement structures can be made operational in conjoint structures by the incorporation of algorithms to represent the subjective judgements made by stakeholders. For reliable use, it requires the algorithms to be compliant with measurement theory in all places.

The basic idea in conjoint measurement is to measure one attribute against another and hence must involve common scales where the scale ends have a defined meaning. In practice, making scales commensurable requires both normalisation onto a 0 to 1 scale and that input data is expressed on a ratio scale. If other scaling systems are used, such as interval and ordinal, Tversky et al. (1988) have shown that they are incompatible with the axioms of measurement theory and commensurable scales cannot be constructed with them.

The abovementioned prerequisite formed the basis for the development of the measurement theory compliant Conjoint Value Hierarchy (CVH) measurement system (see Pike & Roos, 2004a, b; Pike et al., 2005; Garnett et al., 2006; Rødseth et al., 2007; Kinne, 2009).

The application of the CVH follows the following measurement theory compliant process: The object in its context is defined by the stakeholders, taking into strict account the legitimacy of the stakeholder and the implied comparison that the context will provide. A hierarchical measurements system is an ordered triple, a non-empty set $\mathbb{A}$, containing all the attributes (a_i) of the entity, the relationships (r_i) between them, and the operations (o_i) upon them. These are usually expressed as:

$$\mathbb{A}_{i=1}^{n} = \{a_i, r_i, o_i\}$$

This means that for a set containing n elements:

$$\sum_{i=1}^{n} a_i = \mathbb{A} \text{ and } a_i \bigcap_{\substack{i=1\\ j=1\\ i\neq j}}^{n} a_j = 0$$

The only test that can be applied to demonstrate compliance with these conditions is proof by exhaustion. The hierarchical structure constructed along these lines simply describes the object to be measured but nothing more. It shows what ought to be measured.

The second step is to build an operational isomorph. The practical problem that is almost always encountered is that some of the attributes that ought to be measured cannot be easily measured in practice; thus, the stronger condition of homeomorphy cannot be invoked. Thus, the description of the entity to be measured $\left(\mathbb{A}^n_{i=1} = \{a_i, r_i, o_i\}\right)$ appears as an isomorphic measurement structure in which the attributes a_i are replaced in part or in whole by proxies b_i. As the measurement structure is an isomorph, r_i and o are preserved, and the measurement structure is represented by another ordered triple, $\mathbb{B}$, where:

$$\mathbb{B}^n_{i=1} = \{a_i, r_i, o_i\}$$

It is necessary to ensure that the proxies (which can be measured reliably and reproducibly) are acceptable. Since these are not exactly the same as the defined attributes that ought to be measured, it is necessary to test them to ensure that the conditions of completeness and distinctness have not been violated, but most of all that the aggregated meaning of $\mathbb{B}$ approximates to $\mathbb{A}$ in a way that is acceptable to the stakeholders. The method to test this is proof by exhaustion, and the tests are as follows:

Assuming true isomorphism and $a_i \cong b_i$, that is, $a_i \cong b_i$, then $b_i \approx a_i$ and

$$b_i \bigcap_{\substack{i=1\\ j=1\\ i\neq j}}^{n} b_j = 0$$

Given an acceptable isomorphic measurement system $\mathbb{B}$, the measurable attributes are b_i with relationships r_i.

The nature of the binary operations o_i becomes the next issue. The simplest of aggregation algorithms is weighted addition, with aggregated value V of n attributes defined as:

$$V = \sum_{i=1}^{n} W_i V_i \quad \text{where} \quad \sum_{i=1}^{n} w_i = 1$$

The simplicity of the weighted addition algorithm is often problematic, as it does not have the ability to show complex combination behaviours. This is especially important when the loss of performance of one combining attribute could lead to a complete loss of value in the combined higher-level attribute, and this cannot be compensated for by a contribution from the other combining attribute. Marichal (1998) gives an excellent account of aggregation functions and their properties.

When a measurement system is used, the results are dependent to a large degree on the nature of the combination algorithm, which must be selected with care and conform to certain conditions of propositional logic. Failure to do this often introduces catastrophically large and variable errors into calculations. The key propositions that an algorithm must satisfy are those of commutativity and associativity, and they can be proved by algebraic means:

$$(\boldsymbol{f} \circ \boldsymbol{g}) \circ \boldsymbol{h} = \boldsymbol{f} \circ (\boldsymbol{g} \circ \boldsymbol{h}) = \boldsymbol{f} \circ \boldsymbol{g} \circ \boldsymbol{h} \qquad (\text{associativity})$$

$$\boldsymbol{f} \circ \boldsymbol{g} = \boldsymbol{g} \circ \boldsymbol{f} \qquad (\text{commutativity})$$

where $\bigcirc$ is the generalised binary operation of the aggregation function.

The penultimate step in constructing a measurement system is to customise copies of it so that it represents the behaviours of the individual stakeholders. This step ensures compliance with axiological requirements, in that the individual's views are maintained without interference or the averaging of those results from consensus processes. In practice, this means asking for opinions on the relative importance of the attributes, the natures of the attribute combinations, and the limits of performance.

In complex value measurement systems like the CVH, native performance scales are collapsed onto a non-dimensional value scale, which is normalised, between 0 and 1. The task is to define what 0 and 1 mean. It is usual to set 0 as that performance level that just becomes useful—in other words, the threshold of uselessness. The meaning of 1 has two common alternatives: either that it means the best in class or that it is some internally set strategic objective. The choice between them is decided by the user of the CVH, but it is important that the basis for the decision be known.

The final step in producing a measurement system concerns the performance data to be used to operate the measurement system. All performance measures have two parts, the amount and the scale, but it is important to realise that there are many types of scale. If reliable results are to be obtained, then it is important that data are collected on an appropriate scale. For the purposes of proper measurement, only ratio or absolute scales are acceptable.

Bearing in mind the multiplicity of units that may arise and the fact that a measurement system requires a meaningful 0 to 1 scale, all data inputs must be commensurable, which, in practice, means normalisable. Some other conditions are also required of performance data to ensure that the measurement system functions properly. These are that:

$$(\mathrm{X} \geq \mathrm{Y}) \text{ if and only if } (\mathrm{X}+\mathrm{Z}) \geq (\mathrm{Y}+\mathrm{Z}) \qquad (\text{monotonicity})$$

$$(\mathrm{X}+\mathrm{Y}) > \mathrm{X} \qquad (\text{positivity})$$

There exists a natural number n such that:

$$(n\mathrm{X} \geq \mathrm{Y}) \text{ where } (1\mathrm{X} = \mathrm{X}) \text{ and } (n+1)\mathrm{X} = (n\mathrm{X}+\mathrm{X}) \qquad (\text{Archimedean condition})$$

3 Conclusion

In light of the evidence presented in this chapter, the introduction of an intellectual capital taxonomy and measurement framework emerges as a crucial strategy for entities operating within the green economy. The value relevance of both financial and non-financial information in integrated reporting, as systematically reviewed by Veltri and Silvestri (2020), underscores the importance of comprehensive intellectual capital measurement and reporting. The presented framework offers a promising approach to harmonising sustainable development objectives with economic prosperity, a balance that is increasingly vital in today's business landscape.

The proposed taxonomy and measurement system provide organisations with a systematic and detailed methodology for cataloguing and quantifying intellectual assets. This comprehensive approach encompasses a wide range of intangible resources, including human knowledge, organisational processes, and technological assets. By offering a structured framework, the system facilitates a more profound comprehension of these often-elusive resources, thereby augmenting the process of strategic decision-making.

Central to the efficacy of this framework is its development from a 'bottom–up' approach, ensuring precision and clarity in resource classification. This meticulous methodology, coupled with the integration of various resource types—monetary, physical, relational, organisational, and human—into a holistic view, aligns seamlessly with the resource-based perspective prevalent in contemporary management theory.

The measurement aspect of the framework, based on the Conjoint Value Hierarchy (CVH), adheres to the principles of measurement theory. This compliance lends credibility to the system, enabling the representation of complex entities through a hierarchical structure with mutually independent attributes. Such a robust measurement approach enhances the framework's capability to identify critical value creation domains, thereby allowing organisations to align their intellectual capital more effectively with their strategic ambitions.

It is worth noting, however, that the effectiveness of this framework is contingent upon proper implementation and adaptation to specific organisational contexts. The complexity inherent in measuring intangible assets and the necessity for stakeholder buy-in may present challenges during the implementation phase. Nevertheless, these potential hurdles do not diminish the framework's overall value and potential impact.

In conclusion, the assimilation of this intellectual capital schema into the strategic management protocols of green economy ventures is not merely advisable but imperative. It delineates a distinct trajectory for reconciling economic aims with environmental conservation imperatives: a balance that is increasingly critical in today's business environment. Organisations that successfully adopt this strategic framework are likely to navigate the complexities of the contemporary market more adeptly and potentially influence the trajectory of sustainable business practices in the future.

Future research and practical applications of this taxonomy and measurement system hold promise for unlocking the latent potential of intellectual capital. As such, they may serve as a catalyst for sustainable growth and competitive advantage within the green economy. This framework, therefore, represents a significant step forward in our understanding and management of intellectual capital, particularly within the context of sustainable development and the green economy.

References

Alcaniz, L., Gomez-Bezares, F., & Roslender, R. (2011). Theoretical perspectives on intellectual capital: A backward look and a proposal for going forward. *Accounting Forum, 35*(2), 104–117.

Ballow, J., Burgman, R., Roos, G., & Molnar, M. (2004b). *A new paradigm for managing shareholder value*. Accenture Institute for High Performance Business.

Ballow, J. J., Thomas, R. J., & Roos, G. (2004a). Future value: The $7 trillion challenge. *Journal of Applied Corporate Finance, 16*(1), 71–76.

Ballow, J. J., Thomas, R. J., & Roos, G. (2004c). Future value: The $7 trillion challenge. *Outlook, 1*, 28–37.

Cricelli, L., Greco, M., & Grimaldi, M. (2014). An overall index of intellectual capital. *Management Research Review, 37*(10), 880–901.

Dean, A., & Kretschmer, M. (2007). Can ideas be capital? Factors of production in the postindustrial economy: A review and critique. *Academy of Management Review, 32*(2), 573–594.

Dumay, J. (2016). A critical reflection on the future of intellectual capital: From reporting to disclosure. *Journal of Intellectual Capital, 17*(1), 168–184.

Edvinsson, L., & Malone, M. S. (1997). *Intellectual capital: Realizing your company's true value by finding its hidden brainpower*. HarperCollins.

Garnett, H., Pike, S., & Roos, G. (2006, May). The application of conjoint measurement to reveal the real value of research: A case study of an Australian University. In *6th annual conference of the European academy of management*.

Helmholtz, H. (1887). Zählen und Messen. Erkenntnistheoretisch betrachtet. In *Philosophische Aufsätze. Eduard Zeller zu seinem fünfzigjährigen Doctor-Jubiläum gewidmet* (pp. 17–52). Fues's Verlag. (Helmholtz, H. (1887). Counting and measuring. Epistemologically considered. In *Philosophical essays. Dedicated to Eduard Zeller on his fiftieth Doctor Anniversary* (pp. 17–52). Fues's Verlag.).

Keeney, R., & Raiffa, H. (1976). *Decisions with multiple objectives: Preferences and value tradeoffs*. John Wiley & Sons.

Kinne, P. (2009). *Integratives Wertemanagement: Eine Methodik zur Steuerungsoptimierung immaterieller Ressourcen in mittelständischen Unternehmen*. Springer-Verlag.

Krantz, D., Luce, R. D., Suppes, P., & Tversky, A. (1971). *Foundations of measurement, Vol. I, additive and polynomial representations*. Academic Press.

Lavie, D. (2007). Alliance portfolios and firm performance: A study of value creation and appropriation in the US software industry. *Strategic Management Journal, 28*(12), 1187–1212.

Luce, D., Krantz, D., Suppes, P., & Tversky, A. (1990). *Foundations of measurement, Vol. III, representation, axiomatization and invariance*. Academic Press.

Marichal, J. L. (1998). *Aggregation operations for multicriteria decision aid*. Doctoral dissertation, University of Liège.

Menger, C. (1883). *Untersuchungen über die Methode der Socialwissenschaften und der politischen Ökonomie insbesondere*. Verlag von Duncker & Humblot. (Menger, C. (1883). *Studies on the method of social sciences and political economy in particular*. Verlag von Duncker & Humblot).

Narens, L. (1985). *Abstract measurement theory*. MIT Press.
Pike, S., Fernström, L., & Roos, G. (2005). Intellectual capital: Management approach in ICS Ltd. *Journal of Intellectual Capital, 6*(4), 489–509.
Pike, S., & Roos, G. (2004a). Mathematics and modern business management. *Journal of Intellectual Capital, 5*(2), 243–256.
Pike, S., & Roos, G. (2004b, October). Theoretical foundations of intellectual capital measurement and valuation. In *International intellectual capital conference, NCCU* (pp. 11–12).
Rødseth, O. J., Steinbach, C., & Mo, B. (2007, September). The use of technical condition indices in ship maintenance planning and the monitoring of the ship's safety condition. In *Proceedings of the international symposium on maritime, safety, security and environmental protection (SSE)* (pp. 20–21).
Roos, G. (2019). *Optimising resource deployment within the firm: Overcoming theoretical problems with a practical application*. Doctoral Dissertation, University of South Australia.
Scott, D., & Suppes, P. (1958). Foundation aspects of theories of measurement. *Journal of Symbolic Logic, 23*(2), 113–128.
Secundo, G., Ndou, V., Del Vecchio, P., & De Pascale, G. (2020). Sustainable development, intellectual capital and technology policies: A structured literature review and future research agenda. *Technological Forecasting and Social Change, 153*, 119917.
Stabell, C. B., & Fjeldstad, Ø. D. (1998). Configuring value for competitive advantage: On chains, shops, and networks. *Strategic management journal, 19*(5), 413–437.
Stevens, S. S. (1946). On the theory of scales of measurement. *Science, 103*(2684), 677–680.
Suppes, P., Krantz, D., Luce, D., & Tversky, A. (1989). *Foundations of measurement, Vol. II, geometrical, threshold and probabilistic representations*. Academic Press.
Suppes, P., & Zines, J. (1963). Basic measurement theory. In R. Luce, R. Bush, & E. Galanter (Eds.), *Handbook of mathematical psychology* (Vol. 1, pp. 1–76). John Wiley & Sons.
Tversky, A., Slovic, P., & Sattath, S. (1988). Contingent weighting in judgment and choice. *Psychological Review, 95*(3), 371–384.
Veltri, S., & Silvestri, A. (2020). The value relevance of corporate financial and nonfinancial information provided by the integrated report: A systematic review. *Business Strategy and the Environment, 29*(8), 3038–3054.
Zúñiga, G. (2000). *A general theory of value: Axiology in the Central European philosophical tradition*. Doctoral dissertation, State University of New York.

Identifying Intangible Assets in Organizations: A Review of Existing Technology-driven Approaches and Proposal of a New One That Improves IC Visibility

María-Isabel Sánchez-Segura, Fuensanta Medina-Domínguez, and Roxana González-Cruz

Abstract Intellectual capital is a lever for improving a country's gross domestic product, and the value of intangible assets in the digital era is beyond question. The value hidden in every single organization can be exposed by discovering and cataloging intangible assets into the different branches of intellectual capital. How good are current technologies at pinpointing intangible assets? In this chapter, we introduce the technologies that are being used to locate intangible assets and look at how they live up to this challenge. We then describe a new mechanism that we have designed, which has proven, through several case studies, to be very effective for improving the visibility of the intellectual capital of organizations.

1 Introduction

The value of intangible assets, such as knowledge, innovation, copyrights, trademarks, brands and patents, virtualization of work, education, and relationships, is growing and, in turn, improves the company's competitiveness and profits. Intangible assets are related to human capital, technological edge, branding, or labor. Thus, intangible assets are part of organizations and organizational projects, including information technology (IT), where technological innovation has been changing the way information is used. Investment in information and communication

M.-I. Sánchez-Segura (✉) · F. Medina-Domínguez
Computer Science and Engineering Department, Universidad Carlos III de Madrid, Madrid, Spain
e-mail: misanche@inf.uc3m.es; fmedina@inf.uc3m.es

R. González-Cruz
Project Management Department, Telefónica España, Madrid, Spain
e-mail: roxana.gonzalezcruz@telefonica.com

F. Matos et al. (eds.), *Intellectual Capital in a Global Business Landscape*, Contributions to Management Science, https://doi.org/10.1007/978-3-031-86362-2_4

technologies (ICT) and intangible assets is a key source of growth in advanced economies (de Morais et al., 2021).

In this context, there is a need to apply new approaches to obtain business value, achieve business sustainability, as well as strengthen the digital transformation by primarily recycling and reusing the digital data that organizations have created, collected, stored, and shared among employees, stakeholders, partners, and customers. Currently, one of the biggest challenges to the success of most digital transformation processes in companies is to have absolute control over the data. This data is often represented in different formats and can come from a variety of sources, i.e., organizations have semi-structured or unstructured data usually representing people's knowledge about various organizational topics or, in other words, the organization's know-how. However, this knowledge is not always formalized within the company's organizational processes and may or may not be digitized, i.e., the company may or may not use a process mining software tool. Be that as it may, data control poses a great challenge for companies with a view to identifying their intangible knowledge assets (IKAs), which explicitly measure the value of an organization's intellectual capital and without which they cannot discover their hidden value. Thus, companies that have identified their IKAs for transformation and protection have an advantage over their competitors in the market.

But how can companies generate this business value? One concept of intellectual (human, relational, structural) capital asserts that an organization's ability to leverage the dynamics of knowledge assets is at the core of its ability to create value (Schiuma, 2009). For example, Xu et al. (2021) analyzed the nexus between intellectual capital and sustainable growth of firms in three specific industries and concluded that firms that want to excel in efficient sustainable growth must use intangible resources (intellectual capital) to maintain competitive advantage and adjust their intellectual capital investment to dynamic changes in the internal and external operating environment. A review of existing literature in the field of administrative management (Schwarz & Otero, 2018) found that several of the management models and tools developed to assess intellectual capital emphasize the definition of metrics and indicators. In fact, research in this area related to intellectual capital mainly focuses on the evaluation of intangible assets, paying little attention to the first and critical step: the **identification** of intangible assets. Identification is the basis for any analysis and subsequent valuation of intangible assets. This suggests that the current analysis and alignment of business objectives and organizational processes with the valued intangible assets are essentially flawed. This is an obstacle to making sound decisions regarding the company's digitalization and sustainability process, as well as to highlighting the intellectual capital inherent in such IKAs.

Given that business digitalization processes have not been as successful as expected (Behnam et al., 2019) and the drivers of change needed to support digital transformation are IT managers, they should propose and use solutions that combine the identification and valuation of intangible assets with the construction of software solutions to enhance digital business. On this basis, this chapter carries out an analysis of the following disciplines: agile business intelligence, process mining tools, valuation and management of intangible assets, and natural language processing, which are the current ICT techniques that should underpin a good identification of IKAs so that the intellectual capital inherent in such IKAs can be properly measured and, consequently, improved.

2 Context Analysis: Existing Disciplines with the Potential to Empower Intellectual Capital

In the following subsections will be presented the existing disciplines that, due to their nature, have the potential to empower intellectual capital.

2.1 Agile Business Intelligence

One would expect the field of business intelligence (BI) to propose applicable formulas to identify hidden IKAs. Several studies published in the BI literature focus on the successful implementation of BI projects using agile methodologies in the areas of computer science, engineering, economics, and information systems management. However, none identify and relate information and knowledge assets to business objectives. For example:

- Fakir et al. (2021) bring together the most recent work on BI capable of handling all data types. The works considered in this study promote the rapid adaptation of the organization's BI systems to the changes required by the business, thus promoting system flexibility, but the data is not mapped to the company's strategic and business objectives.
- Williams et al. (2017) present a practical guide on how to implement an agile BI project, again improving the flexibility demanded by BI systems. To do this, they analyze Scrum, as the agile methodology best suited to ensure success in the implementation of a BI project. In this way, the development of BI projects will focus on people, as well as providing flexibility in addressing changes in user requirements. After their analysis, they conclude that there are four agile approach factors that are key to improving BI success:
  - User satisfaction: Scrum puts the customer first. Typically, the business can prioritize what it needs from the BI system to align with strategic objectives.
  - Results delivered in frequent iterations: Return on investment (ROI) can be seen early in the project, and project successes/victories are demonstrated on an ongoing basis.
  - Simplicity: The real priorities for project success are broken down into manageable pieces and focused on.

– Continuous improvement: The Scrum team frequently reviews what is working and what is not improving the BI process and deliverables. Stakeholders are the critical voice for improving project results.

Agile business intelligence (ABI) emerged in response to the need for companies to flexibilize and speed up the development of user-focused BI projects with frequently changing requirements and many deliverables throughout the project implementation phase. However, ABI does not specify what data types can be processed. Nor does it provide any steps to define business-critical IKAs. Therefore, their impact on the organization's intellectual capital is not visible. Of note is the research reported by Baars and Hüter (2015) considering structured and semi-structured data. There are also two studies within the area of business administration that provide an agile BI method accounting for all data types (Chang, 2018) and a catalog with agile principles to improve decision-making in organizations (Krawatzeck & Dinter, 2015).

Thus, we find that, although it could be a very powerful resource for identifying and cataloging information and knowledge assets (intangible assets) that are critical for organization according to the different types of intellectual capital, this is not the primary focus of agile business intelligence research, which is instead to help make an organization's BI units more agile to meet the needs of its users.

2.2 Process Mining Tools

Process mining represents a set of techniques that support the analysis, understanding, and improvement of organizational processes based on the analysis of data from the events of a process, known as event logs, which are stored in a software tool during the execution of that process. Three main branches can be identified here: process discovery, compliance checking, and process improvement. In process discovery, the objective is to discover a process model that accurately describes the behavior recorded in an event log, i.e., a model that describes the actual process followed during the execution of that process. In compliance testing, conformance testing is performed to compare a process model with the recorded behavior of that process to identify if there are deviations between the model and the observed behavior. In process improvement, a process model is dynamically enriched with new information about the process based on new analyses of the process model and/or event logs (e.g., detection of critical paths, prediction of process performance indicators, repair/simplification of process models, etc.) (Van Zelst et al., 2019). However, the organization has to have event logs, extracted from a software tool to implement process discovery, i.e., processes have to be automated, which limits its use in organizations with low digital maturity. For example:

- Janssenwillen and Depaire (2018) mention that the field of process mining, and process discovery in particular, has so far focused on the exploration and description of event data using models. Since the resulting models are often based

directly on a sample of event data, the question of whether they also apply to the actual process is often left unanswered. Besides, since the underlying process is unknown in real life, unbiased estimators are needed to assess the system quality of a discovered model and subsequently make assertions about the process. They further describe and discuss an experiment to analyze whether existing metrics of fitness, accuracy, and generalization can be used as unbiased estimators of system fitness and accuracy. The results show that significant biases exist, which means that it is currently almost impossible to objectively measure a model's ability to represent the system.
- Another study by Zerbino et al. (2021) presents a comprehensive review of the literature on process mining, highlighting that process mining is a new type of business analytics and has emerged as a powerful family of process science techniques to analyze and improve the business. However, the works reviewed in this study do not address the analysis of unstructured data or define business-critical information and knowledge assets. Instead, the authors state that "the current scientific literature does not present an up-to-date research agenda that specifies the directions that the application of process mining in Business Management can take."

As mentioned above, process mining requires event logs stored in the organization's information systems to apply sophisticated algorithms based on artificial intelligence to automatically identify new organizational process models. The event logs must be prepared and/or adapted to the format required by the corresponding software tools. Some research has found that process mining is often not very accurate because the event logs may contain noise that affects the analysis performed (Van Zelst et al., 2019). In addition, the organization must have professionals with advanced IT skills to ensure that the software tools used in process mining are deployed correctly in order to effectively map the digitalized processes that the organization needs to analyze to achieve its strategic objective. However, this is not usually the starting point for this type of project.

From the diverse existing literature, Van der Aalst (2012) recognized the discipline of process mining as a potential topic for improving an organization's process models based on the use of event data that are recorded after the execution of activities by people, machines, and software. In this way, process mining techniques use these records to discover, analyze, and improve business processes. Thus, the literature review reveals that Gao et al. (2018) focus on identifying process similarity based on event logs extracted from the organization's software tools, whereas others (Goel et al., 2022; Theis & Darabi, 2019; Liu et al., 2023; Adams et al., 2023; Maggi et al., 2023) focus on verifying data quality and creating algorithms to reduce noise in the extracted event logs, respectively. In this way, we find that the reviewed research works focus on how to extract the event logs of the organization's automated processes, but it would be necessary to specifically improve the process discovery step in order to take into account the organization's strategic objectives and identify which processes to extract. Note also that process mining only considers those processes that are automated within the organization.

Undoubtedly, this field has enormous potential for providing and mapping data that can be categorized as intangible assets to potentially digitizable processes in organizations. This establishes a direct and traceable link between organizational processes and their impact on the organization's intellectual capital.

2.3 Valuation of Intangible Assets

Sanchez-Segura et al. (2022) describe a complete process called Digital Transformation Governance Engineering Process (DTGEP), whose objective is to systematize the valuation of the intangible knowledge assets of an organization to be used as a lever to propose solutions to help all organizations innovate through their digital transformation process. DTGEP has been tested in more than 30 organizations. Even though its effectiveness has been corroborated, the step of the process that involves the identification of critical intangible knowledge assets in the organization is very complex and highly dependent on the expertise of the software engineers who apply DTGEP. Therefore, more systematization is required when deploying the search for critical intangible assets in the organization.

Sanchez-Segura et al. (2021) developed the concept of Intangibles-Driven Business Model Canvas, wherein the critical knowledge assets of an organization have to be placed in the appropriate region of the business model canvas once the assets have been characterized using the Systemic Intangible Process Assets Characterization (SIPAC) methodology. In this way, it is possible to observe how the health status of each intangible asset affects each of the region of the business model.

Sánchez-Segura et al. (2017) applied all the steps of the SIPAC methodology at several IT companies, thus providing a new point of view for decision-making based on process intangible assets.

Sanchez-Segura et al. (2017, 2021, 2022) mainly focus on the valuation of process intangible assets to aid organizational decision-making, but it would be very timely to specifically improve the step of systematic identification of organizational intangible assets, which is the common bottleneck facing all organizations when it comes to properly cataloging their intellectual capital.

2.4 Natural Language Processing (NLP)

According to Varghese and Punithavalli (2022), a word is the smallest indivisible syntactic unit. Words are arranged in sequence to form sentences, which are governed by the grammar of a language. Semantic similarity analysis focuses primarily on meaning. The proper combination of a string of words, phrases, and punctuation marks results in sentences. Each element of a sentence or corpus is considered a token. Each token, even if it is a punctuation mark which may or may not be related to neighboring words, has a meaning. Lexical semantics refers to the meaning of the word, which resides in the arrangement of the context word and the surrounding words in relation to the size of the context word window. Depending on the word network, a word can have more than one meaning.

In this sense, multiple texts can be found in an organization. These texts are formed by a combination of sentences, which may be available in different formats, such as physical (e.g., written on paper) or digital (e.g., contained in any tool or software application). Generally, these texts contain a large amount of semi-structured or unstructured data, generated daily by employees and stakeholders for the development of their activities, and organizations need to control, analyze, and process these data in order to meet their business objectives.

Therefore, Reategui et al. (2022) describe text mining as a research field that encompasses different approaches, such as information retrieval, natural language processing, information extraction, text summarization, supervised and unsupervised learning, probabilistic methods, text stream and social media mining, opinion mining, and sentiment analysis. Their goal is to retrieve relevant information from semi-structured or unstructured data.

Thus, NLP is a branch of artificial intelligence that can be used for the analysis of text and speech produced by humans. It seeks to provide solutions to the concrete problems derived from the attempt to artificially reproduce the patterns with which the human mind and language work in order to transfer them to the relationship between humans and machines (Baez et al., 2022).

Therefore, with NLP, it is possible to analyze semi-structured and unstructured texts that have been generated with large volumes of data (big data). Within this area of NLP, the technique of automatically extracting keywords from a text is a task of great importance. According to Kelebercová and Munk (2022), keyword extraction (KE) is described as a technique for automatically obtaining the most important words from text. This extraction process can identify words or phrases that summarize the document.

The literature review highlights research studies in various areas, applied to specific domains that obtain notable improvements by making use of text mining and NLP techniques for text processing and analysis. In the health sciences field, Machado et al. (2023) present the development of an intelligent Data Driven Intelligence (DDI) extraction system based on pharmacological and toxicological data, which makes use of NLP to analyze unstructured data, whereas Zhao et al. (2020), Heintzelman et al. (2013), Yu et al. (2014), and Orangi-Fard et al. (2022) focus on applying NLP and text mining to analyze text from patient medical records or discharge summaries in order to find important information to help process ongoing medical programs. In the area of computer science, Perovsek et al. (2016), Cunliffe et al. (2022), Tanguy et al. (2016), Wan et al. (2020), Li et al. (2022), and Roitero et al. (2021) focus on applying NLP and text mining to different use cases to provide a solution to a problem, such as the analysis of aviation incident reports (Tanguy et al., 2016) to help aviation safety experts analyze such incidents. However, it is clear from the reviewed literature that the abovementioned studies do not focus on the identification of information and knowledge assets for the business as a pillar to improve strategic decision-making. This discipline is a key piece for advancement in the field of the identification of IKAs for their subsequent cataloging into the different branches of intellectual capital. It is used to analyze both semi-structured and unstructured data to discover hidden behavioral patterns for identifying information and knowledge assets that are relevant to the business.

3 Proposed Methodology: Complement for Process Mining (C4PM) as a Tool to Discover Intellectual Capital

With the idea of enhancing the use of the aforementioned disciplines, namely, agile business intelligence, process mining tools, valuation of intangible assets, and natural language processing, to be able to identify and catalog IKAs by intellectual capital type for visibility, we created the C4PM method (Sanchez-Segura et al., 2022). C4PM integrates four disciplines: agile business intelligence principles and practices, strategic process asset management, systems thinking, and natural language processing. C4PM is a key method to help organizations with the management, protection, and governance of data and information. It provides business capabilities that they can use to act effectively and more accurately on their organizational processes based on the critical IKAs identified and cataloged according to the different types of intellectual capital. As a result, it supports the development of the intellectual capital of organizations, which, as is well known, has an impact on their country's gross domestic product.

Thus, organizations will be able to use C4PM as a standalone method or integrate the approach into their information governance and digital business transformation projects, without having to invest large sums of money. Besides, decision-making on critical IKAs will be more accurate, for example, avoiding economic losses due to information leaks that may occur by having these assets exposed.

C4PM operation can be summarized according to the following steps:

Step 1: Definition of business objectives. Before developing Step 1, it is necessary to have access to and analyze the initial information available within the organization about its organizational processes. Once this information has been gathered, this step consists of identifying and classifying the business objectives according to the strategic business objectives in accordance with the organizational processes provided by the organization. It consists of two activities: Activity 1.1. Identify business objectives and Activity 1.2. Classify business objectives.

Step 2: Systemic conceptualization of the corporate environment. This step consists of identifying the areas that work toward the business objectives of each organizational process, including the actors involved in achieving the business objectives of each of these areas and determining the type of relationship between the actors and the type of knowledge they share in the current corporate environment. It consists of three activities: Activity 2.1. Identify the areas involved,

Table 1 Breakdown of activities for each step of the C4PM

Step 1. Definition of business objectives	Step 2. Systemic conceptualization of the corporate environment	Step 3. Identification of information and knowledge assets
Activity 1.1. Identify business objectives	Activity 2.1. Identify the areas involved	Activity 3.1 Identify information and knowledge assets from the activities of the corporate environment
Activity 1.2. Classify business objectives	Activity 2.2. Identify stakeholders in the corporate environment	Activity 3.2 Identify information and knowledge assets from semi-structured and unstructured data
	Activity 2.3. Graphically represent the corporate environment	

Activity 2.2. Identify actors in the corporate environment, and Activity 2.3. Graphically represent the corporate environment.

Step 3: Identification of information and knowledge assets. This step consists of identifying and classifying the information and knowledge that is transferred among the actors in the corporate environment within each of the processes necessary to carry out the organizational processes. It involves analyzing semi-structured and unstructured data to discover patterns of behavior that lead to the discovery of new information and knowledge assets for the organization classified according to the different branches of intellectual capital. It consists of two activities: Activity 3.1. Identify information and knowledge assets from corporate environment activities and Activity 3.2. Identify information and knowledge assets from semi-structured and unstructured data.

Table 1 shows the activities that make up each step of the C4PM method.

The impact of using C4PM in two case studies to identify and catalog IKAs into the different branches of intellectual capital is summarized below.

4 Application of C4PM in Two Case Studies

Case Study 1: Enron

Enron was founded in the year 1985 with its headquarters located in Houston, Texas. It quickly became the largest natural gas trader in the United States and the United Kingdom (Bondarenko, 2019). This was a multinational company that used to have a large share of the global energy market and, at the same time, developed several products in other industries, such as paper, water, etc. The three main players that led Enron to grow from a conventional gas company in Texas into holding a large share of the world energy market and become the sixth largest business group in the United States over a span of just a few years were Jeffrey Skilling (CEO and COO), Kenneth Lay (founder and CEO), and Andrew Fastow (CFO).

Enron executives employed accounting practices that falsely inflated the company's revenues and, for a time, made it the seventh largest company in the United States. Once the fraud came to light, the company quickly unraveled, filing for bankruptcy on December 2, 2001, wherein nearly 21 000 people became unemployed (Chen, 2019).

As this case was highly publicized worldwide, there is a lot of public information available on the Internet (Chen, 2019). In this regard, it was noted that several groups of researchers had conducted a number of investigations with the e-mail data of the employees of the Enron company. This constitutes significant data that suits the purposes of this research with regard to the application of C4PM.

This dataset used for the application of the proposed method was collected and prepared by the CALO (A Cognitive Assistant that Learns and Organizes) project. CALO was an output of the PAL (Personal Assistant that Learns) framework developed by DARPA, a massive collaborative project led by SRI International (https://pal.sri.com/). It contains data from about 150 users, mostly senior Enron managers, organized in folders. The corpus contains a total of about 0.5 million messages. This data was originally made public and posted on the web, by the Federal Energy Regulatory Commission during its investigation.

The e-mail dataset was later acquired by Leslie Kaelbling at Massachusetts Institute of Technology (MIT), which turned out to have a number of integrity issues. A number of people at SRI, notably Melinda Gervasio, worked hard to correct these problems, and it is thanks to them that the dataset is available. The dataset does not include attachments, and some messages have been removed "as part of a redaction effort due to requests from affected employees." Invalid e-mail addresses were converted to something of the form user@Enron.com whenever possible (i.e., the recipient was specified in some parseable format such as "Doe, John" or "Mary K. Smith") and to no_address@Enron.com when no addressee was specified.

This dataset has been distributed as a resource for researchers interested in improving current e-mail tools or in understanding how e-mail is currently used. The version used in this research corresponds to May 7, 2015 (data compressed to 1.7 GB) (Cohen, 2015).

Summary of the information describing Case Study 1:

- Enterprise: Enron
- Source of data: Public e-mail dataset
- Business goal: To increase the value of the company's shares
- Case study material can be reached here: https://github.com/C4PM-project/C4PM_Caso1_Enron

Part of the company analyzed: Productive model.

Table 2 summarizes the number of valuable IKAs discovered after the application of the C4PM method and their categorization according to their impact on the organization's intellectual capital.

C4PM was validated on the dataset of the e-mail inboxes of 16 of the 142 company employees. E-mail is one of the key elements within any organization, whatever its size, as today's organizations almost always have an e-mail domain to

Table 2 Summary of the uncovered assets in Enron case study

Areas	Type of intellectual capital	Number of assets uncovered
Accounting (20 assets uncovered)	Structural	16
	Human	4
	Relational	0
Investment relations (26 assets uncovered)	Structural	6
	Human	13
	Relational	7

publicize the company in the market and exchange information both inside and outside the company.

Thus, after the application of C4PM, the results from this data source would have allowed Enron to evaluate any information and knowledge assets identified in the areas of accounting (20 discovered assets) and investment relations (26 discovered assets) to redefine its strategic and economic plans, leading to greater success in any digital transformation projects that it might have implemented, bearing in mind it was a large company with many diversified products and services. Therefore, the identification of these assets would have been a key factor in the company's success; it would also have contributed to improving the tools used for the development of its daily operations, as well as to improving relations between internal areas and consequently between employees, since they play a fundamental role in the execution of the company's organizational processes.

Furthermore, having identified and cataloged these assets according to the different intellectual capital branches, the company's level of competitiveness in the market would have improved, since it would have been taking advantage of the knowledge contained in each of these IKAs in a constant, agile, and sustainable manner, contributing to making better strategic decisions. For example, by identifying the human asset of gas system operation procedures within the area of investment relations, it would have been possible to value, safeguard, automate, and update this asset, since the knowledge it contains is the result of having invested resources in the customization of the gas systems that kept this service in operation.

Case Study 2: Instituto Pablo de la Torre

The Instituto Pablo de la Torre (IPT) (https://itpformacionprofesional.com/) is a company that develops its activities in the educational sector as part of the network of official and approved vocational training centers in the province of Seville in Spain. The intermediate-level and higher-level vocational training cycles it offers are specialized in the fields of computer science, administration, and health.

In recent years, the institute has increased its educational offer and is becoming a reference in its sector, as it receives students from different cities in the province, as well as from other parts of Spain and abroad.

It also develops other lines of business in the same sector, such as the school support academy to reinforce the educational performance of primary and secondary school students, as well as for university entrance exams or vocational training preparation courses, with the aim of achieving academic success for its students.

For the application of C4PM in IPT, IPT provided all the required prior information on its organizational processes. The implementation of the C4PM to the IPT case study can be reached here https://github.com/C4PM-project/C4PM_Caso2_InstitucionEducativa.

C4PM used the semi-structured dataset provided by IPT, consisting of e-mails of four of its corporate accounts: one used for communicating issues related to information on the institute's educational offerings (infoitp@itpformacionprofesional.com), another used for communicating issues related to the institute's management (directoritp@itpformacionprofesional.com), another used for administrative matters (aapariciog@itpfp), and another used for issues related to academic coordination (fabudp@itpfp.com). All the abovementioned e-mail accounts record conversations in a real business environment.

The C4PM method was applied in cooperation with the company's CEO, since he was the most relevant actor who had a holistic approach to company management. Therefore, he was well acquainted with the company's mission, vision, strategies, and organizational processes.

From the interviews with the company's CEO, it became clear that he was concerned about developing his activities outside Spain. Therefore, as this situation represented a bottleneck in terms of business growth, the CEO decided that the strategic objective on which he needed the proposed method to be applied was related to expanding his business geographically, opening up new locations not only nationally but also internationally over the next 5 years.

Based on the strategic objective "To expand the company with new locations nationally and internationally in the next 5 years," the following information summarizes the information describing Case Study 2:

Enterprise: Instituto Pablo de la Torre (IPT)
Source of data: e-mail datasets
Business goal: To expand the company with new locations nationally and internationally in the next 5 years
Part of the company analyzed: Productive model and client model

Table 3 summarizes the number of valuable IKAs discovered after the application of the C4PM method and their categorization according to their impact on the organization's intellectual capital.

Note that C4PM identified 42 information and knowledge assets from the analysis of the content of the messages in the inboxes of their four company e-mail addresses. E-mail is one of the key elements within any organization, whatever its size, as today's organizations almost always have an e-mail domain to publicize themselves in the market and exchange information both inside and outside the company.

Table 3 Summary of the uncovered assets in the ITP case study

Areas	Type of intellectual capital	Number of assets uncovered
General management (12 uncovered assets)	Structural	7
	Human	4
	Relational	1
Administrative (12 uncovered assets)	Structural	7
	Human	4
	Relational	1
Academic (14 uncovered assets)	Structural	7
	Human	6
	Relational	1
Marketing and communication (4 uncovered assets)	Structural	2
	Human	1
	Relational	1

Thus, after the application of C4PM, the results of analyzing these data sources have allowed IPT to identify other information and knowledge assets in the areas involved in organizational process enactment, such as general management (12 discovered assets), administration (12 discovered assets), academic (14 discovered assets), and marketing and communication (4 discovered assets). This information and knowledge assets can be used to redefine its strategic and economic plans, promoting greater success in the digital transformation projects that the institute would like to implement, since, being a growing company, it can now more easily adopt changes within its organizational culture that contribute to the expansion of its products and services outside of Spain. Therefore, based on all of the assets identified using C4PM, the company also acquires the capacity to implement plans to improve the quality of the services provided to both internal and external users (e.g., improve the collaborative tools used by the teaching staff, automate some administrative procedures, improve employability plans for students, etc.).

In addition, asset identification brings added value to the business that contributes to increasing the company's level of competitiveness in the market, since it would be taking advantage of the knowledge contained in each of these IKAs in a constant, agile, and sustainable manner, thus improving strategic decision-making. For example, by identifying the human asset of educational resources, the company can value, protect, automate, and keep updated its resources, bearing in mind that the content of many of these resources is the result of having invested in the training of teaching staff in order to improve classes and keep students motivated, thus ensuring the quality of the services provided.

5 Conclusions and Future Work

The key conclusion of this research is that the main tools existing today that could be useful to highlight the IKAs of an organization and their impact on the intellectual capital of organizations, namely, agile business intelligence, process mining, knowledge asset valuation, and natural language processing, have a lot of potential. However, more effort is required with a view to their use for the purpose of empowering intellectual capital measurement.

In sum, the left-hand column in Table 4 shows a list of the needs that organizations have to address in order to identify IKAs within the area of study indicated in the central column, whereas the right-hand column shows a list of the existing methodologies, guidelines, or best practices applied to cover each of these needs.

Thus, the application of C4PM, as described in the reported case studies, identified a large number of assets using only the text from the e-mail inboxes of 16 employees in the Enron case and the inboxes of the four corporate e-mail addresses in the IPT case. Therefore, any organization can use its e-mail dataset to identify assets that are potentially invisible or hidden to the organization. Following these findings, knowledge asset discovery can be recognized as essential for any organization to successfully apply process mining along the path to develop a sustainable, productive, and competitive digital transformation.

Using C4PM, a company will be able to account for all the intangible information and knowledge assets in the form of intellectual capital in order to establish business plans, for example, initiating digital transformation projects with the objective of expanding geographically or diversifying the services offered to its users. This will generate more business value and drive a sustainable and successful digital transformation, when necessary.

As future work, we propose to deploy C4PM at more organizations and use different data sources to identify IKAs to measure organizational intellectual capital primarily for the digital development of organizations.

Table 4 Needs to be addressed in order to identify intangible assets and their respective literature

Needs to be addressed in order to identify intangible assets in an organization	Areas of study	Existing methodologies, guidelines, or best practices applied to meet these needs
Improve data governance and comply with government regulations related to data protection and data quality, such as GDPR, HIPAA, CCPA, PCI, SOX, future regulations	Computer science, information sciences and document management, information security and communications	European Data Governance Regulation (The Data Governance Act aims to increase trust in data sharing, strengthen mechanisms to increase data availability, and overcome technical barriers to data reuse. It entered into force on June 23, 2022 and, after a grace period of 15 months, will be applicable as of September 2023. More information on the official website of the European Union: https://digital-strategy.ec.europa.eu/es/policies/data-governance-act), ISO/IEC 33000, ISO 8000, Data Management Capability Assessment Model (DCAM) (DCAM, or Data Management Capability Assessment Model, is a best practice framework to help develop and maintain a comprehensive data management program. More information at: https://edmcouncil.org/frameworks/dcam/), Alarcos Model for Data Improvement (MAMD) (The Alarcos Model for Data Improvement (MAMD) aims to collect the necessary processes to achieve quality in the three abovementioned dimensions: data management, data quality management, and data governance. More information at: https://alarcos.esi.uclm.es/), Data Management Association (DAMA) (DAMA is the English acronym for Data Management Association, which is an international association for data management professionals. It has had a Spanish chapter, DAMA Spain, since March 2019. More information at: https://www.dama.org/cpages/home)
Improve the identification and valuation of intangible knowledge assets	Computer science, administrative and economic sciences, information sciences and document management	SIPAC methodology for the valuation of intangible assets (Sanchez-Segura et al., 2022) C4PM (complement for process mining) methodology (Sanchez-Segura et al., 2022)
Improve the formalization and digitalization of organizational processes	Computing	Process mining (Aguirre Mayorga, 2017)

References

Adams, J., Pitsch, C., Brockhoff, T., & van der Aalst, W. P. (2023). An experimental evaluation of process concept drift detection. *VLDB Endowment, 16*(8), 2150–8097. https://doi.org/10.14778/3594512.3594517

Aguirre Mayorga, H. S. (2017). *Process mining: Fundamentals and application methodology*. Pontificia Universidad Javeriana.

Baars, H., & Hüter, H. (2015). A framework for identifying and selecting measures to enhance BI-agility. In I. C. Society (Ed.), *Proceedings of the 2015 48th Hawaii international conference on system sciences* (pp. 4712–4721). https://doi.org/10.1109/HICSS.2015.561

Báez, P., Arancibia, A. P., Chaparro, M. I., Bucarey, T., Núñez, F., & Dunstan, J. (2022). Natural language processing for clinical text in Spanish: The case of waiting lists in Chile. *Revista Médica Clínica Las Condes, 33*(6), 576–582. https://doi.org/10.1016/j.rmclc.2022.10.002

Behnam, T., Ed, L., Kirk, G., & Vernon, I. (2019). Digital transformation is not about technology. *Harvard Business Review*, 2–7. https://hbr.org/2019/03/digital-transformation-is-not-about-technology

Bondarenko, P. (2019, October 07). *Enron scandal*. Encyclopædia Britannica, Inc., 1. Retrieved May 10, 2020, from https://www.britannica.com/event/Enron-scandal

Chang, B.-J. (2018). Agile business intelligence: Combining big data and business intelligence to responsive decision model. *Journal of Internet Technology, 19*(6), 1699–1706. https://www.semanticscholar.org/paper/Agile-Business-Intelligence%3A-Combining-Big-Data-and-Chang/82d8ed9d415a46a845485af973dfebb6e8716bfe

Chen, J. (2019, October 06). *Enron*. Retrieved May 10, 2020, from Investopedia: https://www.investopedia.com/terms/e/enron.asp

Cohen, W. W. (2015, May 08). *Enron email dataset*. Retrieved April 2020, from Enron Email Dataset: http://www.cs.cmu.edu/~enronron/

Cunliffe, D., Vlachidis, A., Williams, D., & Tudhope, D. (2022). Natural language processing for under-resourced languages: Developing a Welsh natural language toolkit. *Computer Speech and Language, 72*. https://doi.org/10.1016/j.csl.2021.101311

de Morais, M. O., Gomes, C. F., & Ribeiro, P. C. (2021). Intangible assets in information technology projects: Identification and evaluation. *Investigação bibliotecológica, 35*(86), 203–225. https://doi.org/10.22201/iibi.24488321xe.2021.86.58311

Fakir, M., Mohamed, B., & Rachid, E. (2021). *Business intelligence: 6th international conference, CBI 2021, Beni Mellal, Morocco, May 27–29, 2021, proceedings*. Springer International Publishing. https://doi.org/10.1007/978-3-030-76508-8

Gao, Y., Song, S., Zhu, X., Wang, J., Lian, X., & Zou, L. (2018). Matching heterogeneous event data. *IEEE Transactions on Knowledge and Data Engineering, 30*(11), 2157–2170. https://doi.org/10.1109/TKDE.2018.2815695

Goel, K., Leemans, S. J., Martin, N., & y Wynn, M. T. (2022). Quality-informed process mining: A case for standardised data quality annotations. *ACM Transactions on Knowledge Discovery from Data, 16*(5), 47. https://doi.org/10.1145/3511707

Heintzelman, N. H., Taylor, R. J., Simonsen, L., Lustig, R., Anderko, D., Haythornthwaite, J. A., et al. (2013). Longitudinal analysis of pain in patients with metastatic prostate cancer using natural language processing of medical record text. *Journal of the American Medical Informatics Association, 20*(5), 898–905. https://doi.org/10.1136/amiajnl-2012-001076

Janssenwillen, G., & Depaire, B. (2018). Hacia el descubrimiento de procesos confirmatorios: Making Assertions About the Underlying System. *Ingeniería de sistemas de información y negocios, 61*(6), 713–728. https://doi.org/10.1007/s12599-018-0567-8

Kelebercová, L., & Munk, M. (2022). Search queries related to COVID-19 based on keyword extraction. *Procedia Computer Science, 207*, 2618–2627. https://doi.org/10.1016/j.procs.2022.09.320

Krawatzeck, R., & Dinter, B. (2015). Agile business intelligence: Collection and classification of agile business intelligence actions by means of a catalog and a selection guide. *Information Systems Management, 32*(3), 177–191. https://doi.org/10.1080/10580530.2015.1044336

Li, K., Zhou, C., Luo, X., Benitez, J., & Liao, Q. (2022). Impact of information timeliness and richness on public engagement on social media during COVID-19 pandemic: An empirical investigation based on NLP and machine learning. *Decision Support Systems, 162*. https://doi.org/10.1016/j.dss.2022.113752

Liu, C., Li, H., Zhang, S., Cheng, L., & Zeng, Q. (2023). Cross-department collaborative healthcare process model discovery from event logs. *IEEE Transactions on Automation Science and Engineering, 20*(3), 2115–2125. https://doi.org/10.1109/TASE.2022.3194312

Machado, J., Rodrigues, C., Sousa, R., & Mendes Gomes, L. (2023). Drug–drug interaction extraction-based system: A natural language processing approach. *Expert Systems*, (e13303), 1–12. https://doi.org/10.1111/exsy.13303

Maggi, F. M., Marrella, A., Patrizi, F., & Skydanienko, V. (2023). Data-aware declarative process mining with SAT. *Association for Computing Machinery*. https://doi.org/10.1145/3600106

Orangi-Fard, N., Akhbardeh, A., & Sagreiya, H. (2022). Predictive model for ICU readmission based on discharge summaries using machine learning and natural language processing. *Informatics-Basel, 9*(1). https://doi.org/10.3390/informatics9010010

Perovsek, M., Kranjc, J., Erjavec, T., & Cestnik, B. (2016). TextFlows: A visual programming platform for text mining and natural language processing. *Science of Computer Programming, 121*, 128–152. https://doi.org/10.1016/j.scico.2016.01.001

Reategui, E., Marcio, B., Michel, C., & Rafael, A. d. (2022). Evaluating the performance of SOBEK text mining keyword extraction algorithm. In *Machine learning and knowledge extraction, CD-MAKE 2022, 13480* (pp. 233–243). https://doi.org/10.1007/978-3-031-14463-9_15

Roitero, K., Portelli, B., Popescu, M. H., & Della Mea, V. (2021). DiLBERT: Cheap embeddings for disease related medical NLP. *IEEE Access, 9*, 159714–159723. https://doi.org/10.1109/ACCESS.2021.3131386

Sanchez-Segura, M.-I., Dugarte-Peña, G.-L., Amescua-Seco, A., & Medina-Dominguez, F. (2021). Exploring how the intangible side of an organization impacts its business model. *Kybernetes. Kybernetes, 50*(10), 2790–2822. https://doi.org/10.1108/K-05-2020-0302

Sanchez-Segura, M.-I., González-Cruz, R., Medina-Dominguez, F., & Dugarte-Peña, G.-L. (2022). Valuable business knowledge asset discovery by processing unstructured data. *Sustainability, 14*(20), 12971. https://doi.org/10.3390/su142012971

Sanchez-Segura, M.-I., Medina-Dominguez, F., Dugarte-Peña, G. L., de Amescua-Seco, A., & González Cruz, R. (2022). Engineering sustainable digital transformation projects immune to technical debt. *Kybernetes*. https://doi.org/10.1108/K-06-2022-0875

Sánchez-Segura, M-I., Ruiz-Robles, A., & Medina-Dominguez, F. (2017, de Septiembre de 4). Strategic characterization of process assets based on asset quality and business impact. *Industrial Management & Data Systems, 117*(8), 1720–1737. https://doi.org/10.1108/IMDS-10-2016-0422

Schiuma, G. (2009). The managerial foundations of knowledge assets dynamics. *Knowledge Management Research and Practice*, 290–299. https://doi.org/10.1057/kmrp.2009.21

Schwarz, M., & Otero, E. (2018, April). Literature review of intellectual capital measurement techniques and methods. *UCSA Scientific Journal, 5*(1), 41–60. https://doi.org/10.18004/UCSA/2409-8752/2018.005(01)041-060

Tanguy, L., Tulechki, N., Urieli, A., Hermann, E., & Raynal, C. (2016). Natural language processing for aviation safety reports: From classification to interactive analysis. *Computers in Industry, 78*, 80–95. https://doi.org/10.1016/j.compind.2015.09.005

Theis, J., & Darabi, H. (2019). Behavioral petri net mining and automated analysis for human-computer interaction recommendations in multi-application environments. *Proceedings of the ACM on Human-Computer Interaction, 3*(EICS), 16. https://doi.org/10.1145/3331155

Van der Aalst, W. (2012). Process mining: Overview and opportunities. *ACM Transactions on Management Information Systems, 3*(2), 17. https://doi.org/10.1145/2229156.2229157

Van Zelst, S., Buijs, M., Vázquez-Barreiros, B., Lama, M., & Mucientes, M. (2019, May 28). Repairing alignments of process models. *Business and Information Systems Engineering, 62*, 289–304. https://doi.org/10.1007/s12599-019-00601-7

Varghese, N., & Punithavalli, M. (2022). Semantic similarity extraction on Corpora using natural language processing techniques and text analytics algorithms. In *Proceedings of 2nd international conference on artificial intelligence: Advances and applications* (pp. 163–176). Springer Nature Singapore. https://doi.org/10.1007/978-981-16-6332-1_16

Wan, X., Lucic, M. C., Ghazzai, H., & Massoud, Y. (2020). Empowering real-time traffic reporting systems with NLP processed social media data. *IEEE Open Journal of Intelligent Transportation Systems, 1*, 159–175. https://doi.org/10.1109/OJITS.2020.3024245

Williams, M., Ariyachandra, T., & Frolick, M. (2017). Business intelligence-success through agile implementation. *The Journal of Management and Engineering Integration, 10*(1), 14–21. https://www.journalmei.com/_files/ugd/f76c8e_e5ea95afc7e9468cb279f9b89a825fb1.pdf

Xu, X. L., Li, J., Wu, D., & Zhang, X. (2021). The intellectual capital efficiency and corporate sustainable growth nexus: Comparison from agriculture, tourism and renewable energy sector. *Environment, Development and Sustainability, 23*(11), 16038–16056. https://doi.org/10.1007/s10668-021-01319-x

Yu, S., Kumamaru, K. K., George, E., Dunne, R. M., Bedayat, A., Neykov, M., & Rybicki, F. J. (2014). Classification of CT pulmonary angiography reports by presence, chronicity, and location of pulmonary embolism with natural language processing. *Journal of Biomedical Informatics, 52*, 386–393. https://doi.org/10.1016/j.jbi.2014.08.001

Zerbino, P., Stefanini, A., & Aloini, D. (2021). Process science in action: A literature review on process mining in business management. *Technological Forecasting and Social Change, 172*, 121021. https://doi.org/10.1016/j.techfore.2021.121021

Zhao, K., Shi, N., Sa, Z., Wang, H.-X., & Lu, C.-H. (2020). Text mining and analysis of treatise on febrile diseases based on natural language processing. *World Journal of Traditional Chinese Medicine, 6*(1), 67–73. https://doi.org/10.4103/wjtcm.wjtcm_28_19

A Unified Theory and Ontological Framework of ESG Reporting

Hans-Günter Lindner and Ingo Steinhäuser

Abstract Intangible values, for example, environmental, human, and social metrics and behavior, have become indispensable in the global economy. One of the key global drivers of measuring intangible values is expressed in corporate environmental and social responsibility, mainly through the Environmental, Social, and Governance (ESG) framework. This is leading to a massive shift in the way intangible and financial metrics need to be measured and monitored together. Problems arise when real and intangible values are treated mathematically in the same way. Therefore, a new theory of value is presented that combines nonlinearity and multivalued logic and leads to a new ontology for ESG. This study describes the transfer from theory to practice using an example of an adaptive decision support system that uses fuzzy cognitive maps for multidimensional value maps and for handling incomplete data of ESG measures. It reduces complexity and enables the prediction of intangibles that support decision-makers in evaluating companies according to an ESG framework.

1 Introduction

In a rapidly evolving global market, Environmental, Social, and Governance (ESG) factors have emerged as vital elements for sustainable business practices and investment decisions. The growing emphasis on ESG underscores a collective push toward greater corporate responsibility and transparency, driven by changing

H.-G. Lindner (✉)
TH Köln–University of Applied Sciences, Cologne, Germany
e-mail: hans-guenter.lindner@th-koeln.de

I. Steinhäuser
Thomson Reuters, Washington, DC, USA
e-mail: ingo.steinhaeuser@thomsonreuters.com

F. Matos et al. (eds.), *Intellectual Capital in a Global Business Landscape*,
Contributions to Management Science, https://doi.org/10.1007/978-3-031-86362-2_5

societal values, regulations, and the understanding that ESG factors enhance company viability and performance.

Recent trends show a remarkable surge in ESG data disclosure. Many large companies and organizations are investing in ESG data collection and reporting. Various frameworks, including the newly established International Sustainability Standards Board (ISSB), aim to standardize ESG data collection and reporting, helping organizations navigate sustainability complexities.

Regulatory requirements, such as the Corporate Sustainability Reporting Directive (CSRD) in Europe and forthcoming regulations by the Securities and Exchange Commission (SEC) in the United States, are accelerating ESG standard adoption, emphasizing reporting on greenhouse gas emissions and other sustainability metrics. Additionally, global anti-slavery regulations and deforestation laws show a broader commitment to addressing human rights and environmental issues in business models.

Despite its importance, measuring ESG performance poses challenges due to inconsistent data collection, individual preferences in decision-making, and varying reporting standards. This inconsistency highlights the need for harmonized frameworks to provide reliable, comparable ESG data, enabling informed investment and stakeholder decisions.

In summary, the growing importance of ESG in corporate governance and investment decisions reflects a shift toward sustainable and responsible business practices. Developing standardized and transparent ESG frameworks is crucial for supporting this transition, although challenges remain. The variety in ESG data and measurement methods makes it hard to evaluate companies based on individual numeric and intangible values. This highlights the need for a unified method that can harmonize different rating agency approaches and support individual decision-making.

This article aims to evaluate a decision-making process for ESG that harmonizes different approaches to integrating and comparing intangible and tangible values. It introduces a new theoretical framework designed to achieve this alignment. Additionally, it aims to empower consumers and investors to develop personalized evaluation systems by defining their specific value ranges, thus enabling the seamless application of their preferences using readily available data. As a consequence, we present a prototype with an adaptive decision support system.

2 Methodology

As an initial step, we provide an overview of the importance of ESG, a conceptual framework that leads to a significant shift in how intangibles and traditional economic metrics influence company ratings. ESG users require a comprehensible and individualized perspective based on their preferences and financial portfolios. Consequently, the valuation of intangibles must be user-adaptive.

To address this requirement, we present a unified theory developed and validated by the author over the past decade at TH Köln–University of Applied Sciences. This theory integrates several concepts: a novel definition of values that represent intangibles and real financial metrics, interconnected values as fields surrounding business processes (drawing an analogy from physics), and resulting value maps as learning networks or active ontologies akin to machine learning and artificial intelligence.

To elucidate the unified theory and its practicability in handling regulatory and binding intangibles, we initiated three projects aimed at finalizing our concepts into an adaptive decision support system. In the first phase, we focused on companies in the food and drug category within Refinitiv Eikon database, reducing the available intangible values and developing an initial prototype for a feasibility study. The subsequent step involved broadening the scope and expanding the key value areas. Finally, the results from these prior efforts were utilized to develop and prototype an adaptive decision support system.

3 Environmental, Social, and Governance (ESG)

3.1 The Importance of ESG

Environmental, Social, and Governance (ESG) factors are increasingly used to provide transparency in the workings of organizations. While the collection and the publishing of ESG data is voluntary, an increasing number of public and private organizations are investing in ESG data collection and reporting capabilities. In the United States, nearly two-thirds of respondents are disclosing sustainability information according to the annual survey of sustainability officials (Dow Jones & Company, 2023). Moreover, 95% of all large companies (1283 companies) disclose ESG information according to the third report on ESG disclosures by the International Federation of Accountants (Ho, 2023).

To provide guidance and rules for the collection of ESG data, Various frameworks and standard setting bodies exist: from the UN Global Compact, the Task Force on Climate-related Disclosures (TCFD), Science-based Target Initiative (SBTI Net-Zero Standard) to the recent development of the International Sustainability Standards Board (ISSB) as a consolidating sustainability standard.

The acceleration in adopting these standards is driven by the urgency to adhere to existing and upcoming greenhouse gas (GHG) reporting regulations. In Europe, the Corporate Sustainability Reporting Directive (CSRD) mandates the reporting of greenhouse gas emissions, classified into scope 1, scope 2, and scope 3. It will include 49,000 companies including private organizations (European Commission, n.d.). In the United States, the upcoming SEC regulation is expected to include at least GHG emissions, classified into scope 1 and scope 2.

Not only are environmental regulations the driver of increased ESG data adaptation. Global anti-slavery regulations like the Uyghur Forced Labor Prevention Act (UFLPA), the Act on Corporate Due Diligence Obligations in Supply Chains, and the Corporate Sustainability Due Diligence Directive (CSDDD) are geared to identify potential negative impacts on human rights and environmental rights. In addition, deforestation regulation in the European Union will prohibit the import of commodities like cattle, cocoa, coffee, soy, rubber, and oil palm that were produced on land subject to illegal deforestation.

ESG data plays an important role in the provision of transparency. Various tools and methods exist to collect data that are relevant to any sustainability framework. Such data largely includes corporate disclosures that are expressed in binary form (yes or no answer to a question) or in a numerical way. In addition, ESG benchmarks, news, and controversies are also part of an ESG data framework and are provided by specialist data firms.

3.2 ESG Users

ESG data is increasingly used in the financial industry for investment decision-making. Their main users are banks, Private Equity/Venture Capital (PE/VC) funds, insurance firms, brokerage houses, research organizations, and retail investors. At the beginning of 2020, for example, global sustainable investment reached \$35.5 trillion, which represents 36% of all professionally managed assets according to the Global Sustainable Investment Alliance (GSIA) (Global Sustainable Investment Alliance, n.d.). The GSIA defines sustainable investment as an investment approach that considers "environmental, social and governance (ESG) factors in portfolio selection and management across seven strategies of sustainable or responsible investment."

Financial materiality and consumer demands play an important role in the growth of sustainable assets. Unfortunately, a misleading classification of sustainable assets, a form of greenwashing, contributed to that growth. Both European and US regulators have now revised their sustainable investment figures and incorporated a more rigid approach in calculating sustainable assets. While the financial performance of ESG funds does not provide a clear picture about financial materiality, a different picture emerges when analyzing the correlation between financial performance and ESG on a corporate level. As studies may show conflicting results, it is worthwhile to analyze the results of all available studies. Meta-studies have been conducted to aggregate the findings and results of thousands of studies (Whelan et al., 2021).

In one of the most recent meta-studies, Rockefeller Asset Management in combination with NYU Stern analyzed the results of over a thousand studies from the years 2015 to 2020.

Financial performance has been measured by looking at return on equity (ROE) or return on assets (ROA). The results show a positive correlation in 58% of the cases, and no correlation (neutral) in 13% of the results, 21% with mixed results, and 14% with a negative correlation. Such clear findings demonstrate why the use of ESG in the investment process is continuing to gain traction. It is simply good for business because it reduces business risk across various domains of a corporation and, at the same time, uncovers opportunities for a more energy-efficient business operations.

3.3 ESG Integration

Various forms of integrating ESG in the analysis of companies exist. The Global Sustainable Investment Alliance defines sustainable investment as one that "considers [ESG] factors in portfolio selection and management" and divides ESG investing into the following common strategies for investors (Global Sustainable Investment Alliance, n.d.):

- ESG integration (using ESG data next to financial data)
- Corporate engagement and shareholder action (investor activism to focus on ESG)
- Norm-based screening (screening against minimum standards)
- Exclusionary screening (negative screening)
- Best in class (positive screening)
- Thematic investing (clean energy, social trends, low carbon, etc.)
- Impact investing (generating financial return next to social or environmental return)

The collection of ESG data and its utilization in making investment decisions are significantly shaped by established frameworks that have evolved over time. Regulations, on the other hand, make it mandatory for companies to use this data as a basis for due diligence to ensure compliance. For example, the UFLPA in the United States requires that companies do not source products from the Xinjiang region in China, as these products have likely been produced using forced labor from the Uyghur minority. In conducting supply chain due diligence, companies often use information generated from ESG frameworks.

ESG data collection and provision constitute a critical dimension in ESG, laying the foundational information utilized in the integration process of ESG at financial institutions.

The respective frameworks and standards introduce another dimension utilized to adhere to regulatory requirements.

The interplay of ESG data is visualized in Fig. 1: On one hand, there is the critical importance of ESG data collection and its integration into the investment and decision process at financial institutions. However, the respective frameworks and standards provide guidance and harmonization in the way ESG data is collected. They serve as a good basis for decision-making and compliance with various ESG-related regulations.

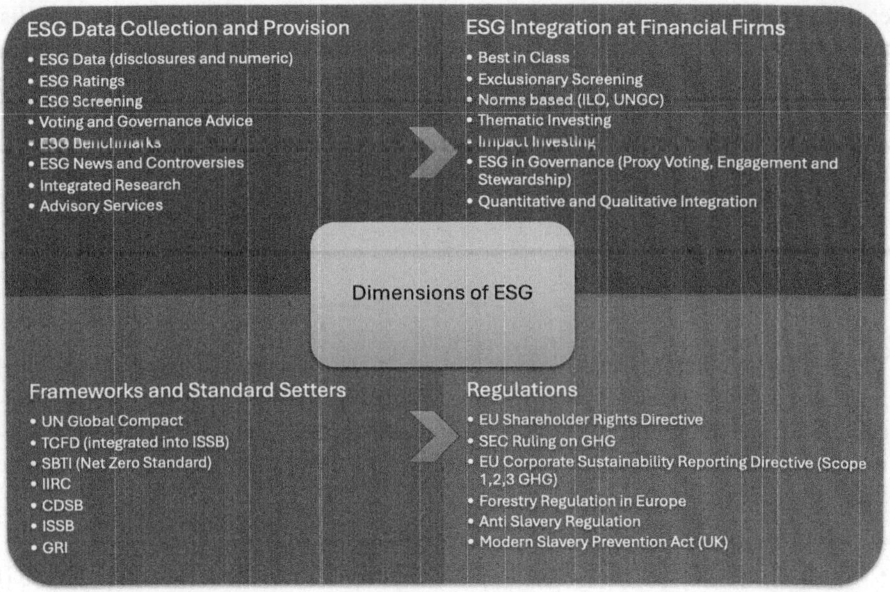

Fig. 1 Four dimensions of ESG

3.4 Problems of ESG Measurement

A primary area of criticism centers on the diverse methodologies used to assess ESG performance. A wide range of data is available for assessing the sustainability performance of companies, but heterogeneous approaches to recording, measuring, and allocating assessments often lead to different results. The three biggest barriers to ESG integration are comparability between companies, the lack of standards, and the cost of integrating and analyzing information (see Amel-Zadeh & Serafeim, 2018, p. 40).

For example, different rating providers came to different conclusions when assessing the oil giant Exxon Mobil, which makes it very difficult to make a clear assessment of a company's ESG performance in individual cases (KNOWESG, n.d.). According to the provider Sustainalytics, Exxon Mobil represents a serious risk on a five-level scale, ranging from negligible risk, low risk, medium risk, high risk, and serious risk (Sustainalytics, n.d.).

Refinitiv gives Exxon Mobil an ESG rating of 66 (good) on a scale from 1 to 100, where:

- 0–25 is poor
- >25–50 is satisfactory
- >50–75 is good
- >75–100 is excellent

MSCI has given a BBB (average) for Exxon Mobil in the following categories:

- CCC and B: Laggard
- BB, BBB, A: Average
- AA and AAA: Leader

Every data provider creates different categories within ESG. Refinitiv, for example, has three environmental subcategories (resource use, emissions, innovation), four social subcategories (workforce, human rights, community, product responsibility) and three governance subcategories (management, shareholders, and corporate social responsibility). In addition, each category has information on controversies, which are summarized in a separate ESG controversy score.

In contrast, MSCI has developed a different approach. Their environmental category includes the subcategories climate change, natural resources, pollution and waste, and opportunities. The social category is subdivided among human capital, product liability, stakeholder opposition, and social opportunities. The governance category includes only two subcategories: corporate governance and corporate behavior (MSCI ESG Categories, n.d.). RepRisk, another ESG provider, exclusively utilizes controversy information to calculate ESG scores.

While some of the underlying data points are often identical, e.g., greenhouse gas emissions, energy efficiency metrics, or water consumption, there are differences in the way controversies are handled or how performance improvement is measured in the actual category score.

The diversity with which ESG ratings are calculated makes it very difficult to assess risks universally. In this respect, ESG ratings differ significantly from the risk assessments of rating agencies.

3.5 *ESG Data Challenges*

According to the CFA Institute, there are many challenges when comparing ESG data. Firstly, there are issues related to disclosure and data, such as data consistency, data scarcity, data incompleteness, and lack of verified data. Most of the data is not reported uniformly for all companies, regions, and economic sectors.

Secondly, there are difficulties with comparability, e.g., lack of comparability between ESG rating agencies and the availability of different accounting standards. Thirdly, comparison between different regions and cultures is difficult; fourthly, the terminology used in measuring and reporting ESG is often inconsistent.

All these factors contribute to heterogeneous ESG valuations and assessments across a variety of ESG data providers. Because of this lack of uniformity, ESG ratings are more comparable to financial analyst ratings when making sell, hold, or buy decisions.

To illustrate this, let us take Exxon Mobil as an example again. Twenty-five investment analysts rated the Exxon Mobil share as follows in September 2023 (Yahoo! finance, n.d.):

- 2 strong buy
- 5 buy
- 11 hold
- 5 underperform
- 2 sell

One of the effective ways in which investors and consumers understand ESG-related data is to compare a company with its peers in the same industry.

MSCI, S&P, and Dow Jones have developed the Global Industry Classification Standard (GICS), which comprises 11 industry sectors, 25 industry groups, 74 industries, and 163 sub-industries. This four-level hierarchical industry classification system enables comparison within an industry or sub-industry and is an important step in creating a degree of standardization for comparing a company with its peers.

3.6 The Need for Individual Decision Support in ESG

ESG investing is often criticized because it is difficult for investors to identify ESG factors and consider them in their investment decisions. The main criticism centers on four areas:

- Overinclusion of underperforming companies: ESG mutual funds and exchange-traded funds (ETFs) frequently include investments in companies that could be considered ethically questionable in one or more ESG dimensions.
- Questionable assessment criteria: The criteria used to evaluate ESG factors are often subjective and may reflect narrow or conflicting ideological and political viewpoints. This can lead to an overemphasis on nonmaterial or sociopolitical factors and may cast doubt on the accuracy of materiality assessments.
- Data quality concerns: The data used to assess ESG factors often comes from the companies themselves and may not be verified or corroborated by third parties. This complicates efforts to validate, compare, and establish standardized ESG information.
- Potential disregard of long-term improvements: Several financial advisors focus more on investment returns than on ESG criteria during the screening process, which could result in the omission of companies with robust ESG practices that emphasize long-term sustainability.

The diversity in ESG performance and measurement methodologies, combined with heterogeneous "big data" that decision-makers must analyze, complicates the process of evaluating companies based on individual values and preferences.

This situation emphasizes the need for a methodology that can reconcile varying approaches from rating agencies and can provide, at the same time, individual decision support.

4 A Unified Theory and Ontological Framework

4.1 *Motivation for a New Theory*

The importance of measuring intangibles for market-oriented ratings is steadily increasing. A study by Ocean Tomo (2020, p. 1) highlights this trend, with the proportion of intangible assets in market value rising from 17% in 1975 to a staggering 90% in 2020. The importance of intangibles for measuring corporate value is closely related to ESG. "Modern accounting standards have not fully kept pace with these changes" (Takatsuki & Yanagi, 2019, p. 2).

As discussed in the previous chapter, ESG factors are a key driver of intangible ratings. However, the challenges associated with measuring ESG metrics are also relevant for measuring other intangibles. Unlike ESG, where established rating agencies provide data, measuring other intangibles remains a challenge.

The biggest problem is the variety of definitions: Knowledge, intellectual capital, intangible assets, intangible capital, intangible values, etc. exist parallelly (Becker, 2005, p. 18; Müller, 2006, p. 8; Kaufmann & Schneider, 2006, p. 26). This problem becomes more complex when we consider multiple translation alternatives. Most of the literature neglects the real meaning of capital and assets in balance sheets, e.g., Sveiby equates capital with assets (Bodrow & Bergmann, 2003, p. 83). Words such as assets and capital are placeholders for value, whereas value is not clearly defined.

Rather than presenting specific actions, much of the literature on intangibles remains vague, lacking in precise definitions and practical examples. For instance, human capital, a principal element of intangibles, lacks a unified approach and detailed engagement with human resources (HR) literature, with measures often selected haphazardly. Occasionally, traditional HR metrics from standard HR reports, such as staff turnover or the number and average age of employees, are cited as indicators of human capital. More perplexingly, measures like "new customers acquired" are identified, even though these do not fall under HR metrics (compare Becker, 2005, p. 153). Kasperzak and Nestler (2010, p. 206) propose various alternatives for assessing human capital, distinguishing between nonmonetary and monetary assessment methods yet only referring to indicators without explicitly naming them. Reilly and Schweihs (1998, p. 20; 2000, p. 442) identify the assembled workforce, employee agreements, and union contracts as valuable components of human capital.

Referring to Edvinsson and Malone, human capital or employee competency pertains to personal capabilities, such as knowledge, experience, and skills, their exchange, and further development through qualification and educational measures. (Kneisel et al., 2012, p. 54). Bodrow and Bergmann (2003, p. 96) enrich the concept by incorporating the dynamics of an intelligent organization, drawing upon Edvinsson's work without explicitly specifying these terms. Nagel (2012, p. 69) characterizes human capital as individual determinants that impact intangible assets, encompassing competencies, skills, capabilities, and motivation. These determinants are illustrated through examples like qualified staff, social skills, motivation and job satisfaction, leadership, management expertise, and dependability. Lastly, Roos et al. (2004) identify top management quality, problem-solving ability, and personnel reputation as aspects of human capital that cannot be standardized for company comparisons.

However, all the definitions and interpretations are vague and provided on a non-binding basis. Consequently, Scholz et al. (2011, p. 57) have compiled over 47 methods specifically for the management and assessment of human capital. They recommend their formula "Die Saarbrücker Formel," asserting that it allows for precise calculation of human capital. Unfortunately, this formula yields a monetary value and fails to consider the qualitative aspects of intangibles. It should be noted that the formula labels "value" as "price" or "costs", and uses the period of employment as the denominator. This results in age discrimination, because older employees longer tenures cause them to recieve lower values. Becker et al. (2007) demystify this formula by listing ten reasons against its use and summarize "Die Saarbrücker Formel thus exemplifies the central shortcomings of many approaches to recording and evaluating human capital: a focus on the past, failure to take account of interdependencies between variables and neglect of the heterogeneity of human capital holders" (translated from German).

The definition problem of human capital stands for the most measures of intangibles. Though there are weak definitions and no standards, various definitions conclude a variety of measuring methods that leads to an additionally higher dilution of content. Formulas, like the Pulic's information coefficient or Tobin's Q, complete with strategic management tools like balanced scorecards or the IC Navigator, which are highly aggregated (see Becker, 2005, p. 40).

The main problems remain. Most of the measuring methods are driven by financial numbers. Measurement methods focus on balance sheets, accounting standards and regulations, or strategy (see van Criekingen et al., 2021). Some methods focus on use or benefit; others solely focus on financial concepts (compare Kasperzak & Nestler, 2010, p. 59). Therefore, the use of classical algebra is necessary to fulfill regulatory accounting standards. Most of the standards call intangibles hidden drivers, but they are obvious like child labor or working conditions. ESG measures are intangibles because of their immaterial nature, but they do not fit into the historical classification of human, relational, and customer values, neither the FASB (Financial Accounting Standards Board) suggestions nor the Schmalenbach-Gesellschaft approach. Some intangibles relate to several clusters, and therefore multivalued logic must be included.

Hunter et al. (2005) criticize the measuring of intangibles and state "Furthermore, since it is generally not clear whether these non-financial indicators are reflections of the activity (cost) expended to generate the asset, or represent forward-looking values to the firm, there are no all-purpose ways to use the data analytically." Finally, Kaufmann and Schneider (2006, p. 39) state that a theoretical model is missing.

Additionally, the technical extraction, transfer, and loading (ETL) process in data warehousing, which is normally used for tangible values, is not able to manage intangibles when they are interconnected as networks. Because of the different nature of real and intangible values, the problem of combination remains. There is a need for a content-based approach that leads to aggregated ontologies, which can be measured and evaluated.

In summary, a new theory requires clear definitions, many-valued logic, the integration of both monetary and nonmonetary values, the modeling values as networks, and therefore calculations beyond classical algebra.

4.2 Definition Problems of Values

The term value has a lot of meanings in different domains. The only common denominator is that values are immaterial. Over the last few centuries, many theories of value have emerged, leading to different meanings that mix the meaning of value with need or benefit, price, and so on.

Axiology, the philosophical study of values, focuses on the concept of the good and the question of what kind of things have value. In contrast to axiology, it is sometimes irrelevant in economics how and why values are created. Another issue is that axiology is influenced by ideas formulated by scientific leaders. In everyday usage, the term value is often employed to denote an amount of money, a level of quality, or significance (Merriam-Webster, n.d.). In mathematics, it is only a number or a measure. In the economic context, value pertains to scarcity, quantifiable significance of economic objects, and the fulfilment of consumer demands. In this area, many authors equate value with benefit. In the social sciences and psychology, values are concerned with what is desirable, and in these fields, values are an aggregate as they often relate to groups through culture or countries. Prominent theories by Shalom H. Schwartz (2017) and Milton Rokeach (1973) present basic values in lists of words with broad meanings, allowing for a wide spectrum of interpretations. Most values are aggregated in nature and lose context for the individual.

To assess companies and their performance, interdisciplinary teams tackle this subject, frequently resulting in a conflation of meanings that complicates precise measurement. Methods of business analytics and data warehousing are used to analyze and aggregate measures, but they are based on classical algebra, which does not address the interrelated and nonlinear nature of intangibles. Therefore, we propose a new theory to solve insufficiencies.

4.3 A New Definition of Values

The new definition of values includes intangible values and shifts the focus sharply toward the individual. The first theorem is as follows: A value is a result of individual perception.

Let us take an example of Refinitiv Eikon. "Targets Diversity and Opportunity," DFO Code SODODP0151, is a value also in the new definition. The description states: “Has the company set targets or objectives to be achieved on diversity and equal opportunity?

- Any objective/target set to increase or promote diversity in the workplace with a time frame.
- Includes information on the promotion of women, minorities, disabled employees, or employment from any age, ethnicity, race, nationality, and religion”.

The measure has a data type of Boolean in Eikon but must be reviewed by an analyst in policy or compliance testing and is therefore a perception of that analyst. Although it is of Boolean nature, the analyst could count the frequency of occurrences for this value and observe that there is a range of fulfilment.

To avoid mixing the meanings, it must be clear that value is not benefit, is not price, is not money (the second theorem). But there is a conversion from values to money. Values can be transformed into benefits through utilization or a process that generates an advantage. A price can only be established in the presence of a market. When market participants reach an agreement on a price, a transaction can occur, facilitating the exchange of money.

The previously mentioned value “Targets Diversity and Opportunity” does not in itself constitute a benefit. Merely setting targets or objectives holds no inherent value. For a benefit to arise, a specific process aimed at achieving these goals must be implemented. This process incurs a cost, calculated based on activities that consume time, resources, and the cost associated with time. The price of this cost is determined within the company, factoring into internal cost accounting, or is externalized through payments to consultants based on hourly rates.

4.4 Ontological Framework: Value Fields and Processes

Values surround processes like electromagnetic fields surround an electric wire. Analogous to quantum mechanics, values are entities within the process field that possess a probability, which can vary in magnitude or position in relation to process activities. This depends on the recipient, who is a participant in the business process. The receiver’s perception can only occur after all facets of the value have been understood, regardless of whether this understanding is implicit or explicit. The explicit method is cognitive, as when the analyst in our example reads the description in Eikon. Implicit understanding happens when an analyst observes activities and finds that these align with their internal model of this value. Subsequently, the ability to articulate this value in words may follow if it has been implicitly perceived.

The values associated with the process are partially interconnected, resulting in a nonlinear system (as per the third theorem). In our example, “Targets Diversity and Opportunity” can be linked to the value “Woman Managers” under DFO Code SODODP019. Such a relationship can be inferred when these two values appear together in time. This simultaneity points to a limitation of conventional measurements across all databases. However, this limitation can be addressed if an analyst asks about the relationships between values. Consequently, a network of interconnected values is established.

The question remains how we can measure the value. When we follow the second theorem, the value is not monetary. To distinguish between immaterial (intangible) from real (tangible) numbers, we propose measuring value using complex numbers.

4.5 *Values as Complex Numbers*

The traditional approach results in intangibles being treated as tangible assets in business practices. Consequently, uniform methods are frequently applied in business valuation, adhering to the same financial principles and guidelines.

The new theory posits that tangible and intangible values differ fundamentally and thus necessitate distinct mathematical approaches for accurate treatment. However, integration between the two is essential. While tangible values can be computed using classical algebra, this method is not suitable for intangible values. Instead, these require analysis within a multidimensional space where they relate to each other to varying degrees. Intangibles are entities connected by causal relationships governed by fuzzy logic and characterized by membership functions. Consequently, the system of values constitutes a fuzzy space, essentially a multidimensional hypercube.

To calculate both tangible and intangible values within a single framework, complex numbers are utilized. Real numbers, which are economically quantifiable, correspond to the x-axis. Immaterial or intangible values—referred to in mathematics as imaginary numbers—correspond to the imaginary y-axis. In Fig. 2, the real number is a and the imaginary number b, resulting in the complex number as $z = a - ib$, where i is the imaginary unit defined by $i^2 = -1$. The total value of a system comprising several values is represented as V = Sum (Real Value) + i*Sum(Intangible Values). The value's magnitude is then determined using the Pythagorean theorem.

When we observe these values over time, a trajectory emerges, enabling tests of stability or compliance analysis. Observations can be conducted through interviews, questionnaires, or process analytics. This provides the opportunity to establish a new two-dimensional controlling system.

In our example "Targets Diversity and Opportunity," the count of occurrences determines the imaginary number, while the sum of money spent on related processes plus the depreciation of resources constitutes the real number. This number is positive because it is treated as an investment. However, this should not be confused with measuring its benefit.

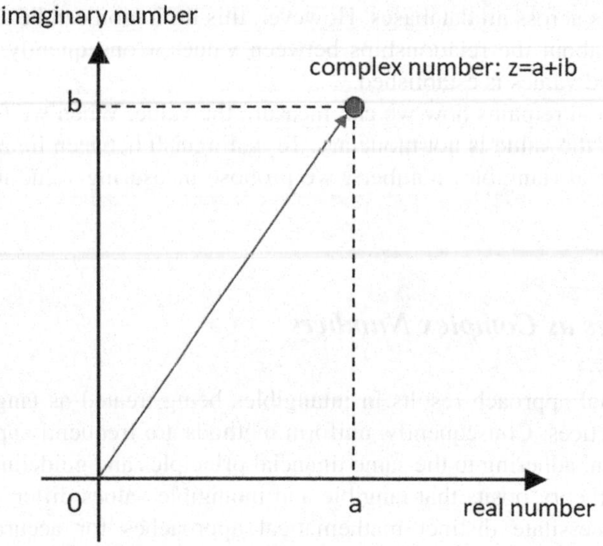

Fig. 2 Complex number for a single two-dimensional value

4.6 Value Maps as Networks

As mentioned earlier, the relationships between values form a network. This can be depicted in a directed graph, functioning like a mental map, which visualizes the strength of impact, for example, in the form of fuzzy cognitive maps (FCMs) (Kosko, 1992). The nodes in the graph represent values and function similar to neurons. The causal relationships are illustrated by arrows. The strength of each relationship is indicated by a plus or minus sign, or a number within the interval [−1; 1] on the arrows. Values may host internal activities that flow through these arrows, akin to how neural activities transfer energy across neural axons and synapses. FCMs are nonlinear hybrid systems that integrate the capabilities of fuzzy logic and neural networks.

FCMs can be built by expert interviews, questionnaires, or process observation. Several maps can be combined to build aggregated knowledge or to expand the knowledge. Figure 3 presents an aggregated selection of social values represented as an FCM during the initial stage, aimed at establishing the adaptive decision support detailed in Sect. 5. Eikon measures are represented as rectangles and aggregated values as hexagons. The arrows are the relationships with strength from the interval between three minus signs and three plus signs.

FCMs act as dynamic ontologies that modify their states in response to activity distribution. They, along with their mechanism of spreading activation, can be utilized to predict system states. When values are assigned to process activities (which should not be confused with neural activities in FCM nodes), value maps evolve into value journeys.

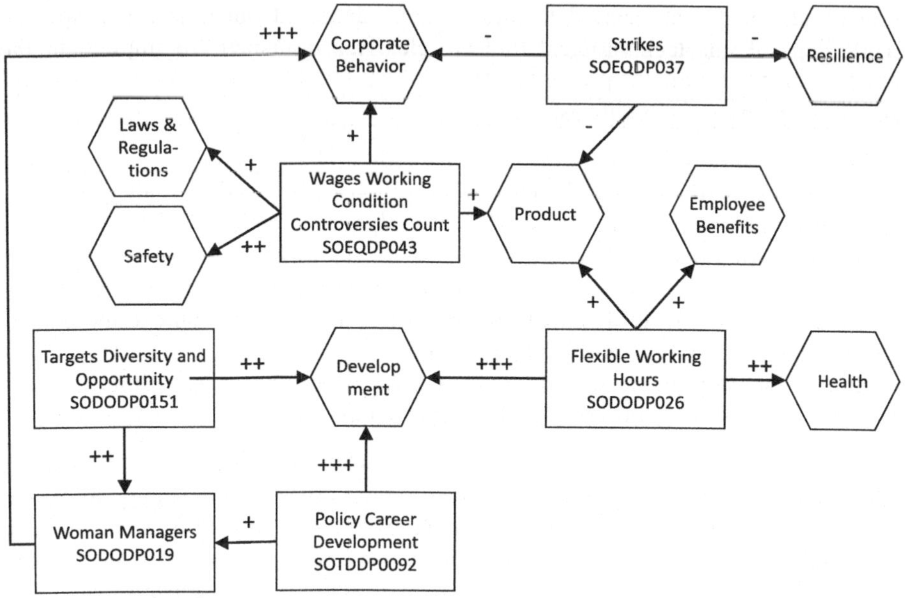

Fig. 3 A partial fuzzy cognitive map for ESG

5 Adaptive Decision Support for ESG Intangibles

5.1 Project Overview

The sheer volume of ESG data, coupled with the comprehensive processes required for data acquisition, presents challenges for both professional and individual investors in the valuation of companies. Considering the societal shift toward a more sustainable lifestyle, sustainable investments are becoming increasingly significant, particularly in assessing social values.

In three projects initiated in July 2020 at TH Köln – University of Applied Sciences, the new value concept was applied using the Eikon database, which includes over 400 ESG metrics (Buchmüller et al., 2020). Together with the project partner PSI Software SE, their web-enabled software Qualicision® was used to build an adaptive decision support system for investors and consumers. The software solution utilizes versatile technology that is applicable across a broad spectrum of fields without being limited to any industry. It intelligently captures, analyzes, and transparently displays conflicting objectives, creating a comprehensive solution for proactive planning, simulation, and optimization (for further explanation of Qualicision®, see Felix, 2021, 2023). Consequently, it highlights and makes visible the most critical information and levers for decision-making.

Qualicision® fosters a synergy between fuzzy modeling and decision support. Within this framework, "fuzzy" refers to the recognition of patterns and the transformation of imprecise data into accurate data and outcomes. The specific work steps of this technological tool are clearly established. To implement the Qualicision® solution, the process under consideration must first undergo an analysis focusing on the following aspects:

1. In the initial step, decision aspects are identified. These encompass all aspects of the process pertinent to decision-making, which are referred to as alternatives or decision alternatives, and those relevant to the decisions themselves, known as decision criteria in Qualicision®.
2. The second step involves analyzing the interdependencies between the alternatives and the criteria. This analysis establishes the decision context and constitutes the core analysis within Qualicision®.
3. In the final step, the analyzed interdependencies are incorporated into the process, a procedure termed the Qualicision® synthesis.

One objective was to simplify complexity to facilitate easier decision-making. Moreover, the data itself does not indicate which criteria significantly influence clients' investment decisions. Beyond a composite score derived from all metrics, these metrics are typically assessed individually. The actual impact of one criterion on others, including the direction and intensity of these relationships, has yet to be documented. This is particularly true for the S-dimension (social), which is not adequately covered due to the limited number of quantifiable criteria available. These criteria are categorized into subcategories: workforce, human rights, community, and product responsibility.

The challenge was to match the intangible aspects of the S-dimension with quantitative data. For the prototypes in Qualicision®, data and decisions were modeled using fuzzy logic. The first FCM was created to model the dependencies of intangible social values. This approach enables a comparison of how data from individual criteria influence the predefined values and goals of investors. Based on individual perspectives and priorities, a ranking for company valuation can be determined in real time while utilizing the application.

This approach allows both professional and individual investors to derive benefits from the application, as the valuation of a company then becomes dependent on the user's perspective. Additional advantages include the time savings afforded by using Qualicision® and an enhanced understanding of the interdependencies, which serve to improve users' mental models.

5.2 A Customer Journey for Adaptive Decision Support

The system's design was inspired by the customer journey of investors (see Fig. 4). Investors seek to invest in companies that align with their personal values. The vast amount of data presents a challenge and can overwhelm users. In response, investors seek advice, and analysts assist in prioritizing their goals and value preferences.

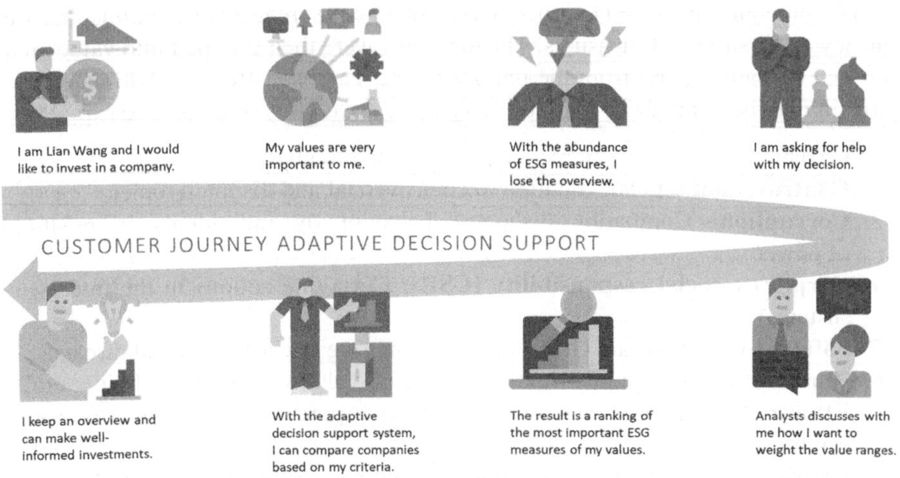

Fig. 4 A customer journey for decision support (Adapted from Buchmüller et al., 2020, p. 40)

5.3 *Data Analysis and Preparation*

Several steps were essential in preparing the data and user goals for Qualicision®. We established an ETL (extract, transform, load) process, simplified complexity, defined relationships, and determined user objectives. The initial analysis was conducted using Excel PivotTable to gain an overview across sectors and to filter out companies that provided enough valuable data for further analysis. In the first project phase, we concentrated on the Food & Drug sector, which encompasses 150 companies, to streamline the number of measures. Through text mining techniques, we extracted ten key values: product, law and regulations, health, safety, development, corporate behavior, privacy, responsibility, employee benefits, and resilience.

In the next phase, we expanded the range of measures to all sectors. At most, companies contributed data for only 14.47% of all the measures. We opted to focus on the data ranging from 7% to 14.47% of all measures because it included ESG controversies of significance. Ultimately, we were able to proceed with 90 ESG measures for further analysis.

The text mining ETL process was executed in Altair AI Studio (RapidMiner) as follows:

1. Read Excel export.
2. Transfer nominal values to text.
3. Extract content.
4. Tokenize.
5. Transform cases.
6. Filter stop words.
7. Generate n-grams.
8. Filter tokens.

The outcome of the ETL process was an Excel spreadsheet detailing the frequency distributions of measures. The measures were then grouped into value areas through domain experts from the university and Thomson Reuters. Ultimately, we streamlined the complexity to 12 primary value areas (Reyelt et al., 2021, p. 23):

1. **Career:** Promotion of employee personal development
2. **Controversial topics:** Attention to controversial and disputed topics
3. **Corruption:** Combating dishonest behavior by individuals in positions of power
4. **Corporate social responsibility (CSR):** Corporate actions in the interest of sustainability
5. **Safety:** Ensuring a safe environment, countering uncertainties and threats
6. **Equality:** Ensuring equal rights for all people of any sexuality, religion, etc.
7. **Ethics:** Appropriate business policies and practices regarding controversial topics
8. **Fairness:** Equality in the treatment of people with the same performance standards
9. **Health:** Well-being in health
10. **Human rights:** Protecting the dignity of every individual/human rights
11. **Quality management:** Constant optimization of the quality of products and services
12. **Workplace environment:** Positive work environment, mutual respect, and mindfulness

5.4 Selection of Values

Eikon categorizes each company according to 148 environmental and 163 social ESG factors that are important measures for company valuation, risk management, and compliance. The third project team successfully developed an adaptive decision support system, enabling both professional and private investors to dynamically construct personalized rankings that align with their unique interests and objectives in real time (Hauser et al., 2022). In this project, we selected factors of high societal relevance, choosing ten measures from the environmental domain and ten from the social domain. This compilation draws upon methodologies for complexity reduction and value areas developed in previous projects.

These 20 measures are presented as percentages or relative numbers to enable comparison across different companies. They serve as examples and are representative of other ESG criteria. The selected criteria are assigned value ranges in accordance with the preceding project phases.

Environmental Measures

1. **Total energy use per million in revenue ($)** calculates the energy usage for every million dollars earned, indicating efficiency in energy consump-

tion relative to revenue. The corresponding value areas are environment and responsibility.

2. **Renewable energy use ratio** assesses the percentage of energy consumption that is sourced from renewable energy, reflecting a company's commitment to sustainable energy use. The corresponding value areas are environment, sustainability, and recycling.
3. **Total water use/million revenue ($)** measures the amount of water utilized for every million dollars of revenue, illustrating water use efficiency. The corresponding value areas are resources and efficiency.
4. **Emission reduction target percentage** outlines the company's targeted percentage decrease in emissions, emphasizing its goals for reducing its carbon footprint. The corresponding value areas are responsibility and sustainability.
5. **Emission reduction target year** identifies the specific year by which the emission reduction targets should be met, underscoring the urgency and timeframe for environmental goals. The corresponding value areas are responsibility and development.
6. **Total CO_2 emissions/million in revenue ($)** estimates the total carbon dioxide emissions generated per million dollars of revenue, serving as a gauge for the company's carbon intensity. The corresponding value areas are environment and efficiency.
7. **Total waste/millions in revenue ($)** compares the total waste output against revenue, where a lower figure indicates higher environmental efficiency in minimizing waste production. The corresponding value areas are resources, environment, and efficiency.
8. **Waste recycled to total waste ratio** reveals the percentage of waste that is recycled, indicating the effectiveness of a company's waste management practices. The corresponding value areas are responsibility, sustainability, and recycling.
9. **Total water pollutant emissions/million in revenue ($)** evaluates the total pollutant emissions to water per million dollars of revenue, measuring the impact on water quality. The corresponding value areas are preservation, environment, and efficiency.
10. **Environmental certification (ISO 14000 or EMS)** determines whether a company holds ISO 14000 or Environmental Management System (EMS) environmental certification, both of which are benchmarks for robust environmental management systems. These certifications are indicators of a company's dedication to continuous environmental performance improvement and adherence to sustainable practices. The corresponding value areas are sensitivity, responsibility, law, and regulations.

Social Measures

1. **Employee satisfaction** is measured as a percentage to estimate the level of contentment among employees. The corresponding value areas are health, career, and workplace environment.

2. **Salary gap** highlights the disparity in wages within a company, expressed as an absolute number. A lower value suggests a more equitable salary structure among all employees. The corresponding value areas are CSR and ethics.
3. **Trade union representation** measures the degree to which employees are represented by unions, indicating the involvement of collective bargaining in the workplace. The corresponding value areas are equality and fairness.
4. **Employee turnover rate** should also be documented to reflect the percentage of employees leaving the company over a certain period. The corresponding value areas are career and workplace environment.
5. **Gender pay gap percentage** is utilized to document disparities in salary between genders, aiming to highlight and address inequality in pay. The corresponding value areas are career, CSR, and ethics.
6. **Female employee rate** is tracked to gauge gender equality within the company. The corresponding value areas are career, equality, and fairness.
7. **Women in management positions** Similarly, the percentage of women in leadership is monitored to assess gender representation at higher levels of decision-making. The corresponding value areas are career, equality, and fairness.
8. **Human rights commitment** is evaluated on a scale from 1 to 12, with higher scores indicating a greater emphasis on and adherence to human rights within the company. The corresponding value areas are career, controversy topics, corruption, fairness, health, human rights, safety, and workplace environment.
9. **Product responsibility** is also assessed on a scale from 1 to 12, where a higher score reflects a stronger commitment to considering the impact of products on consumers and society. The corresponding value areas are CSR and quality management.
10. **Cybersecurity measures** are identified with a binary indicator, where 1 signifies implementation and −1 indicates a lack of cybersecurity practices. The corresponding value area is safety.

5.5 Modelling and Parametrization

In Qualicision®, constructing the model entails four critical steps:

1. **Defining goals:** The initial step involves specifying value areas, termed as goals, which are informed by the ESG criteria and FCM insights. These value areas are then prioritized based on expert evaluations, ensuring a structured approach to goal setting.
2. **Inputting alternatives:** This stage requires the incorporation of ESG metrics, referred to as alternatives, into the model. This process lays the groundwork for evaluating the impact of each ESG measure.
3. **Modelling evaluation functions:** At this point, users are empowered to design fuzzy membership functions through the evaluation function feature. This involves delineating the scope of all integrated ESG measures by their negative and positive impacts, as visualized in Fig. 5.

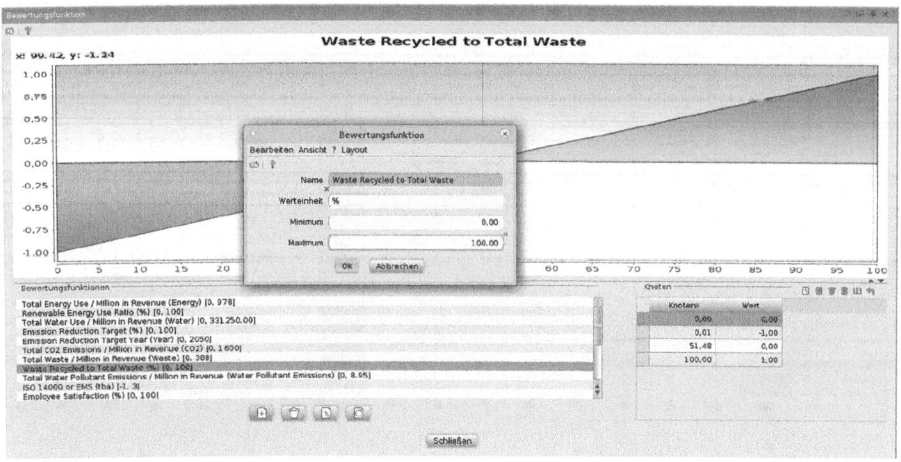

Fig. 5 An exemplary evaluation function (Hauser et al., 2022, p. 27, PSI Software SE)

4. **Editing input tables:** The final step enables the linkage between goals and evaluation functions within a specified range of [−1; 1] through the table editor. This table compiles data from 68 companies across 20 measures. For instance, the measure of energy use is associated with the goal of low energy consumption, illustrating the practical application of aligning specific measures with overarching corporate sustainability goals.

5.6 *Analytical Output*

The system generates multiple types of visual outputs such as the impact matrix, dependency table, and rankings. The primary output is the automatically generated impact matrix, which displays the relationships between ESG measures (rows) and value areas (columns), as illustrated in Fig. 6. Positive relationships are denoted by plus signs, negative relationships by minus signs, and the absence of a relationship by a zero. As an alternative visual representation, numeric values can be displayed instead of plus and minus signs to convey the nature of these relationships.

The second output option is termed the explanatory module, which delineates the auto-associative relationships among the ESG measures, as seen in Fig. 7. This module functions analogously to a FCM but is presented in matrix format. Within this matrix, five distinct cases are identified.

1. Analogy (dark green): This shading signifies criteria that evolve in parallel, both in direction and magnitude. Therefore, cells labelled identically on both axes, such as [1] low energy consumption by [1] low energy consumption, are always marked in dark green, indicating identical developmental trajectories.

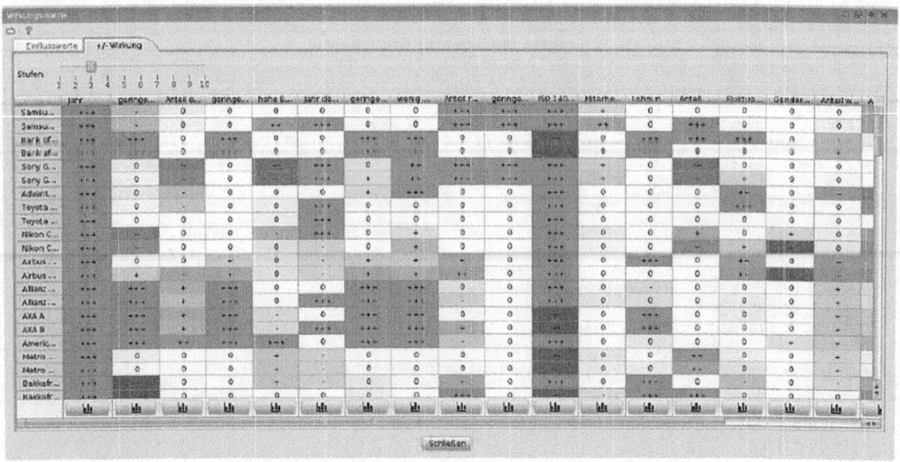

Fig. 6 ESG impact matrix (Hauser et al., 2022, p. 30, PSI Software SE)

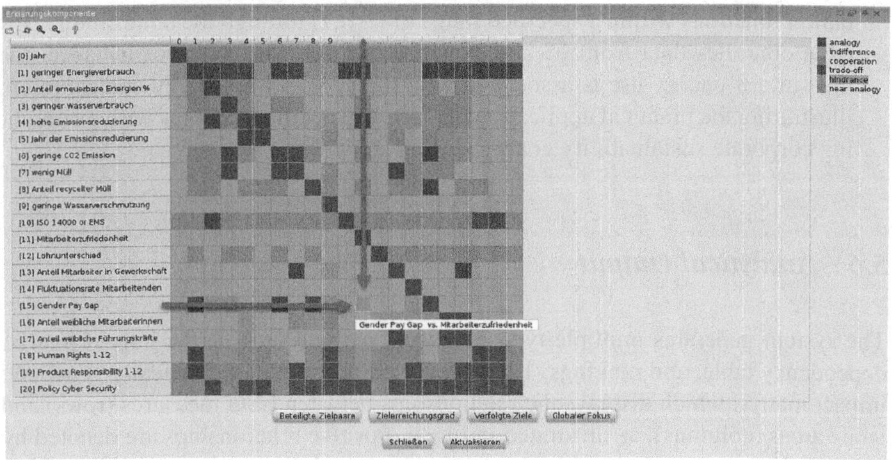

Fig. 7 Visualization of dependencies (Adapted from Hauser et al., 2022, p. 31, PSI Software SE)

2. Cooperation or near analogy (light green): These cells suggest that while the criteria influence each other positively, they may not do so with equal intensity. They move in the same direction, but the degree of impact can vary.
3. Indifference (light blue): This color indicates a lack of influence between two criteria, signifying that their developments are independent of each other.
4. Hindrance (light red): In situations of hindrance, criteria move in opposite directions; as one criterion's value increases, the other's decreases, represented in light red within the matrix.

5. Trade-off (dark red): Cases marked in dark red identify criteria that are mutually exclusive, where the advancement of one criterion directly compromises the other.

This nuanced visualization aids in understanding the complex interplay between various ESG measures and their consequent impact on value areas, offering users a comprehensive overview of associative dynamics.

In the illustration provided in Fig. 7, a notable instance of hindrance is demonstrated between the Gender Pay Gap (Row 15) and Employee Satisfaction (Column 11). This interaction highlights how an increase in the Gender Pay Gap and Employee Satisfaction mutually constrains each other's positive development. Specifically, an expanding gender pay gap adversely and disproportionately impacts employee satisfaction. Conversely, increases in employee satisfaction inherently limit the possibility of widening salary differentials; any attempt to expand the Gender Pay Gap in tandem with increased employee satisfaction would, paradoxically, result in decreased satisfaction among employees. This example underlines the complex and reciprocal negative influence these factors exert on each other.

The sensitivity settings of the matrix can be adjusted through the decision algorithm, allowing for the modulation of relationships to be either more positive or more negative. For instance, should the matrix display an excessive number of cells marked as "indifference," rendering it difficult to draw meaningful conclusions, it is possible to recalibrate the sensitivities. This adjustment ensures that the matrix more accurately reflects the nuances of relationships, enabling clearer insights and decision-making based on the revised data representation.

The decision overview enables an in-depth examination of the relationships between various factors and how each company fares in specific areas, as depicted in the matrix in Fig. 7. All settings previously outlined in Qualicision® are comprehensively presented in the "User-adaptive ranking table" (Fig. 8). Here, companies

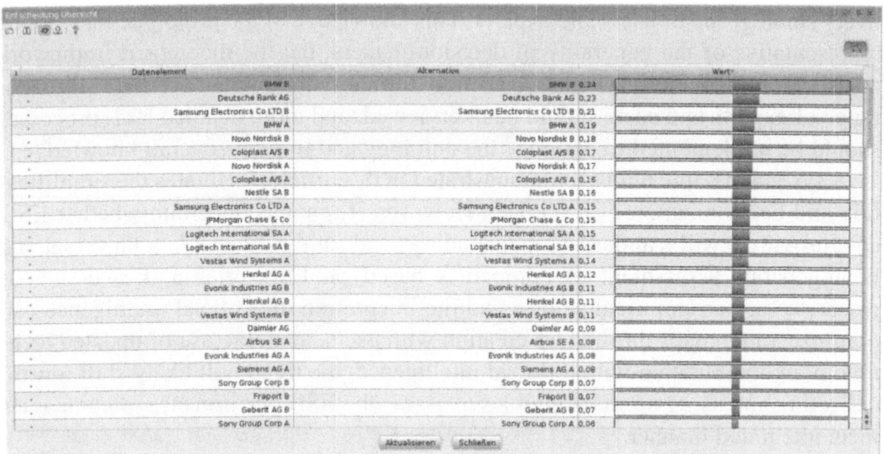

Fig. 8 User-adaptive ranking table (Hauser et al., 2022, p. 34, PSI Software SE)

are ranked based on set priorities for illustrative purposes. Moreover, there is an option to filter the data according to industry sectors.

6 Conclusion and Future Work

In our study, we examined the decision-making process behind company ratings using ESG criteria, which are intangibles. ESG providers have developed a wide array of classification systems that are not only diverse but also segmented into various subcategories. The extensive data collected theoretically enhances transparency through standardizations and frameworks. This should provide investors and consumers with significant insights and allow their preferences to be considered. However, despite the potential for customization based on respective ESG scores and responses, the combination of tangibles and intangibles, complexity, and lack of consistent standards can overwhelm users. Therefore, individualization is crucial to support users in the decision-making process for company ratings.

To overcome these limitations and to fulfill the demand for individualization, this chapter introduces a new theory that unifies tangibles and intangibles based on complex numbers. Intangibles are modelled in fuzzy networks that allow multivalued logic and causal networks, called value maps. It goes beyond classical algebra but enables the combination of tangibles and intangibles. The value maps represent ontologies as fuzzy neural networks that can be used in user-adaptive applications. The practical result of the theory is presented as an adaptive decision support system. In three phases, intangibles from the ESG provider Refinitiv were analyzed and grouped into the network according to the unified theory. Our approach empowers users by reducing complexity and enhancing analysis through causal value maps. Consequently, the company ratings incorporate intangibles in alignment with the decision-makers' preferences. However, we have tested the application with a relatively small group of users and experts. This knowledge of the prototype may not be representative of the generality of decision-makers, but the theoretical framework takes account of future changes and transformation. Moving forward, a broader range of experts and users should be interviewed, and more detailed ETL processes should be implemented to optimize the ontology and improve overall knowledge.

A system of value fields, as demonstrated in this article, facilitates the simplification and harmonization of ESG data. However, it remains uncertain whether ESG data providers will standardize their findings and ratings to enable a universal and homogeneous assessment of companies based on ESG criteria. Based on our research, further empirical studies and the integration of artificial intelligence can optimize value maps through co-creation with users. With the use of updated technology in combination with artificial intelligence, the trend will likely shift toward collecting and using more intangibles to assess the ESG performance of companies in an integrated manner.

References

Amel-Zadeh, A., & Serafeim, G. (2018). Why and how investors use ESG information: Evidence from a global survey. *Financial Analysts Journal, 3*(74), 87–103.

Becker, D. (2005). *Intangible Assets in der Unternehmenssteuerung – Wie Sie weiche Vermögenswerte quantifizieren und aktiv managen*. Gabler.

Becker, M., Labucay, I., & Rieger, C. (2007). Erfassung und Bewertung von Humankapital ¬ Kritische Anmerkungen zur Saarbrücker Formel. *Betriebswirtschaftliche Forschung und Praxis, 01*(2007), 38–58.

Bodrow, W., & Bergmann, P. (2003). *Wissensbewertung in Unternehmen – Bilanzieren von intellektuellem Kapital*. Erich Schmidt.

Buchmüller, A., Hahn, S., Kistner, M., & Lesting, S. (2020). *Strengthening the S in ESG, part II. project report*. TH Köln.

Dow Jones & Company. (2023). *Sustainable Business Survey Report 2023*. WSJ Pro Sustainable Business. Retrieved September 30, 2023, from https://s.wsj.net/public/resources/documents/Pro_SB_Survey_Report_2023.pdf

European Commission. (n.d.). *Corporate sustainability reporting*. Retrieved September 30, 2023, from https://finance.ec.europa.eu/capital-markets-union-and-financial-markets/company-reporting-and-auditing/company-reporting/corporate-sustainability-reporting_en

Felix, R. (2021). Learning of consistent preference relations for decision making and optimization in context of interacting goals. In M. Radko, M. Reformat, M. Štěpnička, & P. Hurtik (Eds.). *Joint proceedings of the 19th world congress of the international fuzzy systems association (IFSA), the 12th conference of the European society for fuzzy logic and technology (EUSFLAT), and the 11th international summer school on aggregation operators (AGOP)* (pp. 266–273). Atlantis Press. https://doi.org/10.2991/asum.k.210827.036

Felix, R. (2023). Machine learned KPI goal preferences for explainable AI based production sequencing. In K. Honda, B. Le, V. N. Huynh, M. Inuiguchi, & Y. Kohda (Eds.), *Integrated uncertainty in knowledge modelling and decision making. IUKM 2023. Lecture notes in computer science* (Vol. 14376, pp. 79–90). Springer. https://doi.org/10.1007/978-3-031-46781-3_8

Global Sustainable Investment Alliance. (n.d.). Retrieved September 30, 2023, from https://www.gsi-alliance.org/

Hauser, L., Cordes, K., & Brand, V. (2022). *Adaptive Entscheidungsunterstützung für den Finanzmarkt, project report*, TH Köln.

Ho, S. (2023, March 1). *Nearly all large global companies disclose ESG information*. Retrieved September 30, 2023, from https://tax.thomsonreuters.com/news/nearly-all-large-global-companies-disclose-esg-information/#:~:text=The%20data%20is%20based%20on,of%201%2C400%20companies%20in%202020

Hunter, L., Webster, E., & Wyatt, A. (2005). Measuring intangible capital: A review of current practice. *Intellectual Property Research Institute of Australia, 15*. https://doi.org/10.1111/j.1835-2561.2005.tb00288.x

Kasperzak, R., & Nestler, A. (2010). *Bewertung von immateriellem Vermögen – Anlässe, Methoden und Gestaltungsmöglichkeiten*. Wiley-VCH.

Kaufmann, L., & Schneider, Y. (2006). Intangible Unternehmenswerte als internationales Forschungsgebiet der Unternehmensführung – Literaturübersicht, Schwerpunkte und Forschungslücken. In K. Matzler, H. H. Hinterhuber, B. Renzl, & S. Rothenberger (Eds.), *Immaterielle Vermögenswerte – Handbuch der intangible Assets* (pp. 23–41). Erich Schmidt.

Kneisel, E., Rößel, C., & Pawlowsky, P. (2012). Meilensteine der IC Entwicklung. In P. Pawlowsky & L. Edvinsson (Eds.), *Intellektuelles Kapital und Wettbewerbsfähigkeit – Eine Bestandsaufnahme zu Theorie und Praxis* (pp. 39–65). Springer Gabler.

KNOWESG. (n.d.). *Exxon Mobil company summary (2023)*. Retrieved September 30, 2023, from https://www.knowesg.com/esg-ratings/exxonmobil

Kosko, B. (1992). *Neural networks and fuzzy systems*. Prentice Hall.

Merriam-Webster. (n.d.). Retrieved September 30, 2023, from https://www.merriam-webster.com/thesaurus/value

MSCI. (n.d.). *The global industry classification standard (GICS®)*. Retrieved September 30, 2023, from https://www.msci.com/our-solutions/indexes/gics

Müller, C. (2006). Wissen, intangible Assets oder intellektuelles Kapital – eine Begriffswelt in Diskussion. In K. Matzler, H. H. Hinterhuber, B. Renzl, & S. Rothenberger (Eds.), *Immaterielle Vermögenswerte – Handbuch der intangible Assets* (pp. 23–41). Erich Schmidt.

Nagel, C. (2012). Intellectual Capital Ansätze in Unternehmen – Erfahrungen aus der Praxis. In P. Pawlowsky & L. Edvinsson (Eds.), *Intellektuelles Kapital und Wettbewerbsfähigkeit – Eine Bestandsaufnahme zu Theorie und Praxis* (pp. 67–96). Springer Gabler.

Ocean Tomo. (2020). *Intangible asset market value study, Chicago*. Retrieved September 30, 2023, from https://oceantomo.com/intangible-asset-market-value-study/

Refinitiv Eikon database. (n.d.). *Definition and explanation*. Retrieved from Database Eikon July 20, 2020.

Reilly, R., & Schweihs, R. (1998). *Valuing intangible assets*. McGraw Hill.

Reilly, R., & Schweihs, R. (2000). *The handbook of advanced business valuation*. McGraw-Hill.

Reyelt, P. C., Kluczynski, K., & Fünfgeld, A.-C. (2021). *Strengthening the S in ESG, part I*. Project report, TH Köln.

Rokeach, M. (1973). *The nature of human values* (p. 28). Collier-Macmillan. Retrieved July 13, 2024, from https://archive.org/details/natureofhumanval00roke

Roos, G., Pike, S., & Fernström, L. (2004). Intellectual capital management, measurement and disclosure. In P. Horváth & K. Möller (Eds.), *Intangibles in der Unternehmenssteuerung* (pp. 127–158). Vahlen.

Scholz, C., Stein, V., & Bechtel, R. (2011). *Human capital management: raus aus der Unverbindlichkeit!* Luchterhand.

Schwartz, S. H. (2017). The refined theory of basic values. In S. Roccas & L. Sagiv (Eds.), *Values and behavior: Taking a cross-cultural perspective*. Springer. Retrieved July 13, 2024, from https://doi.org/10.1007/978-3-319-56352-7_3

Sustainanalytics. (n.d.). *Company ESG risk ratings, Exxon Mobil Corp*. Retrieved September 30, 2023, from https://www.sustainalytics.com/esg-rating/exxon-mobil-corp/1008284584

Takatsuki, Y., & Yanagi, R. (2019). *ESG and intangibles: Driving value creation across companies*. AXA Investment Managers.

van Criekingen, K., Bloch, C., & Eklund, C. (2021). Measuring intangible assets–A review of the state of the art. *Journal of Economic Surveys, 36*(5), 1539–1558.

Whelan, T., Atz, U., van Holt, T., Clark, C., CFA (2021). *ESG AND FINANCIAL PERFORMANCE: Uncovering the relationship by aggregating evidence from 1,000 plus studies published between 2015–2020*. Rockefeller Asset Management, NYU Stern, Center for Sustainable Business. Retrieved September 30, 2023, from https://www.stern.nyu.edu/sites/default/files/assets/documents/NYU-RAM_ESG-Paper_2021%20Rev_0.pdf

Yahoo! finance. (n.d.). *Exxon Mobil corporation (XOM)*. Retrieved September 30, 2023, from https://finance.yahoo.com/quote/xom/analysis

Building a Leadership Culture as an Engine of the Intellectual Capital of Nations and Organizations

Juan Pablo Stegmann

Abstract This chapter discusses how the ten dimensions of our spirituality build a leadership culture and how both these dimensions and leadership culture maximize what Leif Edvinsson describes as the intellectual capital (IC) of nations and organizations, their human, social, process, and renewal capital, which help in promoting economic growth, social justice, organizational success, and social well-being.

This chapter presents a new interdisciplinary framework that relies on the intuition of IC as the backbone to connect political economy, strategic management, cultures, leadership, philosophy, and spirituality.

Our spirituality builds our capacity to perceive phenomena; build our consciousness, knowledge, relationships, ideals, and values; and reinforce human and social capital, which are pillars of IC.

Our spirituality promotes inspiration and creation, reinforcing renewal capital, a pillar of IC.

Our spirituality is an engine of leadership in every person and society, generating transcendence, a vision of the future, a mission, and stronger relationships, building communities that promote continuous individual and social transformation processes, and building IC.

1 Introduction

A leadership culture provides intellectual capital, which, in turn, impacts the political economy and strategic management.

Leif Edvinsson argues that a nation's success depends on its National Intellectual Capital (NIC), composed of human, market, social, renewal, and process capital

J. P. Stegmann (✉)
Keiser University, Florida, USA
e-mail: jstegmann@keiseruniversity.edu

F. Matos et al. (eds.), *Intellectual Capital in a Global Business Landscape*,
Contributions to Management Science, https://doi.org/10.1007/978-3-031-86362-2_6

(Edvinsson, 2002; Edvinsson & Malone, 1999; Lin & Edvinsson, 2012; Roos et al., 1997; Ullberg et al., 2021).

A leadership culture provides resources that maximize NIC, promoting economic growth and social justice.

Leaders provide *human capital* by helping build better knowledge, wisdom, information, ideas, research, creativity, innovation, entrepreneurship, competencies, skills, organizational knowledge, labor productivity, dialogue, social and personality attributes, values, motivation, interdisciplinary science, education, health, and life expectancy.

Leaders provide *market and social capital* by creating relationships and social networks with reciprocity and goodwill norms. The leadership of some individuals encourages others to change their behaviors and to act with leadership as well, generating new norms and cooperative behaviors, reducing transaction costs (costs generated by unpredictable economic interactions between agents), and minimizing the agency problem (agents act with self-interest against the interests of principals), thus promoting growth and prosperity.

Leaders provide market and social capital by supporting institutions, legal systems, constitutional provisions, rules and regulations, law enforcement, property rights, and political structures, reinforcing social behaviors, and helping overcome institutional constraints.

Leaders provide *market and social capital* by supporting culture, generating collaboration and trust; leaders provide shared values and norms of social behavior expressed in personal relationships and vertical and horizontal partnerships; leaders provide a shared sense of civic responsibility, shared social norms, a sense of community, reciprocity, mutually beneficial cooperation, altruism, and emotional support; leaders provide cultural values that influence decisions and promote entrepreneurship and frugality. Leadership promotes attitudes toward hard work, welfare, health care, education, the rule of law, responsibility, personal effort, ethics, reduction of free riding, and effectiveness of institutions.

In the prisoner's dilemma model of game theory, if the first player believes that the second player will act with leadership, then they will act with leadership, as would the rest of society. This is true in all dimensions of political economy: the leadership of some people will encourage others to change their behavior and act with leadership as well.

Leaders provide *market and social capital* by reducing transaction costs, minimizing the agency problem, reducing information asymmetry, lowering information cost, lowering law enforcement costs, lowering costs as a result of bribery and corruption, and lowering the cost of transformation, therefore raising the return on investment, which leads to promoting investment, social entrepreneurship, social innovation, social change, business opportunities, growth, and prosperity.

Leaders provide *market and social capital* by promoting a culture that welcomes investors and promotes goodwill, civic and political freedoms, internationality, trade intensity, social and educational equality, knowledge sharing, and organizational resources.

Leaders provide *renewal and process capital* by providing resources regarding wisdom, transcendence, higher values, the meaning of life, and the power to perform personal and social transformations, social actions, and social change.

2 Statistical Analysis, Part 1: A Leadership Culture Has a Positive Impact on the World of Organizations by Building Resources, IC

Following the intuitions of Bennett Stewart (Stewart, 1991) and Leif Edvinsson (Edvinsson, 2002; Edvinsson & Malone, 1999; Roos et al., 1997), I wrote two doctoral dissertations (Stegmann, 2001, 2005), two research papers (Stegmann, 2007a, 2007b), and four books (Stegmann, 2000, 2002b, 2009, 2023d) and made presentations at several international conferences (Stegmann, 2002a, 2002c, 2003, 2010a, 2010b, 2010c, 2011), which places Edvinsson's IC as the backbone to connect several disciplines: strategic management, political economy, leadership, cultures, philosophy, and spirituality.

My first dissertation, "Using the EVA model for corporate stock investment; Impact of knowledge, growth and monopoly power on economic value" (Stegmann, 2005), investigates the connection between strategic management and economic value creation. This work leads to a new version of strategic management, introducing metrics, economic modeling, systems analysis, and the central role of resources.

This research demonstrates five hypotheses[1] that provide the metrics and framework for analysis to connect strategic management, economic value creation, and IC.

Two of these hypotheses are fundamental: (1) Market power and economic profits are positively correlated. (2) Growth and knowledge are positively correlated.

A firm is a collection of productive resources (Penrose, 1995), assets, capabilities, organizational processes, firm attributes, information, knowledge that improve its efficiency and effectiveness (Barney, 1991), internal capabilities that create knowledge (Grant, 1996) and promote innovation and growth (Teece et al., 1997), and core competencies (Prahalad & Hamel, 2006) that promote competitive advantage (Mahoney & Pandian, 1992; Peteraf, 1993; Wernerfelt, 1984; Winter, 1988)..

The need to invest in resources introduces the need to justify the required economic effort: an investment in resources must create economic value, which means that to be justified, the investment must yield better results than the alternative investments.

[1] Hypothesis 1. Economic profits and growth are not correlated.
Hypothesis 2. Growth and knowledge are positively correlated.
Hypothesis 3. Economic profits and knowledge are not correlated.
Hypothesis 4. Market power and economic profits are positively correlated.
Hypothesis 5. Economic profits and growth are negatively correlated for different levels of knowledge.

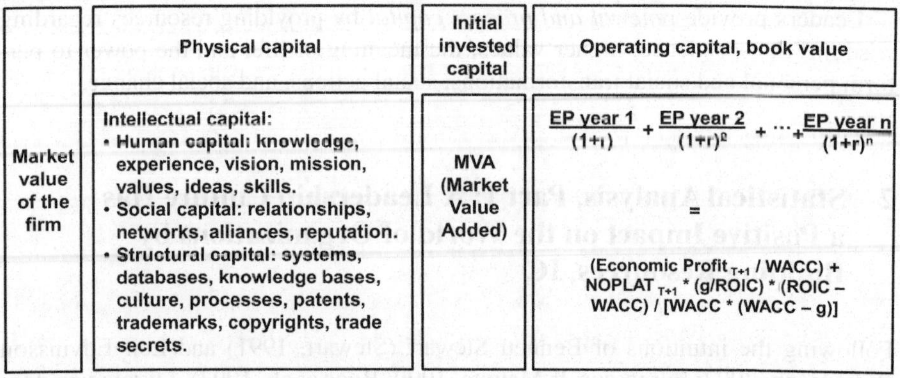

Fig. 1 A leadership culture provides resources that enrich IC, promoting organizational success and social well-being (*EP* economic profits; *r* discount rate; *WACC* weighted average cost of capital; *ROIC* return on invested capital; *g* growth)

To ensure our strategies are correct, we need to connect the strategies with the results: as (Fig. 1) shows, one crucial result of modern organizations is the company's market value.

A company's market value is equal to its initial invested capital, which measures its physical capital, plus its MVA (market value added), which measures its IC.

Physical capital is easy to measure: the company's book value comes from accounting. How do we measure IC?

McKinsey (Copeland et al., 2000) proposes this equation to assess the market value added, which measures the IC:

$$MVA = \left[EPyear1/(1+r)\right] + \left[EPyear2/(1+r)2\right] + \ldots + \left[EPyear\,n/(1+r)n\right]$$

IC is measured by the MVA, which reflects how much investors are willing to pay for a company above its book value based on its future cash generation.

The future cash generation of the company is based on its resources: its IC.

McKinsey[2] (Copeland et al., 2000) formulates the MVA also with this equation that provides crucial insights for our analysis:

[2]According to Copeland et al. (2000), the MVA of a company using a continuing value approach = (Economic Profit T + 1/WACC) + NOPLAT T + 1 * (g/ROIC) * (ROIC—WACC)/[WACC * (WACC—g)] where:

Economic profitT+1 = Invested Capital * (Return on Invested Capital—Opportunity Cost of Capital).

NOPLAT T + 1 = The normalized NOPLAT (net operating profits less adjusted taxes) in the first year after the explicit forecast period.

g = The expected growth rate in NOPLAT in perpetuity.

ROIC = The expected rate of return on net new investment.

WACC = The weighted average cost of capital.

$$MVA = (Economic\ Profit\,T + 1 / WACC) + NOPLAT\,T + 1 * (Growth / ROIC) * (ROIC - WACC) / [WACC * (WACC - Growth)]$$

This equation introduces three terms that help to connect economic value creation with strategic management.

Figure 2 shows the correlations explained earlier: the X-axis measures the economic profits (Return on Invested Capital—Opportunity Cost of Capital) based on competitive strategies; the Y-axis measures growth based on innovation strategies, and the Z-axis reflects the future, the MVA, based on resource strategies.

- *Economic profits are based on competitive strategies. Economic Profits = Return on Invested Capital—Opportunity Cost of Capital.* The X-axis indicates economic profits, which measure the company's profitability compared to the profitability of similar companies. To have positive economic profits, an organization must be more profitable than similar organizations based on its competitive strategies, satisfying its customers better than the competition. The economic profits measure the company's profitability compared to the profitability of similar companies. For example, if the profitability of company A is 15% and the profitability of company B is 10%, company A has economic profits of 5% (15% minus 10%); thus, company A creates economic value. But company B has economic profits of −5% (10% minus 15%), destroying economic value. Economic profits are based on a comparison: to succeed, we need to be better than others by having better resources.

Fig. 2 Connecting strategic management with economic value creation and IC

- *Growth is based on innovation strategies.* The Y-axis indicates sales growth based on the innovation strategies. To grow, an organization must be more innovative than similar organizations based on innovation strategies (new products, new customers, new markets, new businesses, new channels).
- *MVA, market value added, IC, is based on resource strategies.* The Z axis reflects the future, the MVA, based on the resource strategies. To have a positive MVA (present value of future economic profits), an organization needs to have future positive economic profits and growth by having better resources than similar organizations, based on its resource strategies, which support their future competitive and innovation strategies. The MVA reflects the future, that is, what the investors are willing to pay for the firm above its book value based on the expectation that the firm can generate positive economic profits and growth in the future. The MVA is the most significant part of the economic value of modern organizations. Ninety percent of the market value of firms such as Microsoft or Apple is their MVA.

2.1 Modern Strategic Management Supports Edvinsson's Views: The Resources of an Organization, its IC, Promote Economic Value Creation

IC supports competitive strategies. Organizations are successful when they can produce value and generate satisfied customers, employees, and shareholders with solid relationships, resulting in higher sales and margins.

IC supports innovation strategies, product innovation, value chain innovation, diversification, international expansion, acquisitions, and alliances.

IC is vital to predicting whether a company's competitive and innovation strategies will be successful.

3 Statistical Analysis, Part 2: A Leadership Culture Positively Impacts the Political Economy by Building Resources, NIC

My second dissertation, "Epistemological Analysis of Strategic Management and Related Sciences. How Realism Promotes Leadership" (Stegmann, 2020), investigates how a leadership culture correlates better with social outcomes than individualist and collectivist cultures.

It presents a linear correlation statistical analysis that associates cultural values to their degree of individualism, collectivism, and leadership. The statistical analysis correlates cultural values in 60 countries of the World Values Survey (Institute for Comparative Survey Research) with six social outcomes: 1. Gross Domestic Product per capita (World Bank, 2017); 2. The Human Development Index (United Nations Development Programme, 2017); 3. The Index of Economic Freedom (The Heritage Foundation and The Wall Street Journal, 2017); 4. The Corruption Perceptions Index (Corruption Perceptions Index, 2017) published by Transparency International; 5. The Knowledge Index (World Bank Institute, 2017); 6. The Happiness Rankings (Helliwell, 2019).

According to Geert Hofstede, individualism versus collectivism refers to the relationship between the individual and the group. Individualism pertains to societies where the ties between individuals are loose: everyone is expected to look after themselves and their immediate family (Hofstede et al., 2010). Collectivism pertains to societies in which people from birth onward are integrated into strong, cohesive in-groups, which, throughout people's lifetime, continue to protect them in exchange for unquestioning loyalty (Hofstede et al., 2010). A leadership culture considers how individuals have ideals for a better future, have higher-level values as defined by Max Scheler (1973), have the capacity to build relationships and communities with ideals and values, and rely on discernment to make decisions and execute social actions.

Table 1 summarizes the results of the linear correlation statistical analysis.

Table 1 shows that:

- Individualist cultural values correlate positively and negatively with social outcomes; negatively correlated factors (94) outnumber positively correlated factors (26).
- Collectivist cultural values correlate positively and negatively with social outcomes; negatively correlated factors (54) outnumber positively correlated factors (16).
- Cultural values related to leadership have a substantial prevalence of positive correlating factors (73) over negative ones (9).

This statistical analysis provides evidence of the prevalence of leadership cultural values over individualist and collectivist cultural values.

Table 1 Results of the linear correlation statistical analysis

Cultural values	Individualism	Collectivism	Leadership
Positive correlation factors (greater than 0.3)	26	16	73
Negative correlation factors (lower than −0.3)	94	54	9
Average of all correlation factors	−0.12	−0.18	0.11

Source: Stegmann (2020)

3.1 Modern Political Economy Supports Edvinsson's Views: The Resources of a Nation, its NIC, Promote Economic Growth and Social Justice

A book (Stegmann, 2023d) that I wrote investigates how the science of political economy explains that a nation's success depends on its resources, which Leif Edvinsson has summarized as NIC to promote economic growth and social justice. A leadership culture maximizes the NIC.

Economic growth requires resources in terms of *human capital*, namely, knowledge, information, ideas, skills, social and personality attributes, creativity, and health, according to Smith (1982), Solow (1957), Mankiw et al. (1992), Romer (1986), Samuelson (1971), Jones (1971), Heckscher and Ohlin (1933), Barro (1996), Becker (1993), Mincer (1974), and Schultz (1971), among other authors.

Economic growth requires *social capital*, including institutions, relationships, social networks, bonding, values, a culture of trust, collaboration, norms of reciprocity, goodwill, alliances, and reputation, according to Olson (1996), Putnam (2000), Fukuyama (1996), Commons (1931), and North (1990, 1992), among other authors.

Social justice involves solidarity, which requires resources to promote social well-being. As Sachs (2006) defends, extreme poverty can be eliminated if richer countries provide primary capital to the poor to help them escape the poverty trap, *as well as human and social capital, business, infrastructure, natural*, and public institutions, and knowledge. As Sen (1997, 1999) states, to achieve well-being, a person needs to be able to function, which requires capabilities (resources).

According to Bruni and Zamagni (2016), social justice involves subsidiarity, which requires resources to be shared to promote social well-being.

3.2 Conclusions of the Statistical Analyses: The Positive Interaction between Leadership and IC

The intuition of IC as a measure of MVA provides a powerful explanation of the positive impact of a leadership culture.

Introducing a leadership culture in organizations helps to make decisions that consider the long-term dimension.

A leadership culture helps build:

- *Human capital*, as employees and other stakeholders, may be willing to contribute more knowledge based on trust, shared values, shared mission, and shared willingness to execute social action.
- *Social capital*, by establishing more stable and stronger relationships, trust, and collaboration among stakeholders.

- *Structural capital* with committed stakeholders who work harder, build efficiency, and improve processes.

The leadership of organizations and nations can impact NIC, which then can positively impact aggregate demand and supply, involve more economic agents, and raise production and sales volumes.

Focusing on the future may positively impact the economic value of the company by raising its MVA, its IC:

- Leadership provides resources: consciousness, rational intelligence (IQ), emotional intelligence (EQ), spiritual intelligence (SQ), wisdom, transcendence, connectedness, values, relationships, discernment, and capacity to transform and execute social actions.
- Those resources enrich the IC of the organization.
- IC positively impacts the future, ensuring organizational success, creating economic value, and promoting social well-being.

4 Explanation of the Conclusions of the Statistical Analysis: Spirituality Is an Engine of Leadership and a Driver of IC

We all have an extraordinary power of transformation, a power to build a better reality, a power to become leaders.

That power arises from our spirituality, which connects us with ourselves and others, developing our consciousness, knowledge and relationships, and ideals and values, leading to personal and social transformation.

A book in four volumes that I wrote, *Leadership: A Journey Toward World Peace* (Stegmann, 2023a, 2023b, 2023c, 2023d), investigates how our spirituality has ten dimensions that build our leadership: (1) the cognitive dimension, (2) the transcendental dimensions, (3) the axiological dimension, (4) the religious dimension, (5) the relational dimension, (6) the discernment dimension, (7) the existential dimension, (8) the transformational dimension, (9) the healing dimension, and (10) the social action dimension.

Leadership is an ability, a capacity, and a process that starts with cognitions that may be generated by a person or the community, impacting each other and affecting interpersonal behaviors. These ten dimensions of our spirituality build our leadership:

1. The ability to create a *vision* of society's future, promoting transcendence, goodness, beauty, and truth. Our spirituality and greatness drive our visions, raising the level in promoting transcendence, goodness, beauty, and truth and "participating" in God's reality toward perfection.
2. The ability to build *missions*, values, purpose, identity, commitment, and societal role. Our spirituality and greatness drive our missions, values, purpose in life,

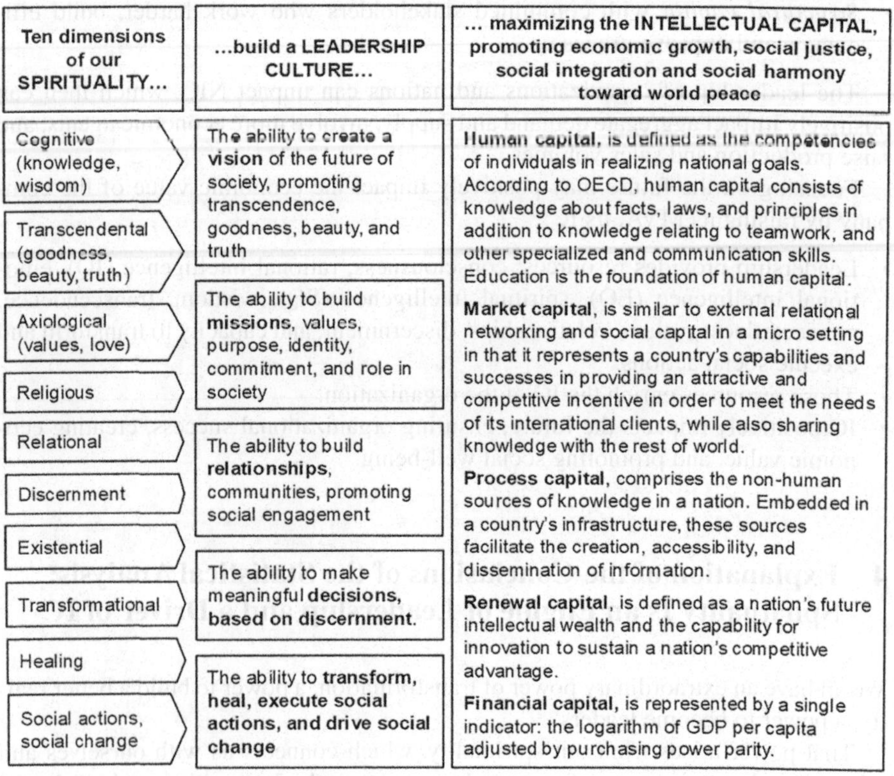

Fig. 3 Connecting spirituality, leadership, political economy, and strategic management, relying on IC

role in society, vocation, will, commitment, identity, energy, and motivation to positively impact society.

3. The ability to build *communities* and relationships, promoting social engagement. Our spirituality and greatness drive our relationships and communities with God (for religious persons) and others, promoting social engagement: the power to communicate, build emotional intelligence, reach the hearts of others, inspire, and build community, teams, and relationships.
4. The ability to make meaningful decisions based on *discernment*. Our spirituality and greatness drive our ability to find meaning, make meaningful decisions, and discern.
5. The ability *to transform, heal, and execute social actions* and drive social change. Our spirituality and greatness drive our ability to transform persons and communities, heal, execute social actions, and drive social change.

Figure 3 presents a conceptual framework that connects these intuitions:

The following analysis is based on this framework. It discusses how these ten dimensions of our spirituality and a leadership culture maximize the IC of nations and organizations, promoting economic growth, social justice, organizational success, and social well-being, explaining the results of the statistical analyses presented earlier.

4.1 *The Cognitive Dimension of Spirituality, Driver of IC*

When we are silent, reflect, meditate, and contemplate, we strengthen our consciousness and capacity to listen to words, perceive phenomena and organize them, enlighten our knowledge, and inspire wisdom.

This connects internally and with others and enriches our communication by accessing personal and community knowledge, understanding symbols, discovering universal truths, and building shared knowledge and ideals in diversity and complexity.

This leads to building personal and organizational knowledge, which reinforces *human capital.*

This capacity to connect helps us build relationships by perceiving and connecting with others, understanding them, and generating feelings, emotions, and empathy. This also reinforces what Daniel Goleman (2005) defines as emotional Intelligence, which helps understand the environment and people and develop empathy. Emotional intelligence involves competencies such as self-awareness, social awareness, empathy, the ability to join intelligence, and emotions as critical dimensions of leadership, promoting a positive impact on persons and organizations. Emotional Intelligence promotes humanism, social integration, and social harmony, which are components of *social capital.*

This capacity to build symbols reinforces what Buzan (2012) defines as spiritual intelligence: understanding the meanings and values, going to the roots, questioning the boundaries, transforming, and creating. This promotes creativity, innovation, and entrepreneurship, which are components of *renewal capital.*

4.2 *The Transcendental Dimension of Spirituality, the Power to Appreciate and Create Transcendence, Driver of IC*

Anyone can appreciate transcendence during the day: anyone can enjoy a beautiful landscape, the beauty of children, reading of a good book, and the joy of beautiful music; anyone can contemplate the magnificence of the universe, the galaxies that are hundreds of millions of light-years away, the massive stars; anyone can contemplate the microcosm, the perfection of our bodies, and their biology.

The appreciation of transcendence can lead us to become creators of transcendence, goodness, beauty, and truth and become agents of transformation: through our work, giving life, creating families, creating and performing music, and many other ways.

This is the backbone of our ideals, what leadership calls the vision of the future, which applies to business organizations and nations.

The creation of transcendence, the ideals, and the vision of the future lead persons, organizations, and nations to create IC: *human capital* to transform reality, *social capital* with people sharing the search for transcendence, *renewal capital* in creating a new reality, and *process capital* in executing it.

4.3 The Axiological Dimension of Spirituality, Driver of IC

Any person can experience how our consciousness helps us be connected with reality, our inner selves, and others. Any person can experience the role of consciousness to have a whole life: we educate our children to exercise their consciousness to live a life of integrity.

Consciousness and connectedness lead to discovering that we all have transcendence; we are valuable.

Phenomenologists explain how spirituality builds values:

- For Max Scheler (1973), consciousness connects a person internally and to the external reality, discovering values, building values based on love and sympathy, the human heart, and promoting greatness. Values and value ranks promote greatness, recognizing spiritual values (justice, rights, aesthetics, values of goodness, beauty, and truth) as the highest values, promoting greatness and leading to peace and harmony.
- For Buber (2008), our spirituality helps us connect with the other: human relationships are manifestations of spirituality.
- For Heidegger (1927), we are members of a human community, sharing experiences and impacting each other, a society in dialogue.
- For Dietrich von Hildebrand (2009), our spirituality connects with the heart, the voice of the personal soul, the root of all affectivity, and empathy; values are the unifying force that builds communities.
- For Stein (1989), our spirituality promotes empathy and builds community.
- For Arendt (1958), our consciousness leads to social integration and human relationships toward world peace.
- For Lévinas (1969), our consciousness, the human face, and expression lead to encounters; ethics is based on values, relationships, and sensibility.
- For Wojtyla (1979), everyday life spirituality leads to discovering the person's value and the primacy of love.
- For Bouyer (1961), consciousness and values reintegrate spirituality, psychology, affections, and religiosity, crucial to promoting happiness, emotional health, social integration, social harmony, and personal and social transformation.

- For Etcheverry Boneo (1969), values are transformational: values create in us a desire to act, arouse in us a specific emotion, a particular affection, an attitude, transforming us and our behaviors; values transform cultures and build communities; values transform relationships and reality. Values transform our affections, attitudes, behaviors, and ways we relate to others and the world, transforming reality and impacting persons' and communities' lives. Values become part of ourselves, transforming us as persons, communities, our worldviews, and psycho-ethical structures.

Values are the core of an organization's mission, the second component of the leadership of an organization, our role in society, and the source of commitment and energy.

Values are engines of transformation, promoting new knowledge, *human capital.*

Values promote *social capital* and social engagement, sharing higher values, promoting sympathy, and discovering the community's value. Values promote personal and social integration, social engagement, and social commitment.

Values reinforce the power to transform, heal, and execute social actions, drive social change, and *build renewal and process capital.*

4.4 The Religious Dimension of Spirituality, Driver of IC

Any person may appreciate transcendence, goodness, beauty, and truth and may discover the Creator's "participation," leading to a central aspect of our spirituality: building our relationship with the Creator.

Religious people build relationships with God by collaborating with his creation, transforming reality, making reality more beneficial to humankind, promoting social engagement, performing social actions, creating communities, and building IC.

Religiosity promotes *process and renewal capital*: we collaborate with God as efficient causes, makers, artisans, and manufacturers. We collaborate with God as formal causes, imitating God's perfections and promoting social action based on God's image. We collaborate with God as the final cause, as our final goal is seeking God as the ultimate goodness, beauty, and truth.

Religiosity promotes *renewal capital*: Hermans (1994) presents an interesting perspective on how our religiosity promotes creativity. Mysticism is a process parallel to creativity; mysticism leads to human encounter, to dialogue, which fosters creativity; mysticism integrates the self, an engine of creativity; mysticism invites symbolism, which empowers creativity; and mysticism promotes encounters, which promote a process of change.

4.5 The Relational Dimension of Spirituality, Driver of IC

Any person can experience that consciousness leads to discovering the person's value, inspiring love among persons, and building relationships and communities.

According to phenomenology, every act of consciousness we perform is "consciousness of" something or others: consciousness makes us relational. We give value to intentional feelings and build love, interest, and attraction. Consciousness generates intersubjectivity; builds relationships; integrates families, couples, and friendships; and helps people escape isolation.

Relationships help us to build *human capital*: shared organizational knowledge.

Relationships foster empathy and love, which promote social engagement, the will to transform and heal, and drive social actions that lead to social change. This, in turn, enables the building of effective teams, connecting with vulnerable individuals, and establishing organizations with a social orientation.

Relationships motivate us to generate transformation and social action and help us build *renewal and process capital*.

4.6 The Discerning Dimension of Spirituality, Driver of IC

Modern higher education and strategic management promote critical thinking to make decisions.

In a dissertation (Stegmann, 2020), I investigated how we often rely on our discernment in our daily lives, concluding that people rely more on discernment than on critical thinking.

Discernment builds *human capital*: it relies on richer personal and community knowledge. Discernment is phenomenological; it relies on our rational intelligence and emotional and spiritual intelligence. Our spirituality builds connections, to listen to our customers, employees, and stakeholders, to understand them, to know how they feel, and to empathize with them. Discernment confronts the ideas and their sources, searching reliable sources, wise people, respected scriptures, communities that have balanced responses, dialogue with respected communities, people with moral authority, and role models. Discernment confronts our knowledge with the knowledge of wise people, respected scriptures, and people with moral authority.

Discernment builds *renewal and process capitals*: discernment is transcendental; we make decisions based on our desire to journey toward transcendence and create transcendence.

Discernment builds *renewal and process capitals*: it relies on values when we ponder the value of an idea, whether it leads to the right direction, choosing the right road that leads to life, goodness, beauty, truth, freedom, and happiness, and when we ponder the values of the person that generated that idea, the legitimacy of the sources of information, its authority, reliability, and trustfulness. For religious people, discernment involves our relationship with God, which generates motions of the soul, the motivation to build a better world.

Discernment builds *social capital*: it relies on the power to create and recreate social organizations, communities, with people who share the same cognitions, the same ideals, the same values, and the same religiosity.

Discernment builds *renewal and process capitals* based on its power to find the meaning of our existence and the capacity to deal with suffering; its power to transform, create, recreate, reform, and integrate the persons and communities, fostering virtues; its power to produce emotional and physical health; and its power to perform social actions, to generate social change..

4.7 The Existential Dimension of Spirituality, Driver of IC

Any person can discover that spirituality has an existential dimension: it helps us find the meaning of our lives and understand our lives as a journey with a past, present, and future, as Heidegger describes (Heidegger, 1927).

The existential dimension of our spirituality promotes transformation, as each dimension of spirituality described above may help us to overcome or transform suffering and build *renewal and process capital.*

The wisdom produced by spirituality may build *social capital*, to help us understand our and others' suffering and fight to overcome it..

Spirituality, wisdom, ideals, values, and relationships may help us overcome suffering, transform our lives, and build *renewal and process capital.*

A community with values and love may lead us to help others or lead others to help us, to suffer with the suffering person, promoting social engagement, people with shared meanings, shared sensibility, shared sufferings, and the need to connect with others; suffering leads to others' company, overcoming suffering building *social, renewal, and process capitals.*

Acting with discernment may help make decisions that positively impact the person and community, promoting transformation, healing, social action, and social change, overcoming our suffering or helping others overcome their suffering, and building *social, renewal, and process capital.*

4.8 The Transformational Dimension of Spirituality, Driver of IC

Any person can experience how our spirituality is transformational: a silent force, energy, and inspiration drive a transformation process. Our spirituality provides the power to transform all aspects of our lives: our consciousness leads us to life journeys, to discover something that we consider sacred, which drives our passions and priorities. That discovery leads us to create, develop, and elevate. Our spirituality builds our values, relationships, and loves; we become more committed, concerned for others, and engaged, changing our behaviors.

Spirituality drives transformation processes that promote deeper awareness, silence, simplicity, inner rest, harmony, peace, happiness, and freedom, developing meanings, values, and virtues.

Religions lead to transformations; they promote the golden rule, ethics, and values, as well as compassion, love, generosity, concern for others, sympathy, and respect. They strengthen us to tolerate the suffering that accompanies transformation, healing, and social action.

Our power to transform may build *renewal and process capital.*

Our power to transform may build relationships and communities, promoting social engagement, teams, task forces, and people willing to transform communities that need such transformation power, building *social capital.*

4.9 The Healing Dimension of Spirituality, Driver of IC

Any person can experience that spirituality heals the soul and the body, helps them live in the present, reduces anxiety, provides the will to heal, let go, and release the unconscious, leading to personal inner peace, healing relationships, and overcoming addictions.

Any person can experience that spirituality provides a shelter to survive the complexities of our existence; provides peace, energy, and life; and helps to fight and overcome suffering, accept reality actively, and accept limitations.

This leads to building *human capital*, clarifying our ideas and enriching our knowledge, helping us to discover our true selves, which is a central factor in most psychotherapies, especially in cognitive therapy; spirituality plays a central role in Bowen Family System Therapy, learning to be mature, differentiated, living our lives as a journey toward goodness, beauty, truth, and love; spirituality plays a central role in the Enneagram, helping us to build relationships based on the wisdom that spirituality provides to overcome our shadow areas; spirituality helps us to find meanings, which is central to logotherapy; it helps us to transforms us, especially our behaviors, which are deemed central in behavior modification therapies; it plays a central role on the Twelve Steps, the most used therapy to heal addictions.

Our capacity to promote health may promote *social capital* by building relationships and communities and promoting social engagement between healers and people who need healing.

Our capacity to promote health is a resource that may promote *renewal and process capital* by positively impacting our ideals and values, promoting transcendence, and relying on our healing power to heal society spiritually, emotionally, and physically. Becoming aware of our power to heal provides IC: it builds confidence, faith, hope, and energy which enlighten, inspire, and energize our lives, promoting transcendence, values, purpose, identity, commitment, social engagement, relying on our power to heal, to build teams, task forces, with those willing to heal, and those that need such healing, promoting cooperation, compassion, solidarity, and social action.

4.10 The Social Action Dimension of Spirituality, Driver of IC

Any one of us may experience how spirituality leads to social action by connecting us with our souls and others' souls, alerting us to the need for compassion.

There is a mutual need between spirituality and action.

Spirituality leads to social action: it fortifies, enlarges, and motivates us to do good works for others; meditation leads to an engaged spirituality of people sharing their being and nurturing their compassion and justice; silent prayer makes us alert to the need for compassionate and loving action in the pursuit of justice.

Social action nurtures our spirituality, prayer, and liturgy; social action is a requirement of spirituality: contemplation without action is like a fantasy without substance; the active life is a preparation for the contemplative life.

Our capacity to perform social actions builds *human, renewal, and process capital* by positively impacting our ideals, values, purpose, identity, commitment, and societal role.

Our capacity to perform social actions builds *social capital*, connecting us with others, alerting us to the need for compassion, caring for each member of the community, and the need for compassionate and loving action to serve the community, execute social actions, and drive social change, building relationships and communities, promoting social engagement building teams with social action agents and communities that need social action.

5 Final Reflections

Our spirituality and leadership maximize the IC of nations and organizations, promoting their success.

Spirituality and leadership culture are crucial for the political economy. The political agenda should not focus on the battle between the right and the left; the real topic of discussion should become how to educate society on the role of spirituality and leadership so that we can all contribute our human, social, renewal, and process capital, promoting economic growth and social justice.

Spirituality and leadership culture are crucial for the strategic management of organizations and the business world. Leaders should prioritize how our spirituality and leadership can contribute to human capital, social capital, and structural capital, to promote organizational success and social well-being.

References

Arendt, H. (1958). *The human condition*. University of Chicago Press.
Barney, J. (1991). Firm resources and sustained competitive advantage. *Journal of Management, 17*(1), 99–120. https://doi.org/10.1177/014920639101700108
Barro, R. J. (1996). *Determinants of economic growth: A cross-country empirical study*. NBER Working Papers, Article 5698. https://ideas.repec.org//p/nbr/nberwo/5698.html
Becker, G. S. (1993). *Human capital: A theoretical and empirical analysis, with special reference to education*. University of Chicago Press. https://doi.org/10.7208/chicago/9780226041223.001.0001
Bouyer, L. (1961). *Introduction to spirituality*. Desclee Company.
Bruni, L., & Zamagni, S. (2016). Civil economy: Another idea of the market. *Agenda Publishing*. https://doi.org/10.2307/j.ctv5cg8w2
Buber, M. (2008). *I and thou* (R. G. Smith, Trans.). Martino Publishing.
Buzan, T. (2012). *The power of spiritual intelligence*. Thorsons.
Commons, J. R. (1931). Institutional economics. *History of Economic Thought Articles, 21*, 648–657.
Copeland, T. E., Koller, T., & Murrin, J. (2000). *Valuation: Measuring and managing the value of companies* (3rd ed.). McKinsey & Company Inc. John Wiley & Sons, Inc.
Edvinsson, L. (2002). *Corporate longitude: What you need to know to navigate the knowledge economy*. Financial Times Prentice Hall.
Edvinsson, L., & Malone, M. S. (1999). *Intellectual capital: Realizing your company's true value by finding its hidden brainpower* (1st ed.). Harper Business.
Etcheverry Boneo, L. M. (1969). El Cristianismo frente a la actual cosmovisión: Conocimiento, juicio, valoración y acción. Pro-manuscrito y Pedagogía para una visión del mundo.
Fukuyama, F. (1996). *Trust: The social virtues and the creation of prosperity*. (1. Free Press paperback ed). Free Press.
Goleman, D. (2005). *Emotional intelligence: Why it can matter more than IQ*. (10th anniversary trade pbk. ed). Bantam Books.
Grant, R. M. (1996). Toward a knowledge-based theory of the firm. *Strategic Management Journal, 17*(S2), 109–122. https://doi.org/10.1002/smj.4250171110
Heckscher, E., & Ohlin, B. (1933). *International and inter-regional trade*. Harvard University Press.
Heidegger, M. (1927). *Being and Time*. Max Niemeyer Verlag.
Helliwell, J. F., Layard, R., & Sachs, J. D. (2019). *World happiness report 2019*. Sustainable development solutions Network.
Hermans, H. J. M. (1994). Buber on mysticism, may on creativity, and the dialogical nature of self. *Studies in Spirituality, 0*, 279–305. https://doi.org/10.2143/SIS.4.0.2014683
Hofstede, G., Hofstede, G. J., & Minkov, M. (2010). *Cultures and organizations: Software of the mind: Intercultural cooperation and its importance for survival (Revised and expanded third edition)*. McGraw-Hill.
Jones, R. W. (1971). A three-factor model in theory, trade, and history. In J. N. Bhagwati, R. W. Jones, R. A. Mundell, & J. Vanek (Eds.), *Trade, balance of payments and growth*. North-Holland Publishing Company.
Lévinas, E. (1969). *Totality and infinity: An essay on exteriority* (23rd printing). Duquesne Univ. Press [u.a.].
Lin, C. Y. Y., & Edvinsson, L. (2012). National intellectual capital model and measurement. *International Journal of Knowledge-Based Development, 3*(1), 58. https://doi.org/10.1504/IJKBD.2012.045570
Mahoney, J. T., & Pandian, J. R. (1992). The resource-based view within the conversation of strategic management. *Strategic Management Journal, 13*(5), 363–380. https://doi.org/10.1002/smj.4250130505
Mankiw, N. G., Romer, D., & Weil, D. (1992). A contribution to the empirics of economic growth. *Quarterly Journal of Economics, 107*(May), 407–437.

Mincer, J. A. (1974). The human capital earnings function. *NBER Chapters*, 83–96.

North, D. C. (1990). *Institutions, institutional change, and economic performance*. Cambridge University Press.

North, D. C. (1992). *Transaction costs, institutions, and economic performance*. ICS Press.

Olson, M. (1996). Distinguished lecture on economics in government: Big bills left on the side walk: Why some nations are rich, and others poor. *Journal of Economic Perspectives, 10*(2), 3–24. https://doi.org/10.1257/jep.10.2.3

Penrose, E. (1995). *The theory of the growth of the firm* (3rd ed.). Oxford University Press. https://doi.org/10.1093/0198289774.001.0001

Peteraf, M. A. (1993). The cornerstones of competitive advantage: A resource-based view. *Strategic Management Journal, 14*(3), 179–191. https://doi.org/10.1002/smj.4250140303

Prahalad, C. K., & Hamel, G. (2006). The Core competence of the corporation. In D. Hahn & B. Taylor (Eds.), *Strategische Unternehmungsplanung—Strategische Unternehmungsführung: Stand und Entwicklungstendenzen* (pp. 275–292). Springer. https://doi.org/10.1007/3-540-30763-X_14

Putnam, R. D. (2000). *Bowling alone: The collapse and revival of American community*. Proceedings of the 2000 ACM Conference on Computer Supported Cooperative Work, 357. https://doi.org/10.1145/358916.361990.

Romer, P. M. (1986). Increasing returns and long-run growth. *Journal of Political Economy, 94*(5), 1002–1037. https://doi.org/10.1086/261420

Roos, J., Roos, G., Dragonetti, N. C., & Edvinsson, L. (1997). *Intellectual Capital*. Palgrave Macmillan. https://doi.org/10.1007/978-1-349-14494-5

Sachs, J. (2006). *The end of poverty: Economic possibilities for our time*. Penguin Books.

Samuelson, P. A. (1971). Ohlin was right. *The Swedish Journal of Economics, 73*(4), 365. https://doi.org/10.2307/3439219

Scheler, M. (1973). *Formalism in ethics and non-formal ethics of values: A new attempt toward the foundation of an ethical personalism*. (M. S. Frings & R. L. Funk, Trans.). Northwestern University Press.

Schultz, T. W. (1971). *Investment in Human Capital. The role of education and of research*. The Free Press, A Division of The Macmillan Company. 10022 ($8).

Sen, A. (1997). Human capital and human capability. *World Development, 25*(12), 1959–1961.

Sen, A. (1999). *Development as freedom*. Oxford University Press USA–OSO.

Smith, A. (1982). An inquiry into the nature and causes of the wealth of nations. In R. H. Campbell, A. S. Skinner, & W. B. Todd (Eds.), *The Glasgow edition of the works of Adam Smith*. Oxford University Press.

Solow, R. M. (1957). Technical change and the aggregate production function. *The Review of Economics and Statistics, 39*(3), 312. https://doi.org/10.2307/1926047

Stegmann, J. P. (2000). Gestión Estratégica Moderna. Instituto de Estudios para la Excelencia Competitiva.

Stegmann, J. P. (2001). *An integrative and modern approach to business strategy and entrepreneurship based on value based management and knowledge management. Becoming a learning organization*. [Doctoral Dissertation]. Pacific Western University.

Stegmann, J. P. (2002a). *An integrative and modern approach to business strategy and entrepreneurship, based on value based management and knowledge management*. Second International Research Seminar.

Stegmann, J. P. (2002b). *Estrategia Empresarial Moderna—Para Crecer, Modernizarse, Internacionalizarse y Competir Con Exito en el Nuevo Entorno*. Instituto de Estudios para la Excelencia Competitiva.

Stegmann, J. P. (2002c). The foundations of strategic management: Relationship between growth, economic value creation, knowledge creation and monopoly power. In *2002 Academy of International Business (AIB) Southeast Asia and Australia Regional Conference*.

Stegmann, J. P. (2003). *An integrative approach to modern strategy, based on value based and knowledge*. Third International Research Seminar.

Stegmann, J. P. (2005). *Using the EVA model for corporate stock investment; impact of knowledge, growth and monopoly power on economic value. An investigation on 168 U.S. firms*. [Doctoral Dissertation]. University of Warsaw.
Stegmann, J. P. (2007a). An integrated view of strategic management. *Journal of Interdisciplinary Economics, 18*(4), 275–302. https://doi.org/10.1177/02601079X07001800402
Stegmann, J. P. (2007b). Toward an integrated strategic management. *Journal of Interdisciplinary Economics, 18*(1), 35–69. https://doi.org/10.1177/02601079X07001800103
Stegmann, J. P. (2009). *Strategic value management: Stock value creation and the management of the firm*. J. Wiley & Sons. https://doi.org/10.1002/9781118268087
Stegmann, J. P. (2010a). Gestión estratégica y valor.
Stegmann, J. P. (2010b). Personal values versus stock value maximization. In *Conflicts and solutions. 70th Annual Meeting of the Academy of Management*.
Stegmann, J. P. (2010c). Strategic value management. A new generation of strategic management thinking. In *SMS 30th Annual Conference*.
Stegmann, J. P. (2011). The social side of capitalism towards an interdisciplinary view of business ethics. *Norwich University*. https://doi.org/10.13140/RG.2.2.26522.24003
Stegmann, J. P. (2020). *Epistemological analysis of strategic management and related sciences. How realism promotes leadership* [Doctoral Dissertation. Ph.D. in Humanities for the contemporary world. Specialization in Philosophy]. Universitat Abat Oliba.
Stegmann, J. P. (2023a). *Leadership: A journey toward world peace–our leadership transforms decision making, promoting organizational success, and social Well-being* (Vol. 1). En Route Books and Media, LLC.
Stegmann, J. P. (2023b). *Leadership: A journey toward world peace–our leadership transforms decision making, promoting organizational success, and social Well-being* (Vol. 2). En Route Books and Media, LLC.
Stegmann, J. P. (2023c). *Leadership: A journey toward world peace–our leadership transforms decision making, promoting organizational success, and social Well-being* (Vol. 3). En Route Books and Media, LLC.
Stegmann, J. P. (2023d). *Leadership: A journey toward world peace–our leadership transforms decision making, promoting organizational success, and social Well-being* (Vol. 4). En Route Books and Media, LLC.
Stein, E. (1989). *On the problem of empathy* (3rd ed.). ICS Publications.
Stewart, G. B. (1991). *The quest for value: A guide for senior managers (34 print)*. Harper Business.
Teece, D. J., Pisano, G., & Shuen, A. (1997). Dynamic capabilities and strategic management. *Strategic Management Journal, 18*(7), 509–533. https://doi.org/10.1002/(SICI)1097-0266(199708)18:7<509::AID-SMJ882>3.0.CO;2-Z
The Heritage Foundation & The Wall Street Journal. (2017). *Index of economic freedom* [Dataset].
Transparency International. (2017). *Corruption perceptions index* [Dataset].
Ullberg, E., Edvinsson, L., & Yeh-Yun Lin, C. (2021). *Intangible asset gap in global competitiveness: Mapping and responding to the new economy*. Springer International Publishing. https://doi.org/10.1007/978-3-030-55666-2
United Nations Development Programme. (2017). Human Development Index [Dataset].
Von Hildebrand, D. (2009). *The nature of love*. St. Augustine's Press.
Wernerfelt, B. (1984). A resource-based view of the firm. *Strategic Management Journal, 5*(2), 171–180. https://doi.org/10.1002/smj.4250050207
Winter, S. (1988). Knowledge and competence as strategic assets. In *The competitive challenge: Strategies for industrial renewal (Teece, D.)*. Ballinger Publishing.
Wojtyla, K. (1979). *The acting person*. Reidel.
World Bank. (2017). *GDP per Capita* [Dataset].
World Bank Institute. (2017). *Knowledge index* [Dataset].

The Impact of the Domestic Environment on the Relationship Between a Firm's Intellectual Capital and Innovation

Edyta Skarzyńska and Joanna Paliszkiewicz

Abstract This article analyzes the impact of the domestic environment on the relationship between a firm's intellectual capital and its ability to innovate, emphasizing that a firm's competitiveness depends on both the assets it possesses and the external factors that regulate its use. Two factors at the national level—the availability of skilled labor and the system of appropriation—are key features of the domestic environment that can shape how intellectual capital affects a firm's innovativeness. The national climate combines factors (or country-level resources) and institutions that shape the ability of companies to pool resources at the firm level and extract value from them. The study aims to provide a deeper and more comprehensive understanding of how intellectual capital affects company performance, focusing on the impact of country conditions. The availability of skilled labor and the appropriation system significantly impact the relationship between intellectual capital and innovation by determining the ability to utilize and protect intellectual capital, which can stimulate or inhibit a company's innovation processes. This study will provide additional valuable input to strategic management by examining how combinations of country-level factors and firm-level resources jointly contribute to understanding firm performance. The results show that the more favorable the country's environment is, the less impact human and structural capital have on a company's innovation. In contrast, relational capital retains its influence in more and less favorable conditions. This can help professionals target specific aspects of intellectual capital that have the most significant impact in their context.

E. Skarzyńska (✉) · J. Paliszkiewicz
Management Institute, Warsaw University of Life Sciences, Warsaw, Poland
e-mail: edyta_skarzynska1@sggw.edu.pl; joanna_paliszkiewicz@sggw.edu.pl

F. Matos et al. (eds.), *Intellectual Capital in a Global Business Landscape*,
Contributions to Management Science, https://doi.org/10.1007/978-3-031-86362-2_7

1 Introduction

In the available literature on the knowledge-based perspective in the context of companies, there is a widespread belief that knowledge is a key strategic resource that significantly affects company performance (Grant, 1996; Spender, 1996). This approach assumes that intellectual capital, which combines various sources of knowledge, such as employee competencies and relationships between people and management systems (referred to as human capital, relational capital, and structural capital, respectively), plays a key role in shaping an organization's ability to innovate (Subramaniam & Youndt, 2005; Barrena-Martínez et al., 2020). Based on the resource approach (Barney, 1991), this stream of research understands intellectual capital as one of those rare, unique, and difficult-to-imitate firm-level resources that allow companies to achieve competitive advantage. A company's competitive advantage is based not only on its valuable assets but also on the external circumstances surrounding the acquisition and usage of these resources. Integrating both internal and external factors affecting a company will better clarify the sources of a company's competitive advantage. Each company exhibits varying levels of innovative capacity, where the ability to absorb knowledge based on a unique combination of resources gives companies their distinctive profile (Jansen et al., 2005; Nieto & Quevedo, 2005; Subramaniam & Youndt, 2005; Engelman et al., 2017).

The domestic environment plays an important role as a contextual factor that can explain the relationship between firm-specific resources and firm performance, particularly for emerging economies and the international arena in general (e.g., Meyer et al., 2009; Hoskisson et al., 2013; Kafouros & Aliyev, 2016). In this context, Wan (2005) and Wan and Hoskisson (2003) have proposed a theoretical framework that describes the domestic environment as consisting of factors (i.e., country-level resources) and institutions that collectively affect the ability of firms to acquire and use firm-level resources. A better understanding of these conditions can broaden intellectual capital theory and the knowledge-based perspective of firms, make it more contextually flexible (Bamberger, 2008; Whetten, 2009), and help practitioners guide their managerial efforts to develop the intellectual capital components that are most meaningful to their environment. Building on Wan and Hoskisson's theoretical framework (Wan & Hoskisson, 2003; Wan, 2005), two key country-level factors are presented, such as the availability of skilled labor and the appropriation system, which shape the impact of intellectual capital on firm innovation. The availability of skilled labor has been depicted as the availability of competent workers in a country's labor market (Chacar et al., 2010; Kwan & Chiu, 2015) and the appropriation system as a set of measures to protect innovations from being copied (Hurmelinna-Laukkanen & Puumalainen, 2007).

Among the myriad assets available on the market, a proficient and capable workforce stands out as a key factor that can either enhance or limit the impact of intellectual capital on a company's ability to innovate—human capital and organizational capital foster investment in research and development (R&D) and the generation of various patent applications. Moreover, macroeconomic factors, industry specifics, and firm differentiation influence the relationship between intellectual capital and innovation activity, making intellectual capital an incentive and selection criterion for firm innovation in typical developing countries (Ren & Song, 2021). Indeed, the quality of the skills of a company's workforce is not only the result of the company's investment in developing the competencies of its personnel but also depends on the availability of such a workforce in the labor market. This includes the variety of skills, their level of sophistication, and the number of available highly skilled workers (Kwan & Chiu, 2015). These skilled workers are a key asset, enabling a company to use its intellectual capital effectively and efficiently. For example, a company's ability to leverage business relationships (i.e., relational capital) to enhance its ability to innovate depends on the employees' skills who build these relationships (Kamprath & Mietzner, 2015). Similarly, the effectiveness of a company's internal organizational structures and knowledge repositories (i.e., structural capital) depends on the employees' skills who use these resources (Garavan et al., 2001; Bowman & Swart, 2007). Ultimately, the utility of the knowledge stored in the employees' minds (i.e., human capital) increases when these employees can collaborate with knowledgeable and skilled colleagues, as innovation is often the result of a joint effort (Nonaka & Takeuchi, 1995; Ritter & Gemünden, 2003).

In the context of the various features of the institutional environment, it is worth paying special attention to the importance of the appropriation system in accordance with a country's laws to effectively manage an organization's knowledge base and innovation efforts (Su et al., 2016). An appropriation system is "a combination of available and effective means of protecting intangible assets and innovations, their profitability and increased returns" (Hurmelinna-Laukkanen & Puumalainen, 2007, p. 95). An appropriate institutional environment that ensures the protection of intellectual property rights and promotes fair competition by establishing a legal framework governing agreements and contracts is an important factor in supporting a strong appropriation system (Hurmelinna-Laukkanen & Puumalainen, 2007; Hurmelinna et al., 2007; Murphy et al., 2012). Promoting knowledge patenting and licensing at the institutional level can increase knowledge diversity and enable companies to adapt, combine, and exploit ideas, contributing to better innovation performance (Galunic & Rodan, 1998; Zhong & Sun, 2020). Registered patents are companies' most commonly used formal appropriation tool, encouraging firms to integrate and leverage their knowledge across markets, resulting in increased innovation (Bahl et al., 2021). In addition, a robust appropriation system ensures that cooperating partners treat each other fairly when sharing new ideas. This fosters fair competition and creates more opportunities for innovation, as companies feel safer collaborating with less fear that their secrets and images will be illegally used (Ritala et al., 2015). Thus, when the legal framework supports a strong appropriation regime by promoting fair competition and protecting intellectual assets, a company's intellectual capital plays a more pronounced role in driving a company's innovation.

The availability of a skilled workforce and an appropriation system are important for creating a favorable innovation environment that supports the development of intellectual capital and stimulates innovation activities in companies. A national environment that promotes the development of a skilled workforce and effective appropriation systems can influence companies' development strategies, encouraging them to focus on innovation as a key factor of competitiveness. In addition, the study sets out to determine whether a favorable national environment (both in terms of resource availability and less formal institutions) influences firm innovation and how the availability of skilled labor at the national level and the appropriation system affect the relationship between firm-level intellectual capital and innovation performance. The literature in the area was first reviewed, and the research methodology was described. Then, a review and classification of the results were conducted. Finally, the implications of our findings for both research and management are discussed, and directions for future research are suggested.

2 Literature Review

2.1 *Intellectual Capital*

At the beginning of the twenty-first century, numerous studies confirmed the important role of knowledge and intellectual capital in modern companies operating in the knowledge economy (Roos & Roos, 1997; Bontis, 1998; Edvinsson, 1997; Edvinsson et al., 2004; Anderson & Wincoop, 2003; Marr & Roos, 2005; Erickson & Rothberg, 2009; Dumay, 2016). Stewart (2002) argues that intellectual capital is the third "big idea" in management over the past two decades, along with total quality management and reengineering. As a result, companies that effectively manage their intellectual resources have gained a competitive advantage over those that focus less on managing them (Wiig, 1997). Intellectual capital is an intangible asset organizations hold that can contribute to future value creation (Hunter et al., 2005). In intellectual capital research, one can observe a growing variety of aspects of knowledge and resources considered (Serenko & Bontis, 2013).

Within the knowledge economy, intellectual capital plays an important role as a key determinant of a company's ability to consistently increase its value (Serenko & Bontis, 2009, 2017). Various researchers, including Torre et al. (2020), emphasize that intellectual capital is the amount of general knowledge used in business processes to achieve competitive advantage (Reed et al., 2006; Subramaniam & Youndt, 2005; McDowell et al., 2018). In contrast, the preferred definition in corporations is the possession of relationships with objectives, professional knowledge, experience, and technological skills used to gain a competitive advantage for the organization. Intellectual capital encompasses intangible assets, such as resources, competencies, and capabilities, which affect company performance and generate value (Edvinsson, 1997). In addition, Sullivan (1999) identifies intellectual capital as intangible assets that consist of human knowledge, skills, experience, abilities, and customer relationships that benefit companies in the marketplace. Kim et al. (2015) emphasize that intellectual capital is a nonmonetary resource that affects a company's financial position. It is worth noting that intellectual capital is a complex set of assets of knowledge, practical competence, and experience that contribute to the value of a company (Rehman et al., 2021). Intellectual capital can be divided into general components, such as human, structural, and relational (Wang et al., 2016). Studies commonly use indicators to measure intellectual capital, including social, human, relational, and structural (Asiaei et al., 2018). With this in mind, most studies analyze human, structural, and relational capital while ignoring renewal capital. Theoretically, each of these intellectual capital components has a positive impact on firm innovation (Subramaniam & Youndt, 2005; Kianto et al., 2017; McDowell et al., 2018; Bananuka et al., 2023). In terms of individual IC components, Khalique et al. (2018) documented that human, structural, and relational capital are significantly related to firm performance.

Both knowledge that is public and accessible and knowledge that remains hidden and difficult to access play an important role in the development of intellectual capital. Moreover, each intellectual capital component—human, relational, structural, and renewal—is essential for organizational effectiveness and development (Ahmed et al., 2020; Tran et al., 2022). It is worth noting that these components require different types of organizational support. It is particularly important to understand how these components are created through formal and informal knowledge accumulation processes, considering the influence of corporate culture and leaders' motivation for transformation. These factors lead to the creation of intellectual capital and, as a result, influence organizational innovation (Matricano, 2020). Different components of intellectual capital and different synergies between them have been observed to influence innovation-related outcomes (as can be seen in the works of (Subramaniam & Youndt, 2005; Wu et al., 2008; Buenechea-Elberdin et al., 2018; Kianto et al., 2017). For example, some researchers suggest that managers should focus on developing relational capital to promote innovation, arguing that new ideas for innovation emerge in response to market demand (Zhang & Lv, 2015). Meanwhile, other studies emphasize that human capital is a key element of innovation, as it is people who can challenge the status quo, generate new ideas and innovations (Zhang & Lv, 2015), and flexibly acquire new needed skills (e.g., Youndt & Snell, 2004).

2.2 Innovations

Ensuring the continued prosperity and increasing productivity of economies is a priority for governments. It is pointed out that these goals can be achieved by promoting innovation in business communities. This is particularly important for developing economies, which have limited opportunities for growth based on "capacity building" and cost competition. Accordingly, much research has been conducted in the early twenty-first century on organizational innovation in economics, strategic management, human resource management, and marketing (Aas & Pedersen, 2010; Armbruster et al., 2008). Rose et al. (2009) note that innovation has been recognized as an important driver of economic growth, often allowing organizations to provide higher-quality products and services at lower costs. In this context, Edvinsson et al. (2004) and Vincent et al. (2005) emphasize that this effect contributes significantly to sustainable competitive advantage. In addition, Amidon (1997) suggests that innovation generates competitive and collaborative advantages in organizations.

Different interpretations and aspects of organizational innovation must lead to clear conclusions in the literature. Armbruster et al. (2008) note the lack of unanimity in defining "organizational innovation." On the other hand, Jinchveladze et al. (2009) argue that researchers from different fields are developing their perspectives and identifying with the complex nature of organizational innovation. Damanpour and Gopalakrishnan (1998) provided an earlier quantitative perspective on corporate innovation. According to their definition, organizational innovation involves creating, cultivating, and implementing novel ideas or methodologies in organizations. Vincent et al. (2005), however, argue that this definition needs to be revised because it focuses on the internal variables of organizations and their impact on organizational innovation. The relationships between these factors and innovation are more complex and may be relatively constant across studies and contexts. A more comprehensive approach to collecting and interpreting innovation data can be found in the *Oslo Manual*. It defines innovation as the introduction of new and better production and supply processes. In the third edition of this manual in 2005, this definition was expanded to include new organizational methods in business practices, workplace organization, and external relations. In this context, Ngoc Ca (2009) suggests that innovation is not only different types of activities but also continuous improvement during the implementation process. This includes the learning activities necessary to work effectively within a technological system. To help understand this concept, the Organization for Economic Cooperation and Development (OECD) suggests that the novelty of innovation should be viewed in the context of companies (Mel et al., 2009). Armbruster et al. (2008) note that innovation is a complex phenomenon that includes technical (new products, new production methods) and nontechnical (new markets, new organizational forms) aspects (Alhaimer, 2021). We can also distinguish between product innovation (new products or services) and process innovation (new production methods or organizational forms) (Alabdullah & Kanaan-Jebna, 2023). Ngoc Ca (2009) defines invention as the initial creation of an idea for a new product or process, while innovation is the attempt to bring that idea to life. "Radical innovations" are fundamental and revolutionary changes that require a clear departure from existing practices and existing technology or the introduction of new technologies.

On the other hand, "incremental innovations" are minor improvements or simple changes in operations over a long period of time (Jinchveladze et al., 2009; Li et al., 2023). To achieve optimal organizational structure and efficiency, Fonseca et al. (2019) identify human capital as an important element in the innovation process. Similarly, Diebolt and Hippe (2022) analyzed the impact of human capital on innovation and long-term economic growth in the European region.

Previous research must sufficiently consider the importance of the managers' role and strategic decision-making approach in supporting knowledge-based collaboration (Audretsch & Belitski, 2020). Innovation (Khan et al., 2019), organizational learning (Rehman, Bhatti, & Chaudhry, 2019a), and organizational capabilities (Rehman, Mohamed, & Ayoup, 2019b) have a significant impact on performance.

2.3 *Institutional Environment*

The need to pay more attention to intellectual capital research in the context of the domestic environment may stem from the initial rooting of this research in the resource-based approach to the firm (Penrose, 1959; Barney, 1991). Because this approach focuses on internal sources of competitive advantage and interfirm differentiation (Barney, 1991; Mahoney & Pandian, 1992), it has been criticized for overlooking the impact of the external environment (Priem & Butler, 2001). In response to these issues, the field of strategic management has initiated a study of the importance of the external environment and the potential it offers to leverage a company's unique resources (Miller & Shamsie, 1996; Kim & Hoskisson, 2015). Studies have shown that the domestic environment can play an important role as a moderating factor in the relationship between firm-specific intellectual capital resources and firm performance (e.g., Kim et al., 2015; Kafouros & Aliyev, 2016). Accordingly, our research focuses on the national context, recognizing it as an important country-level contextual element influencing how effectively a firm can leverage its intellectual capital.

Incorporating ideas from the institutional field (North, 1990), Wan and Hoskisson (2003), along with Wan (2005), introduced the concept of a domestic environment consisting mainly of factors and institutions. According to their theory, differences in the availability and quality of these factors and different institutional structures create different opportunities and constraints for companies doing business. In response to these conditions, companies choose different strategies for acquiring resources, developing skills, and achieving results (Wan, 2005). In other words, according to Wan and Hoskisson (2003) and Wan (2005), the domestic environment encompasses both the resource context, which offers firms operational sources, and the institutional context, which shapes firms' decisions to use those resources. Later, Kim and Hoskisson (2015) called this approach the competitive advantage resource environment. The global discussion on the possible impact of the Sustainable Development Goals on the business landscape and related corporate growth is extensive. It revolves around achieving a harmonious balance between meeting business expansion requirements and protecting future generations' interests, environmental protection, and sustainable practices (Vasylieva et al., 2019; Holotová et al., 2020; Mentel et al., 2020). Lu et al. (2008) proposed a theory that assumes that the institutional environment influences knowledge resources and firms' ability to innovate by determining what types of knowledge can be accumulated and how these can be acquired and used and through incentives for knowledge creation, transfer, and application. Bilgili et al. (2016) suggested that the national environment shapes firms' learning strategies and choice of external knowledge sources, influencing the associated costs. Empirical evidence suggests that the institutional context affects the relationship between knowledge creation capacity and firm performance (Su et al., 2016) and intangible assets' impact on foreign subsidiaries' development (Kafouros & Aliyev, 2016).

In this framework, if the national environment is rich in a particular resource, many companies in an area may want to exploit that resource and take advantage of it. This has been confirmed in the international business literature, which shows that multinational companies move across national borders to take advantage of local resource advantages (Kedia & Mukherjee, 2009; Mukherjee et al., 2019). While not all firms in a country necessarily have equal access to resources, the widespread availability of assistance makes it relatively easy and economical for firms to acquire them when they see competitors using them (Kim & Hoskisson, 2015). As a result, if a resource is widely available in the market, it is likely to be held by many firms, making it less unique and scarce and, therefore, less valuable in creating a sustainable competitive advantage (Barney, 1991). On the other hand, if a company can obtain a scarce resource in its domestic environment, it gains a comparative advantage over its competitors. At the same time, the institutional environment, which influences the management and strategies of resources, can support or limit their optimal use (Oliver, 1997). This environment includes legal rules and government structures (i.e., formal institutions), as well as ideology and culture (i.e., informal institutions) (Kaufmann et al., 2018). The institutional environment can impose constraints, determining the range of company resource options (Oliver, 1997).

Additionally, institutions affect a company's ability to utilize resources and reap their full benefits (Peng et al., 2009; Kafouros & Aliyev, 2016). For example, in economic countries with well-established rules of law, companies operate more confidently because managers clearly understand regulations. Companies can use legal procedures to resolve conflicts (Elango & Lahiri, 2014). On the other hand, companies may be reluctant to invest in countries where the rule of law is weak because they fear that their property rights are not adequately protected.

This two-dimensional framework and its components have been widely used to study the interaction between firm-level resources and the domestic environment in predicting firm performance (e.g., García-García et al., 2017; Zhu et al., 2019). We suggest that this framework is also useful for describing the external environment for developing and using firm-level intellectual capital across countries. Although the various elements of intellectual capital represent specific resources belonging to the firm, the ability to acquire them depends on the availability of renewed sources in the external environment. The resource-based perspective assumes that firms can acquire knowledge resources through accumulated experience and learning by doing (Oliver, 1997) or acquire them in the factor market (Barney, 1991). Accordingly, the availability of knowledge resources in the factor market plays a key role in the development of a company (Phonthanukitithaworn et al., 2023). The effective and efficient use of accumulated intellectual capital by a company depends on the regulation of the institutional environment, which determines what actions a company can take with regard to this intangible resource and how it can do so. We, therefore, use Wan and Hoskisson's framework (Wan & Hoskisson, 2003; Wan, 2005) to understand how the domestic environment shapes the relationship between a firm's intellectual capital and its ability to innovate.

3 Methodology

The survey was conducted in Poland. The target population was a broad group of companies from many industries and regions; this was done to maximize the variables' variability and increase the results' generality. We only considered companies with at least 100 employees since such organizations will likely have formalized management and innovation systems. National databases were used to identify companies. Data collection took place from July 2023 to August 2023. All data was collected through telephone interviews. A random sampling approach was used. In total, 158 responses were received, and the majority of respondents held managerial positions, indicating their expertise. Each data point corresponds to a unique company. The companies represented a variety of sectors, including manufacturing, wholesale and retail trade, various service industries, transportation, and warehousing. Data collection and analysis was done using SmartPLS 3.2.8. The survey used scales covering nine items to measure three key components of intellectual capital. All of these scales were assessed by asking survey participants to express their opinions on the extent to which various statements relating to the dimensions of intellectual capital apply to the organization they represent. A 5-point Likert scale was used for this purpose, with participants expressing their opinions anchored on "strongly agree" or "disagree."

The human capital scale included three items adapted from Bontis's (1998) and Yang and Lin's (2009) work. The three structural capital items were based on the work of Kianto (2008) and Kianto et al. (2010), while the three relational capital items were taken from the work of Kianto (2008). In the context of intellectual capital resources, exploratory factor analysis was first conducted using a varimax rotation to ensure that the various intellectual capital resources could be used as separate constructs. The reliability of these constructs was then tested, and Cronbach's alpha was above the acceptable threshold level of 0.70 (see Nunnally, 1978) for all categories (human capital Cronbach's alpha, 0.82; structural capital Cronbach's alpha, 0.71; relational capital Cronbach's alpha, 0.77). A scale to measure innovation was used, which was from the work of Weerawardena (2003). In this case, study participants were asked to rate the success of their company compared to the success of their competitors in generating different types of innovations. The scale, which took the form of a Likert scale, allowed ratings on a scale of 1 (very poor) to 5 (very good) and included four different items. The questionnaire was tested with managers and a panel of experts to ensure the scale items' wording was clear and understandable. We then gave our respondents full anonymity to encourage them to answer honestly.

Table 1 Demographic description of the study sample

		Percentage share (%)
Gender	Female	35
	Male	65
Age range	18–26 years	1
	27–35 years	8
	36–45 years	38
	Over 45 years old	53
Province	Dolnośląskie	5.8
	Kujawsko-Pomorskie	3.2
	Lubelskie	13.4
	Lubuskie	8.2
	Łódzkie	9.5
	Małopolskie	1.8
	Mazowieckie	19.7
	Opolskie	2.5
	Podkarpackie	5.0
	Podlaskie	1.2
	Pomorskie	9.4
	Śląskie	5.0
	Świetokrzyskie	4.4
	Warminsko-Mazurskie	3.7
	Wielkopolskie	1.3
	Zachodniopomorskie	6.0
City size	Village	7
	City up to 50,000	12
	A city with a population of 50,000 to 150,000	20
	A city with a population of 150,000 to 500,000	26
	A city of more than 500,000 inhabitants	35

Table 1 shows the demographic description of the respondents. In total, 158 company representatives participated in the survey, of which 35% were women and 65% were men. As for the managerial positions, 53% of the respondents declared their age above 45 years, and 38% indicated a range of 36–45 years. The characteristics of the survey sample took into account the size of the province and city. More than 33% of respondents were representatives of companies from the Mazowieckie and Lubelskien provinces.

We controlled for three variables to eliminate the influence of factors other than intellectual capital on firm innovation. First, following the approach of Kianto et al. (2017), we included the size of firms, which was measured as the number of employees reported by survey participants. Second, we controlled for the level of sophistication of firms' R&D, following the approach of Cohen and Levinthal (1990), which was measured by assessing the proportion of research personnel to the total number of employees. Third, we took into account the nature of services, as

Table 2 Evaluation of measurements

		Descriptive formulation of elements	Average	SD
Control	Size	Number of employees	4492	5782.39
	Intensity of scientific and research work	Percentage of R&D personnel %.	6.72	4.839
	Servit. Grade	Share of service sales %	37.07	17.142
Independent variables	Human capital	Our employees are highly skilled in their work	4.475	0.746
		Our employees are highly motivated to work	4.070	0.911
		Our employees have a high level of expertise	3.842	0.736
	Structural capital	Our company has efficient and adequate information systems	3.443	0.778
		Our company has tools and facilities to support collaboration among employees	3.563	0.569
		Our company has extensive knowledge of documents and databases	3.696	0.646
	Relational capital	Our company and its external stakeholders (customers, suppliers, and partners) understand each other well	3.880	0.793
		Our company and its external stakeholders often work together to solve problems	3.981	0.761
		Cooperation between our company and its external stakeholders is going well	4.006	0,753
Dependent variable	Innovation	To what extent has your company successfully created innovation in the following areas over the past year compared to competitors?		
		Products and services for customers	3475	0,645
		Production methods and processes	3215	0,545
		Management practices	3380	0,701
		Business models	3133	0,815

previous studies (e.g., Kianto et al., 2010) have suggested that companies in manufacturing and service industries may exhibit different configurations of intellectual capital components, affecting their performance (Table 2).

The results of the baseline model show that all components of intellectual capital significantly influence innovation performance, with relational capital having the strongest influence and human capital the weakest. Moreover, the higher the intensity of R&D activities, the better the company's innovation performance compared to its competitors (Table 3).

Table 4 shows the availability of skilled labor according to the IMD index. The average score of the selected indicators is 4.05.

Table 3 Correlation matrix

	1	2	3	4	5	6	7
1. Size	1.000						
2. R&D intensity	0.048	1.000					
3. Degree of servitization	**0.075*****	**−0.013****	1.000				
4. Human capital	**0.086****	**0.065***	**−0.240***	1.000			
5. Structural capital	**0.162*****	**0.049***	**0.052***	**0.062*****	1.000		
6. Relational capital	**0.118****	**−0.065***	**−0.136***	**0.067*****	**0.068****	1.000	
7. Innovation performance	**0.000*****	**0.044*****	**−0.212****	**0.078*****	**0.089****	**0.141****	1.000

***$p < 0.001$, **$p < 0.01$, *$p < 0.05$ (based on one-tailed tests)

Table 4 Availability of skilled labor and relevant IMD indicators in Poland

IMD index	Average 2022
Indicators of availability of skilled labor	
1. Skilled labor is readily available	3.75
2. Qualified engineers are available on the job market	4.53
3. Digital/technological skills are readily available	3.59
4. Competent senior managers are readily available	4.31
Average score of IMD indicators	4.05

4 Discussion

The impact of intellectual capital on firm performance has been studied by examining the role of country conditions. The results suggest that when skilled labor is available in a country, the impact of human and structural capital on a firm's innovation performance weakens. This is consistent with the prediction that a firm's ability to increase the impact of its intellectual capital on innovation and outperform its competitors will be lower when this opportunity becomes less unique and more common. Research on the role of the resource environment suggests that the effectiveness of firm-specific intellectual capital may be determined by the availability of resources in the market. This support is consistent with the concept put forward by Wan (2005), Wan and Hoskisson (2003), and Kim and Hoskisson (2015). However, our results also indicate that not all firm-specific resources are the same, as some are unique (e.g., relational capital), and the effectiveness of these resources does not necessarily depend on the external resource environment. With confidence that intellectual property rights are effectively protected, employees may be more cautious about sharing their knowledge inside and outside the company. They are concerned about the accidental disclosure of knowledge and the associated negative consequences (Ritala et al., 2015). However, the potential risk of knowledge leakage can overshadow the benefits of sharing knowledge between companies at various industry meetings, including trade shows, exhibitions, or other formal and informal events (Hamel, 1991; Ritala et al., 2015). Some studies indicate that a more rigorous appropriation system can also have negative effects. Although the goal of such a system is to prevent unwanted transfer of ideas, it can also restrict the flow of knowledge in situations that would be beneficial (Hurmelinna et al., 2007). For example, due to strong intellectual property protection, employees may be less inclined to share their knowledge inside and outside the company, fearing accidental disclosure and the resulting consequences (Ritala et al., 2015).

Moreover, in environments with robust misappropriation systems, extensive noncompete agreements are often used, in which employees agree not to work for competing companies after leaving their previous jobs. When IPR protection systems are weak and require greater protection, companies choose partners based on other criteria. They often form networks with noncompeting companies to access complementary resources and combine different forms of knowledge (Dahlander & Wallin, 2006; Hurmelinna et al., 2007; Lee & Cavusgil, 2006). Both types of partnerships, although in different ways, foster innovation. Thus, while the complex mechanisms affecting the impact of relational capital on innovation performance may differ, the overall effect remains positive across different appropriation contexts.

5 Summary

In summary, the results suggest that the more favorable the domestic environment (both in terms of availability of resources and less formal institutions), the lower the influence of human and structural capital on firm innovation. In contrast, relational capital retains its influence in more and less favorable conditions. These findings shed new light on research regarding the impact of intellectual capital on performance, putting it in context. A study by Subramaniam and Youndt (2005) found that relational capital has a significant and beneficial impact on various aspects of innovation performance, while the impact of human and structural capital on these outcomes is variable, depending on the type of innovation and may be insignificant or even negative. The study's contribution to the strategic management literature emphasizes that to understand the performance of firms at the corporate level, it is necessary to consider firm-level resources in the context of the country's overall environment. Our research supports theoretical concepts such as that of Wan and Hoskisson (2003), Wan (2005), Peng et al. (2009), and Kim and Hoskisson (2015) by providing empirical evidence on how the availability of skilled labor at the country level and the appropriation system affect the relationship between firm-level intellectual capital and innovation performance. Managers should focus primarily on investing in the development of relational capital to increase innovation in their companies. This is because this aspect of intellectual capital still significantly impacts whether we are talking about strong or weak appropriation systems and whether we operate in resource-rich or poorer markets. Our study was based on data analysis from a single country, so we had a limited variety of country-level variables and their combinations. The value of future research could come from applying our conceptual framework to other countries with different environmental conditions or to more countries to increase the overall utility of our findings. Later research could also explore additional features of country environments or different combinations of them, for example, by analyzing countries with government regulations, both direct and indirect. The literature indicates that industry specifics can be an important external factor affecting the effectiveness of resources available at the firm level. The study only considered the legal framework supporting the appropriation system as part of the institutional environment. It is therefore recommended that future research consider both formal and informal elements. Despite these limitations, the results contribute to developing an intellectual capital-based perspective in corporate research. Existing literature suggests that industry characteristics may be another important external factor that can explain the effectiveness of firm-level resources. They demonstrate the importance of the country-level environmental factor in understanding the impact of intellectual capital on firm performance, overcoming some of the discrepancies observed in previous studies and opening up new research perspectives in the context of this important resource.

References

Aas, T. H., & Pedersen, P. E. (2010). The firm-level effects of service innovation: a literature review. *International Journal of Innovation Management, 14*(05), 759–794.

Ahmed, S. S., Guozhu, J., Mubarik, S., Khan, M., & Khan, E. (2020). Intellectual capital and business performance: the role of dimensions of absorptive capacity. *Journal of Intellectual Capital, 21*(1), 23–39.

Alabdullah, T. T. Y., & Kanaan-Jebna, A. (2023). The Mediating Role of Innovation on the Relationship between Supply Chain Management and Company Performance in the Kingdom of Bahrain. *Journal of Humanities, Social Sciences and Business, 3*(1), 160–176.

Alhaimer, R. S. (2021). The role of social media in the innovation and per- formance of kuwaiti enterprises in the food sector. *Journal of Theoreti- cal and Applied Electronic Commerce Research, 16*(6), 1960–1972.

Amidon, D. M. (1997). *Innovation strategy for the knowledge economy the ken awakening*. Butterworth-Heinemann.

Anderson, J. E., & Wincoop, E. (2003). Gravity with gravitas: a solution to the border puzzle. *American Economic Review, 93*(1), 170–192.

Armbruster, H., Bikfalvi, A., Kinkel, S., & Lay, G. (2008). Organizational innovation: The challenge of measuring non-technical innovation in large-scale surveys. *Technovation, 28*(10), 644–657.

Asiaei, K., Jusoh, R., & Bontis, N. (2018). Intellectual Capital and performance measurement systems in Iran. *Journal of Intellectual Capital, 19*(2), 294–320.

Audretsch, D. B., & Belitski, M. (2020). The role of R&D and knowledge spillovers in innovation and productivity. *European Economic Review, 123*, 103391.

Bahl, M., Lahiri, S., & Mukherjee, D. (2021). Managing internationalization and innovation tradeoffs in entrepreneurial firms: Evidence from transition economies. *Journal of World Business, 56*(1), 101150.

Bamberger, P. (2008). Beyond contextualization: Using context theories to narrow the micro–macro gap in management research. *Academy of Management Journal, 51*, 839–846.

Bananuka, J., Tauringana, V., & Tumwebaze, Z. (2023). Intellectual capital and sustainability reporting practices in Uganda. *Journal of Intellectual Capital, 24*(2), 487–508.

Barney, J. B. (1991). Firm resources and sustained competitive advantage. *Journal of Management, 17*, 99–120.

Barrena-Martínez, J., Cricelli, L., Ferr'andiz, E., Greco, M., & Grimaldi, M. (2020). Joint forces: Towards an integration of intellectual capital theory and the open innovation paradigm. *Journal of Business Research, 112*, 261–270.

Bilgili, T. V., Kedia, B. L., & Bilgili, H. (2016). Exploring the influence of resource environments on absorptive capacity development: The case of emerging market firms. *Journal of World Business, 51*, 700–712.

Bontis, N. (1998). Intellectual capital: an exploratory study that develops measures and models. *Management Decision, 36*(2), 63–76.

Bowman, C., & Swart, J. (2007). Whose human capital? The challenge of value capture when capital is embedded. *Journal of Management Studies, 44*, 488–505.

Buenechea-Elberdin, M., Saenz, J., & Kianto, A. (2018). Knowledge management strategies, intellectual capital, and innovation performance: a comparison between high-and low-tech firms. *Journal of Knowledge Management, 22*(8), 1757–1781.

Chacar, A. S., Newburry, W., & Vissa, B. (2010). Bringing institutions into performance persistence research: Exploring the impact of product, financial, and labor market institutions. *Journal of International Business Studies, 41*, 1119–1140.

Cohen, W. M., & Levinthal, D. A. (1990). Absorptive capacity: A new perspective on learning and innovation. *Administrative Science Quarterly, 35*, 128–152.

Dahlander, L., & Wallin, M. W. (2006). A man on the inside: Unlocking communities as complementary assets. *Research Policy, 35*, 1243–1259.

Damanpour, F., & Gopalakrishnan, S. (1998). Theories of organizational structure and innovation adoption: the role of environmental change. *Journal of Engineering and Technology Management, 15*(1), 1–24.

Diebolt, C., & Hippe, R. (2022). *Human capital and regional development in Europe*. Springer International Publishing.

Dumay, J. (2016). A critical reflection on the future of intellectual capital: from reporting to disclosure. *Journal of Intellectual Capital, 17*(1), 168–184.

Edvinsson, L. (1997). Developing intellectual capital at Skandia. *Long Range Planning, 30*(3), 366–373.

Edvinsson, L., Dvir, R., Roth, N., & Pasher, E. (2004). Innovations: the new unit of analysis in the knowledge era: The quest and context for innovation efficiency and management of IC. *Journal of Intellectual Capital, 5*(1), 40.

Elango, B., & Lahiri, S. (2014). Do market-supporting institutional characteristics explain firm performance? Evidence from emerging markets. *Thunderbird International Business Review, 56*, 145–155.

Engelman, R. M., Fracasso, E. M., Schmidt, S., & Zen, A. C. (2017). Intellectual capital, absorptive capacity and product innovation. *Management Decision, 55*(3), 474–490.

Erickson, G. S., & Rothberg, H. N. (2009). Intellectual capital in business-to-business markets. *Industrial Marketing Management, 38*(2), 159–165.

Fonseca, E., Yankovskaya, L., Martins, A. F., Fishel, M., & Federmann, C. (2019, August). *Findings of the WMT 2019 shared tasks on quality estimation*. In Proceedings of the Fourth Conference on Machine Translation (Volume 3: Shared Task Papers, Day 2) (pp. 1–10).

Galunic, D. C., & Rodan, S. (1998). Resource recombinations in the firm: Knowledge structures and the potential for Schumpeterian innovation. *Strategic Management Journal, 19*, 1193–1201.

Garavan, T. N., Morley, M., Gunnigle, P., & Collins, E. (2001). Human capital accumulation: The role of human resource development. *Journal of European Industrial Training, 25*, 48–68.

García-García, R., García-Canal, E., & Guill, M. F. (2017). Rapid internationalization and long-term performance: The knowledge link. *Journal of World Business, 52*, 97–110.

Grant, R. M. (1996). Toward a knowledge-based theory of the firm. *Strategic Management Journal, 17*, 109–122.

Hamel, G. (1991). Competition for competence and interpartner learning within international strategic alliances. *Strategic Management Journal, 12*, 83–103.

Holotová, M., Nagyová, L., & Holota, T. (2020). The impact of environmen- tal responsibility on changing consumer behaviour—Sustainable mar- ket in Slovakia. *Economics and Sociology, 13*(3), 84–96.

Hoskisson, R. E., Wright, M., Filatotchev, I., & Peng, M. W. (2013). Emerging multinationals from mid-range economies: The influence of institutions and factor markets. *Journal of Management Studies, 50*, 1295–1321.

Hunter, L., Webster, E., & Wyatt, A. (2005). Measuring intangible capital: a review of current practice. *Australian Accounting Review, 15*(36), 4–21.

Hurmelinna-Laukkanen, P., & Puumalainen, K. (2007). Nature and dynamics of appropriability: Strategies for appropriating returns on innovation. *R&D Management, 37*, 95–112.

Hurmelinna, P., Kylaheiko, K., & Jauhiainen, T. (2007). The Janus face of the appropriability regime in the protection of innovations: Theoretical re-appraisal and empirical analysis. *Technovation, 27*, 133–144.

Jinchveladze, T., Zschockelt, F., Van Velzen, M., & Looise, J. K. (2009). *The role of intangible assets in the relationship between HRM and innovation: A theoretical and emperical exploration*.

Jansen, J. J. P., Van Den Bosch, F. A. J., & Volberda, H. W. (2005). Managing potential and realized absorptive capacity: how do organizational antecedents matter? *Academy of Management Journal, 48*(6), 999–1015.

Kafouros, M., & Aliyev, M. (2016). Institutions and foreign subsidiary growth in transition economies: The role of intangible assets and capabilities. *Journal of Management Studies, 53*, 580–607.

Kamprath, M., & Mietzner, D. (2015). The impact of sectoral changes on individual competences: A reflective scenario-based approach in the creative industries. *Technological Forecasting and Social Change, 95*, 252–275.

Kaufmann, W., Hooghiemstra, R., & Feeney, M. K. (2018). Formal institutions, informal institutions, and red tape: A comparative study. *Public Administration, 96*, 386–403.

Kedia, B. L., & Mukherjee, D. (2009). Understanding offshoring: A research framework based on disintegration, location and externalization advantages. *Journal of World Business, 44*, 250–261.

Khalique, M., Bontis, N., Shaari, J. A. N. B., Yaacob, M. R., & Ngah, R. (2018). Intellectual capital and organisational performance in Malaysian knowledge-intensive SMEs. *International Journal of Learning and Intellectual Capital, 15*(1), 20–36.

Khan, S.N., Hussain, R.I., Rehman, S.-u., Maqbool, Q., Engku ALI, E.I. and Numan, M. (2019), "The mediating role of innovation between corporate governance and organizational performance: moderating role of innovative culture in Pakistan textile sector", Cogent Business and Management, Vol. 6 1, p. 1631018.

Kianto, A. (2008). Development and validation of a survey instrument for measuring organizational renewal capability. *International Journal of Technology Management, 42*, 69–88.

Kianto, A., Hurmelinna-Laukkanen, P., & Ritala, P. (2010). Intellectual capital in serviceversus product-oriented companies—What's the difference? *Journal of Intellectual Capital, 11*, 305–325.

Kianto, A., Saenz, J., & Aramburu, N. (2017). Knowledge-based human resource management practices, intellectual capital and innovation. *Journal of Business Research, 81*, 11–20.

Kim, H., & Hoskisson, R. E. (2015). A resource environment view of competitive advantage. *Emerging Economies and Multinational Enterprises (Advances in International Management), 28*, 95–140.

Kim, H., Hoskisson, R. E., & Lee, S.-H. (2015). Why strategic factor markets matter: New multinationals' geographic diversification and firm profitability. *Strategic Management Journal, 36*, 518–536.

Kwan, L. Y. Y., & Chiu, C. Y. (2015). Country variations in different innovation outputs: The interactive effect of institutional support and human capital. *Journal of Organizational Behaviour, 36*, 1050–1070.

Lee, Y., & Cavusgil, S. T. (2006). Enhancing alliance performance: The effects of contractual-based versus relational-based governance. *Journal of Business Research, 59*, 896–905.

Li, Z., Huang, Z., & Su, Y. (2023). New media environment, environmental regulation and corporate green technology innovation: Evidence from China. *Energy Economics, 119*, 106545.

Lu, Y., Tsang, E. W. K., & Peng, M. W. (2008). Knowledge management and innovation strategy in Asia Pacific: Toward an institution-based view. *Asia Pacific Journal of Management, 25*, 361–374.

Mahoney, J. T., & Pandian, J. R. (1992). The resource-based view within the conversation of strategic management. *Strategic Management Journal, 13*, 363–380.

Marr, B., & Roos, G. (2005). Chapter 2–A strategy perspective on intellectual capital. In M. Bernard (Ed.), *Perspectives on intellectual capital* (pp. 28–41). Butterworth-Heinemann.

Matricano, D. (2020). The effect of R&D investments, highly skilled employees, and patents on the performance of Italian innovative startups. *Technology Analysis & Strategic Management, 32*(10), 1195–1208.

McDowell, W. C., Peake, W. O., Coder, L., & Harris, M. L. (2018). Building small firm performance through intellectual capital development: Exploring innovation as the black box. *Journal of Business Research, 88*, 321–327.

Mel, S. D., McKenzie, D., & Woodruff, C. (2009). *Innovative firms or innovative owners? Determinants of innovation in micro, small, and medium enterprises*. Forschungsinstitut zur Zukunft der Arbeit, Institute for the Study of Laboro.

Mentel, G., Vasilyeva, T., Samusevych, Y., Vysochyna, A., Karbach, R., & Streimikis, J. (2020). The evaluation of economic, environmental and energy security: Composite approach. *International Journal of Global Environmental Issues, 19*(1–3), 177–195.

Meyer, K. E., Estrin, S., Bhaumik, S. K., & Peng, M. W. (2009). Institutions, resources, and entry strategies in emerging economics. *Strategic Management Journal, 30*, 61–80.

Miller, D., & Shamsie, J. (1996). The resource-based view of the firm in two environments: The Hollywood film studios from 1936–1965. *Academy of Management Journal, 39*, 519–543.

Mukherjee, D., Lahiri, S., Ash, S. R., & Gaur, A. S. (2019). Search motives, local embeddedness, and knowledge outcomes in offshoring. *Journal of Business Research, 103*, 365–375.

Murphy, M., Perrot, F., & Rivera-Santos, M. (2012). New perspectives on learning and innovation in cross-sector collaborations. *Journal of Business Research, 65*, 1700–1709.

Ngoc Ca, T. (2009). Learning by networking with multinationals: A study of the Vietnamese automotive industry. In M. G. A. J. Woo (Ed.), *Fuelling economic growth: The role of public–private sector research in development* (pp. 219–261). Practical Action Publishing Ltd..

Nieto, M., & Quevedo, P. (2005). Absorptive capacity, technological opportunity, knowledge spillovers, and innovative effort. *Technovation, 25*(10), 1141–1157.

Nonaka, I., & Takeuchi, H. (1995). *The knowledge-creating company: How Japanese companies create the dynamics of innovation*. Oxford University Press.

North, D. C. (1990). *Institutions, institutional change and economic performance*. Cambridge University Press.

Nunnally, J. C. (1978). An overview of psychological measurement. In *Clinical diagnosis of mental disorders: A handbook* (pp. 97–146).

Oliver, C. (1997). Sustainable competitive advantage: Combining institutional and resource-based views. *Strategic Management Journal, 18*, 697–713.

Peng, M. W., Sun, S. L., Pinkham, B., & Chen, H. (2009). The institution-based view as a third leg for a strategy tripod. *Academy of Management Perspectives, 23*, 63–81.

Penrose, E. T. (1959). *The theory of the growth of the firm*. Wiley.

Phonthanukitithaworn, C., Srisathan, W. A., Ketkaew, C., & Naruetharadhol, P. (2023). Sustainable development towards openness SME innovation: Taking advantage of intellectual capital, sustainable initiatives, and open innovation. *Sustainability, 15*(3), 2126.

Priem, R., & Butler, J. (2001). Is the resource-based view a useful perspective for strategic management research? *The Academy of Management Review, 26*, 22–40.

Reed, K. K., Lubatkin, M., & Srinivasan, N. (2006). Proposing and testing an intellectual capital-based view of the firm. *Journal of Management Studies, 43*, 867–893.

Rehman, S.-U., Bhatti, A., & Chaudhry, N. I. (2019a). Mediating effect of innovative culture and organizational learning between leadership styles at third-order and organizational performance in Malaysian SMEs. *Journal of Global Entrepreneurship Research, 9*(1), 1–24. https://doi.org/10.1186/s40497-019-0159-1

Rehman, S.-U., Kraus, S., Shah, S. A., Khanin, D., & Mahto, R. V. (2021). Analyzing the relationship between green innovation and environmental performance in large manufacturing firms. *Technological Forecasting and Social Change, 163*, 120481.

Rehman, S.-U., Mohamed, R., & Ayoup, H. (2019b). The mediating role of organizational capabilities between organizational performance and its determinants. *Journal of Global Entrepreneurship Research, 9*(1), 1–23.

Ren, S., & Song, Z. (2021). Intellectual capital and firm innovation: incentive effect and selection effect. *Applied Economics Letters, 28*(7), 617–623.

Ritala, P., Olander, H., Michailova, S., & Husted, K. (2015). Knowledge sharing, knowledge leaking and relative innovation performance: An empirical study. *Technovation, 35*, 22–31.

Ritter, T., & Gemünden, H. G. (2003). Network competence: Its impact on innovation success and its antecedents. *Journal of Business Research, 56*, 745–755.

Roos, G., & Roos, J. (1997). Measuring your company's intellectual performance. *Long Range Planning, 30*(3), 413–426.

Rose, S., Shipp, S., Lal, B., & Stone, A. (2009). In S. A. T. P. Institute (Ed.), *Frameworks for Measuring Innovation: Initial Approaches* (Vol. 06). Athena Alliance.

Serenko, A., & Bontis, N. (2009). Global ranking of knowledge management and intellectual capital academic journals. *Journal of Knowledge Management, 13*(1), 4–15.

Serenko, A., & Bontis, N. (2013). Global ranking of knowledge management and intellectual capital academic journals: 2013 update. *Journal of Knowledge Management, 17*(2), 307–326.

Serenko, A., & Bontis, N. (2017). Global ranking of knowledge management and intellectual capital academic journals: 2017 update. *Journal of Knowledge Management, 21*(3), 675–692.

Spender, J. C. (1996). Making knowledge the basis of a dynamic theory of the firm. *Strategic Management Journal, 17*, 45–62.

Stewart, T. A. (2002). *The Wealth of Knowledge: Intellectual Capital and the Twenty-First Century Organization*. Currency Doubleday.

Su, Z., Peng, M. W., & Xie, E. (2016). A strategy tripod perspective on knowledge creation capability. *British Journal of Management, 27*, 58–76.

Subramaniam, M., & Youndt, M. A. (2005). The influence of intellectual capital on the types on innovative capabilities. *Academy of Management Journal, 48*, 450–463.

Sullivan, P. H. (1999). Profiting from intellectual capital. *Journal of Knowledge Management, 3*(2), 132–143.

Torre, C., Tommasetti, A., & Maione, G. (2020). Technology usage, intellectual capital, firm performance and employee satisfaction: the accountants' idea. *The TQM Journal.*

Tran, N. P., Dinh, C. T. H., Hoang, H. T. T., & Vo, D. H. (2022). Intellectual Capital and Firm Performance in Vietnam: The Moderating Role of Corporate Social Responsibility. *Sustainability, 14*, 12763.

Vasylieva, T., Lyulyov, O., Bilan, Y., & Streimikiene, D. (2019). Sustainable economic development and greenhouse gas emissions: The dynamic impact of renewable energy consumption, GDP, and corruption. *Ener- gies, 12*(17), 3289.

Vincent, L. H., Bharadwaj, S. G., & Challagalla, G. N. (2005). *Does Innovation Mediate Firm Performance?: A Meta-Analysis of Determinants and Consequences of Organizational Innovation* (p. 34). College of Management, Georgia Tech.

Wan, W. P. (2005). Country resource environment, firm capabilities, and corporate diversification strategies. *Journal of Management Studies, 42*, 161–182.

Wan, W., & Hoskisson, R. (2003). Home country environments, corporate diversification strategies, and firm performance. *The Academy of Management Journal, 46*, 27–45.

Wang, Z., Sharma, P. N., & Cao, J. (2016). From knowledge sharing to firm performance: a predictive model comparison. *Journal of Business Research, 69*(10), 4650–4658.

Weerawardena, J. (2003). Exploring the role of market learning capability in competitive strategy. *European Journal of Marketing, 37*, 407–429.

Whetten, D. A. (2009). An examination of the interface between context and theory applied to the study of Chinese organizations. *Management and Organization Review, 5*, 29–55.

Wiig, K. M. (1997). Integrating intellectual capital and knowledge management. *Long Range Planning, 30*(3), 399–405.

Wu, W. Y., Chang, M. L., & Chen, C. W. (2008). Promoting innovation through the accumulation of intellectual capital, social capital, and entrepreneurial orientation. *R&D Management, 38*, 265–277.

Yang, C., & Lin, C. (2009). Does intellectual capital mediate the relationship between HRM and organizational performance? Perspective of a healthcare industry in Taiwan. *International Journal of Human Resource Management, 20*, 1965–1984.

Youndt, M. A., & Snell, S. A. (2004). Human resource configurations, intellectual capital, and organizational performance. *Journal of Managerial Issues, 16*, 337–360.

Zhang, H. Y., & Lv, S. (2015). Intellectual capital and technological innovation: The mediating role of supply chain learning. *International Journal of Innovation Science, 7*, 199–210.

Zhong, Q., & Sun, Y. (2020). The more the better? Relational governance in platforms and the role of appropriability mechanisms. *Journal of Business Research, 108*, 62–73.

Zhu, H., Ma, X., Sauerwald, S., & Peng, M. W. (2019). Home country institutions behind cross-border acquisition performance. *Journal of Management, 45*(4), 1315–1342.

Value Cocreation in Big Data Value Networks: Identifying and Analyzing the Interdependency of Actors and Roles

Devrim Yurdaanık-Eskiyerli and Oana Gavrila

Abstract In today's manufacturing industry, servitization and the adoption of Industry 4.0 technologies have emerged as key drivers of competitive advantage. This chapter explores how the integration of cloud computing, big data analytics, and smart manufacturing technologies facilitates value cocreation within big data value networks, improving strategic and organizational capabilities. Through a detailed single case study of a technology service provider (TSP) specializing in predictive maintenance solutions in the North Brabant region of the Netherlands and utilizing data collected through surveys and interviews, we explain the complex relationship between technology providers, manufacturing firms, and end users. Our analysis reveals that effective collaboration, founded in a mutual understanding of needs and value drivers, optimizes value creation across the network. Key findings highlight the role of digital servitization in generating intangible assets, such as technological know-how and relational capital, which are critical for sustaining a competitive edge. The study emphasizes the importance of aligning value propositions across network actors to bring out the full potential of big data and advanced technologies in the manufacturing domain. By providing an in-depth analysis of the TSP's case and its interactions within the value network, this chapter contributes to a deeper understanding of the mechanisms underlying value cocreation in the context of Industry 4.0.

D. Yurdaanık-Eskiyerli (✉) · O. Gavrila
Fontys International Business Studies, Research Group Business Innovation, Venlo, The Netherlands
e-mail: d.eskiyerli@fontys.nl; o.gavrila@fontys.nl

F. Matos et al. (eds.), *Intellectual Capital in a Global Business Landscape*, Contributions to Management Science, https://doi.org/10.1007/978-3-031-86362-2_8

1 Introduction

Advanced technologies such as the predictive capabilities offered by big data analytics (BDA), an essential element of Industry 4.0, make the value chain complex in all sectors, including manufacturing (Gröger, 2018). Asset and process digitization makes the value chain more data-centric, leading to newer processes such as the data value chain (DVC) and big data value chain (BDVC).

Data-oriented value creation involves complementarity among suppliers, partners, service providers, and end users who form a value network. Collaboration replaces competition in a new paradigm for value creation through technology that contributes to a firm's intellectual capital by generating intangible assets, primarily the knowledge acquired by employees in utilizing advanced technologies, the knowledge gained and invested by the firm in its systems, and relational capital formed through external relationships and alliances. Manufacturing firms often collaborate with technology service providers (TSPs) to harness the value of technology.

This chapter explores the role of TSPs in smart maintenance via original equipment manufacturers (OEMs) employing advanced architectures and data-driven methods for efficient predictive diagnostics. We aim to demonstrate that BDVC relationships are more intricate and interwoven than traditional value chains, and thus, creating value through these relationships requires understanding different value chain nodes. In the subsequent sections, we review the role of big data in manufacturing, particularly in predictive maintenance, and how digital servitization and technology outsourcing create value in intangible assets for the OEMs in a BDVC environment. Then, we present a case study highlighting the relationships between the actors in a BDVC environment. Finally, this chapter proposes a value proposition model for predictive maintenance technology providers, emphasizing their role in BDVCs, where value extends indirectly to OEMs' customers.

2 Big Data in Manufacturing and Predictive Maintenance

Before the advent of BDA, reactive maintenance led to production losses, spurring preventive strategies for scheduled upkeep (Rokhforoz et al., 2021). Nevertheless, machine degradation modeling complexity led to condition monitoring and big data. Today, manufacturing systems can employ advanced technologies such as controllers, sensors, robotics, and artificial intelligence to enhance production and repair times (Kolberg & Zühlke, 2015). Embedded sensors gather data on equipment, quality, and logistics for analysis, offering insights for decision-making. Assets autonomously track sensor, operational, maintenance, environmental, and health data, yielding a product's lifecycle insights, wear pattern recognition, and maintenance guidance (Sezer et al., 2018).

As a result, equipment harm can be anticipated and prevented by early predictive maintenance, thus reducing downtime and costs while improving reliability (Ghaleb et al., 2020; Haarman et al., 2017; Sezer et al., 2018; Zonta et al., 2020). Predictive maintenance, in turn, can help optimize overall equipment effectiveness (OEE), technical availability, and equipment usage (Sezer et al., 2018) and, therefore, has a massive positive impact on the production process and quality management. This comprehensive view, known as "smart maintenance," supports data-driven decisions, enhancing efficiency, cost reduction, and revenue growth (Nunes et al., 2017; Pereira & Romero, 2017).

Despite the enormous advantages of smart maintenance, small- and medium-sized enterprises need to catch up in digital transformation due to costs, resources, and technology-related apprehensions (Del Giudice et al., 2021a). For such businesses to fully reap the benefits of smart maintenance, they either need to develop in-house capabilities or cooperate with TSPs.

3 Digital Servitization, Intellectual Capital, and Technology Outsourcing

Manufacturing firms and OEMs increasingly offer different service options alongside their existing products or even transform them into service-based offerings to increase customer value (Baines & Lightfoot, 2012) and generate additional revenue (Fliess & Lexutt, 2019). Manufacturers can now utilize BDA to monitor their products in real time and offer predictive maintenance. This "development of new services and/or the improvement of existing ones using digital technologies" has been termed digital servitization (Paschou et al., 2020). Although digital servitization can potentially create value for all actors in the network relationship, for example, by preventing unexpected costly machine failures for the customers and increasing revenue for the manufacturers, such value should be recognized and shared fairly by all actors for digital servitization to be utilized effectively.

Product-service systems (PSS) is a concept developed from servitization and defined as "a marketable set of products and services capable of jointly fulfilling a user's need" (Mont, 2002). Customers' preparedness and desire to purchase complicated PSS is a common determinant of how well a company's servitization plan works (Morgan et al., 2019). However, given the nonlinear relationship between servitization and performance and the multiplicity of moderators that influence it, a company's performance outcome remains unpredictable (Burton et al., 2017). In addition to managing the production of complex products, companies must now enhance their value proposition by offering new services (Khanra et al., 2021).

Moreover, formulating a new value proposition introduces several challenges, most prominently the differences in the perceived importance of value creation among users and service providers. Therefore, value expectations should be carefully considered during the solution design process. A relevant, well-defined value proposition is crucial to developing long-lasting relationships with users, and its relevance should be maintained over time. The contribution of our study is identifying how big data changes the relationship between the actors of the value chain.

Services are generated in service ecosystems (actor-to-actor networks), which is the central theme of service-dominant logic. In service ecosystems, value is no longer created by one actor but increasingly through cocreation (Lusch & Nambisan, 2015), where each actor adds incremental value to the network while concentrating on their core competencies (Bovet et al., 2000). Understanding the underlying value network of ecosystems is crucial as digitalization has altered the nature of firm relationships prevalent in the twentieth century; industries can no longer be classified as suppliers, customers, and competitors (Biem & Caswell, 2008; Peppard & Rylander, 2006; Pil & Holweg, 2006).

With the emergence of Industry 4.0 and big data, more complex chains and relationships have been emerging and led to the creation of the concept of value networks, "a set of relatively autonomous units that can be managed independently, but operate together in a framework of common principles and service level agreements"(Peppard & Rylander, 2006). Service-oriented and nonphysical sectors now commonly use the value network concept (Peppard & Rylander, 2006). Business collaboration has become easier because of platform structures and enabling technologies. In this sense, a digital business ecosystem can be described as a social and technological environment where individuals, organizations, and digital technologies enable and develop value through digital platforms (Senyo et al., 2019).

Indeed, digitizing organizational processes yields greater efficiency and utilizes an often-neglected resource: data (Parviainen et al., 2017). Intangible assets are, therefore, not well suited to the traditional value chain concept, which must be modified to incorporate a data-centric approach rather than a product- or process-centric one. In a data-centric value chain, the physical and digital worlds are merging because of digitalization (Faroukhi et al., 2020; Hanelt et al., 2015). Although value in both traditional value chains and value networks is created from the relationships in the networked economy, a network perspective considers relationships part of a larger whole, comprising a network of interdependent relationships (Peppard & Rylander, 2006).

Value cocreation can only occur through the interactive engagement between the provider and the customer within the process of creating value (Mostafa, 2015; Ramaswamy, 2008). Recent academic discussions in this area emphasize this perspective and the need for a deeper comprehension of the cocreation (Mostafa, 2015; Ramaswamy, 2008). Despite the widespread acknowledgment of its significance, the concept of value cocreation remains vague, with variations in its interpretation and application across different academic inquiries (Dey et al., 2016). Furthermore, there is a gap in empirical insights regarding the practical aspects of value cocreation and the role of digitalization in value cocreation (Echeverri & Skålén, 2011; Vargo & Lusch, 2008). In their work, Lenka et al. (2017) examine how manufacturing companies transitioning toward a servitization strategy increasingly rely on developing digitalization capabilities to interact and cocreate value with customers. They conceptualize digitalization capabilities into three subcomponents:

intelligence capability (the ability to configure hardware components to sense and capture information with minimal human intervention), connect capability (the ability to connect digitalized products through wireless communication networks), and analytic capability (the ability to transform captured data into actionable insights). These capabilities enable value cocreation with customers through perceptive and responsive mechanisms, highlighting the critical role of digital technologies in facilitating this process in a business-to-business (B2B) context. This demonstrates how digitalization capabilities enable manufacturing firms to cocreate value with their customers, offering a framework that shows the mechanisms through which these capabilities support the value cocreation process.

The value creation driven by technology adoption has a multidimensional impact on a firm's intellectual capital, generating various intangible assets. The intangible assets include the explicit outcomes of technological integration and the tacit knowledge accumulated and refined during the process of using advanced technologies (Saunders & Brynjolfsson, 2016). These intangible assets are essential in enhancing a firm's competitive advantage and long-term viability (Bontis, 1998). Foremost among these intangible assets is the experiential knowledge accrued by the firm's employees as they navigate the intricacies of innovative technologies in their daily operational contexts. This knowledge represents a combination of practical insights, creative problem-solving, and refined technical skills, all of which create intellectual capital that reinforces the firm's innovation capabilities and adaptability (Sveiby, 1997).

To explain the full potential of these advanced technologies and the intangible assets they cultivate, manufacturing firms frequently engage in collaborative partnerships with specialized TSPs. These providers serve as enablers for technical guidance and innovative solutions that align with the firm's specific needs and objectives (Cenamor et al., 2019a). The collaboration between manufacturing firms and TSPs embodies a mutual relationship that catalyzes value extraction from technology adoption. This partnership facilitates not only the transfer of technical expertise but also the cocreation of novel strategies and the exploration of new technological territories.

TSPs from digital ecosystems have started offering computing infrastructures and applications as a service in the form of cloud computing, service orientation, digital platforms, and new business models built on these platforms (Rabelo et al., 2020). Therefore, all TSPs would constitute diverse digital ecosystems. As a digital service, TSPs make their technology assets (software services and, indirectly, their required computing infrastructure) available as a service to companies while retaining their autonomy and legal independence (Rabelo et al., 2008). They also own and provide the software services' implementations, descriptions, and technical and business support. OEMs can face challenges when integrating such collaborators into their business models, overcoming which will require a robust understanding of the value of such relationships and alleviating their concerns about collaborating.

In summary, the value generation catalyzed by integrating advanced technologies is a multidimensional phenomenon that resounds throughout a firm's intellectual capital. The knowledge accrued through technological utilization, the refinement of internal systems to accommodate these innovations, and the cultivation of relational capital through collaborative alliances reinforce the creation of intangible assets. As manufacturing firms strive to utilize the potential of these technologies, their strategic collaborations with TSPs function as key enabler for realizing tangible outcomes from intangible endeavors. This dynamic interplay enhances a firm's competitive advantage and positions it at the frontline of innovation in contemporary manufacturing.

Considering this dynamic landscape and the impact of advanced technologies on the industry, this study explores the relationship between big data, digital servitization, intellectual capital, and technology outsourcing through a comprehensive case study and survey-based investigation involving 33 companies. By examining real-world cases and garnering insights from the experiences and strategies of industry players, this article aims to contribute to the ongoing discourse on leveraging advanced technologies for value creation as an intangible asset in the manufacturing domain. Specifically, this study identifies and analyzes two different but interlocking value proposition canvases, where the user of one value proposition canvas becomes the provider of the second value proposition canvas. Additionally, we aim to identify the fits and misfits between the value propositions of the actors and how to align them to create value as an intangible asset.

4 Methodology for Empirical Analysis of Data Management Approaches of OEMs

The Case Study.

For the empirical investigation, the case study analyzed is a TSP (hereinafter referred to as the "Tech Company") engaging in predictive maintenance from the North Brabant region of the Netherlands. The region was selected because it is renowned as the technology hub of the Netherlands; it is the location of the Brainport Eindhoven, where knowledge institutes, start-ups, and high-tech manufacturing companies are situated.

Tech Company is an early-stage start-up offering industrial measurement solutions for translating physical signals into insights through sensors and data analytics. Their team is experienced in building corporate-scale Industrial Internet of Things (IIoT) solutions and developing a range of machine learning algorithms—from financial pricing tasks to quality assurance by visual inspection of industrial production. The company is also designing a connected wireless measurement device to collect data from analog sensors on unconnected machines. This device can analyze a customer's use case and build a pilot solution to add value to the link between an IIoT solution and the end user. Their data science team can develop turnkey solutions and algorithms tailored to customers' needs.

Tech Company supports IIoT applications by providing solutions for heterogeneous environments and old unconnected machines, security concerns, limited operational technology (OT) capabilities at scale, and poor collaboration between information technology (IT) and OT. To address these issues, Tech Company offers a three-dimensional solution:

1. *Asset management software*: Their software treats machines and systems as assets that generate data and trigger events to take necessary actions for optimal performance. Tech Company is working on its first release to aid both manufacturers and end users in digitizing critical asset data sets and log events and states. In addition, Tech Company created a software as a service (SaaS) hub on Microsoft Azure cloud that OEM, its customers, and partners can securely access. This hub contains pages where all the critical data regarding an asset, identifiable using a unique QR and six-digit codes, is easily accessible to all stakeholders.
2. *Remote monitoring hardware and service*: Tech Company's edge device is connected to Docker-style software that can run on any server or edge computer for database and PLC/DCS system connection. It easily connects to the machines' existing data acquisition interface and runs edge analytics, adding unconnected and critical data resources to their service via transparent sensor units. The wireless and connected hardware turns old, unconnected brown tech into a data-driven infrastructure without replacing the existing machinery.
3. *Data science as a service*: The Tech Company's team helps build the first data models in the pilots and then encourages the clients to develop their solutions on no-or-low-code platforms.

Therefore, the Tech Company has a SaaS offering for predictive maintenance, asset management, data analytics, and a hardware component built into OEM equipment at their customer sites. By offering additional services based on their hardware, Tech Company is aiming to servitize their product.

As Tech Company's software solution is still being developed, the company needs to understand the requirements of OEMs to achieve their goal. In manufacturing, an OEM serves the role of a supplier (Belkadi et al., 2016), engaging in product manufacturing (Narkhede et al., 2020). Collaborating with component suppliers, they produce and market products to distinct customer segments (Dahlquist & Griffith, 2014) and thus hold product branding and manage marketing (Zhai et al., 2007). The product range and collaborations by OEMs vary, driven by organizational focus and context (Dahlquist & Griffith, 2014). In supply chain management, OEMs lead the planning, design, implementation, and maintenance of an exclusive supply chain section (Dath et al., 2010). Therefore, OEM activities span competition, customer processes, procurement, supply chain, logistics, manufacturing, management, and performance (Dath et al., 2010). OEMs contribute to competitive advantage in diverse market challenges via distinct competencies and core manufacturing components (Belkadi et al., 2016).

Moreover, a poor product-market fit in the current value proposition may be a barrier between the Tech Company and the OEMs. The individual connections between actors in the network are crucial to their competitive positions (Peppard & Rylander, 2006). The OEMs manufacture machinery and sell it to their customers,

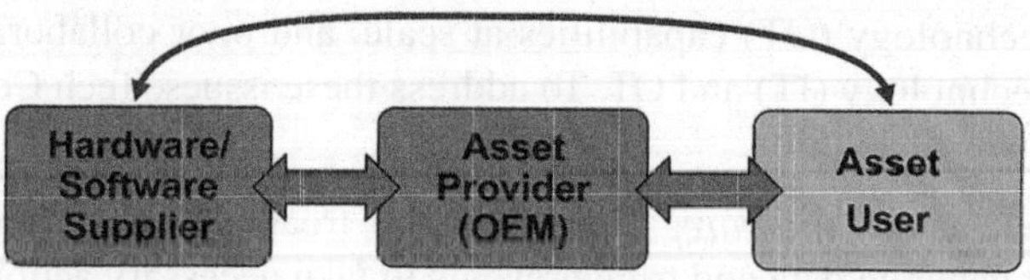

Fig. 1 Value creation network

called the "end users" or "asset owners." On the other hand, OEMs themselves are also the customers of the TSPs, such as our Tech Company (Fig. 1). Since the Tech Company is engaged with a multitude of actors and relationships, the value that it creates needs to be helpful for the OEM and indirectly to the OEM's customers. In such a multiactor network, the design and creation of value becomes more complicated and intricate.

5 Methodology, Data Collection, and Analysis

For this study, we utilized a case study methodology. Case study methodology has been shown to facilitate a more detailed description of a phenomenon (Siggelkow, 2007), a deeper exploration of the subject (Dyer & Wilkins, 1991), and a reassessment of old theoretical relationships (Yin, 2013), which are in line with the objectives of this study. We also used a collaborative research design, incorporating business perspectives while contributing to a theory (Freytag & Young, 2017). The case study benefits from previous theoretical findings and aims to expand them with empirical findings from the business.

Central to our investigation was a survey designed to gather insights from Dutch original equipment manufacturers (OEMs), focusing on their current practices, challenges, and attitudes toward digital technologies in predictive maintenance and servitization. Our survey setup was guided by secondary research and industry expert opinions, who have contributed to selection of the survey topics.

The primary focus of the secondary research was to identify the key challenges that a typical TSP was experiencing when working with the OEMs on the topic of utilizing predictive maintenance-related services. The topics have also been cross-checked by two industry experts. The first expert (expert 1) is the chief executive officer of the Tech Company with 25 years of experience in machine manufacturing and wireless measurement systems, and the other one is an industry expert and academic (expert 2) with 41 years of experience in industrial and high-tech products and services, as well as servitization.

The secondary research revealed that the adoption of predictive maintenance by OEMs is hindered by several key challenges. Despite the growing interest in predictive maintenance, its implementation is often hindered by a lack of internal knowledge, reliance on legacy maintenance systems, and systematic guidance (Wagner & Hellingrath, 2021). The disruption levels experienced in OEMs due to machine failure can be significant, leading to disorganization and production delays (Sobaszek et al., 2020). Predictive maintenance, which involves the use of big data analytics and AI to anticipate machine failures, can play a crucial role in preventing these disruptions (Lee et al., 2016). Gatica et al. (2016), Lee et al. (2020), and Ren and Zhao (2015) also highlight the need for data analytics and intelligent maintenance systems in optimizing maintenance operations. Pertselakis et al. (2019) highlight the importance of integrating equipment data from various sources, including legacy systems and operational data, to develop effective predictive maintenance models. This is further supported Patwardhan et al. (2016), who emphasize the potential of big data technologies in enabling the shift from preventive to predictive maintenance. Nacchia et al. (2021) provide a comprehensive overview of the use of machine learning methods in predictive maintenance, with a focus on the increasing availability of data and the use of statistical tests to uncover root causes of problems. These studies jointly point to the need for advanced data analytics, intelligent systems, and automation as key enablers for the successful adoption of predictive maintenance by OEMs.

Based on the secondary research and expert opinions, also taking into account the Tech Company's problems in connection to the OEMs, the topic guide for the survey has been determined:

- *Digitizing data sets*
  - Overview of current methods of data digitization practices
  - Communication methods of critical machine-related data to customers
- *Predictive maintenance and servitization*
  - Insight into the predictive maintenance process and technology adoption
  - Methods of tracking the performance of the machines
  - Types of maintenance service offered
  - The time frame and willingness to integrate machine intelligence/remote connectivity to track machine performance
- *Keeping machines and equipment up to date*
  - Processes for managing software/firmware updates
  - Communication tools used to send the latest software and firmware version
  - Strategies to minimize downtime during updates
  - Communication with customers regarding updates
  - Solutions to update-related challenges.
- *OEM gains, pains, and jobs*
  - Value of pain points of the OEMs in the relationship with the end user

The target population for this study comprised firms that are actively integrating Industry 4.0 technologies or interested in doing it, to enhance their service offerings through digital servitization. The selection of companies for participation in the survey was guided by a set of criteria developed to ensure a representative sample of the manufacturing industry's diverse sectors. These criteria were as follows:

1. *Industry sector*: Firms must be actively engaged in the manufacturing sector, with a focus on integrating digital technologies for predictive maintenance.
2. *Size and scale*: A mix of small, medium, and large enterprises was chosen to capture varied perspectives and experiences with digital servitization.
3. *Geographical location*: Companies were selected in the Brainport region, which is known as the technology and manufacturing center of the Netherlands.
4. *Technology adoption level*: Firms demonstrating varying levels of technology adoption—from early to advanced stages—were included to explore a broad spectrum of experiences and strategies in digital servitization.

A preliminary list of potential participants was compiled through industry database provided by Brabantse Ontwikkelings Maatschappij (BOM-Brabant Development Agency), an enterprise support agency aiming for the development of businesses in the region. This list was refined based on our selection criteria, resulting in a targeted group of companies that would be invited to participate in the survey. Afterwards, we have decided to participate in the Vision Robotics & Motion Trade Fair and Congress, held in 's Hertogenbosch on June 8, 2022, where we identified that the companies with our selection criteria would be attending. Trade shows gather essential stakeholders from specific industries or technological domains with the main aim of sharing insights into emerging trends and innovations within their sector. Consequently, these gatherings have become a focal point of interest for scholars in business and management, aiming to investigate the strategies and practices of companies (Gibson, 2023). This trade fair annually attracts manufacturing companies driven by technology in the region, where developments in sensors and other Industry 4.0 technologies are shared. Therefore, this forum served as an ideal location to carry out our survey. Out of 100 participated in the trade fair, 33 machine manufacturing OEMs participated in the survey.

The survey was developed to cover key aspects of digital servitization and predictive maintenance within the manufacturing sector. The survey method was chosen over interviews based on the need for broad coverage across the business-to-business (B2B) sector, within the constraints of time and resources available for the study. The companies were selected through a purposive sampling method, aiming to include a diverse range of perspectives and key industry players, who have interest in highly specialized and niche topic of predictive maintenance in machine manufacturing. Therefore, a sample size of 33 is sufficient to identify trends and patterns, especially when the population under study is relatively homogenous in terms of their technological orientation and market environment.

The survey followed the topic guide initially formulated and comprised 14 questions (digitizing the data sets: two questions, predictive maintenance and servitization: four questions, keeping machines and equipment up to date: two questions, OEM gains, pains, and jobs: six questions) designed to understand what value Tech Company can create for the OEMs and, based on that, to identify the gaps in the Tech Company's value proposition. Our study employed a cross-sectional design, and each response

OEMs is treated as an independent data point. The study did not incorporate repeated measurements or longitudinal data, as the focus was to capture the current view of OEM practices toward digital technologies in predictive maintenance.

The survey comprised both closed- and open-ended questions. The survey analysis involved calculating percentages from the survey responses, a quantitative method that provides a high-level overview of the data. This involved summarizing responses to each question or statement in the survey to understand the distribution of opinions, behaviors, or characteristics among the respondents. The analysis focused on understanding the mechanisms through which digital technologies facilitate value cocreation in the context of predictive maintenance services. Descriptive statistics of the survey responses are also provided in the analysis. All statistics were performed using Microsoft Excel in Office 365. Distribution of frequency, mean scores (M), and standard deviations (SD) were determined from the results of the survey. The descriptive statistics are reported by the notation of $M \pm SD$.

Insights gained from the analysis were used to develop a model through the value proposition canvas, illustrating the relationship between technology adoption, value cocreation, and servitization in the manufacturing industry.

Once quantitative analysis identified key trends and patterns, these responses are transferred into the value proposition canvas. The transfer to the value proposition canvas is based on categorization and prioritization of survey items within each response.

The value proposition canvas (Fig. 2) is a crucial tool in business model design that aids in creating value propositions that resonate with customers' needs (Osterwalder et al., 2015). It comprises the customer profile and the value proposition sides, and the aim is to align the two, achieving fit through stages: problem-solution fit (addressing key jobs, pains, and gains), product-market fit (positive customer response), and business model fit (scalable and profitable model). The customer profile dissects a specific customer segment into their jobs, pains, and gains. Customer jobs represent tasks customers aim to accomplish, pains denote adverse outcomes and obstacles, and gains signify desired outcomes and benefits. It is vital to prioritize and rank these aspects according to their importance and relevance. On the value proposition side, products and services are categorized and listed as "essential" or "nice to have." Pain relievers explain how offerings address specific pains, focusing on significant ones. Similarly, gain creators elucidate how products and services generate desired customer gains.

The survey responses from the OEMs are first categorized into different aspects of the value proposition canvas. This was done by analyzing the responses and classifying them into the segments of the canvas that best represented the implications of the answers. The categories used were "Value Proposition of the OEM," "Customer Profile of the OEM Customers," and "Customer (OEM) Profile." Afterwards, we collaborated with expert 2 where his role was to provide an in-depth analysis of the responses and help prioritize the survey items based on their relevance and impact on the industry. The expert's insights served to align the identified values with the components of the Canvas, ensuring that each survey item was placed correctly in terms of the "Jobs," "Pains," and "Gains" it represented. The

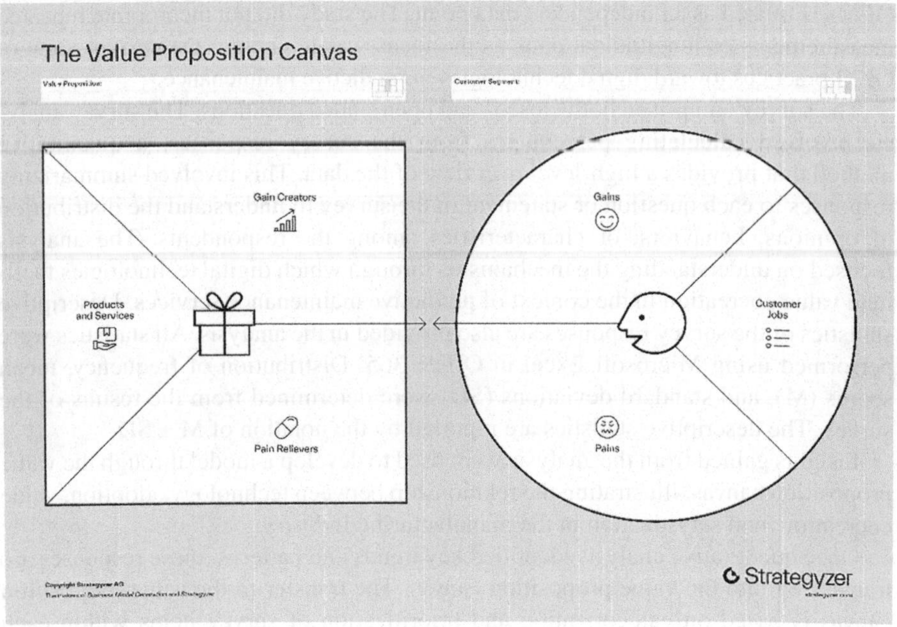

Fig. 2 Value proposition canvas

expert prioritized each item based on his extensive knowledge and current industry trends, so that the most critical aspects from the survey were addressed in the value proposition canvas. The aim was to create a clear and compelling value proposition that would resonate with the OEMs and their customers, highlighting the benefits and solutions provided by the Tech Company. The draft of the value proposition canvas went through several iterations, also involving expert 1, with the experts providing feedback on the relevance and impact of the proposed value propositions. Based on the categorized survey data and with the guidance of the expert, we further developed the "Value Proposition of the Tech Company." This process involved mapping the OEM's needs and the corresponding services that the Tech Company could provide to address those needs effectively. The alignment was achieved by creating connections between the OEM's "Jobs" and the Tech Company's services that would alleviate the "Pains" and enhance the "Gains."

6 Results

6.1 Digitizing the Data Sets

In the first question in the survey asking the OEMs how they store the machine-related data sets, there were four possible answers: print on paper (category 0), using product life cycle management (PLM) software (category 1), using enterprise

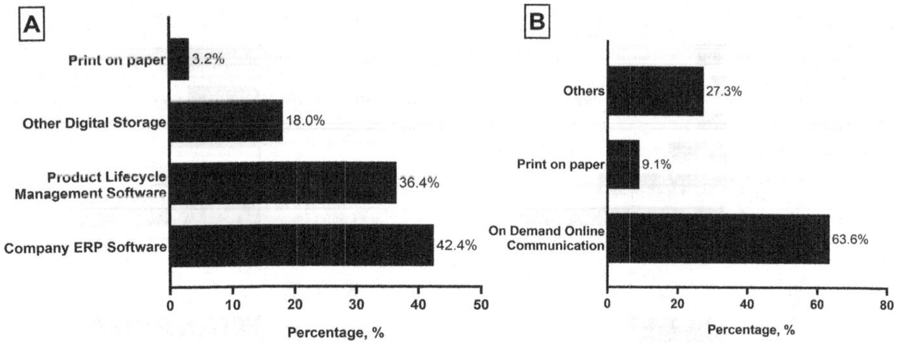

Fig. 3 (**a**) Method of storing machine-related data sets. Other digital storages include SWiM system, notion, data centers, cloud, or local devices. (**b**) Methods of communicating critical machine-related data to customers. Online communication includes emails and digital platforms such as notion. Others include one-on-one conversations, guided tours, customer networks, phone calls, meetings with the customer after management approves, or a combination of the above, depending on the application

resource planning (ERP) software (category 2), or other digital software (category 3). Our survey indicated that most OEMs (42.4%) have either their own ERP software to store the data sets of their machines or use PLM software to keep all documentation of products digitally (36.4%) (Fig. 3a). The rest of the companies use other types of public or private software to keep their data sets, except for one company that keeps their asset documentation on paper (Fig. 3a). $M = 1.76 \pm 0.79$ indicates that that on average, the response is closer to category 2 and the 95% confidence interval for the mean is between 1.48 and 2.04.

For the second question in the survey asking the OEMs their methods of communicating critical machine-related data to customers, there were three possible answers: print on paper (category 0), online communication (category 1), and others (category 2). Most companies (63.6%) use a digital environment such as email or other online communication methods to communicate critical information about machines to third parties, while 9.1% still use printed copies of the product documentation (Fig. 3b). The figures for the mean and standard deviation are $M = 1.12 \pm 0.54$ indicating that that the average response is closer to category 1. The 95% confidence interval for the mean is 0.93 to 1.31.

6.2 *Predictive Maintenance and Servitization*

When asked how the OEMs track machine performance at their customers' sites, there were six possible answers: no connection with the machine (category 0), repair/maintenance when needed (category 1), remotely monitor and fix (category 2), monitor remotely with predictive maintenance (category 3), both remotely monitor and fix and monitor remotely with predictive maintenance (category 4), and

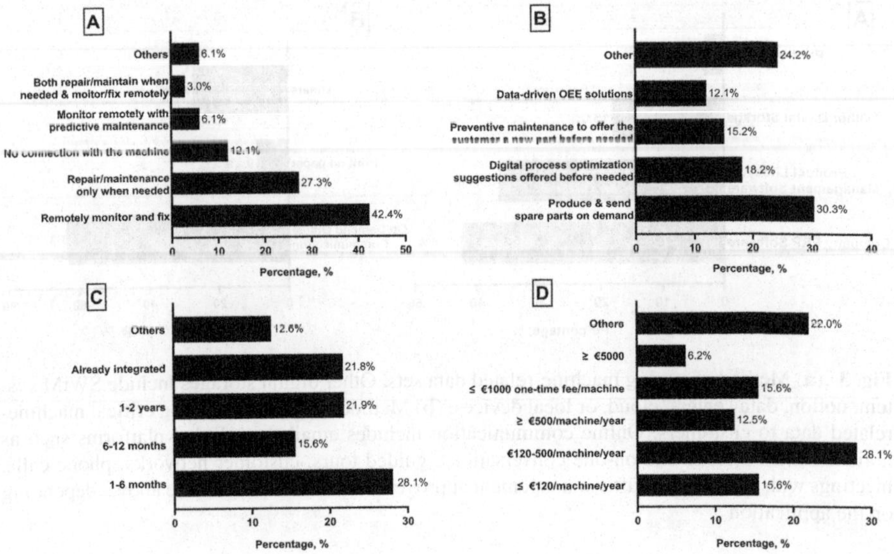

Fig. 4 (**a**) Methods of tracking the performance of the machines at the customer's site. Others include not applicable, depends on the customer, and would offer cloud solution (Festo AX), but concerned with customer data privacy. (**b**) Types of maintenance service offered. Others include only sales, service level agreements, selling maintenance contracts, solutions, or commissioning, leaving it to the customer, and none of the above. (**c**) The time frame for integrating machine intelligence/remote connectivity to track the condition of the machines and assets at the customer sites. Others include on-demand, not planned, and depending on the customer. (**d**) Amount willing to invest per machine to increase its capacity for remote connectivity and machine intelligence. Others include depends, not sure, and not much

others (category 5). For this question, 42.4% indicate they monitor and fix machines remotely, 27.3% indicate they only have on-site access to machine performance when a repair or maintenance is needed, 12.1% of OEMs did not have any connection to machines at the customers' site, and only 6.1% of OEMs monitored the customer's machine remotely and offered predictive maintenance (Fig. 4a). The mean and standard deviation numbers are $M = 1.88 \pm 1.34$. Thus, the mean response is closer to category 2, but the standard deviation is relatively high, indicating most responses are falling in the categories 1, 2, or 3. The 95% confidence interval for the mean is 1.41 to 2.35.

When asked about the types of maintenance services offered, there were five possible answers: produce and send a new spare part (category 1), digital process optimization suggestions (category 2), predictive maintenance suggestions to offer a new part before it breaks down (category 3), data-driven OEE solutions (category 4), and others (category 0). Here, under half of the OEMs engaged in some form of monitoring over the customer's machine to be able to provide them with maintenance: 18.2% offer digital process optimization suggestions based on the customer's machine and quality data, 15.2% use preventive maintenance services to recommend a new part before it is needed, and 12.1% offer data-driven overall equipment efficiency (OEE) solutions (Fig. 4b). In contrast, 30.3% of OEMs produced and sent a new spare part at their customers' request (Fig. 4b). On average, the response is closer to category 2: M = 1.60 ± 1.34, but SD is also relatively high; i.e., the responses are mostly falling in categories 1 or 2. The 95% confidence interval for the mean is between 1.13 and 2.07.

Regarding plans to integrate machine intelligence/remote connectivity to track the condition of the machines and assets at the customer sites, there were five possible answers: already integrated (category 0), 1–6 months (category 1), 6 to 12 months (category 2), 1–2 years (category 3), and others (category 4). Here, 28.1% of the OEMs indicated within 1 to 6 months, 15.6% within 6 to 12 months, 21.9% within 1 to 2 years, and 21.8% already had integrated machine intelligence and remote connectivity (Fig. 4c). The mean and standard deviation of the responses for this question is M = 1.82 ± 1.40, and the 95% confidence interval for the mean is 1.32 to 2.32. Mean response is close to category 2, but also considering the standard deviation, the responses tell us that most of the respondents are planning to integrate planning to integrate predictive maintenance between 1 month to 2 years.

In terms of amount of investment per machine per year to offer remote connectivity and machine intelligence, there were six possible answers: €120–€500 machine/year (category 1), up €1000 one-time fee/machine (category 2), more than €500 machine/year (category 3), €5000 and more (category 4), and others (category 0). Here, 28.1% of OEMs indicated they would invest €120–500, 15.6% would invest up to €120, and only 6.2% would invest €5000 or more; 15.6% indicated they would make a one-time investment per machine of up to €1000 (Fig. 4d). The 95% confidence interval for the mean figure is 1.26 to 2.32. Mean response is close to category 2, where M = 1.79 ± 1.49, but also considering the standard deviation, the responses tell us that most of the respondents are planning to spend between €120 and more than €500/year.

Interestingly, there was no correlation between the costs per machine for connectivity and machine intelligence with the time horizon to establish this capability. For example, among the respondents who plan to institute such capability in a short time (1 to 6 months), the cost estimates were distributed equally between the first four categories. One respondent even predicted that they would invest around €5000 for remote connectivity and machine intelligence capability in less than 6 months. Similarly, respondents who indicated they would acquire remote connectivity/machine intelligence for their assets in the long term (1 to 2 years) also had almost equal distribution among forecasted costs per asset.

6.3 Keeping Machines and Equipment up to Date

When asked about communication tools used to send the latest software/firmware version, there were five possible answers: on-site updates/upgrades (category 1), products do not need an update (category 2), email announcement (category 3), on the air update (category 4), and not informing (category 5). Here, 42.4% of OEMs did so remotely by contacting the machine controller, 21.2% sent an email with a web link or attachment, 18.2% ensured their service staff visited the customer to update the software, and 15.2% of respondents stated that their products did not require software updating (Fig. 5a). The mean response, M = 2.82 ± 1.26, is close to category 3, but also considering the standard deviation of the responses, the

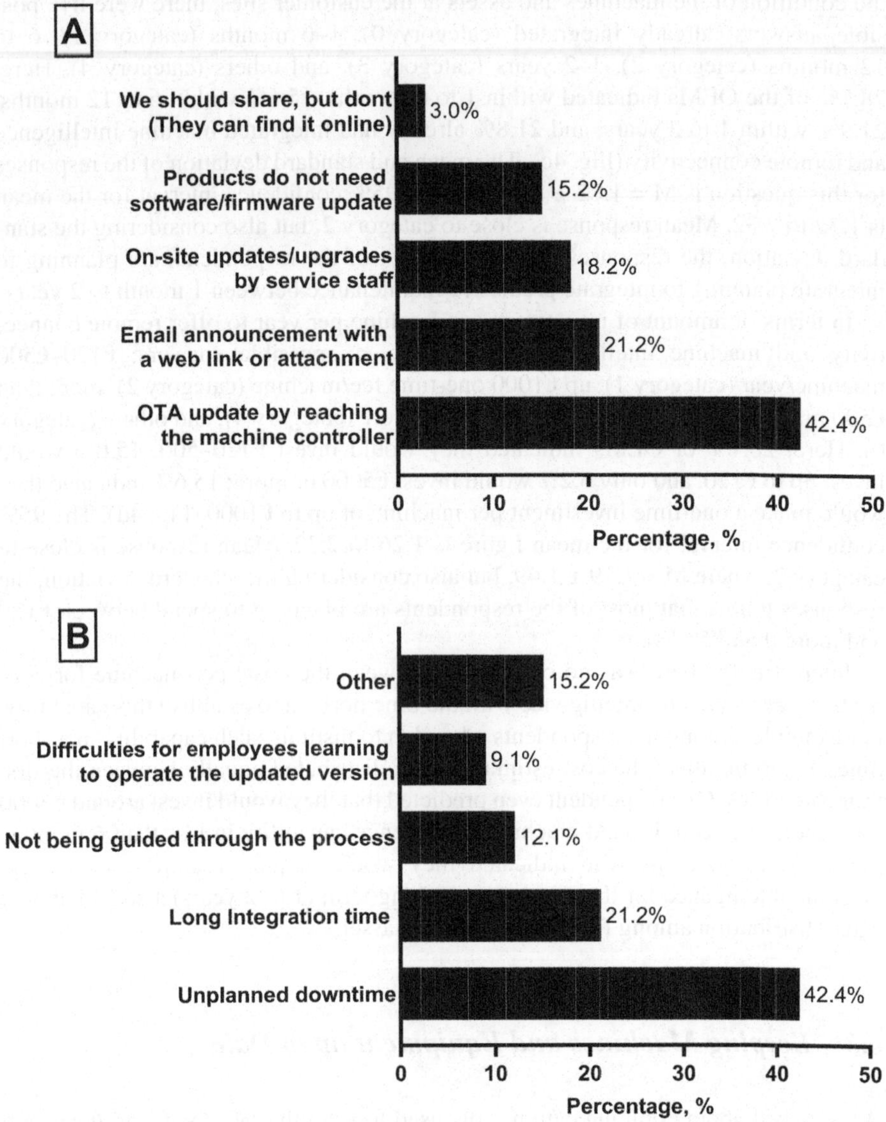

Fig. 5 (**a**) Communication tools used to send the latest software and firmware version. (**b**) Level of disruption customers have encountered due to a lack of or an unsuccessful update in software or firmware

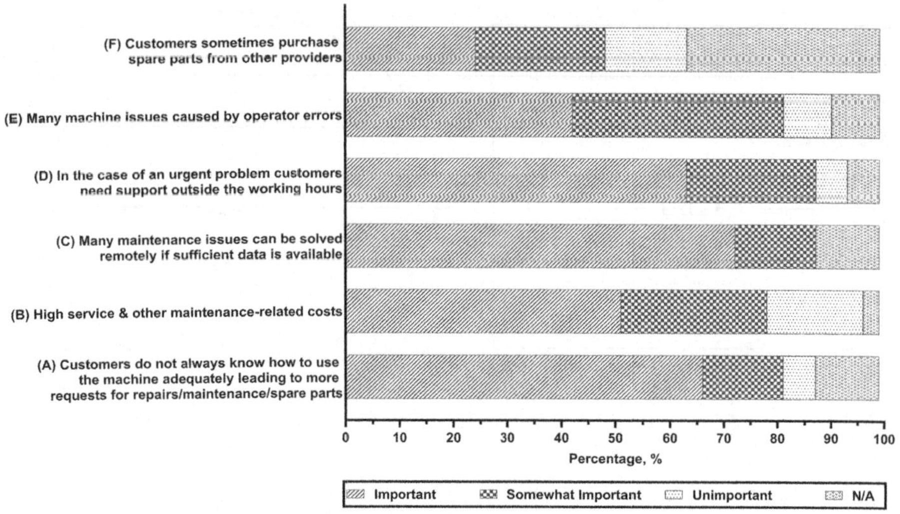

Fig. 6 Pain points in the relationship with the end user, based on how important it is for the OEM to find a solution to the issue. N/A = not applicable

respondents tell us that responses are spread among categories 2, 3, or 4. The 95% confidence interval for the mean is between 2.37 and 3.27.

When asked, the level of disruption OEM customers experience due to lack of or an unsuccessful update in the software or firmware, there were five possible answers: long integration time (category 1), not being guided through the process (category 2), unplanned downtime (category 3), difficulties for employees learning to operate the updated version (category 4), and other (category 5). Interestingly, 42.4% of OEMs also indicated that their customers experienced unplanned downtime because of a lack of or unsuccessful software updates (Fig. 5b). The mean and standard deviation are $M = 2.09 \pm 1.28$ indicating that average response is category 2, but taking the standard deviation into account, it is fair to say that respondents state categories 1, 2, and 3 are the main levels of disruption. The 95% confidence interval for the mean number lies between 1.64 and 2.54.

6.4 *Gains, Pains, and Jobs of the OEM Customers*

We also asked the OEMs about the importance of pain points in the relationship with the end user. We asked them to rank the pain points as unimportant (category 1), important (category 2), somewhat important (category 3), or not applicable (category 0), based on their perceived value for finding solutions for the specific pain points.

Over 80% of OEMs viewed the lack of customer expertise on the supplied products, leading to more maintenance and spare parts requests as an important or somewhat important pain for customers (Fig. 6, bar a). The average of the responses is

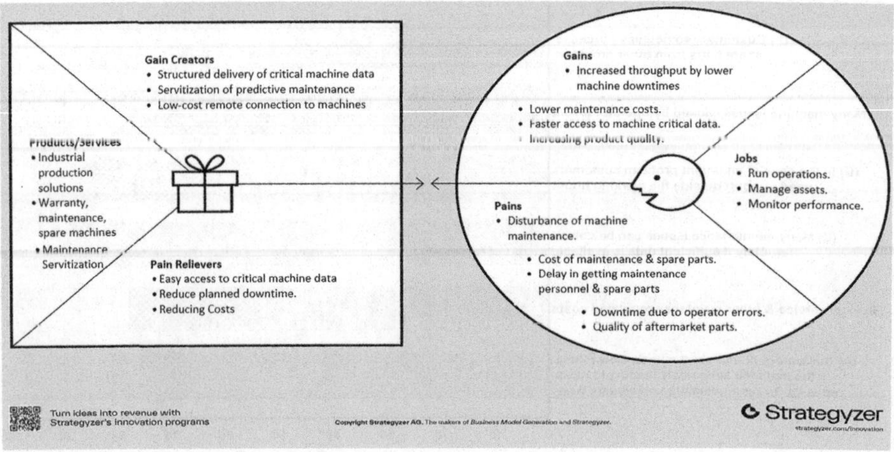

Fig. 7 Value proposition canvas for the OEMs and their customers

very close to category 2, where M = 1.85 ± 0.83. The 95% confidence interval for the mean result is between 1.56 and 2.14.

Additionally, the cost of maintenance and spare parts for customers was viewed as a customer pain point by over three-quarters of the OEMs (Fig. 6, bar b) as indicated by the mean and standard deviation of responses: M = 2.03 ± 0.77. The 95% confidence interval for the mean number is between 1.77 and 2.30.

In a related point, 88% of the OEMs indicated that sufficient data, if available, could solve many maintenance issues remotely, indicating a potential pain reliever for their customers (Fig. 6, bar c). The mean number is very close to category 2: M = 1.91 ± 0.80. The 95% confidence interval for the mean figure is between 1.63 and 2.19.

Further, OEMs almost universally viewed the mismatch between customer operating hours and the provision of maintenance services as a customer pain (Fig. 6, bar d) with a mean of M = 2.06 ± 0.74, where the 95% confidence interval for the mean is 1.80 to 2.32.

OEMs also overwhelmingly think that many machine issues are caused by customer operator errors (Fig. 6, bar e). This significant customer pain may be attributable, at least in part, to unplanned downtime, disruption, and potentially expensive maintenance calls; the mean is between category 2 and 3: M = 2.12 ± 0.92, and the 95% confidence interval is between 1.80 and 2.44.

Finally, under half of OEMs (48%) believe that the purchase of aftermarket parts by customers affects the product's quality, indicating that this is not commonly evaluated to be a pain for customers by OEMs (Fig. 6, bar f). The mean of responses is M = 1.36 ± 1.22, and 95% confidence interval for the mean is between 0.93 and 1.79.

6.5 *Value Proposition Canvas for the OEMs and their Customers*

We analyzed the responses to the survey through the lens of the value proposition canvas to develop the OEM customer profile in terms of products, pain relievers, and gain creators.

Given that 97% of OEMs maintained the data sets of their products in digital form, digitization of critical data related to asset status and performance as a gain creator and pain reliever for customers is well understood by OEMs. However, a considerable number of OEMs do not have a structured method of delivering critical information about their products to their customers in a definite time window. This can lead to some customers having access to necessary information earlier while others remain unaware and disappointed. Moreover, over one-third of OEMs (39%) do not use any digital method for delivering critical information. Therefore, the delivery process of critical information is not controlled and error-prone—a crucial customer pain point. A more structured approach to critical data delivery that covers all the customers would be an OEM gain creator, ensuring that the OEM is protected against customer dissatisfaction due to late delivery of critical product or service information.

Regarding predictive maintenance and digital servitization, an almost equal division exists between companies tracking machine performance at the customer site (42.4%) and companies that do not (39.3%). This insight is validated in the answers to the subsequent question, which show that 45.5% of OEMs offer some maintenance service based on remote monitoring, while 30.3% do not.

The unpredictable failure of OEM products at the customer site is an obvious pain for the customer. Unplanned downtime resulting from any built-in redundancy in the customer facility might mean significant disruption, loss of revenue, and customer goodwill for OEMs. By relieving this pain, OEMs can increase the market share of their product. Furthermore, by reclaiming some of the benefits derived from the reduced disruption for the customer, OEMs can servitize their products and increase their revenue. Thus, the servitization of predictive maintenance as a new product would be a gain creator for the OEM.

Understanding the barriers that prevent OEMs from relieving customer pain and creating customer gain is essential. Most OEMs are not ready to spend significant one-off investment to achieve predictive maintenance through connected sensors and machine intelligence. They favor a pay-as-you-go model to significant up-front investment to gain such a capability, preferring a fee per machine per year rather than a one-time expense.

OEM pain relievers and gain creators discussed above were integrated to develop the value proposition canvas for the OEMs and their customers (Fig. 7).

6.6 Value Proposition Canvas for the Tech Company and OEMs

The value proposition relationship between the Tech Company and the OEMs relies on the ability of the Tech Company to provide services (products, pain relievers, and gain creators) that assist OEMs with their jobs, pains, and gains. In this respect, the OEMs have specific jobs, the most important being the need to increase revenues through selling more products and services. Secondly, OEMs need to increase customer satisfaction by increasing the quality of their offerings, thereby increasing the economic output of their customers. More specifically, OEMs need to increase the throughput of their equipment at customer premises by reducing downtime and operator errors and ensuring correct and optimal operation. Additionally, OEMs need to enhance the service portfolio to grow revenue. Thus, digital servitization of relevant jobs creates service value for their customers. OEMs can achieve this by offering preventive and predictive maintenance services, digitizing the data related to their equipment, and creating robust and structured methods to share digital data with their customers.

The OEM pains are directly related to its customer's (end user) pains: Although mostly digitized, our survey indicated that the critical data is not communicated with customers in a timely and structured way, which may lead to unexpected equipment failure due to incomplete or outdated information, increased downtime, and ultimately customer dissatisfaction. Operator errors can further increase unscheduled machine downtime or reduce throughput. Moreover, servicing machinery at customer premises is expensive, especially outside business hours. Although preventive maintenance would be ideal in this context, the Tech Company is unaware of the probability of equipment failure even when the machine is connected and remotely accessible.

The OEM gains are also related to end user gains. Among the most important OEM gains are greater customer loyalty and sales due to the higher perceived quality of OEM offerings. Additionally, increased sales from smart service offerings such as predictive maintenance with the introduction of servitization could be a significant OEM gain. Moreover, predictive maintenance of customer equipment through remote connectivity and machine intelligence would reduce OEM or asset users' costs, especially if the contract is based on outputs. Better feedback on the present equipment's performance at the customer premises would also make them aware of next-generation products.

Our survey results indicate that OEMs are more interested in machine intelligence to improve customer communication and loyalty than in gaining additional service revenues. This does not necessarily mean OEMs do not care about additional revenues but is more indicative that the surveyed OEMs are lagging in the servitization area significantly. In this context, Tech Company's SaaS supports the creation of additional service revenues for the OEM, as well as more uptime and performance for end users. The survey results indicate that almost half of the OEMs do not use remote monitoring for their assets and do not offer maintenance services

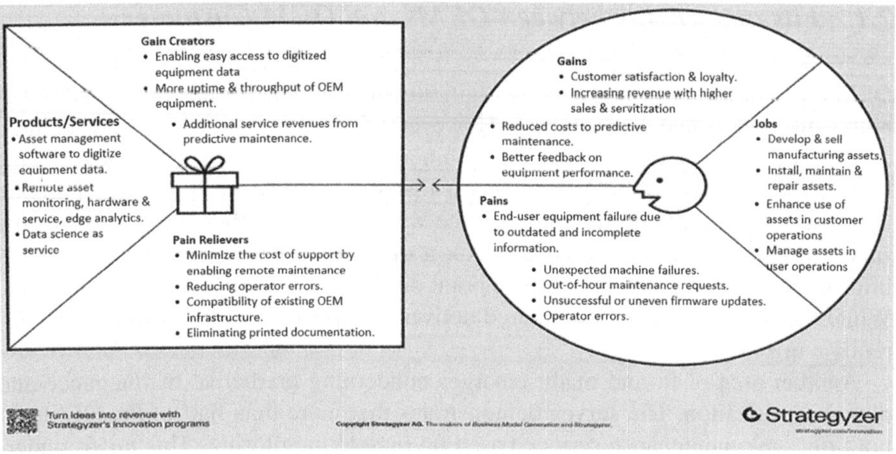

Fig. 8 Value proposition canvas for the Tech Company and the OEMs

using machine intelligence. Furthermore, end users encounter issues such as unplanned downtime or long integration time due to a lack of or unsuccessful updates on their assets bought from the OEM.

As discussed in the preceding section, Tech Company's current value proposition is centered on three key components: (i) asset management software, (ii) remote equipment monitoring hardware and service, and (iii) data science as a service. Considering the customer profile of OEMs, Tech Company could relieve their pains through its asset tracking and management software. High costs associated with customer visits/service trips could be reduced by enabling customers (end users) and OEM employees to access asset pages for information helpful in remotely solving maintenance issues, ensuring better machine utilization by customers, and minimizing after-hours requests of customer support.

Based on these insights, we can derive the Tech Company's current value proposition (Fig. 8). With better access to data sets to all stakeholders, the Tech Company can offer several pain relievers to OEMs, including minimizing support costs by enabling remote maintenance, reducing operator errors, eliminating printed documentation, and providing compatibility with the existing OEM infrastructure.

7 Discussion

Our analysis, conducted through the lens of the value proposition canvas, reveals both fits and misfits in the relationships between the OEMs, their customers (end users or asset owners), and the Tech Company. The OEM customer profile has been dissected in terms of products, pain relievers, and gain creators, shedding light on crucial aspects of their needs and priorities.

7.1 Fits and Misfits between OEMs and OEM Customers

OEMs recognize the significance of digitizing critical data for customers, acting as both gain creators and pain relievers. However, misfits arise regarding the structured delivery of vital product information within a defined time frame. The lack of such structured communication leads to access disparities to crucial information among customers, potentially disappointing some while favoring others. Furthermore, the survey highlights that many OEMs lack a digital approach to delivering critical information, creating a customer pain point due to unreliability and potential errors. While the potential gain of structured delivery is apparent, implementation is currently a misfit.

Another area of fit and misfit emerges concerning predictive maintenance and digital servitization. The survey demonstrates that more than half of the OEMs do not offer any maintenance service based on remote monitoring. This misfit underscores potentially unrealized benefits for both OEMs and customers. By addressing this misfit and offering predictive maintenance services, OEMs can relieve the pain of unexpected failures for customers, improving customer satisfaction and increasing market share. Simultaneously, OEMs can gain additional revenue through service offerings.

Most OEMs have already integrated or plan to integrate machine intelligence and/or remote connectivity in the short term. However, respondents' (~28%) indications to offer machine intelligence/remote connectivity in 1 to 6 months could also suggest these companies have an unrealistic view of the complexity of integrating machine intelligence with their services. Machine intelligence is only helpful with large data sets where the correlations between sensor readings and machine failures can be reliably detected. Accumulating and digitizing such large data sets would typically require more than 6 months. We can assume that respondents with a longer time horizon (>6 months) for integrating connectivity and machine intelligence into their assets are late adopters of remote monitoring technology and offering machine intelligence/predictive maintenance solutions is almost impossible without the connectivity infrastructure.

On the other hand, OEMs indicated that over 40% of their customers experienced unplanned downtime because of a lack of unsuccessful software updates. Customers struggle with such updates because they are primarily hardware vendors and lack required software quality controls. Moreover, they may be unable to tailor updates to their customers' configuration. The lack of adequate asset monitoring (including configuration information, installed sensor readings, or throughput) may also cause extra downtime for their customers and expensive customer site visits during system updates.

Most OEMs also recognized the lack of sufficient data for remote maintenance as a potential pain for their customers. The lack of data can refer to both preinstallation data about the product and data through remote monitoring during operation on the customer premises. The latter requires both remote connectivity and sensor placement to measure equipment performance during regular operation. Most

OEMs also seem aware that a short-term increase in customer revenue through maintenance or spare parts orders harms the OEMs' business in the long term. Further, the mismatch between the customer operating hours and the provision of maintenance services emerged as a prominent customer pain. The wait time for maintenance personnel could mean longer downtime and lost revenue for the customer. Finally, most OEMs perceive customer operator error as a common cause of machine issues leading to unplanned downtime, disruption, or potentially expensive maintenance calls. Therefore, this may be a significant customer pain.

7.2 Fits and Misfits between Tech Company and OEMs

The end user's pains identified in this study are potential opportunities for the OEMs to offer new products through servitization (e.g., via predictive maintenance) to relieve these pains, especially in developed markets with high labor costs. This, in turn, represents an opportunity for the Tech Company as a facilitator for OEMs. Therefore, Tech Company, as a facilitator for OEMs, aims to align its products, pain relievers, and gain creators with the OEM's needs. There is good evidence from research (He et al., 2020) and industry that customers care about a service such as those offered by the Tech Company. However, our study also identified several gaps between Tech Company and the OEMs, resulting in misfits arising in their current value proposition.

7.3 The Gap between Tech Company and the OEMs

Based on the value proposition design model, there are three stages of market fit (Osterwalder et al., 2015):

1. *Problem-solution fit*: The company has evidence that customers care about specific jobs, pains, and gains and has designed a value proposition that addresses them, but the company does not yet have customers.
2. *Product-market fit*: The company has evidence that their products and services, pain relievers, and gain creators are creating customer value and getting traction in the market and thus acquire customers more quickly than their competitors.
3. *Business model fit*: The company has evidence that its value proposition can be embedded in a profitable and scalable business model.

Currently, the Tech Company is in the problem-solution fit stage, trying to achieve a product-market fit, but it does not have customers yet. However, it seems to focus on elements that are not high priority or even relevant to OEMs, while those that are more relevant are not emphasized enough. Accordingly, Tech Company's value proposition and the OEM customer profile (see Fig. 8) were analyzed to understand misalignments between Tech Company products and OEM jobs, pains, and gains.

The Tech Company indeed addresses all customer (OEM) jobs with its value proposition. Their service furthers the information sharing between OEMs and their customers (end users), integrating connectivity to equipment, offering predictive maintenance services to OEM customers (end users or asset owners), and increasing the performance of assets for them. However, when it comes to pain and pain relievers, the value proposition of Tech Company focuses more on digitizing equipment data, which most OEMs are already performing on their own. Other pain relievers of Tech Company can further assist OEMs with their pains, but this is not emphasized in its value proposition. For instance, the availability of data asset pages to all stakeholders and an easy-to-use platform that can minimize the costs of service trips, support solving maintenance issues remotely, and improve operator performance are not clearly stated.

Furthermore, increasing uptime and performance for end users and creating additional service revenues help companies improve customer communication and loyalty. It also diminishes the level of disruption to the end user since these assets are located s at the end user's site. However, the Tech Company does not currently emphasize these gain creators. Consequently, OEMs may not correctly evaluate the value and effectiveness of Tech Company's pain relievers.

Therefore, while Tech Company's service addresses OEM's jobs, pains, and gains, it may not be apparent from the current value proposition to OEMs. This might explain why OEMs do not see the full value in purchasing and using Tech Company's SaaS. By redesigning Tech Company's value proposition based on the survey results and the created OEM customer profile, the company can better emphasize what is relevant for OEMs and achieve a better fit.

The renewed value proposition needs to focus less on digitizing data sets of assets and more on relieving OEMs' pains regarding costly service trips, after-hours support, machine operation, and operator mistakes, as well as solving maintenance issues remotely. These elements are all interconnected, as better machine usage and remote maintenance decrease the need for service trips, thus decreasing costs. With fewer requests for customer support, there will be less need for support outside of working hours. Regarding gain creators, the link between machine connectivity and improved customer communication and loyalty should be emphasized. By clarifying the beneficial nature of machine connectivity and predictive maintenance for both the OEM and the end user, the creation of additional service revenues for OEMs can be emphasized. Through this process, Tech Company can attain a product-market fit, effectively aligning their offerings with the needs and priorities of OEMs, thereby fostering successful collaborations and generating value in the relationship.

Value creation is an intangible asset that drives the success of the value network comprising OEMs, the Tech Company, and OEM customers. In this interconnected value network, value creation translates into enhanced customer satisfaction, increased revenues, and improved relationships. Addressing misfits and optimizing the value proposition allows for realizing potential gains, such as improved communication, reduced downtime, and increased market share. The role of Tech Company as a facilitator highlights the significance of creating value that resonates with OEMs' priorities and concerns. Ultimately, value creation acts as the glue that binds together the OEMs, the Tech Company, and OEM customers, creating a mutual relationship that benefits all parties involved. The path toward achieving a product-market fit for Tech Company rests on the ability to craft a value proposition that aligns seamlessly with the needs and aspirations of OEMs. The value network can thrive through this alignment, leading to mutual success and lasting partnerships.

The potential of digital servitization within OEM and TSP collaborations, while promising, also encounters several challenges that must be acknowledged. Firstly, the rapid pace of technological advancements can outstrip an organization's capacity to adapt and integrate new solutions, creating a gap between capabilities and potential benefits. This is particularly true for SMEs that may lack the resources or expertise to fully leverage advanced digital tools. Moreover, market dynamics, including competition, regulatory changes, and evolving customer expectations, can impact the implementation and success of digital servitization initiatives. In such an environment, the view of the current value proposition may require continuous alignment with market and technological trends. Moreover, the potential of digital servitization to reshape value chains is not insulated from the influence of regulatory frameworks and economic policies. In regions where data governance and privacy regulations are stringent, OEMs and TSPs face complex compliance environments, which could either block innovation or stimulate the development of robust digital solutions. On the contrary, in environments with supportive policies for digital transformation, OEMs and TSPs may find a suitable environment ground for scaling digital servitization models.

8 Conclusion

This chapter contributes to the existing literature by introducing and demonstrating the innovative use of the value proposition canvas as a tool for identifying and aligning relationships within value networks. By analyzing two interlocking value proposition canvases among multiple actors, including TSPs, OEMs, and end users, this study provides valuable insights into the dynamics of value creation and intangible asset development.

The novel approach of utilizing the value proposition canvas as a means to trace and understand value creation networks offers a new perspective on how organizations can optimize their collaborative efforts. This method not only enhances our understanding of the complex relationships between actors within value networks but also emphasizes the importance of aligning these relationships for maximizing the creation of value and intangible assets.

The findings presented in this article serve as a resource for researchers, practitioners, and organizations seeking to achieve a product-market fit and enhance their competitiveness in contemporary business landscapes. By emphasizing the significance of effective collaboration and communication within value networks and by leveraging intangible assets through aligned value propositions, this research opens new opportunities for future studies in the field of business strategy and innovation.

It is also important to consider the broader research surrounding digital transformation challenges. While our study highlights the benefits of digital servitization and technology outsourcing, alternative viewpoints emphasize significant barriers faced by SMEs due to resource constraints. Del Giudice et al. (2021b) discuss these concerns related to costs, resources, and technological adaptation that may inhibit SMEs from fully leveraging smart maintenance and digital transformations. Furthermore, the effectiveness of predictive maintenance, as argued by Zonta et al. (2020), is not universally positive and varies greatly depending on industry-specific factors, technologies used, and data quality. Moreover, the concept of value cocreation is beneficial in many contexts as our research suggests, but it is also met with skepticism regarding its complexity and potential for conflict among stakeholders, which may dilute its benefits. This perspective is supported by Cenamor et al. (2019b), who highlight the challenges in managing cocreation processes effectively. In addition, there are organizational and cultural barriers that may prevent the full utilization of Industry 4.0 technologies, necessitating substantial organizational adaptation to realize potential benefits, a challenge discussed by Hanelt et al. (2015). Additionally, Raddats et al. (2017) provide a critical view on the economic impacts of servitization, suggesting potential negative consequences such as an overreliance on service revenues, which may not be as stable as product-based revenues.

9 Limitations and Scope for Further Research

This cross-sectional study is carried out in a representative sample of 33 companies in the region of North Brabant, in the Netherlands. Although the selected sample size is highly homogenous and concentrated, a bigger sample size, a longitudinal or a comparative study of different regions or industries, could yield additional perspectives to see how the context affects value cocreation in big data networks. Additionally, further research can also include whether an industry benchmark or standards can be applied to serve as a frame of reference to see how relationships in big data networks hold in comparison to our study.

Acknowledgments We extend our gratitude to Frank Marks for his invaluable contributions to the data analysis and insights into industry dynamics.

References

Baines, T., & Lightfoot, H. (2012). Made to serve. *John Wiley & Sons Ltd.* https://doi.org/10.1002/9781119207955

Belkadi, F., Messaadia, M., Bernard, A., & Baudry, D. (2016). Collaboration management framework for OEM—Suppliers relationships: A trust-based conceptual approach. *Enterprise Information Systems, 11*(7), 1018–1042. https://doi.org/10.1080/17517575.2016.1250166

Biem, A., & Caswell, N. (2008). A value network model for strategic analysis. In *Proceedings of the 41st Annual Hawaii International Conference on System Sciences (HICSS 2008)* (p. 361). https://doi.org/10.1109/HICSS.2008.43

Bontis, N. (1998). Intellectual capital: An exploratory study that develops measures and models. *Management Decision, 36*(2), 63–76. https://doi.org/10.1108/00251749810204142

Bovet, D., Martha, J., & Consulting, M. M. (2000). *Value nets: Breaking the supply chain to unlock hidden profits*. John Wiley & Sons Ltd.. https://books.google.com/books?id=dJsFh-LIKEkC

Burton, J., Story, V. M., Raddats, C., & Zolkiewski, J. (2017). Overcoming the challenges that hinder new service development by manufacturers with diverse services strategies. *International Journal of Production Economics, 192*, 29–39. https://doi.org/10.1016/j.ijpe.2017.01.013

Cenamor, J., Parida, V., & Wincent, J. (2019a). How entrepreneurial SMEs compete through digital platforms: The roles of digital platform capability, network capability and ambidexterity. *Journal of Business Research, 100*, 196–206. https://doi.org/10.1016/j.jbusres.2019.03.035

Cenamor, J., Parida, V., & Wincent, J. (2019b). How entrepreneurial SMEs compete through digital platforms: The roles of digital platform capability, network capability and ambidexterity. *Journal of Business Research, 100*, 196. https://doi.org/10.1016/j.jbusres.2019.03.035

Dahlquist, S. H., & Griffith, D. A. (2014). Multidyadic industrial channels: Understanding component supplier profits and original equipment manufacturer behavior. *Journal of Marketing, 78*(4), 59–79. https://doi.org/10.1509/jm.13.0174

Dath, T. N. S., Rajendran, C., & Narashiman, K. (2010). An empirical study on supply chain management in India: The perspective of original equipment manufacturers and suppliers. *European Journal of Industrial Engineering, 4*(1), 2–39. https://doi.org/10.1504/ejie.2010.029568

Del Giudice, M., Scuotto, V., Papa, A., Tarba, S. Y., Bresciani, S., & Warkentin, M. (2021a). A self-tuning model for smart manufacturing SMEs: Effects on digital innovation. *Journal of Product Innovation Management, 38*(1), 68–89. https://doi.org/10.1111/jpim.12560

Del Giudice, M., Scuotto, V., Papa, A., Tarba, S. Y., Bresciani, S., & Warkentin, M. (2021b). A self-tuning model for smart manufacturing SMEs: Effects on digital innovation. *Journal of Product Innovation Management, 38*(1). https://doi.org/10.1111/jpim.12560

Dey, B. L., Pandit, A., Saren, M., Bhowmick, S., & Woodruffe-Burton, H. (2016). Co-creation of value at the bottom of the pyramid: Analysing Bangladeshi farmers' use of mobile telephony. *Journal of Retailing and Consumer Services, 29*, 40. https://doi.org/10.1016/j.jretconser.2015.10.009

Dyer, W. G., & Wilkins, A. L. (1991). Better stories, not better constructs, to generate better theory: A rejoinder to Eisenhardt. *Academy of Management Review, 16*(3), 613. https://doi.org/10.5465/amr.1991.4279492

Echeverri, P., & Skålén, P. (2011). Co-creation and co-destruction: A practice-theory based study of interactive value formation. *Marketing Theory, 11*(3), 351. https://doi.org/10.1177/1470593111408181

Faroukhi, A. Z., El Alaoui, I., Gahi, Y., & Amine, A. (2020). Big data monetization throughout big data value chain: A comprehensive review. *Journal of Big Data, 7*(1), 3. https://doi.org/10.1186/s40537-019-0281-5

Fliess, S., & Lexutt, E. (2019). How to be successful with servitization—Guidelines for research and management. *Industrial Marketing Management, 78*, 58–75. https://doi.org/10.1016/j.indmarman.2017.11.012

Freytag, P. V., & Young, L. (2017). *Collaborative research design: Working with business for meaningful findings*. In Collaborative Research Design: Working with Business for Meaningful Findings. https://doi.org/10.1007/978-981-10-5008-4.

Gatica, C. P., Koester, M., Gaukstern, T., Berlin, E., & Meyer, M. (2016). *An industrial analytics approach to predictive maintenance for machinery applications*. IEEE International Conference on Emerging Technologies and Factory Automation, ETFA, 2016-November. https://doi.org/10.1109/ETFA.2016.7733608.

Ghaleb, M., Taghipour, S., Sharifi, M., & Zolfagharinia, H. (2020). Integrated production and maintenance scheduling for a single degrading machine with deterioration-based failures. *Computers & Industrial Engineering, 143*, 106432. https://doi.org/10.1016/j.cie.2020.106432

Gibson, R. (2023). *International trade fairs and inter-firm knowledge flows: Understanding patterns of convergence-divergence in the technological specializations of firms*. In International trade fairs and inter-firm knowledge flows: Understanding patterns of convergence-divergence in the technological specializations of firms. https://doi.org/10.1007/978-3-031-20557-6.

Gröger, C. (2018). Building an industry 4.0 analytics platform. *Datenbank-Spektrum, 18*(1), 5–14. https://doi.org/10.1007/s13222-018-0273-1

Haarman, M., Mulders, M., & Vassiliadis, C. (2017). Predictive maintenance 4.0: Predict the unpredictable. *PwC and Mainnovation, 4*.

Hanelt, A., Piccinini, E., Gregory, R. W., Hildebrandt, B., & Lutz, M. (2015). *Digital transformation of primarily physical industries exploring the impact of digital trends on business models of automobile manufacturers*. 12th International Conference on Wirtschaftsinformatik, April 2016.

He, L., Xue, M., & Gu, B. (2020). Internet-of-things enabled supply chain planning and coordination with big data services: Certain theoretic implications. *Journal of Management Science and Engineering, 5*(1), 1–22. https://doi.org/10.1016/j.jmse.2020.03.002

Khanra, S., Dhir, A., Parida, V., & Kohtamäki, M. (2021). Servitization research: A review and bibliometric analysis of past achievements and future promises. *Journal of Business Research, 131*, 151–166. https://doi.org/10.1016/j.jbusres.2021.03.056

Kolberg, D., & Zühlke, D. (2015). Lean automation enabled by industry 4.0 technologies. *IFAC-PapersOnLine, 48*(3), 1870–1875. https://doi.org/10.1016/j.ifacol.2015.06.359

Lee, C. K. M., Cao, Y., & Ng, K. K. H. (2016). *Big data analytics for predictive maintenance strategies*. In Supply Chain Management in the Big Data Era. https://doi.org/10.4018/978-1-5225-0956-1.ch004.

Lee, J., Ni, J., Singh, J., Jiang, B., Azamfar, M., & Feng, J. (2020). Intelligent maintenance systems and predictive manufacturing. *Journal of Manufacturing Science and Engineering, Transactions of the ASME, 142*(11). https://doi.org/10.1115/1.4047856

Lenka, S., Parida, V., & Wincent, J. (2017). Digitalization capabilities as enablers of value co-creation in Servitizing firms. *Psychology and Marketing, 34*(1), 92. https://doi.org/10.1002/mar.20975

Lusch, R. F., & Nambisan, S. (2015). Service innovation: A service-dominant logic perspective. *MIS Quarterly, 39*(1), 155–175. https://doi.org/10.25300/misq/2015/39.1.07

Mont, O. K. (2002). Clarifying the concept of product–service system. *Journal of Cleaner Production, 10*(3), 237–245. https://doi.org/10.1016/s0959-6526(01)00039-7

Morgan, T., Anokhin, S. A., & Wincent, J. (2019). New service development by manufacturing firms: Effects of customer participation under environmental contingencies. *Journal of Business Research, 104*, 497–505. https://doi.org/10.1016/j.jbusres.2019.06.017

Mostafa, R. B. (2015). Value co-creation in industrial cities: A strategic source of competitive advantages. *Journal of Strategic Marketing, 24*(2), 144. https://doi.org/10.1080/0965254X.2015.1076885

Nacchia, M., Fruggiero, F., Lambiase, A., & Bruton, K. (2021). A systematic mapping of the advancing use of machine learning techniques for predictive maintenance in the manufacturing sector. In applied sciences (Switzerland) (Vol. 11, Issue 6). https://doi.org/10.3390/app11062546.

Narkhede, B. E., Raut, R. D., Roy, M., Yadav, V. S., & Gardas, B. (2020). Implementation barriers to lean-agile manufacturing systems for original equipment manufacturers: An integrated decision-making approach. *The International Journal of Advanced Manufacturing Technology, 108*(9–10), 3193–3206. https://doi.org/10.1007/s00170-020-05486-5

Nunes, M. L., Pereira, A. C., & Alves, A. C. (2017). Smart products development approaches for industry 4.0. *Procedia Manufacturing, 13*, 1215–1222. https://doi.org/10.1016/j.promfg.2017.09.035

Osterwalder, A., et al. (2015). *Value proposition design: How to create products and services customers want*. John Wiley & Sons.

Parviainen, P., Tihinen, M., Kääriäinen, J., & Teppola, S. (2017). Tackling the digitalization challenge: How to benefit from digitalization in practice. *International Journal of Information Systems and Project Management, 5*(1), 63. https://doi.org/10.12821/ijispm050104

Paschou, T., Rapaccini, M., Adrodegari, F., & Saccani, N. (2020). Digital servitization in manufacturing: A systematic literature review and research agenda. *Industrial Marketing Management, 89*, 278–292. https://doi.org/10.1016/j.indmarman.2020.02.012

Patwardhan, A., Verma, A. K., & Kumar, U. (2016). A survey on predictive maintenance through big data. *Lecture Notes in Mechanical Engineering*. https://doi.org/10.1007/978-3-319-23597-4_31

Peppard, J., & Rylander, A. (2006). From value chain to value network. *European Management Journal, 24*(2–3), 128–141. https://doi.org/10.1016/j.emj.2006.03.003

Pereira, A. C., & Romero, F. (2017). A review of the meanings and the implications of the industry 4.0 concept. *Procedia Manufacturing, 13*, 1206–1214. https://doi.org/10.1016/j.promfg.2017.09.032

Pertselakis, M., Lampathaki, F., & Petrali, P. (2019). Predictive maintenance in a digital factory shop-floor: Data mining on historical and operational data coming from manufacturers' information systems. *Lecture Notes in Business Information Processing, 349*. https://doi.org/10.1007/978-3-030-20948-3_11

Pil, F., & Holweg, M. (2006). Evolving from value chain to value grid. *MIT Sloan Management Review, 47*, 72–80.

Rabelo, R. J., Gusmeroli, S., Camarinha-Matos, L. M., & Picard, W. (2008). *The Ecolead collaborative business infrastructure for networked organizations*. 451–462. https://doi.org/10.1007/978-0-387-84837-2_47.

Rabelo, R. J., Ruiz, H. A., Cancian, M. H., Camarinha-Matos, L. M., Afsarmanesh, H., & Ortiz, A. (2020). *For a dynamic web services discovery model for open ecosystems of software providers*. 83–97. https://doi.org/10.1007/978-3-030-62412-5_7.

Raddats, C., Zolkiewski, J., Story, V. M., Burton, J., Baines, T., & Ziaee Bigdeli, A. (2017). Interactively developed capabilities: Evidence from dyadic servitization relationships. *International Journal of Operations and Production Management, 37*(3), 382. https://doi.org/10.1108/IJOPM-08-2015-0512

Ramaswamy, V. (2008). Co-creating value through customers' experiences: The Nike case. *Strategy and Leadership, 36*(5), 9. https://doi.org/10.1108/10878570810902068

Ren, S., & Zhao, X. (2015). *A predictive maintenance method for products based on big data analysis*. https://doi.org/10.2991/meita-15.2015.71.

Rokhforoz, P., Gjorgiev, B., Sansavini, G., & Fink, O. (2021). Multi-agent maintenance scheduling based on the coordination between central operator and decentralized producers in an electricity market. *Reliability Engineering & System Safety, 210*, 107495. https://doi.org/10.1016/j.ress.2021.107495

Saunders, A., & Brynjolfsson, E. (2016). Valuing information technology related intangible assets. *MIS Quarterly, 40*(1), 83–110. https://www.jstor.org/stable/26628385

Senyo, P. K., Liu, K., & Effah, J. (2019). Digital business ecosystem: Literature review and a framework for future research. *International Journal of Information Management, 47*, 52–64. https://doi.org/10.1016/j.ijinfomgt.2019.01.002

Sezer, E., Romero, D., Guedea, F., Macchi, M., & Emmanouilidis, C. (2018). An industry 4.0-enabled low cost predictive maintenance approach for SMEs. In *2018 IEEE International Conference on Engineering, Technology and Innovation (ICE/ITMC)* (pp. 1–8). https://doi.org/10.1109/ICE.2018.8436307

Siggelkow, N. (2007). Persuasion with case studies. *Academy of Management Journal, 50*(1), 20. https://doi.org/10.5465/AMJ.2007.24160882

Sobaszek, Ł., Gola, A., & Świć, A. (2020). Time-based machine failure prediction in multi-machine manufacturing systems. *Eksploatacja i Niezawodnosc, 22*(1). https://doi.org/10.17531/ein.2020.1.7

Sveiby, K. E. (1997). *The new organizational wealth: Managing & Measuring Knowledge-based Assets*. Berrett-Koehler Publishers. https://www.bkconnection.com/books/title/the-new-organizational-wealth?

Vargo, S. L., & Lusch, R. F. (2008). Service-dominant logic: Continuing the evolution. *Journal of the Academy of Marketing Science, 36*(1), 1. https://doi.org/10.1007/s11747-007-0069-6

Wagner, C., & Hellingrath, B. (2021). Supporting the implementation of predictive maintenance. *International Journal of Prognostics and Health Management, 12*(1). https://doi.org/10.36001/ijphm.2021.v12i1.2933

Yin, R. K. (2013). Case study research: Design and methods. *Applied Social Research Methods Series, 18*(2), 54. https://doi.org/10.1097/00001610-199503000-00004

Zhai, E., Shi, Y., & Gregory, M. (2007). The growth and capability development of electronics manufacturing service (EMS) companies. *International Journal of Production Economics, 107*(1), 1–19. https://doi.org/10.1016/j.ijpe.2006.03.009

Zonta, T., da Costa, C. A., da Rosa Righi, R., de Lima, M. J., da Trindade, E. S., & Li, G. P. (2020). Predictive maintenance in the industry 4.0: A systematic literature review. *Computers & Industrial Engineering, 150*, 106889. https://doi.org/10.1016/j.cie.2020.106889

Intellectual Capital as Strategic Tool for Managing the Dynamic Relationship Between Knowledge Losses and Gains

Lídia Neumann Potrich, Graciele Tonial, Paulo Maurício Selig, Jaime Miranda Junior, and José Leomar Todesco

Abstract Global rapid transformations require continuous and systematic adaptations of organizations. To this end, intangible assets play a central role in organizational sustainability and competitiveness. Considering the intrinsic elements of the company's structure, corporate relationships, and professionals, knowledge is considered a critical success factor. Due to various reasons, this knowledge can be lost over time, posing an organizational risk. To mitigate the impact, it is relevant to create reactive and preventive actions. The risk of knowledge loss is constant and, therefore, needs to be assessed more dynamically. It is important to consider some seemingly contradictory but complementary aspects, such as knowledge gains. Analyzing the relationship between knowledge losses and gains from the perspective of intellectual capital enables the management of intellectual capital to create strategies for maximizing knowledge gains in the face of the risk of loss. Leveraging gains can provide conditions for organizations to remain enduring and adaptive. Therefore, the central objective of this chapter is to analyze how scientific studies relate to knowledge losses and gains and how they are interrelated with the intellectual capital of organizations. It aims to classify knowledge losses and gains within the structures of intellectual capital to identify new approaches to intellectual capital management, considering the analysis of knowledge assets in an expanded manner. Intellectual capital management practices are presented as a way to actively address these contradictions.

L. N. Potrich (✉) · P. M. Selig · J. M. Junior · J. L. Todesco
Engineering and Knowledge Management, Federal University of Santa Catarina (USFC), Florianópolis, Brazil
e-mail: lidia.potrich@gmail.com; pauloselig@gmail.com; jaimemjunior@gmail.com; tite@stela.org.br

G. Tonial
University of the West of Santa Catarina (UNOESC), Joaçaba, Brazil
e-mail: graciele.tonial@unoesc.edu.br

F. Matos et al. (eds.), *Intellectual Capital in a Global Business Landscape*, Contributions to Management Science, https://doi.org/10.1007/978-3-031-86362-2_9

1 Introduction

In the current global scenario, characterized by continuous and multifaceted changes, organizational agility demands that organizations pursue strategic alternatives for their survival through rapid adaptations. The ability to continuously adjust a business's strategic direction is a critical factor (Eller et al., 2020; Holbeche, 2023). According to Hirose and Sawaragi (2020) and Reiman et al. (2021), the sophistication of digital technologies, the data revolution, the digitization of market and work relations, and the demands and challenges of the new society contribute to factors that increase organizational complexity. These changes compel companies to seek strategic alternatives to adapt and remain economically viable.

In conjunction with the turbulent and dynamic environment, it is evident that the digitization of physical assets and work processes enables companies to advance their information systems (Ribeiro et al., 2021). This transformation impacts the agility of production systems while also increasing vulnerability to disruptions in communication and information—a factor that can lead to knowledge loss. Consequently, it is understood that knowledge management practices can help mitigate these losses, as the management of intellectual capital aims to create and develop intellectual assets through strategies that enhance organizational value (Stefano et al., 2014).

Considering this scenario, it becomes necessary to observe the risks that affect organizations, such as the loss of knowledge resources. Companies face disruptions in their processes, with impacts at both strategic and operational levels (Daghfous et al., 2023).

Digitalization can bring many benefits to knowledge workers; however, the destruction of value appears to be stronger, as noted by Vuori et al. (2019). The results of this study demonstrate that knowledge utilization is negatively affected by information overload, making knowledge retrieval difficult. In other words, according to the authors, these factors impede the efficient use of organizational knowledge. Additionally, Smuts (2024) suggests that the mechanization of learning and knowledge creation—stemming from digital technology—limits the capacity of human thought. Consequently, the development and enhancement of tacit knowledge are lost.

Durst and Leyer (2014) observe that a significant portion of knowledge within organizations is of a tacit nature, residing in the skills and competencies of individuals. Therefore, the risks of knowledge loss are substantial, especially if companies do not create strategies for sharing among organizational members. To reduce this risk, the authors propose strategies for identifying knowledge risks associated with people, which serve as the starting point for the creation of specific processes for knowledge sharing and management.

Knowledge loss is a scarcely explored aspect in the strategic management of organizations, as noted by Massingham (2008). The sequence of their studies supports that knowledge loss has a negative impact on organizational issues, interfering with its performance. Research conducted over 5 years in a public institution indicates decreased productivity and performance, resource cuts, a breakdown in customer trust, decreased quality and quantity of work, increased time needed to acquire skills and knowledge, and slower task completion. Additionally, it heightens the risk associated with activities and reduces the ability to manage risks. Ultimately, knowledge loss creates knowledge gaps, decreasing the organizational knowledge base (Massingham, 2018).

However, Wensley and Navarro (2015) assert that through the identification of knowledge losses, management can counteract negative impacts, encouraging them to create change processes and incorporate strategic knowledge. Knowledge loss is a potential risk but serves as a source for the creation of new knowledge structures. Additionally, Massingham (2018) suggests that employee turnover fosters growth for those remaining and allows for the introduction of new knowledge. Therefore, there are knowledge gains for organizational structures. Thus, it is understood that managing knowledge systematically, intentionally, and explicitly is crucial for maximizing efficiency and return on the organization's knowledge assets (Wiig, 1997).

Potrich et al. (2022) assert that investing in resources that enhance knowledge across all organizational spheres strengthens organizational resilience, considering the challenges imposed by current transformations. In this context, intellectual capital gains prominence. It consists of a combination of intangibles capable of generating efficiency, growth, renewal, and organizational stability.

As knowledge is shared, these resources grow (Sveiby, 2001), thus becoming a measure of security for organizational survival. Knowledge, the more it is shared, the more it grows, whereas tangible assets, the more they are used, the more they diminish. Lerro et al. (2014) acknowledge that organizations' ability to create value is no longer solely linked to robust and efficient systems. It is increasingly related to defining adaptable systems, capable of leveraging their intellectual capital and dealing with emerging market demands and challenges through changes and transformations.

Changes occur on a large scale and impact organizations. Transformations in operational environments, such as digitization, coping with the COVID-19 pandemic, remote work, and sustainability maintenance, demand new understandings of the nature of intangibles, such as intellectual capital (Kianto & Cabrilo, 2022). Because value creation is closely related to intellectual capital. Organizational success depends on the management of its knowledge resources (Stamenkova & Trpeski, 2020).

Furthermore, by highlighting the impact that knowledge loss brings to organizations, it is important to touch upon the potential gains they have. According to Nonaka and Takeuchi (2021), the current scenario in which companies are embedded, where growth needs drive high-speed changes, requires modifications in the traditional approach to their strategies. According to the authors, surviving at this crossroads and in this era of unknowns demands new foundations, purposes, and strategies from companies. For this, they suggest the adoption of new practices, such as recognizing dynamic duality. In other words, acknowledging that seemingly distinct and opposing elements are mutually complementary.

Thus, while the risks of knowledge loss may lead to negative outcomes, if the right strategy is applied to mitigate them, they can also represent significant opportunities for cost savings or business development. In this way, this exploratory chapter identifies the relationship between knowledge losses and gains and intellectual capital, presenting strategies for managing intellectual capital to enhance knowledge gains and mitigate loss. According to Daghfous et al. (2023), the impact of knowledge loss can be mitigated by organizational knowledge management practices and initiatives. With this, the aim is to support management in making informed decisions, considering aspects that enable greater conditions for organizational adaptation and survival. Additionally, it seeks to present new relationships for intellectual capital management considering the dynamism of the environment and high competition.

2 Intellectual Capital and Management Intellectual Capital

The term intellectual capital (IC) is used broadly (Petty & Guthrie, 2000), and there are many definitions regarding its conceptualization (Ferenhof et al., 2015). According to Buenechea-Elberdin et al. (2018), research on IC has evolved through three stages: from the 1980s to the mid-1990s, the focus was on raising awareness and demonstrating the importance of the topic; from the mid-1990s to the early 2000s, the objective was to manage and measure IC and analyze its influence on financial results; and the third stage involved understanding IC in practice.

Edvinsson (2013) indicates that there are two perspectives regarding IC analysis. In the first, it is considered as invisible elements that need to be accounted for and measured. In the second, it is perceived as a strategic ecosystem capable of creating sustainable value. This research considers the strategic value of IC, aligning with the author's second perspective, which views intellectual capital as a strategic asset. It also aligns with the third wave of studies, which analyze its pragmatic aspect.

Considering the second view, the main authors in the field are Edvinsson and Sullivan (1996), Sveiby (1997), Roos and Roos (1997), Stewart (1997), Edvinsson and Malone (1998), and Bontis (1998). Their definitions are similar. They all understand IC as an intangible organizational resource in which knowledge is the key element. It is knowledge that creates value, competitive advantage, and sustainability.

The creation of intellectual capital, according to Nahapiet and Ghoshal (1998), occurs through the process of generating new knowledge (arising from interactions) and the combination of existing knowledge. This combination arises from experiences and exchanges among different parties, involving the transfer of individual and/or collective knowledge.

Corroborating this, Kianto (2007) states that IC can be understood as a reservoir of knowledge. Even though it is intangible, it can be located and identified, making it the organization's property. From another perspective, it is understood that knowledge emerges from interactions among people. Its essence lies in the organization's ability to develop and leverage intangible assets for value creation. Thus, it is a continuous and emergent process (Kianto, 2007; Kianto & Waajakoski, 2010).

The study by Ferenhof et al. (2015) identified 83 models for identifying the dimensions of intellectual capital. However, the research asserts that the three main dimensions of analysis are human capital (HC), structural capital (SC), and relational capital (RC).

Human capital refers to the knowledge of individuals, manifesting in competencies, skills, qualifications, know-how, innovation, and creativity (Edvinsson & Malone, 1998; Guthrie et al., 2012; Kianto & Cabrilo, 2022; Petty & Guthrie, 2000; Sveiby, 2001). It is considered the primary intangible resource because people are the main actors in businesses (Edvinsson, 2013; Kianto et al., 2013; Sveiby, 2001). According to Bontis (1998), HC is essentially a tacit knowledge, which is difficult to be codified by organizations.

Recently, Kianto and Cabrilo (2022) present new propositions for IC. Regarding human capital (HC), they argue that digital competencies are crucial, given the skills required to work in the digital age. Self-leadership is also deemed a valuable competency, considering digital work contexts and performance needs. Lastly, temporary work or other forms of employment should be recognized as significant aspects of HC. According to the authors, workers who create value for a company should be counted as part of its human capital, regardless of having a formal contract with the company.

Structural capital pertains to the values invested in organizational structures and internal processes. It represents the accumulated, embedded, and distributed knowledge within organizations and their systems, encompassing culture, management systems, and information systems (Bontis, 1998; Edvinsson & Malone, 1998; Guthrie et al., 2012; Kianto & Cabrilo, 2022; Stewart, 1997). Kianto and Cabrilo (2022) suggest that open digital culture and entrepreneurial culture are important aspects for value creation, forming a crucial facet of structural capital to be considered. This necessitates active knowledge and information management.

Lastly, relational capital is recognized in the values invested in relationships, focusing on social connections and networks that bind them (Kianto & Waajakoski, 2010). Knowledge is available through the relationship networks among its members (internal relational capital) and is embedded in the company's external relationships, such as with customers, suppliers, partners, stakeholders, and other connections (Bontis, 1998; Edvinsson & Malone, 1998; Kianto & Waajakoski, 2010). Concerning external RC, Kianto and Cabrilo (2022) include relationships with value cocreators (such as users, freelancers, virtual teams, and temporary workers), which are essential for open innovation.

The management of intellectual capital (ICM) allows companies to evaluate the potential of intangible value within organizations. Hence, it is crucial to define and integrate systematic intellectual capital management goals with knowledge processes. ICM is about constructing and managing intangible assets from the perspective of the organization's management strategies (Wiig, 1997).

According to Stefano et al. (2014) and Lerro et al. (2014), the objective of ICM is to create and develop intellectual assets through strategies that enhance the organization's value. To realize gains, it is necessary to transform knowledge domains into profitable products and services, as well as dynamically renew capabilities.

ICM is complex because there is no perfect method for its measurement (Matos, 2013). Therefore, the development and exploration of knowledge assets remain a challenge for companies. As per Lerro et al. (2014), intellectual capital management often arises from sporadic or singular actions and does not always respond to planned strategies. According to them, many companies do not deeply identify, evaluate, or measure the results and impacts of intellectual capital management projects and initiatives. However, performance and competitive advantage resulting from intellectual capital are only possible through its management (Lerro et al., 2014; Matos, 2013; Matos & Lopes, 2008).

Stefano et al. (2014) state that culture is the central element in intellectual capital management. It provides the conditions and enables the creation and retention of knowledge. According to the authors, knowledge only grows and develops when there are effective actions.

It is important that ICM strategies are communicated throughout the entire organization since it involves the connection of all its elements and segments. Overcoming the challenge of integrating skills, experience, and organizational culture is necessary to develop capabilities and competencies in a way that makes it difficult for other organizations to replicate them (Mitchell, 2010). As such, some ICM practices enhance performance and provide competitive advantages. Table 9.1 provides some examples.

Table 9.1 Intellectual capital management practices

Dimensions	Management practices	Authors
Human capital	Investments in education; fostering creativity and innovation among employees; competency development; tacit knowledge-sharing practices; ongoing training programs	Edvinsson and Malone (1998), Stewart (1997), Sullivan (1998), Bontis (2001), Matos and Lopes (2008), Kianto et al. (2013), Stefano et al. (2014) and Cassol et al. (2016)
Structural capital	Knowledge-sharing and creation practices; adoption of new technologies; waste control mechanisms; leadership development; intellectual property creation; investment in databases; organizational culture dissemination practices; process improvements; tools and strategies that transform individual knowledge into assets; communities of practice; knowledge mapping development	Edvinsson and Malone (1998), Stewart (1997), Matos and Lopes (2008), Kianto et al. (2013), Stefano et al. (2014) and Cassol et al. (2016)
Relational capital	Prospecting new customers; building stable organizational and individual relationships; customer satisfaction assessment; participation in associations and events; partnership development	Edvinsson and Malone (1998), Stewart (1997), Matos and Lopes (2008), Kianto et al. (2013), Stefano et al. (2014) and Cassol et al. (2016)

Authors (2024)

3 Knowledge Loss and Knowledge Gain

The analysis of knowledge losses and gains stems from the recognition of the importance of dynamic duality, as observed by Nonaka and Takeuchi (2021). It pertains to elements that appear distinct and opposing but interact and exchange with each other, creating something new through experience. Therefore, it is important to actively adopt and cultivate contradictions, paradoxes, and opposites, making this duality part of the organizational culture.

Considering the strategic importance of knowledge for organizations, knowledge loss is considered an organizational risk. Risks associated with knowledge refer to the likelihood of any loss stemming from the identification, storage, or protection of knowledge, which decreases the strategic or organizational efficiency of the company (Perrott, 2007). According to Ferenhof et al. (2015), it is fundamental for organizations to avoid such risks, as knowledge enables them to innovate their business processes, goods, and services.

However, Billington (1997) asserts that if risk assessments are more thorough, not only negative consequences but also positive ones can be identified. The same aspect can have different meanings depending on the organization. The author points to growth and improvement opportunities arising from the use of innovation, entrepreneurship, and initiative as one of the dimensions of risk. In addition, Jennex (2014) states that, although risks to knowledge management may lead to negative outcomes, they also present opportunities for the economy and business development.

Regarding knowledge loss, it is considered as the "diminished capacity for effective action or decision-making in a specific organizational context (p.13). Loss causes both material and immaterial impacts, occurring at the individual, group, and organizational levels" (Delong & Storey, 2004).

According to Jennex (2014), studies that present the origins and causes of organizational knowledge loss reveal retirement, turnover, temporary and/or permanent incapacity, changes in position or role, failure to capture critical knowledge, failure in knowledge repositories, and forgetfulness as the main aspects. Additionally, problems in databases that lead to information exclusion, document losses, lack of standardization, and documentation about processes also result in knowledge loss (Abdul-Rahman et al., 2007; Durst & Leyer, 2014; Massingham, 2018).

It is recognized that these internal factors pose risks to knowledge. However, other studies indicate that factors external to the organization can also lead to knowledge loss, for example, mergers, outsourcing, or acquisitions. This occurs when these strategic changes disrupt the sequence of processes or products, creating knowledge gaps. Moreover, when there is inadequate management of these processes, friction arises among the new team members, leading to professional exits and losses of critical knowledge after the completion of the outsourcing contract (Alaranta & Jarvenpaa, 2010; Alaranta & Martela, 2012; Cha et al., 2009; Nkwocha et al., 2010).

Knowledge loss significantly impacts the organization, especially knowledge-intensive companies, as knowledge is a source for productive processes. Studies conducted in this context point to a decrease in organizational performance and innovative capacity (Sulaiman et al., 2016). The loss of tacit knowledge leads to issues in product development, propensity for errors, decreased productivity, and customer problems (Licorish & Macdonell, 2015; Nassif & Robillard, 2017; Nkwocha et al., 2010; Rigby et al., 2016).

According to Massingham (2008), the primary strategy for measuring the impact of knowledge loss is to identify how key employees create organizational value from their knowledge and how the remaining employees utilize it in their work. In his study, he identified that knowledge loss resulted in losses in human capital (through decreased productivity and output), losses in structural capital (due to decreased organizational learning), losses in relational capital (from disruption of external knowledge flows), and losses in social capital (as knowledge loss impacted contributions to organizational memory).

Sumbal et al. (2018) identify that the loss of valuable employees brings both financial and nonfinancial consequences, such as the competitive advantage of organizations. Jennex (2014) states that the costs for replacing knowledge workers are high as they possess specialized knowledge, which typically requires significant investments.

Due to the negative impacts of knowledge loss, some companies develop measures to control this risk or create processes that ensure organizational knowledge, generating knowledge security strategies (Potrich, 2019). Thus, the risk of loss can also produce positive factors, although few studies delve into and analyze this perspective and these outcomes.

Stauss et al. (2011) address the relationship between organizational losses and gains through the merger process between two organizations. They identified gains and losses of both tacit and explicit knowledge. However, the greatest gains were at the level of explicit knowledge, while losses were at the level of tacit knowledge, corroborating with the aforementioned authors. To mitigate losses, the authors suggest that strategies for capturing essential information and disseminating knowledge should be implemented throughout the merger process, before, during, and after.

Wensley and Navarro (2015) and Massingham (2018) indicate that the departure of professionals from the company opens up opportunities for new employees to incorporate their knowledge into the organization, bringing new insights to the organizational structures. Potrich (2019) suggests that some organizations, upon realizing that certain critical knowledge has been lost, identify ways to acquire it or acquire new knowledge. This leads to the creation of new knowledge and opportunities for adjustments and renewals.

Furthermore, through knowledge loss, the organization can eliminate individuals with undesirable performance. In other words, employees who are not meeting expectations, when they leave the organization, generate organizational benefits (Daghfous et al., 2023).

Because turnover is a source of knowledge loss, Starke et al. (2003) assessed the impact of the departure of key employees. In this research, it was found that organizational performance was not affected. Furthermore, the remaining employees exhibited greater confidence in filling the knowledge gaps left by those who departed.

It is notable that studies on knowledge loss are more prominent in the literature. However, even with this imminent and present risk, organizations survive and adapt. Therefore, it is important to understand how this occurs to identify knowledge gains. In other words, "although the risks of knowledge loss may lead to negative outcomes, if the right strategy is applied to eliminate them, they can also represent significant opportunities for cost savings or business development" (Jennex & Durcikova, 2013, p. 3479).

Intellectual capital and its structures can serve as support pillars for recognizing this duality, to strengthen gains and mitigate loss. The next section presents an analysis of the interplay between knowledge losses and gains and intellectual capital and how CI management interacts with these aspects.

4 Relationship of Intellectual Capital and Knowledge Loss and Knowledge Gain

In order to identify the relationships between knowledge loss, gain, and intellectual capital, a convergence of themes was sought in the literature. To achieve this, an investigation was conducted using the Scopus, Web of Science, and IEEE Explore databases, utilizing the following keywords: "knowledge loss," "knowledge lost," and "knowledge gain." Additionally, searches were conducted in the same databases using the keywords "knowledge loss," "knowledge lost," and "intellectual capital." These searches revealed a scarcity of publications on knowledge gains. Similarly, studies analyzing the relationship between knowledge losses, gains, and intellectual capital are scarce. Therefore, this chapter will provide a theoretical discussion on the subject based on the existing literature.

Regarding the causes of knowledge loss, it was noted that the main aspects relate to people, organizational structure, and issues involving external organizational relationships, in other words the elements that constitute and represent human capital, structural capital, and relational capital.

Thus, it is suggested that when IC is not managed properly, it poses an organizational risk, which occurs through knowledge loss. To illustrate this relationship, Table 9.2 presents the main causes of knowledge loss highlighted in the literature, classified according to the dimensions of intellectual capital.

Table 9.2 reveals that a significant portion of the literature considers employee turnover as the primary source of knowledge loss, whether due to retirement or other reasons. The combination of other factors, such as internal changes that remove the worker from their previous role, geographic relocation, or temporary changes, suggests that aspects related to human capital exert a significant influence on organizational knowledge loss. This finding corroborates the studies of Daghfous et al. (2023) and on the analysis of knowledge loss. Both authors indicate that one of the main drivers of organizational knowledge loss is employee turnover.

Table 9.2 Causes of knowledge loss classified within the dimensions of intellectual capital

Causes	Authors
Human capital	
Retirement	Scott (2007), Massingham (2008), Ghahfarokhi and Zakaria (2009), Bleich et al. (2009), Hu (2010), Jennex and Durcikova (2013), Fronza et al. (2013), Makore and Eresia-Eke (2014), Jennex (2014), Caldas et al. (2015), Bratianu and Leon (2015), Bhattacharjee et al. (2015), Sumbal et al. (2018), Geeraerts et al. (2018) and Bento and Garotti (2019)
Turnover	Massingham (2008), Hafida (2008), Jennex (2014), Gulati and Srivastava (2014), Sulaiman et al. (2016), Lin et al., 2016, Rigby et al. (2016),Constantinou and Mens (2017), Nassif and Robillard (2017), Nkomo et al. (2018), Rashid et al. (2017), Sedano et al. (2017), Sumbal et al. (2018), Potrich (2019), Mirsaeedi and Rigby (2020), Su et al. (2021) and Kazemi et al. (2022)
Downsizing	Stauss et al. (2011)
Incapacity (temporary or permanent)	Jennex (2014)
Internal position change/work rotation	Jennex and Durcikova (2013), Jennex (2014), Lin et al. (2016), Sedano et al. (2017) and Sumbal et al. (2018)
Geographical change (work units) and/or geographical distance	Lin et al. (2016), Sedano et al. (2017), Sumbal et al. (2018) and Al Hafidz and Sensuse (2019)
Structural capital	
Management process failure	Viana et al. (2015)
Failure to capture critical knowledge	Jennex (2014)
Failure in knowledge repositories	Jennex (2014), Durst and Leyer (2014) and Massingham (2018)
Forgetting	Jennex (2014)
Lack of documentation on process	Durst and Leyer (2014)
Limited knowledge sharing	Durst and Leyer (2014)
Lack on standardization in work process	Abdul-Rahman et al. (2007)
Relational capital	
Mergers and acquisitions	Stauss et al. (2011) and Alaranta and Martela (2012)
Outsourcing	Cha et al. (2009), Alaranta and Jarvenpaa (2010) and Nkwocha et al. (2010)

Authors (2024)

In this regard, it is considered that the organized and strategic management of people should take into account the value they bring to the business, especially as they are the main repositories of tacit knowledge. Therefore, investing in internal relationships contributes to mitigating this risk (Constantinou & Mens, 2017; Mariano et al., 2018; Shen & Ke, 2017).

Understanding the organization's response when employees with rare knowledge leave helps to grasp the impact of the loss, enabling the structuring of effective actions (Massingham, 2008). Additionally, identifying the critical knowledge of departing professionals is necessary to create appropriate retention strategies. In other words, knowing what to retain is a prerequisite for the effectiveness of these actions (Sulaiman et al., 2016; Sumbal et al., 2018).

One example is the practices of human capital management, which can involve the sharing of tacit knowledge. These occur through interactions among members of the organization, wherein knowledge that cannot be explicitly articulated circulates among individuals during interaction. This practice supports human capital management as it promotes the creation of new individual knowledge. This is corroborated by Mazorodze and Buckley (2020), who indicate that knowledge transfer tools enabling the sharing of tacit knowledge are a strategy for knowledge retention.

Bhattacharjee et al. (2015) assert that implementing a culture of knowledge sharing helps in preserving organizational memory. This suggests that, although turnover may occur, investment in internal relationships mitigates the issue.

Aspects related to organizational culture and organizational memory pertain to structural capital. Studies reveal that when there are failures in knowledge retention (whether through processes or database failures), knowledge will be lost. These gaps in the structures of structural capital have been shown to be significant for knowledge loss.

Hu (2010) points out that the most effective form of knowledge transfer occurs through human relationships. The results of his study indicate that lost knowledge is particularly related to experiential knowledge (know-how). In order for this knowledge to circulate within the organization, some practices of structural capital management are suggested: training, paired activities, internal communication strategies, knowledge-sharing strategies, communities of practice, employee training and guidance, incorporation of technologies, and development of best practices have shown promise (Altarawneh & Altarawneh, 2017; Massingham, 2018; Mazorodze & Buckley, 2020).

These practices can bring benefits to this risk. In addition to the exchange and absorption of knowledge, it is suggested that the impact generated by failures in knowledge capture be mitigated. Licorish and MacDonell (2015) also reinforce the mitigation of loss through the development of paired activities. Moreover, other research corroborates the relevance of training as a strategy for mitigating knowledge loss (Rashid et al., 2017; Rigby et al., 2016; Shen & Ke, 2017).

Among the dimensions of IC, the one that showed the lowest occurrence of aspects related to knowledge loss is relational capital. However, it is worth noting that according to studies by Cha et al. (2009), Alaranta and Jarvenpaa (2010), Nkwocha et al. (2010), Stauss et al. (2011), and Alaranta and Martela (2012), in poorly managed merger, acquisition, and outsourcing processes, the risks of knowledge loss can be significant.

This occurs due to strained relationships and friction between old and new employees, leading to their departure. The enhancement of stable organizational and individual relationships is a practice of relational capital management that can contribute to improving interorganizational relations, reducing the chances of knowledge loss in these areas. Shen and Ke (2017) suggest that this happens when high levels of trust are promoted.

The data from Table 9.2 suggest that the management of intellectual capital should focus on managing human capital and structural capital as the main strategy for mitigating knowledge loss, because the most significant situations leading to knowledge loss relate to these two capitals.

It is emphasized that some IC management practices show promise as they impact knowledge across all three spheres of IC, for example, knowledge-sharing practices, development programs, and investment in databases, tools, and strategies that transform individual knowledge into assets; communities of practice; and knowledge mapping (Edvinsson & Malone, 1998; Stewart & Intelectual, 1998; Matos & Lopes, 2008; Kianto et al., 2013; Stefano et al., 2014; Cassol et al., 2016).

At this point, leadership also plays a central role in knowledge retention. The study by Sumbal et al. (2018) indicates that it is the management's role to identify critical areas of lost knowledge and specific knowledge of those leaving so that they can be shared. As well as creating actions and investing in resources for knowledge sharing and codification, such as technological infrastructure and the development of relationship networks. In addition to managing knowledge, it is possible to strengthen organizational memory structures (Mariano et al., 2018). In other words, practices of intellectual capital management should be promoted and encouraged by leadership, ensuring better results in the face of loss.

An interesting aspect to consider relates to the new environmental characteristics, which result from the adaptations that business models have made. Remote work and geographical distance among organization members are already a common reality for many companies. However, as Table 9.2 indicates, some studies claim that distance between professionals can lead to knowledge loss.

At this point, the relevance of what Kianto and Cabrilo (2022) state about the need to understand IC in light of the new socioenvironmental context is reinforced, developing new propositions for its classic version. Considering the digital age, the authors state that self-leadership is a relevant characteristic in human capital. Additionally, open digital culture strengthens structural capital as it is an important source in value creation. For this reason, they assert that active management of knowledge and information in this digital age is even more important. This understanding aligns with studies on mitigating knowledge loss, especially emphasizing the importance of knowledge management (Massingham, 2018).

The review by Daghfous et al. (2023) on knowledge loss indicates that this risk can impact organizational performance not only negatively but also positively. As organizations recognize the factors that lead to loss, they develop a series of strategies to mitigate it, which can lead to improved organizational performance.

Once knowledge is lost, it must be reacquired. In the midst of this, new knowledge can bc generated and created, bringing renewal to companies. Additionally, due to the negative impacts of loss, some companies develop actions to control this risk or processes that ensure organizational knowledge, creating strategies such as knowledge security. Zieba (2016) asserts that it is necessary to manage and retain knowledge, emphasizing the need to introduce knowledge security in organizations. In this aspect, structural capital can provide support.

The establishment of the classification of knowledge losses within the structures of IC allowed for a similar understanding of knowledge gains. Recognizing the causes and consequences enables companies to create risk mitigation strategies. Consequently, some organizational aspects gain strength and are enhanced, even though there are damages on one side. Table 9.3 identifies the knowledge gains, which are also classified within the structures of IC.

Table 9.3 reveals the limited number of studies presenting knowledge gains. This data was also noted by Daghfous et al. (2023), stating that the impacts of knowledge loss can be positive or negative, but most studies focus on the negative aspects.

Table 9.3 Knowledge gains resulting from knowledge loss-generating situations

Gains	Authors
Human capital	
Tacit and explicit knowledges	Stauss et al. (2011)
Emotional support among organizational members	Stauss et al. (2011)
Opportunity to incorporate individual knowledge into organization	Wensley and Navarro (2015) and Massingham (2018)
Growth of remaining employees	Starke et al. (2003), Wensley and Navarro (2015) and Massingham (2018)
Creation of human capital development practices	Potrich et al. (2022)
Structural capital	
Development of processes for knowledge retention and knowledge security strategies	Potrich (2019) and Potrich et al. (2022)
Creation of new organizational knowledge	Stauss et al. (2011), Potrich (2019), Wensley and Navarro (2015) and Massingham (2018)
Organizational renewal	Potrich (2019)
Financial benefits	Stauss et al. (2011) and Jennex and Durcikova (2013)
Creation of knowledge repositories	Stauss et al. (2011)
Development of new policies and processes	Stauss et al. (2011)
Development of a knowledge-sharing culture	Stauss et al. (2011)
Business development	Jennex and Durcikova (2013)
Utilization of new technologies	Potrich et al. (2022)
Relational capital	
Increase and investment in interpersonal relationships	Stauss et al. (2011) and Potrich et al. (2022)

Authors (2024)

Additionally, Table 9.2, which exposes the sources and causes of knowledge loss, highlights the significance of human capital as a central aspect of loss. However, the same studies that present human factors as a source of knowledge loss reveal greater gains for the organization's structure, in other words in structural capital.

This observation indicates that knowledge losses and gains do not occur dialectically when analyzed from the perspective of intellectual capital. Nor do they occur in a direct, one-to-one manner (e.g., losses and gains to human capital). This dynamic happens systematically, where all factors and aspects interact. This initial analysis may suggest that strengthening a particular capital can mitigate the friction occurring in another.

One of the main findings from this data suggests that strengthening structural capital compensates for risks related to human capital. Organizations need to strengthen the knowledge present in their structure so that the impacts resulting from the departure of professionals are not as concerning to the business.

When individual knowledge is shared among people, absorbed into organizational processes, and circulates within the organization's culture, companies face fewer financial and nonfinancial risks originating from knowledge loss. They become less dependent on individual professionals and can focus their efforts on effective employee retention programs. This data is consistent with the study by Daghfous et al. (2023), which indicates that enhancing and strengthening the organization's structure can reduce the risks of loss.

The possession of knowledge within organizational structures and its active development increases the competitiveness of the company, generating these gains (Hussinki et al., 2017). Strategies to mitigate knowledge loss should consider retaining critical knowledge within the organization (Daghfous et al., 2023). Therefore, increasing structural capital can ensure gains and reduce losses.

The gains to SC generate indirect impacts on HC. The more robust the structural capital, i.e., the mechanisms and structures of the organization, the better the conditions to support employees and their intellectual and business performance. If the organization has weak procedures and systems, human capital will not reach its maximum potential. Therefore, SC is the link that allows human capital to be measured and developed (Bontis, 1998).

It is perceived that in this context of knowledge losses and gains, the relationships between HC and SC are dialectical. Mitigating knowledge loss through HC leads to gains in organizational structures. Strengthening organizational structures reduces the risks associated with knowledge loss through HC.

Thus, intellectual capital directly contributes to the relationship between knowledge losses and gains through practices of managing human and structural capital. Regarding relational capital, it has shown to be less impacted, both in terms of loss and gains. As stated by Papagiannidis et al. (2020), finding creative and technological solutions for organizational processes is of utmost importance for organizational sustainability. Therefore, IC management practices play a central role.

5 Conclusions and Guidelines

This study contributes to advancing the debate on the relationship between knowledge losses and gains and evaluates how intellectual capital management contributes to this relationship through theoretical research. To this end, the main causes leading to knowledge loss were identified in previous studies and then classified into IC structures. Additionally, possible organizational gains occurring after losses were identified and also classified according to IC structures.

In these aspects, it was evident how human and structural capital are strongly related to knowledge losses and gains. Weakening human capital management may influence knowledge losses to occur. However, conversely, strengthening structural capital management can mitigate knowledge losses, as most loss mitigation strategies focus on organizational structures. When analyzing the main knowledge gains, these also appear to be greater for elements of structural capital.

The findings indicate that there is an important relationship between intellectual capital and knowledge losses and gains. The risks associated with knowledge loss have consequences for organizations. However, analyzing them through intellectual capital can support the mitigation of this risk.

As presented in the previous section, practices related to managing structural capital show promise in mitigating knowledge loss, as they support the creation of new knowledge. Therefore, through these strategies, it is necessary to develop a culture of learning and knowledge sharing to ensure knowledge retention and the creation of new knowledge.

In this sense, it becomes evident that new perspectives on intellectual capital should be considered as a resource to address the challenges organizations face. Managing intellectual capital retains critical knowledge and creates new strategies and processes for businesses, leading to better market adaptations in response to knowledge-related risks.

Practices that strengthen and share tacit knowledge are of paramount importance. They help the organization respond to risks and also to a rapidly changing environment. When the main knowledge losses relate to people-related aspects, investing in training and strengthening structural capital is as relevant as investing solely in human capital. Because structural capital has been shown to provide support against the dangers that weaknesses in human capital can pose to the organization. Investing in internal relational capital also plays the same role.

When threats related to knowledge are identified, it is necessary to consider all spheres of the organization, increasing the conditions for facing them in an organic and systemic way. This ensures not only the mitigation of risk but also the possibilities of organizational gains.

These practices should not only be reactive, right when the risk is identified. But they should also occur preventively. Therefore, strengthening intellectual capital ensures better conditions for mitigating knowledge loss and maximizing its gains. Actions that consolidate each of its dimensions prove to be important allies for quick and accurate responses. Regarding human capital, practices that enhance internal relationships show promise. For structural capital, investment in knowledge security, databases, the development of a learning culture, and knowledge sharing are significant allies. Finally, practices that foster trust relationships among interorganizational professionals contribute to knowledge gains and mitigate the impact of losses.

In this investigation, a new perspective on IC was identified. The greater the investment in managing intellectual capital, the greater the organizational preparedness to face known and even unknown adversities, considering the risks associated with knowledge. This is achieved through strengthening internal knowledge structures.

The discussion regarding intellectual capital is consolidated and robust, while the discussion concerning the risks related to knowledge loss and gains is still in its early stages. However, these new ways of understanding IC can support organizations in their resilience by retaining knowledge losses and maximizing gains. This is because the dynamism of the environment in which organizations operate can influence these risks.

Ultimately, the relationship between knowledge losses and gains with intellectual capital is revealed. However, it is not possible to make generalizations about specific IC practices for mitigating loss and maximizing gain. Each organization must consider its reasons for loss, identifying all factors involved. Organizational culture should be taken into account to propose the best IC practices, aiming to achieve the primary objective: organizational sustainability.

It is important to emphasize that the context of this study is theoretical and exploratory. Research that delves into and analyzes gains in the face of losses is still scarce. In this sense, this study contributes to advancing the discussion on the relationship between these topics. Therefore, it is suggested that future research pragmatically evaluates these relationships and confirms the interplay between the elements presented.

It is believed that future research could be timely to advance theoretical discussions as well as empirical research on the topic. Therefore, it is suggested that qualitative exploratory analyses may identify relevant practices and factors regarding how IC management can mitigate losses and contribute to knowledge gains. Research in knowledge-intensive companies may be feasible to test the relationship between these topics, both with quantitative and qualitative validation.

References

Abdul-Rahman, H., Danuri, M. S. M., Wah, L. W., Zakaria, N., & Rahim, F. A. M. (2007) Using project learning to enhance the value of construction projects. In *CME 25 Conference Construction Management and Economics* (p. 1645).

Al Hafidz, M. U., & Sensuse, D. I. (2019). The effect of knowledge management system on software development process with scrum. In *2019 3rd international conference on informatics and computational sciences (ICICoS)* (pp. 1–6). IEEE.

Alaranta, M., & Jarvenpaa, S. L. (2010). Changing IT providers in public sector outsourcing: Managing the loss of experiential knowledge. In *2010 43rd Hawaii international conference on system sciences* (pp. 1–10). IEEE.

Alaranta, M., & Martela, E. (2012). Knowledge gaps in post-merger integration of software maintenance processes: A case study. In *The European conference on information systems management* (p. 9). Academic Conferences International Limited.

Altarawneh, I. I., & Altarawneh, K. (2017). Knowledge management practices and intellectual capital: A case from Jordan. *International Journal of Business, 22*(4), 341–367.

Bento, F., & Garotti, L. (2019). Resilience beyond formal structures: A network perspective towards the challenges of an aging workforce in the oil and gas industry. *Journal of Open Innovation: Technology, Market, and Complexity, 5*(1), 15.

Bhattacharjee, K. K., Shankar, R., & Gupta, M. P. (2015). Knowledge loss at Institute of Higher Learnings in Technologies in India. In *2015 IEEE international conference on industrial engineering and engineering management (IEEM)* (pp. 1480–1484). IEEE.

Billington, J. (1997). A few things every manager ought to know about risk. *Harvard Management Update, 2*(3), 1–12.

Bleich, M. R., Cleary, B. L., Davis, K., Hatcher, B. J., Hewlett, P. O., & Hill, K. S. (2009). Mitigating knowledge loss: A strategic imperative for nurse leaders. *JONA: The Journal of Nursing Administration, 39*(4), 160–164.

Bontis, N. (1998). Intellectual capital: An exploratory study that develops measures and models. *Management Decision, 36*(2), 63–76.

Bontis, N. (2001). Assessing knowledge assets: A review of the models used to measure intellectual capital. *International Journal of Management Reviews, 3*(1), 41–60.

Bratianu, C., & Leon, R. D. (2015). Strategies to enhance intergenerational learning and reducing knowledge loss: An empirical study of universities. *Vine, 45*(4), 551–567.

Buenechea-Elberdin, M., Kianto, A., & Sáenz, J. (2018). Intellectual capital drivers of product and managerial innovation in high-tech and low-tech firms. *R&D Management, 48*(3), 290–307.

Caldas, C. H., Elkington, R. W., O'Connor, J. T., & Kim, J. Y. (2015). Development of a method to retain experiential knowledge in capital projects organizations. *Journal of Management in Engineering, 31*(5), 04014083.

Cassol, A., Gonçalo, C. R., & Ruas, R. L. (2016). Redefining the relationship between intellectual capital and innovation: The mediating role of absorptive capacity. *BAR-Brazilian Administration Review, 13*.

Cha, H. S., Pingry, D. E., & Thatcher, M. E. (2009). Determining a Firm's optimal outsourcing rate: A learning model perspective. In *2009 42nd Hawaii international conference on system sciences* (pp. 1–10). IEEE.

Constantinou, E., & Mens, T. (2017). An empirical comparison of developer retention in the RubyGems and npm software ecosystems. *Innovations in Systems and Software Engineering, 13*, 101–115.

Daghfous, A., Amer, N. T., Belkhodja, O., Angell, L. C., & Zoubi, T. (2023). Managing knowledge loss: A systematic literature review and future research directions. *Journal of Enterprise Information Management, 36*(4), 1008–1031.

DeLong, D. W., & Storey, J. (2004). *Lost knowledge: Confronting the threat of an aging workforce*. Oxford University Press.

Durst, S., & Leyer, M. (2014, September). How can SMEs assess the risk of organisational knowledge?. In *LWA* (pp. 299–309).

Edvinsson, L. (2013). IC 21: Reflections from 21 years of IC practice and theory. *Journal of Intellectual Capital, 14*(1), 163–172.

Edvinsson, L., & Malone, M. S. (1998). *Capital intelectual: descobrindo o valor de sua empresa pela identificação de seus valores internos*. Makron Brooks.

Edvinsson, L., & Sullivan, P. (1996). Developing a model for managing intellectual capital. *European Management Journal, 14*(4), 356–364.

Eller, R., Alford, P., Kallmünzer, A., & Peters, M. (2020). Antecedents, consequences, and challenges of small and medium-sized enterprise digitalization. *Journal of Business Research, 112*(sn), 119–127. https://doi.org/10.1016/j.jbusres.2020.03.00

Ferenhof, H. A., Durst, S., Zaniboni Bialecki, M., & Selig, P. M. (2015). Intellectual capital dimensions: State of the art in 2014. *Journal of Intellectual Capital, 16*(1), 58–100.

Fronza, I., Janes, A., Sillitti, A., Succi, G., & Trebeschi, S. (2013). Cooperation wordle using pre-attentive processing techniques. In *2013 6th international workshop on cooperative and human aspects of software engineering (CHASE)* (pp. 57–64). IEEE.

Geeraerts, K., Tynjälä, P., & Heikkinen, H. L. (2018). Inter-generational learning of teachers: What and how do teachers learn from older and younger colleagues? *European Journal of Teacher Education, 41*(4), 479–495.

Ghahfarokhi, A. D., & Zakaria, M. S. (2009). Knowledge retention in knowledge management system. In *2009 international conference on electrical engineering and informatics* (Vol. 2, pp. 343–347). IEEE.

Gulati, V. P., & Srivastava, S. (2014). Knowledge management strategy and structure in service sector. In *2014 international conference on computational science and computational intelligence* (Vol. 1, pp. 334–338). IEEE.

Guthrie, J., Ricceri, F., & Dumay, J. (2012). Reflections and projections: A decade of intellectual capital accounting research. *The British Accounting Review, 44*(2), 68–82.

Hafida, B. (2008). Designing a virtual organizational memory-a case study. In *2008 international workshop on advanced information Systems for Enterprises* (pp. 25–30). IEEE.

Hirose, T., & Sawaragi, T. (2020). Extended FRAM model based on cellular automaton to clarify complexity of socio-technical systems and improve their safety. *Safety Science, 123*, 104556.

Holbeche, L. (2023). *The agile organization: How to build an engaged, innovative and resilient business*. Kogan Page Publishers.

Hu, L. T. (2010). Same bed, but different dreams? Comparing retired and incumbent police officers' perceptions of lost knowledge and transfer mechanisms. *Crime, Law and Social Change, 53*, 413–435.

Hussinki, H., Ritala, P., Vanhala, M., & Kianto, A. (2017). Intellectual capital, knowledge management practices and firm performance. *Journal of Intellectual Capital, 18*(4), 904–922.

Jennex, M. E. (2014). A proposed method for assessing knowledge loss risk with departing personnel. *VINE: The journal of Information and Knowledge Management Systems, 44*(2), 185–209.

Jennex, M. E., & Durcikova, A. (2013). Assessing knowledge loss risk. In *2013 46th Hawaii international conference on system sciences* (pp. 3478–3487). IEEE.

Kazemi, F., Lamothe, M., & McIntosh, S. (2022). Exploring the notion of risk in code reviewer recommendation. In *2022 IEEE international conference on software maintenance and evolution (ICSME)* (pp. 139–150). IEEE.

Kianto, A. (2007). What do we really mean by the dynamic dimension of intellectual capital? *International Journal of Learning and Intellectual Capital, 4*(4), 342–356.

Kianto, A., & Cabrilo, S. (2022). Challenging the IC theory: Suggestions for some ways forward. *European Conference on Knowledge Management, 23*(1), 611–618.

Kianto, A., & Waajakoski, J. (2010). Linking social capital to organizational growth. *Knowledge Management Research & Practice, 8*, 4–14.

Kianto, A., Andreeva, T., & Pavlov, Y. (2013). The impact of intellectual capital management on company competitiveness and financial performance. *Knowledge Management Research & Practice, 11*(2), 112–122.

Lerro, A., Linzalone, R., & Schiuma, G. (2014). Managing intellectual capital dimensions for organizational value creation. *Journal of Intellectual Capital, 15*(3), 350–361.

Licorish, S. A., & MacDonell, S. G. (2015). Communication and personality profiles of global software developers. *Information and Software Technology, 64*, 113–131.

Lin, T. C., Chang, C. L. H., & Tsai, W. C. (2016). The influences of knowledge loss and knowledge retention mechanisms on the absorptive capacity and performance of a MIS department. *Management Decision, 54*(7), 1757–1787.

Makore, S., & Eresia-Eke, C. (2014). The role of knowledge management in organisational performance. In *Proceedings of the 15th European Conference on Knowledge Management* (pp. 1240–1248).

Mariano, S., Casey, A., & Olivera, F. (2018). Managers and organizational forgetting: A synthesis. *The Learning Organization, 25*(3), 169–179.

Massingham, P. (2008). Measuring the impact of knowledge loss: More than ripples on a pond? *Management Learning, 39*(5), 541–560.

Massingham, P. R. (2018). Measuring the impact of knowledge loss: A longitudinal study. *Journal of Knowledge Management, 22*(4), 721–758.

Matos, F. (2013). Intellectual capital management: From theoretical model to a practice model. In L. Garcia, A. Rodrigues-Castellanos, & J. Barrutia-Guenaga (Eds.), *Proceeding of the 5th European conference on intellectual capital, University of the Basque Country* (pp. 266–278). Curran Associates, Inc.

Matos, F., & Lopes, A. (2008). Gestão do capital intelectual: A nova vantagem competitiva das organizações. *Comportamento organizacional e gestão*, 233–245.

Mazorodze, A. H., & Buckley, S. (2020). A review of knowledge transfer tools in knowledge-intensive organisations. *South African Journal of Information Management, 22*(1), 1–6.

Mirsaeedi, E., & Rigby, P. C. (2020). Mitigating turnover with code review recommendation: Balancing expertise, workload, and knowledge distribution. In *Proceedings of the ACM/IEEE 42nd international conference on software engineering* (pp. 1183–1195).

Mitchell, H. J. (2010). A model for managing intellectual capital to generate wealth: a thesis presented in partial fulfilment of the requirements for the degree of Doctor of Philosophy in Business, Massey University, Albany, New Zealand. *Doctoral dissertation, Massey University.*

Nahapiet, J., & Ghoshal, S. (1998). Social capital, intellectual capital, and the organizational advantage. *Academy of Management Review, 23*(2), 242–266.

Nassif, M., & Robillard, M. P. (2017). Revisiting turnover-induced knowledge loss in software projects. In *2017 IEEE international conference on software maintenance and evolution (ICSME)* (pp. 261–272). IEEE.

Nkomo, M. W., Thwala, W. D., & Aigbavboa, C. O. (2018). Human resource management and effects of mentoring on retention of employees in the construction sector: A literature review. In *Advances in human factors in training, education, and learning sciences: Proceedings of the AHFE 2017 international conference on human factors in training, education, and learning sciences, July 17–21, 2017, the Westin Bonaventure hotel, Los Angeles, California, USA 8* (pp. 207–217). Springer International Publishing.

Nkwocha, A., Hall, J. G., & Rapanotti, L. (2010). Design rationale capture in the globalised enterprise: An industrial study. In *2010 fifth international conference on software engineering advances* (pp. 284–289). IEEE.

Nonaka, I., & Takeuchi, H. (2021). Strategy as a way of life. *MIT Sloan Management Review, 63*(1), 56–63.

Papagiannidis, S., Harris, J., & Morton, D. (2020). WHO led the digital transformation of your company? A reflection of IT related challenges during the pandemic. *International Journal of Information Management, 55*(sn), 102165–102170.

Perrott, B. E. (2007). A strategic risk approach to knowledge management. *Business Horizons, 50*(6), 523–533.

Petty, R., & Guthrie, J. (2000). Intellectual capital literature review: Measurement, reporting and management. *Journal of Intellectual Capital, 1*(2), 155–176.

Potrich, L. N. (2019). Riscos da perda de conhecimento vinculado a fatores humanos em empresas intensivas em conhecimento. Florianópolis, 2019. Mestrado em Engenharia e Gestão do Conhecimento. Universidade Federal de Santa Catarina.

Potrich, L. N., Selig, P. M., Matos, F., & Giugliani, E. (2022). Organisational resilience in the digital age: Management strategies and practices. In *Resilience in a digital age: Global challenges in Organisations and society* (pp. 59–70). Springer International Publishing.

Rashid, M., Clarke, P. M., & O'Connor, R. V. (2017). Exploring knowledge loss in open source software (OSS) projects. In *Software process improvement and capability determination: 17th international conference, SPICE 2017, Palma de Mallorca, Spain, October 4–5, 2017, proceedings* (pp. 481–495). Springer International Publishing.

Reiman, A., Kaivo-oja, J., Parviainen, E., Takala, E. P., & Lauraeus, T. (2021). Human factors and ergonomics in manufacturing in the industry 4.0 context–a scoping review. *Technology in Society, 65*, 101572.

Ribeiro, D., Almeida, A., Azevedo, A., & Ferreira, F. (2021). Resilience in industry 4.0 digital infrastructures and platforms. In: *Advances in manufacturing technology XXXIV: Proceedings of the 18th international conference on manufacturing research, incorporating the 35th National Conference on manufacturing research, 7–10 September 2021, University of Derby, Derby, UK*. IOS Press (p. 390).

Rigby, P. C., Zhu, Y. C., Donadelli, S. M., & Mockus, A. (2016). Quantifying and mitigating turnover-induced knowledge loss: Case studies of chrome and a project at Avaya. In *Proceedings of the 38th international conference on software engineering* (pp. 1006–1016).

Roos, G., & Roos, J. (1997). Measuring your company's intellectual performance. *Long Range Planning, 30*(3), 413–426.

Scott, K. A. (2007). Managing the threat of lost knowledge through technology and teamwork. *Nursing Administration Quarterly, 31*(1), 17–21.

Sedano, T., Ralph, P., & Péraire, C. (2017). Software development waste. In *2017 IEEE/ACM 39th international conference on software engineering (ICSE)* (pp. 130–140). IEEE.

Shen, B., & Ke, Y. (2017). Causes analysis and risk control of firm knowledge loss. *International Journal of System Assurance Engineering and Management, 8*, 2001–2008.

Smuts, C. (2024). The myth of being modern: Digital machines and the loss of discovery. *Curator: The Museum Journal, 67*(1), 329–351.

Stamenkova, L. P., & Trpeski, P. (2020). Impact of intelectual capital on the value of the organization. *Knowledge-International Journal, 38*(1), 219–225.

Starke, F. A., Dyck, B., & Mauws, M. K. (2003). Coping with the sudden loss of an indispensable employee: An exploratory case study. *The Journal of Applied Behavioral Science, 39*(2), 208–228.

Stauss, K., Ferguson, A., & North, A. (2011). Bridging two worlds: Using knowledge management theory to understand the merging of two non-profit organisations. *Journal of Information & Knowledge Management, 10*(04), 301–314.

Stefano, N. M., Casarotto Filho, N., Freitas, M. D. C. D., & Martinez, M. A. T. (2014). Gestão de ativos intangíveis: implicações e relações da gestão do conhecimento e capital intelectual. *Perspectivas em Gestão & Conhecimento, 4*(1), 22–37.

Stewart, T. A. (1997). *Intellectual capital: The new wealth of organization*. Doubleday.

Stewart, T. A., & Intelectual, C. (1998). *A nova vantagem competitiva das empresas*. Tradução de.

Su, J., Bai, Q., Sindakis, S., Zhang, X., & Yang, T. (2021). Vulnerability of multinational corporation knowledge network facing resource loss: A super-network perspective. *Management Decision, 59*(1), 84–103.

Sulaiman, M. S. B., Nordin, A., & Noor, N. L. M. (2016). A review of knowledge retention frameworks for knowledge intensive organization. In *2016 international conference on information management and technology (ICIMTech)* (pp. 106–111). IEEE.

Sullivan, P. H. (1998). *Profiting from intellectual capital: Extracting value from innovation*. John Wiley & Sons.

Sumbal, M. S., Tsui, E., Cheong, R., & See-To, E. W. (2018). Critical areas of knowledge loss when employees leave in the oil and gas industry. *Journal of Knowledge Management, 22*(7), 1573–1590.

Sveiby, K. E. (1997). The intangible assets monitor. *Journal of Human Resource Costing & Accounting, 2*(1), 73–97.

Sveiby, K. E. (2001). A knowledge-based theory of the firm to guide in strategy formulation. *Journal of Intellectual Capital, 2*(4), 344–358.

Viana, D., Conte, T., Marczak, S., Ferreira, R., & de Souza, C. (2015). Knowledge creation and loss within a software organization: An exploratory case study. In *In 2015 48th Hawaii international conference on system sciences* (pp. 3980–3989). IEEE.

Vuori, V., Helander, N., & Okkonen, J. (2019). Digitalization in knowledge work: The dream of enhanced performance. *Cognition, Technology & Work, 21*(2), 237–252.

Wensley, A. K., & Navarro, J. G. C. (2015). Overcoming knowledge loss through the utilization of an unlearning context. *Journal of Business Research, 68*(7), 1563–1569.

Wiig, K. M. (1997). Knowledge management: An introduction and perspective. *Journal of Knowledge Management, 1*(1), 6–14.

Zieba, M. (2016). Knowledge safety in small and medium-sized service companies: Case study analysis. In *Proceedings of the European conference on knowledge management* (pp. 984–991).

Monitoring Cities' Sustainability Based on Intellectual Capital Indicators

Florinda Matos and Valter Vairinhos

Abstract Technology advancements, particularly those related to the Internet of Things (IoT), artificial intelligence, open databases, and big data concepts, have resulted in citizens becoming more sophisticated, demanding, and informed. Consequently, they require more sustainable city governance, encompassing not only tangible assets but also intangible assets such as knowledge and intellectual capital.

This chapter aims to analyze the problem of monitoring the relationship between regions' intellectual capital and their sustainable management, sketching the formulation of a dynamical model for that purpose. The basic concept is that it makes sense to assume that each territorial unit (city, region, etc.) has its own intellectual capital and that the sustainability of that unit depends on it.

In this chapter, alternatives for modeling and monitoring this relationship are identified and a static (fixed-time) and simple example of this problem, using Portuguese official open data, is used to illustrate the kind of problems involved.

F. Matos (✉)
DINÂMIA'CET-IUL – ISCTE – University Institute of Lisbon, Lisbon, Portugal

ICLab – ICAA – Intellectual Capital Association, Santarém, Portugal

The New Club of Paris, Vienna, Austria
e-mail: florinda.matos@iscte-iul.pt

V. Vairinhos
ICLab – ICAA – Intellectual Capital Association, Santarém, Portugal

CINAV – Naval Research Centre - Escola Naval, Almada, Portugal
e-mail: valter.vairinhos@icaa.pt

F. Matos et al. (eds.), *Intellectual Capital in a Global Business Landscape*, Contributions to Management Science,
https://doi.org/10.1007/978-3-031-86362-2_10

1 Introduction and Structure of the Chapter

The sustainability—or long-term performance and survival—of a city or any territorial unit, such as a region, depends on the formulation and implementation of policies (governance) that ensure the quality of life for its inhabitants, as well as sustained economic and social performance. This implies that effective governance requires the ability to formulate and solve problems based on the available knowledge, also known as intellectual capital (IC). If we consider a city or territorial unit as an intelligent, living entity—one that possesses a mind and can learn and produce knowledge—then Fig. 10.1 (see Sect. 10.3) reflects the hypothesis that the sustainability of these units is influenced by, or dependent on, their intellectual capital. In other words, the ability to formulate and solve problems, as embodied in a unit's level of intellectual capital, directly affects the sustainability or long-term viability of those cities and territorial units.

The current relevance attributed to the problems of computer security associated with the capture and statistical analysis of big data that results from individual or collective choices (consumption, habits, opinions, political decisions, personal relationships) allows the identification, characterization, study, and evaluation of new threats to individual freedom and, therefore, to democracy. Thus, any attempt to condition the IC of individuals, countries, or other territorial units has strategic relevance because it can condition and redirect future individual or collective behavior in unacceptable directions serving third-party aims. Since IC is associated with the ability to use preexisting knowledge to formulate and solve new problems, the conditioning of this IC is a strategic theme at all levels. Monitoring IC and its relations with related processes is strategically relevant and an increasingly important topic in a specific country's economic, social, and defense fields. The study of the relationship between the sustainability of territorial units and IC is an obvious example and relevant instance of these relations, hence the survival interest of monitoring them.

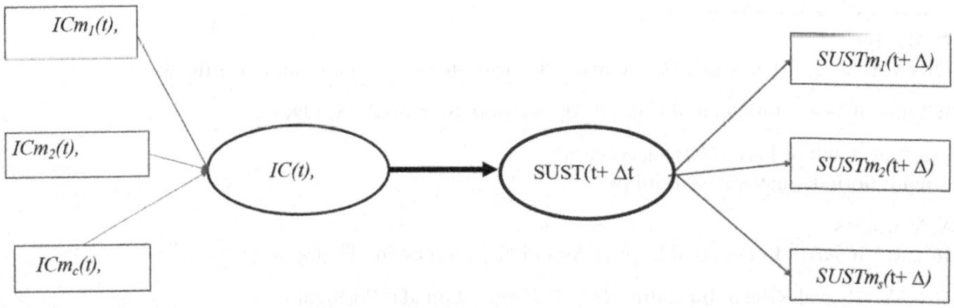

Fig. 10.1 Theoretical structural model (represented by ellipses) designed to monitor the hypothetical relationship between IC(t) and SUST(t), which is modeled as a reflective latent process. The measurement model comprises the observed values of manifest variables (represented by rectangles), which are time series data resulting from observing units at successive time points

Both "city intellectual capital" (CIC) and "sustainability of a city" (SUST) are abstract concepts representing real or existing entities that cannot be observed directly but only through their observable manifestations. This means that latent variables must express or represent these intangible realities in the mathematical models that specify their relations. The concepts of "sustainability" and "intellectual capital" are abstract representations of those intangible realities, related through mathematical models—as illustrated by Fig. 10.1 (see Sect. 10.3). These models express the world views or representations of the world shared and accepted by groups of citizens, decision-makers, scientists, philosophers, or mathematicians. They do not represent the truth but only hypothetical representations of the world these groups believe in and share. Their accuracy, effectiveness, and usefulness are evaluated from the quality of responses, predictions, and decisions made using them.

Therefore, these representations of the world must be logically consistent, mathematically sound, and valid, meaning they must not contradict the empirical knowledge derived from observed data. It is essential to validate these models using appropriate statistical procedures to identify any changes in reality that might necessitate the reformulation or replacement of the models with more accurate representations of the world. This validation is crucial for monitoring the state of the world, allowing for the detection of any continuities or changes that would require adjustments in decision-making processes, whether to maintain reliance on the existing models or to signal the need for modifications.

The main points of this chapter can be summarized as follows:

- First, it seeks to provide empirical evidence for the research hypothesis that "investments in the intellectual capital of territorial units with their own governing bodies such as cities, municipalities, and regions influence the long-term sustainability of the environmental, economic, and social policies adopted by the governance units of these same units."
- Second, it outlines and illustrates an empirical methodology designed to monitor the specified relationship between intellectual capital and long-term sustainability, where "long-term" refers to a period sufficient for the maturation and emergence of the outcomes resulting from these sustainability decisions.

2 Literature Review

According to a 2016 United Nations report, it is estimated that by 2030, 60% of the world's population will live in urban regions, with one in every three individuals residing in cities with a population of at least 500,000. Additionally, a 2018 World Bank report states that 55% of the global population already resides in urban areas. Extensive studies have focused on cities, particularly on the concept of smart cities (e.g., Albino et al., 2015; Dameri, 2013). However, it is important to recognize that the majority of cities do not yet possess the characteristics of a smart city.

Urban living requires the presence of constructed surroundings, and the need for resources continues to increase, primarily as a result of fast urbanization. This urbanization drives the need for the development of new residential areas, the expansion of constructed environments, the enhancement of transportation systems, and the increase in service provision (Juaidi et al., 2019). Urban areas are intricate and necessitate contributions from various fields, such as urban planning, public safety, urban design, and transportation engineering (Bai & Krumdieck, 2019). An additional commonly encountered challenge in urban areas is the equilibrium between urban growth and the need to address issues such as air pollution, traffic congestion, and security, among other factors, which significantly impact the overall quality of life (Juaidi et al., 2019). Whether related to city sustainability or not, city indicators have various benefits. They promote transparency in governance, establish measurable targets, track progress toward those targets, communicate potential benefits of investments, and support decision-making processes (Huovila et al., 2019). Sustainability indicators have the capacity to serve as significant instruments for evaluating and controlling the effects of human activities on the surrounding ecosystems (Silva et al., 2019).

A sustainable city can be regarded as a sentient being able to reason and learn, thus justifying the concepts of intellectual production and intellectual capital (Matos, 2015; Matos & Vairinhos, 2017; Matos et al., 2017a, b). Intellectual capital is anticipated to substantially impact both the innovation processes and the sustainability, as stated by Matos et al. (2017a, b). This reciprocal exchange could occur in both directions: firstly, IC serves as a vital asset for the effective and productive establishment of a city, as it primarily relies on innovation, technology, knowledge dissemination, communication, and citizen engagement; secondly, the city provides a broader platform for testing and implementing IC strategies.

The study of intellectual capital in macroeconomics began in the early 2000s when researchers and certain governments, particularly those of Denmark and the Netherlands, recognized the importance of understanding and quantifying the intellectual capital of nations, regions, and cities. Several of these studies have significantly contributed to the recognition of the importance of assessing intellectual capital on a large scale. The primary aim of these studies is to provide guidance on economic development (e.g., Andriessen & Stam, 2004). However, it is widely acknowledged that the models used to assess intellectual capital, which are often adapted from commercial models, have numerous deficiencies (e.g., Ståhle & Ståhle, 2012; Lazuka, 2012).

When examining the intellectual capital models used in cities or smaller urban areas, a need for more literature on the subject is uncovered. Some of the authors include Viedma (2003, 2004), Carrillo (2004), Rodríguez-Nuñez & Periáñez-Cañadillas (2017), Ergazakis & Metaxiotis (2011), Navarro et al. (2011), Alfaro López and Nevado (2013), Dameri and Ricciardi (2015), Matos & Vairinhos (2016) and Matos et al. (2017a, b).

Research on the relationship between intellectual capital and city sustainability remains extremely limited. Even after more than two decades since the initial proposals for models to monitor intellectual capital, there is still no consensus or standardization in this area.

This chapter will utilize two crucial tools: the concept of "sustainability," which was first introduced in the Brundtland Report (WCED, 1987) and later popularized by the United Nations 2030 Agenda for Sustainable Development in 2015, and open data, which encompasses not only government data but also data sets published by nongovernmental organizations, private agencies, and research institutions. These data sets are typically made available in a centralized and standardized format.

3 Methodology and Model Formulation

The general problem of monitoring the relationship between the intellectual capital of a region and its sustainability is, technically, a dynamic problem involving time. Assuming that it makes sense to speak of the IC of a city or region and that a methodology for its observation is available, the statistical methodology to tackle this problem—modeling, estimation, and prediction—is the so-called "dynamic structural equations" (DSMs) (see Asparouhov et al. (2017) and Driver et al. (2017)).

Considering only a static version of this problem relating the observations of units—regions of Portugal (see Sect. 10.4)—in two occasions separated by Δ years and used as an exploratory and illustrative example, a suitable modeling methodology to be employed is structural equation modeling (SEM) and its estimation using partial least squares (PLS), as described in Wold (1982), Bollen (1989), Tenenhaus et al. (2005), Esposito et al. (2010), Sanchez (2013), and Rigdon et al. (2017).

Let IC(t) represent the intellectual capital of an individual or collective entity at time t.

Let SUST(t) represent the state of sustainability of an individual or collective entity, such as a city or region, at time t.

IC(t) and SUST(t) are variables that are not directly observable (intangibles), whose manifestations in the world are observable through measurements and whose results occur in the form of data time series. This means that both processes can be modeled by latent variables or latent processes since they are both functions of time.

Sustainability is an outcome of individual decision-making or governance decision-making processes of those collective entities and, therefore, presupposes that those relevant entities are associated with a capacity for intellectual creation and problem-solving based on the available knowledge and aiming to pursue specific objectives. This means that the entity's future sustainability, being the outcome of previous governance decisions resulting from reasonings and analysis processes acting on previous information and knowledge, depends on or is influenced or caused by the entity's intellectual capital state at the decision time.

It is assumed that the available data is in the form of time series recorded by the official statistical systems—and that IC(t) and SUST(t) are modeled in a reflective perspective: the observed data being manifestations or indicators of processes that are not directly observable. Specifically, let ICm1(t), ICm2(t),... ICmc(t) be the reflective manifest variables of IC(t) and SUSTm1(t), SUSTm2(t),... SUSTms(t) be the reflective manifest variables associated with SUST(t), observed at the individual/unit level.

The intellectual capital of a specific territorial unit, existing at some moment t, manifested through the data observed at that moment and place, explains decisions whose outcomes can only be observed after a specific interval of time has elapsed, needed for the implementation and maturation of the decisions and its consequences to take place.

For some specific unit, the outcomes of sustainability decisions made at time t—using intellectual capital available at that time—can only be manifested through observations at a later time $t + \Delta$, after a minimum interval Δ has elapsed, needed for its effects to take place.

For example, let $t = 1, 2, \ldots \Delta$ (years). If the decision was taken at t to build a waste treatment station, the time needed for its construction and operational use would be at least $\Delta = 3$ years.

In this context, the aim is to monitor the relationship between IC(t) and SUST($t + \Delta$) using data observed along the interval $t \ldots t + \Delta$.

This means that, ideally, the model specified in Fig. 10.1 must be estimated using as evidence the observations of the available time series over successive periods of Δ years assuming, to simplify, Δ to be constant.

The key question to address here is as follows: for each territorial unit, is there empirical evidence to suggest that the sustainability observed at $t + \Delta$ reflects a significant effect of the intellectual capital existing at t?

A static example of this scenario is presented below, relating IC(t) and SUST($t + \Delta$) with $t = 2011$, $t + \Delta = 2021$, and $\Delta = 10$ years—the interval between national censuses in the Portuguese statistical system. The data is available on the PORDATA platform (https://www.pordata.pt/).

It should be emphasized that when we refer to observed variables as manifestations of IC(t) and SUST(t), we are specifically referring to territorial units, such as cities or regions, represented by their respective governance bodies. These governance bodies are the entities responsible for collecting and storing data, analyzing available information, generating new knowledge, formulating and solving problems, and making decisions. In this context, it is assumed that these governing bodies work for cities and other collective entities in an analogous way to how the human brain generates human intellectual capital (Matos and Vairinhos 2016, 2017; Matos et al. 2019).

4 Data

The data used in the following analysis was obtained from the PORDATA platform (https://www.pordata.pt/municipios) based on data from the Portuguese Census and other sources published by the Portuguese National Institute of Statistics (INE).

Initially, the study considered using data from all 308 municipalities in Portugal (Caldas, 2019). However, due to the small size of many of these municipalities and the high concentration of missing values for most observable variables, this approach was ultimately discarded.

After several trials, it was decided to use data corresponding to the 39 subregions at the NUTS 3 level. According to the European regulations, NUTS means Nomenclature of Territorial Units for Statistical Purposes. The third level—NUTS 3—is a subdivision of the second level, the second level is a subdivision of the first level, and the first level is a subdivision of the Member States. With larger populations, these subregions provided more reliable observed values for the selected manifest variables, significantly reducing the incidence of missing data. Nevertheless, 16 of these units were excluded, primarily those corresponding to the Azorean islands and specific subregions, such as Serra da Estrela, whose outlier behavior significantly affected the interpretation of the results.

The final data set—detailed in Table 10.1—retained for analysis 23 units (rows) and 12 variables (columns). The variables are grouped into two categories: seven manifest variables for intellectual capital and five manifest variables for sustainability. These variables represent yearly expenditures deemed relevant for the construction and maintenance of intellectual capital, as well as expenditures reflecting concerns with the environment and quality of life in the selected units. The expenditure values were standardized as euro per inhabitant by dividing the total expenditure in each category by the aggregated population of the unit.

In the model presented in Fig. 10.1 and Table 10.1, the complete list of variable names and meanings are the following:

- Intellectual capital manifests:
  - ICm1 = PatCult_2001 (Cultural Heritage—2001)
  - ICm2 = PubLit_2001 (Literary Publications—2001)
  - ICm3 = Musica_2001 (Music—2001)
  - ICm4 = ArtCenicas_2001 (Performing Arts—2001)

Table 10.1 Structure of the data set (23 rows × 12 columns) retained for analysis

Units	PatCult_2001	PubLit_2001	Musica_2001	…	ProtRuidoVib_2011
Alentejo Central	1.65	3.30	7.29	…	0.00
Alentejo Litoral	4.69	9.28	8.39	…	0.00
Algarve	0.90	1.01	0.70	…	0.00
Grande Lisboa	0.15	0.14	0.07	…	0.00
Grande Porto	0.13	0.16	0.19	…	0.00
Lezíria do Tejo	1.38	1.96	1.71	…	0.00
…	…	…	…	…	…
Médio Tejo	0.52	1.78	1.25	…	0.00
Minho-Lima	1.09	1.79	1.15	…	0.00
Oeste	0.36	0.90	0.79	…	0.00
Pinhal Litoral	0.96	0.87	0.64	…	0.00
Tâmega	0.47	0.35	0.41	…	0.00

Some units and columns were omitted for space considerations

– ICm5 = ActSocCult_2001 (Cultural Associations—2001)
– ICm6 = RecintCult_2001 (Cultural Places—2001)
– ICm7 = JogosEDesp_2001 (Games and Sports—2001)

- Sustainability manifests:

– SUSTm1 = GestResid_2011 (Waste Management—2011)
– SUSTm2 = ProtSolosAgSubt_2011 (Soil and Groundwater Protection—2011)
– SUSTm3 = ProtRuidoVib_2011 (Noise and Vibration Protection—2011)
– SUSTm4 = ProtBiodivePisag_2011 (Biodiversity and Landscape Protection—2011)
– SUSTm5 = OutrosDomin_2011 (Other Areas—2011)

These expenditures represent yearly investment decisions made in cultural aspects (such as libraries, museums, magazines, and cultural activities in general) or in areas related to the sanitation and well-being of the population. These investments reflect concerns about the cultural and intellectual development of the populations.

Although there are no universally accepted scales to measure intellectual capital and sustainability for these units—similar to the situation for countries—it is believed that the defined latent variables serve as useful proxies for the empirical analysis presented here.

The quality of the data, particularly the abundance of missing values, is highly dependent on the nature of the territorial unit and the significance of each manifest variable. For example, in large metropolitan areas such as Lisbon and Porto, investments in soil and groundwater protection in 2011 may be less significant than those in noise and vibration protection in the same year. In contrast, in predominantly agricultural areas like Alentejo, the opposite is true.

This variability is also reflected in the results (see Sect. 10.5, Fig. 10.2), where small population regional units are highlighted, in contrast to the apparent downplaying of larger population centers.

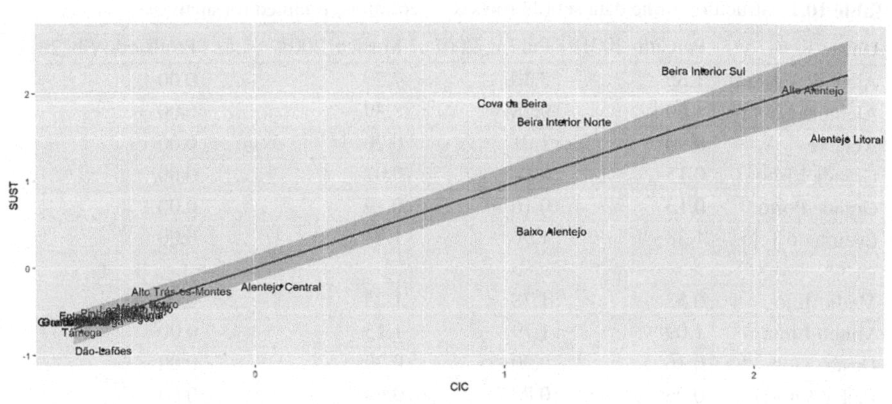

Fig. 10.2 SUST estimated scores as a function of CIC estimated scores. The points are labeled with the names of Portuguese regions corresponding to NUTS 3

5 Estimation of the Model and Discussion of the Results

The model formulated and illustrated in Fig. 10.1 was estimated using the R-package plspm (Gaston Sanchez, 2013). As shown in Table 10.2, the two blocks of manifest variables associated with the latent variables CIC and SUST exhibit very high homogeneity indicators. This suggests a strong tendency toward one-dimensionality, meaning each block effectively represents a single underlying variable. The goodness of fit for this model is 0.78.

Figure 10.2 is a scatter plot showing the estimated scores/values of the latent variable SUST as a function of the latent variable CIC, calculated using the R package plspm (Gaston Sanchez, 2013).

The graph includes the corresponding regression line, given by the equation $SUST = 0.941 \times CIC + 0.000$ ($R2 = 0.887$), along with a confidence band at 90%.

The numerical estimation of this static model of structural equations, namely, the quality of the fit and the results expressed in Fig. 10.2 of the relationship between CIC (2001) and SUST(2011), seems to suggest that there is empirical support for the initial question: "does it makes sense to predict the sustainability of regions using intellectual capital as an independent variable or predictor?"

However, given the evident data limitations, this work should be considered exploratory, and its results should be interpreted with caution.

The primary limitations underlying this cautious stance are as follows:

- The small number of observations in the retained data set (23 observations).
- For some variables, there is interaction between the nature of the observed units and the meaning of the manifest variables. For example, noise control makes perfect sense for large population groups but makes little sense for agricultural regions.
- The presence of a large number of missing values forced the elimination from this study of territorial units with a small number of inhabitants; no attempt was made to "correct" this issue.
- The choice of the manifest variables associated with the two latent variables was largely conditioned by data availability.

Table 10.2 One-dimensionality measures for the two blocks of latent variables (Sanchez 2013)

Latent	Mode	No. of manifests	C. Alpha	DG.rho	eig1	eig2
CIC	A	7	0.948	0.959	5.4	0.915
SUST	A	5	0.735	0.735	2.35	0.96

Key terms: Latent—Latent Variables; Mode A—Reflective; C. Alpha—Cronbach's Alpha; DG. rho—Dillon-Goldstein's Rho; eig1, eig2—Largest Eigenvalues (1 and 2)

6 Conclusions and Future Work

Given the identified limitations, the results presented should be viewed as an initial attempt, constrained by the quality of the available data, to model the relationship between intellectual capital and sustainability for territorial units—such as cities and regions. Only after results in this area have been further consolidated will it be meaningful to address issues related to the temporal evolution (monitoring) of these relationships and to conduct statistical inference, which are relevant only for well-established models and high-quality data.

Future research, conducted with more extensive and higher quality data, ideally within the framework of a well-supported research project, will be necessary to develop dynamic models. These models would allow for the effective monitoring of these relationships, making methodologies such as those proposed by Asparouhov (2017) and Driver (2017) more applicable.

References

Albino, V., Berardi, U., & Dangelico, R. M. (2015). Smart cities: Definitions, dimensions, and performance. *Journal of Urban Technology, 22*(1), 3–21.

Alfaro López, J. L., & Nevado, D. (2013). A theoretical intellectual capital model applied to cities. *Amfiteatru Economic, 15*(34), 455–468.

Andriessen, D., & Stam, C. (2004). Intellectual capital of the European Union: Measuring the Lisbon agenda. *Holland University of professional education, de Baak—Management Centre VNO-NCW: Centre for Research in Intellectual Capital*. [Online]. Retrieved January 26, 2018, from https://www.bvekennis.nl/Bibliotheek/05-0048_Measuring_Lisbon_agenda.pdf.

Asparouhov, T., Hamaker, E. L., & Muthén, B. (2017). Dynamic structural equation models. *Structural Equation Modeling: A Multidisciplinary Journal, 25*(3), 359–388. https://doi.org/10.1080/10705511.2017.1406803

Bai, M., & Krumdieck, S. (2019). Transition engineering of transport in megacities with case study on commuting in Beijing. *Cities, 96*, Article 102452.

Bollen, K. A. (1989). *Structural equations with latent variables*. Wiley.

Caldas, P. (2019). *O rating municipal português (RMP)*.

Carrillo, F. J. (2004). Capital cities: A taxonomy of capital accounts for knowledge cities. *Journal of Knowledge Management, 8*(5), 28–46.

Dameri, R. P. (2013). Searching for smart city definition: A comprehensive proposal. *International Journal of Computer Technology and Applications, 11*(5), 2544–2551.

Dameri, R. P., & Ricciardi, F. (2015). Smart city intellectual capital: An emerging view of territorial systems innovation management. *Journal of Intellectual Capital, 16*(4), 860–887.

Driver, C. C., Oud, J. H. L., & Voelkle, M. C. (2017). Continuous time structural equation modeling with R package ctsem. *Journal of Statistical Software, 77*(5). https://doi.org/10.18637/jss.v077.i05

Ergazakis, K., & Metaxiotis, K. (2011). Formulating integrated knowledge city development strategies: The KnowCis 2.0 methodology. *Knowledge Management Research & Practice, 9*, 172–184.

Esposito Vinzi V., Chin W.W., Henseler J., Wang W. (2010) Handbook of Partial Least Squares: Concepts, Methods and Applications. Springer.

Huovila, A., Bosch, P., & Airaksinen, M. (2019). Comparative analysis of standardized indicators for smart sustainable cities: What indicators and standards to use and when? *Cities, 89*, 141–153.

Juaidi, A., AlFaris, F., Saeed, F., Salmeron-Manzano, E., & Manzano-Agugliaro, F. (2019). Urban design to achieve sustainable energy in residential neighborhoods in arid climates. *Journal of Cleaner Production, 228*, 135–152.

Lazuka, V. (2012). National intellectual capital: Concept and measurement. *Master thesis, School of Economics and Management*, Lund University.

Matos, F. (2015). Cities auditing model. In R. Giaffreda, D. Cagáňová, Y. Li, R. Riggio, & A. Voisard (Eds.), *Internet of things. IoT infrastructures. IoT360 2014. Lecture notes of the Institute for Computer Sciences, social informatics and telecommunications engineering* (Vol. 151). Springer.

Matos, F., & Vairinhos, V. (2016). *Monitoring the intellectual capital of cities. In Theory and applications in the knowledge economy - TAKE 2016* (pp. 714–725).

Matos, F., & Vairinhos, V. M. (2017). Intellectual capital management as a driver of competitiveness and sustainability. *Journal of Intellectual Capital, 18*(3).

Matos, F., Vairinhos, V. M., Dameri, R. P., & Durst, S. (2017a). Increasing smart city competitiveness and sustainability through managing structural capital. *Journal of Intellectual Capital, 18*(3), 693–707.

Matos, F., Vairinhos, V., & Osinski, M. (2017b). Intellectual capital management as an indicator of sustainability. In *European conference on knowledge management* (pp. 655–663) Academic Conferences International Limited.

Matos, F., Vairinhos, V., Durst, S., & Dameri, R. P. (2019). Intellectual capital and innovation for sustainable smart cities: The case of N-tuple of helices. In F. Matos, V. Vairinhos, P. M. Selig, & L. Edvinsson (Eds.), *Intellectual capital management as a driver of sustainability*. Springer. https://doi.org/10.1007/978-3-319-79051-0

Navarro, J. L. A., Ruiz, V. R. L., & Peña, D. N. (2011). A theoretical intellectual capital model applied to cities. In *Proceedings of the European conference on intellectual capital* (pp. 17–25) Academic Conferences International Limited.

Rigdon, E. E., Sarstedt, M., & Ringle, C. M. (2017). On comparing results from CB-SEM and PLS-SEM: Five perspectives and five recommendations. *Marketing ZFP, 39*(3), 4–18. https://doi.org/10.15358/0344-1369-2017-3-4

Rodríguez-Nuñez, E., & Periáñez-Cañadillas, I. (2017). Intellectual capital as the fostering factor for sustainable smart urban development in the Basque autonomous community. In B. Ortiz & D. P. B. Yàbar (Eds.), *Sustainable smart cities* (pp. 31–47). Springer.

Sanchez, G. (2013). *PLS path modeling with R. Trowchez Editions*. http://www.gastonsanchez.com/PLSPath Modeling with R.pdf

Silva, L., Prietto, P., & Korf, E. (2019). Sustainability indicators for urban solid waste management in large and medium-sized worldwide cities. *Journal of Cleaner Production, 237*, Article 117802.

Ståhle, S., & Ståhle, P. (2012). Towards measures of national intellectual capital: An analysis of the CHS model. *Journal of Intellectual Capital, 13*, 164–177.

Tenenhaus, M., Esposito Vinzi, V., Chatelin, Y. M., & Lauro, C. (2005). PLS path modelling. *Computational Statistics & Data Analysis, 48*(1), 159–205.

United Nations. (2016). *The sustainable development agenda*. http://www.un.org/sustainabledevelopment/

Viedma, J. M. (2003). CICBS: Cities' intellectual capital benchmarking system. A methodology and a framework for measuring and managing intellectual capital of cities. A practical application in the city of Mataró. *Journal of Knowledge Management Research & Practice, 2*(1).

Viedma, J. M. (2004). CICBS: A methodology and a framework for measuring and managing intellectual capital of cities. A practical application in the city of Mataró. *Knowledge Management Research & Practice, 2*(1), 13–23.

Wold, H. (1982). Soft modeling: The basic design and some extensions. In K. G. Joreskog & H. Wold (Eds.), *Systems under indirect observations: Causality, structure, prediction. Part 2* (pp. 1–54). Holland.

World Bank. (2018). *Urban population (percentage of total population). United Nations Population Division*. World Urbanization Prospects: 2018 Revision. https://data.worldbank.org/indicator/SP.URB.TOTL.IN.ZS

World Commission on Economic Development (WCED). (1987). *Our common future*. Oxford University Press.

Reflections from the Literature on Applying the Intellectual Capital Lens on the Micro, Meso, and Macro Levels

Göran Roos

Abstract This chapter provides a comprehensive overview of intellectual capital (IC) and its application at the micro, meso, and macro levels. It traces the historical development of IC theory and practice from its origins in firm-level management to its expansion to industries and nations. The constituent parts, objectives, and insights gained from applying the IC lens at each level are examined. Key models for measuring and managing IC are reviewed, along with critiques of the IC approach. The unique benefits of the IC perspective are highlighted, while also acknowledging its limitations. The chapter concludes by reflecting on future directions for IC research and practice, including opportunities to refine measurement frameworks, address global challenges, and leverage new technologies. Overall, this analysis demonstrates the continued relevance of IC as a framework for understanding and leveraging intangible assets to drive value creation, innovation, and competitiveness across organisational, sectoral, and national contexts.

G. Roos (✉)
Intellectual Capital Services Limited, Buckingham, UK

Institute for Sustainability, Energy and Resources (ISER), The University of Adelaide, Adelaide, Australia

School of Communication, Leadership and Marketing, Kristiania University College—Ernst G Mortensen Foundation, Oslo, Norway

Centre for Business Performance, Cranfield School of Management, Cranfield University, Bedford, UK
e-mail: goran@roos.org.uk

F. Matos et al. (eds.), *Intellectual Capital in a Global Business Landscape*, Contributions to Management Science, https://doi.org/10.1007/978-3-031-86362-2_11

1 A Brief History of Applying Intellectual Capital at the Micro, Meso, and Macro Levels

The concept of intellectual capital (IC) has evolved significantly over the past few decades, with its application expanding from the micro level of individual firms to the meso level of industries and sectors and finally to the macro level of national economies.

The origins of IC can be traced back to the early 1990s, when scholars and practitioners began recognising the importance of IC resources in creating value for organisations. Pioneering works by Sveiby (1997), Edvinsson and Malone (1997), and Roos et al. (1997) laid the foundation for the field by defining and categorising IC into human, structural, and relational capital. These early contributions emphasised the need for firms to identify, measure, and manage their IC resources alongside traditional financial metrics.

In the late 1990s and early 2000s, the application of IC at the firm level gained momentum, with companies like Skandia and Dow Chemical implementing IC frameworks to enhance their strategic decision-making and reporting (Bontis, 1999). Researchers developed various measurement models, such as the Intangible Asset Monitor (Sveiby, 1997), the IC Index (ICI) (Roos & Roos, 1997), and VAIC (Pulić, 1998) to help organisations quantify and monitor their IC performance.

Empirical studies during this period provided evidence of the positive impact of IC on firm performance, innovation, and competitiveness (Bontis et al., 2000; Youndt et al., 2004). The resource-based view (RBV) of the firm further underscored the strategic importance of IC resources in achieving sustainable competitive advantage (Barney, 1991).

As the understanding of IC deepened at the micro level, researchers began exploring its application at the meso level of industries, sectors, and regions in the early 2000s. Studies by Bounfour (2003) and Pomeda et al. (2002) examined the role of IC in driving innovation and competitiveness within specific industries and regions.

The concept of regional innovation systems (Cooke et al., 1997) and industrial clusters (Porter, 1998) provided a framework for understanding how IC contributes to the development of specialised knowledge, skills, and networks within geographically concentrated industries. Researchers emphasised the importance of collaborative learning, knowledge spillovers, and supportive institutional environments in fostering the growth of IC at the meso level (Maskell & Malmberg, 1999; Saxenian, 1994).

Empirical studies in various industries, such as banking (Cabrita & Bontis, 2008), information technology (Seleim et al., 2004), and manufacturing (Hervas-Oliver & Dalmau-Porta, 2007), demonstrated the positive impact of IC on sectoral performance and regional competitiveness. These findings highlighted the need for policies and strategies that promote the development of IC within and across industries.

The application of IC at the macro level of national economies gained traction in the late 1990s and early 2000s, as governments and international organisations recognised the importance of IC resources in driving economic growth and competitiveness. Early works by Edvinsson and Stenfelt (1999) and Bontis (2004a, b) conceptualised the notion of national intellectual capital (NIC) and proposed frameworks for its measurement.

The World Bank's knowledge assessment methodology (KAM) (Chen & Dahlman, 2006) and the OECD's work on knowledge-based economies (OECD, 1996) further underscored the significance of IC in the context of national development. These initiatives provided tools and benchmarks for assessing the knowledge assets of countries and guiding policy decisions.

Empirical studies on NIC revealed its significant impact on national economic performance, competitiveness, and innovation capacity (Lin & Edvinsson, 2010; Ståhle et al., 2015). The global financial crisis of 2008–2009 further highlighted the importance of IC in building resilience and adaptability in the face of economic shocks (Lazuka, 2012).

Later, the application of IC at the macro level expanded to include considerations of sustainability, social progress, and inclusive growth (Käpylä et al., 2012; Mačerinskienė & Aleknavičiūtė, 2017). Researchers have explored the links between NIC and the United Nations' Sustainable Development Goals (United Nations, 2015), emphasising the role of knowledge, innovation, and human capital in achieving long-term prosperity and well-being (Secundo et al., 2020).

The historical development of IC theory and practice demonstrates its continued relevance and applicability across the micro, meso, and macro levels of analysis. From its origins in firm-level management and reporting, IC has evolved into a comprehensive framework for understanding and leveraging IC resources in the context of industries, regions, and nations.

2 What Are the Constituent Parts of Intellectual Capital Used at the Micro, Meso, and Macro Levels

At each level of analysis—micro, meso, and macro—IC is typically divided into three main components: human capital, structural capital (sometimes also called organisational capital on the micro level), and relational capital (Andriessen, 2003; Bounfour, 2003; Edvinsson & Malone, 1997; Roos et al., 2005; Sullivan, 2000; Sveiby, 1997).

At the micro level, human capital involves the knowledge, skills, abilities, and attributes of employees that contribute to value creation (Becker, 1964; Bontis, 1998; Hanushek & Woessmann, 2008; Nguyen & Doan, 2020; Roos et al., 1997). Structural capital encompasses the nonhuman storehouses of knowledge within an organisation and includes organisational processes, patents and other IP, databases, and IT systems that support efficient functioning and knowledge retention as well as organisational culture, which consists of shared values, norms, and behaviors shaping the work environment and influencing employee performance (Bontis et al., 2000; Edvinsson & Malone, 1997; Ferreira et al., 2021; Radonić et al., 2021; Roos et al., 1997). Relational capital captures the value of an organisation's relationships with external stakeholders, such as customers, suppliers, and partners (Bontis, 1998; Maskell & Malmberg, 1999; Nahapiet & Ghoshal, 1998; Nguyen & Doan, 2020); it also captures things like reputation, which reflects the perceived value and trustworthiness of an organisation's products or services in the marketplace (Edvinsson & Malone, 1997). The effective integration of structural capital with digital technologies and innovation frameworks significantly enhances organisational agility and resilience (Mouritsen et al., 2001; Martınez-Torres, 2006). The literature finds that human capital directly contributes to both exploratory and exploitative innovation, relational capital facilitates the flow of knowledge and collaboration essential for leveraging both new and existing knowledge for innovative purposes, and structural capital supports and enhances innovative activities, with an understanding of the specific mechanisms of these interactions helping organisations strategically manage their intellectual resources to balance exploratory and exploitative innovation effectively (Zhang et al., 2022; Ali et al., 2023).

At the meso level, IC encompasses the collective skills and expertise of the workforce (human capital) within an industry or region including talent pool size, density, and distribution (Canning & Pedroni, 2008; Cooke et al., 1997; Subramaniam & Youndt, 2005); industry-wide infrastructure and technological advancements including education institutions (Cooke et al., 1997; OECD, 2001; Subramaniam & Youndt, 2005) (structural capital); and networks, including supply networks and lead customers, and alliances within the industry (relational capital) (Bontis, 1998; Maskell & Malmberg, 1999). These elements facilitate innovation, efficiency, and sector-wide growth (Kovács & Lippai-Makra, 2023).

At the macro level, IC includes the collective education, skills, and health of the population (human capital); national infrastructure, innovation systems, and regulatory frameworks (structural capital); and international relationships, trade agreements, and diplomatic ties (relational capital). These components are fundamental for national productivity, economic stability, and global competitiveness (Arshad et al., 2023; Bontis, 1998; Canning & Pedroni, 2008; Cooke et al., 1997; Maskell & Malmberg, 1999; Nguyen & Doan, 2020; OECD, 2001; Subramaniam & Youndt, 2005; Vo & Tran, 2024).

While the specific elements and characteristics of constituent dimensions of IC vary across the three levels and across the different frameworks and models developed, they all contribute to the development of knowledge, innovation, and competitiveness. By understanding and nurturing the constituent dimensions of IC, organisations, industries, and nations can unlock the full potential of their IC resources and thrive in an increasingly complex and interconnected world.

3 What Are the Objectives of Applying the Intellectual Capital Lens at the Micro, Meso, and Macro Levels

The application of the IC lens at the micro, meso, and macro levels aims to enhance understanding and management of IC resources that contribute to value creation, competitiveness, and sustainability (Bounfour, 2002; Edvinsson & Malone, 1997; Roos et al., 2005). By focusing on these key components of intellectual capital, organisations, industries, and nations can identify and nurture the less visible drivers of their success, enabling them to adapt to challenges and achieve long-term prosperity.

At the micro level, the primary goal is to enhance competitiveness. Human capital impacts workforce productivity and innovation (Ali, 2023; Hanushek & Woessmann, 2008), while structural capital supports the efficient functioning of economic activities (Rana & Hossain, 2023; Roos et al., 2005). Relational capital is an essential enabler of organisational value creation (Martínez-Falcó et al., 2023; Roos et al., 2005). The IC lens fosters innovation, maintains competitive advantage, and enables business model innovation to increase organisational value creation (O'Connor & Roos, 2018; Roos, 2019). Focusing on human capital development and enhancing structural capital improves innovation capabilities and identifies strategic investment areas for technological advancements and stronger market positioning (Edvinsson & Malone, 1997; Lin & Edvinsson, 2010). Applying the IC perspective optimises resource use by prioritising investments in IC resources with high returns (Bontis et al., 2000; Sullivan, 2000), aiding in strategic planning by aligning strategies with IC resources (Bontis, 1998). Additionally, developing methodologies for measuring and reporting the value of IC resources helps track progress and make informed decisions (Burgman et al., 2005; Edvinsson & Malone, 1997; Pike & Roos, 2007; Sveiby, 1997). Studies further support the integration of IC management with environmental, social, and governance considerations to enhance organisational sustainability and stakeholder value (Martínez-Ferrero & García-Sánchez, 2017; Vitolla et al., 2019). Moreover, advances in IC performance measurement and the application of multiple theoretical perspectives, such as transaction cost economics and resource dependence theory, can provide a more comprehensive understanding of IC's impact on organisational performance (Evans et al., 2015).

At the meso level, the focus is on enhancing performance, innovation, and competitiveness of sectors or subsystems of the national economy. This involves investing in human capital development, establishing research and development facilities, and fostering collaborations between firms and academic institutions to increase innovation capabilities (OECD, 2001; Subramaniam & Youndt, 2005; Windle et al., 2023). Effective management of relational capital can improve efficiency and foster collaboration, thereby reducing transaction costs, improving quality, and enhancing overall competitiveness (Bontis, 1998; Marco-Lajara et al., 2022; Maskell & Malmberg, 1999). The IC lens helps industries ensure regulatory compliance and maintain credibility by focusing on structural capital, such as legal and regulatory frameworks, to establish standards and protect intellectual property (OECD, 2001; Tuunanen et al., 2023). Emphasising relational capital facilitates industry collaboration through knowledge sharing, developing common standards, and advocating for favourable policies (Bontis, 1998). Enhancing human capital by investing in specialised training programs and promoting continuous learning ensures that the workforce remains skilled, adaptable, and competitive amidst technological advancements and changing market demands (Subramaniam & Youndt, 2005). Moreover, integrating digital transformation strategies with IC management can further enhance sectoral innovation and productivity (Sucena et al., 2024; Vitolla et al., 2019). Applying diverse research methods, including social network analysis and mixed-methods research design, can also provide a deeper understanding of relational capital and its impact on sectoral performance (Evans et al., 2015).

At the macro level, the IC lens is applied to manage IC resources as critical drivers of productivity, competitiveness, economic growth, and sustainable development (Bounfour & Edvinsson, 2005). By investing in education, research and development, and innovation, nations can enhance their human, structural, and relational capital, leading to increased economic output and competitiveness (Bontis, 2004a, b). The IC perspective aligns with sustainable development goals by emphasising the importance of IC resources in achieving long-term economic, social, and environmental sustainability (Adams & Simnett, 2011). The IC framework provides valuable insights for policymakers and strategic planners, helping governments design better policies to foster economic growth, innovation, and social development (Bontis, 2004a, b). Developing standardised methodologies for measuring and reporting IC resources is crucial for informed decision-making and resource allocation, enabling accurate tracking of progress and identification of areas for improvement (Canning & Pedroni, 2008). Nations can promote innovation and technological advancement by leveraging their IC through fostering creativity, investing in research and development, protecting intellectual property rights, and encouraging knowledge transfer between academia and industry (Lin & Edvinsson, 2010). Additionally, the integration of IC with national policies on digitalisation and sustainability can significantly enhance global competitiveness and resilience (Kovács & Lippai-Makra, 2023; Vitolla et al., 2019). Applying a mixed-methods research approach can also provide more comprehensive insights into the role of IC in national economic development (Evans et al., 2015).

The growing importance of sustainability and social responsibility has led to the integration of environmental, social, and governance (ESG) factors into IC management and reporting (Vitolla et al., 2020). Organisations at all levels are increasingly recognising the need to consider the impact of their activities on stakeholders and the environment. Incorporating ESG considerations into IC management enhances reputation, mitigates risks, and creates long-term value for all stakeholders (Martínez-Ferrero & García-Sánchez, 2017).

4 What Are the Insights Gained by Applying the Intellectual Capital Lens at the Micro, Meso, and Macro Levels

At the micro level, the IC perspective offers an enhanced understanding of value creation beyond traditional financial metrics (Marr & Roos, 2005). Studies and cases have demonstrated that effective IC management significantly contributes to organisational performance, innovation, competitiveness, and market valuation (Peppard & Rylander, 2001; Chen et al., 2005; Subramaniam & Youndt, 2005; Calisir et al., 2010; Khan, 2018; Roos & Gromova, 2020). IC assessments provide valuable insights for strategic decision-making, enabling firms to align their strategies with IC and allocate resources effectively (Roos, 2019; Roos et al., 1997, 2005). Aligning IC strategies with business models maximises economic, financial, and organisational performance (Baima et al., 2021). Research highlights the mediating role of IC in strategic management's impact on performance, emphasising its importance in informing strategic decisions (Richard & Akhtar, 2017). The IC lens promotes innovation and creativity by leveraging IC resources (Nonaka & Takeuchi, 1995). Effective IC management fosters sustainable competitive advantage (Biedenbach et al., 2019; Nahapiet & Ghoshal, 1998). The IC approach also integrates IC resources into sustainability strategies, aligning economic, social, and environmental goals (Zambon, 2002). Studies have shown that IC positively impacts business sustainability and financial performance, as seen in the nexus between environmental corporate social responsibility, green intellectual capital, and green innovation in Chinese automobile firms (Li et al., 2023) and the impact of structural capital on financial performance in Nigerian nonfinancial service firms (Umar & Dandago, 2023). The IC lens provides a comprehensive framework for enhancing organisational performance by optimising the use of all resources (Roos, 2019).

At the meso level, leveraging shared IC enhances collective innovation capabilities within a network or industry, leading to new offerings and processes (Kianto et al., 2014). The IC approach underscores the importance of knowledge sharing, collaborative learning, and developing specialised skills and infrastructure within sectors (Nedoluzhko, 2018). Firms benefit from optimised resource sharing, improved productivity, and cost savings by pooling IC (Zhang et al., 2019). This collective IC strengthens competitive advantage, enhances adaptability, and improves responsiveness to market changes (Subramaniam & Youndt, 2005; Zhang et al., 2019). Powerful agglomeration economic benefits are generated through synergistic interaction between larger more specialised labor pools, increasingly efficient use of shared infrastructure alongside processes and systems that promote knowledge retention and innovation, and proximity to customers and suppliers, which lowers costs and improves supply chain efficiency and facilitates collaboration and knowledge spillovers between firms and employees (Bolter & Robey, 2020)—all in all good management of IC at the meso level.

At the macro level, a nation's IC drives economic growth and competitiveness (Bounfour & Edvinsson, 2005). Investing in education, research, and development is essential for building and sustaining robust IC (Bontis, 2004a, b). Effective management and use of IC require supportive policies, institutions, and infrastructure (Ståhle & Bounfour, 2008). IC assessments guide strategic investments in R&D and innovation, helping countries identify areas for increased funding or collaboration to enhance competitiveness (Lin & Edvinsson, 2010). National IC significantly influences economic performance, explaining up to 70% of the variance in developing countries (Seleim & Bontis, 2013). Strong national relational capital is crucial for attracting foreign direct investment and establishing beneficial trade relationships (Käpylä et al., 2012). Maintaining robust IC helps countries withstand economic shocks, as seen in Israel's resilience during the financial crisis (Lin & Edvinsson, 2013). Policies focusing on education, health, and infrastructure enhance national IC and contribute to economic performance and social well-being (Bontis, 2004a, b). Integrating social capital, which includes mutual trust, common values, and networks, further enhances the impact of IC on national performance (Lu et al., 2014). Managing IC is crucial for improving quality of life and economic growth (Labra & Paloma Sánchez, 2013).

In summary, at the firm level, IC enhances value creation, informs strategic decision-making, fosters innovation, and contributes to sustainable competitive advantage (Ferreira et al., 2021). At the sector level, IC promotes collaborative innovation, optimises resource sharing, strengthens competitive positioning, and improves overall performance (Hussain et al., 2023). At the national level, IC drives economic growth, competitiveness, and resilience, while informing policies related to education, research and development, and international trade and investment (Vo & Tran, 2024).

5 Overview of Models Used to Measure and Manage Intellectual Capital on the Micro, Meso, and Macro Levels

Measuring IC is crucial for understanding and managing the IC resources that drive value creation and competitiveness at the micro, meso, and macro levels. Various models and frameworks have been developed to assess and quantify IC, each with its own strengths and limitations.

At the micro level, several models have been proposed to measure and manage IC. These models include the Value Added Intellectual Coefficient (VAIC), developed by Pulić (1998), which measures the efficiency of value creation by calculating the value added by IC and capital employed providing an overall measure of IC efficiency (Pulić, 2000). The balanced scorecard (BSC), introduced by Kaplan and Norton (1992), integrates financial and nonfinancial metrics, including IC components, to provide a balanced view of an organisation's performance (Kaplan & Norton, 1992; Rafiq et al., 2020). The Skandia Navigator, developed by Edvinsson (1997), categorises IC into human capital and structural capital, further divided into customer and organisational capital, using indicators to provide a holistic view of IC resources (Edvinsson & Malone, 1997). The Intangible Asset Monitor (IAM), proposed by Sveiby (1997), classifies intangibles into external structure, internal structure, and individual competence, using indicators to measure each category (Sveiby, 1997). The IC Index (ICI), developed by Roos and Roos (1997), combines financial and nonfinancial indicators to assess the value of IC, providing an aggregated measure for benchmarking and comparative analysis (Roos et al., 1997). The IC Navigator, finalised in Roos (2019), creates a numerical and visual representation of resource deployment and value creation, aiding strategic analysis and decision-making by depicting how different resources interact and transform (Peppard & Rylander, 2001; Roos et al., 1997).

At the meso level, measuring IC involves assessing the collective intellectual resources of firms within a specific industry or region. The Industry Intellectual Capital Index (IICI) adapts firm-level IC measurement models to the industry level, assessing the aggregate IC of firms within an industry and providing insights into comparative IC performance to inform policy decisions and strategic investments (Käpylä et al., 2012). The Regional Intellectual Capital Index (RICI) measures the IC of a specific geographic region as well as interactions within the innovation ecosystem to guide regional development strategies (Martins Rodriguez & Martí, 2006). The Intellectual Capital Benchmarking System (ICBS), developed by María Viedma Marti (2001), benchmarks the IC of cities and regions across human, process, market, and renewal and development capital, enabling comparisons and identifying best practices in IC management. Data envelopment analysis (DEA) is a nonparametric method used to evaluate the relative efficiency of decision-making units, such as firms or industries, based on their inputs and outputs, providing insights into optimal IC resource allocation and areas for improvement (Afzal & Lawrey, 2012).

At the macro level, measuring IC involves assessing the IC resources of entire economies and their contribution to economic growth and competitiveness. The National Intellectual Capital Index (NICI), developed by Bontis (2004a, b), measures the hidden values of nations based on human, market, process, renewal, and trust capital, allowing for cross-country comparisons (Bontis, 2004a, b; Dženopoljac et al., 2022). The Intellectual Capital Monitor (ICM) provides a structured approach to assessing and reporting IC (Labra & Paloma Sánchez, 2013; Navarro et al., 2011). The World Bank's knowledge assessment methodology (KAM) evaluates a country's readiness for the knowledge economy across four pillars: economic incentive and institutional regime, education and human resources, innovation system, and ICT infrastructure (Chen & Dahlman, 2006; Cojanu et al., 2010; Gorji & Alipourian, 2011). The Inclusive Wealth Index (IWI) measures sustainable development potential by considering produced, natural, and human capital (Endo & Ikeda, 2022; Magliarditi et al., 2019; Xue et al., 2022). The Value Added Intellectual Coefficient (VAIC) model assesses the efficiency of value creation by IC at the national level, providing consistent results across different contexts (Nadeem et al. 2017a, b). Other models include the modified NICI by Užienė (Dženopoljac et al., 2022), the principal component analysis (PCA) model (Navarro et al., 2011), and the Corrado, Hulten, and Sichel (CHS) model (Ståhle & Ståhle, 2012). Benchmarking methodologies such as NICI, ICM, ICI, NIC40, and ELSS compare national IC against best practices or other nations to identify strengths and weaknesses (Januškaitė & Užienė, 2016). A systematic literature review by Labra and Paloma Sánchez (2013) highlighted the nascent state of national IC literature at the time and the need for further theoretical and empirical work.

Other models have further expanded the landscape of IC measurement across levels. The Holistic Value Approach (HVA) (Pike & Roos, 2004), Conjoint Value Hierarchy (CVH) (Pike et al., 2005), and the Intellectual Capital Dynamic Value Model (ICDVM) (Andriessen, 2004) provide comprehensive frameworks for assessing intangible assets. The Strategic Intellectual Capital Management (SICM) model (Roos & Roos, 1997), the developed measurement routines (MR) (Johanson et al., 2001), and the IC Navigator (Roos, 2019) offer additional tools for managing IC effectively.

The measurement of IC at the micro, meso, and macro levels involves various models and frameworks that capture the value of intangible assets, helping organisations, industries, and nations assess the contributions of human, structural, and relational capital to economic performance, innovation, and competitiveness, thus enabling informed decision-making and strategic management of intellectual capital.

6 Critique of Intellectual Capital at the Micro, Meso, and Macro Levels

The critique of intellectual capital (IC) discuss the following:

- The lack of a universally accepted definition and taxonomy complicates the application and comparison of IC frameworks across different contexts (Kaufmann & Schneider, 2004; Marr & Chatzkel, 2004; Andreou et al., 2007; Nazari & Herremans, 2007; Roos & Pike, 2007; Gogan & Draghici, 2013; Malinowska-Olszowy, 2013; Gogan, 2014; Kizil & Arslan, 2019).
- Conceptual overlap among IC components, such as human, structural, and relational capital, leads to inconsistent interpretations and applications (Hashim et al., 2015; Nerdrum & Erikson, 2001; Noordin & Mohtar, 2013; Pap et al., 2021; Wang, 2011). The intangibility and subjectivity of IC components further complicate objective quantification (Andriessen, 2003; Bontis, 2001; Bontis et al., 1999; Campbell et al., 2017; El Borsaly et al., 2023; Long Kweh et al., 2013; Sveiby, 1997; Sveiby, 2010; Yang & Lin, 2009).
- Measurement challenges arise due to the lack of standardised metrics and reliance on proxy indicators that may not accurately represent IC resources (Freeman, 2002; Andriessen, 2004; Khalifa & Khalid, 2015; Pirozzi & Ferulano, 2016). Traditional financial metrics often fail to capture IC's value, leading to potential underestimation or misrepresentation (Afzal & Lawrey, 2012; Cenciarelli et al., 2018; El Borsaly et al., 2023). Data availability and reliability issues hinder accurate IC assessment, particularly in developing nations (Bontis,

2004a, b; Lin & Edvinsson, 2013; Hussinki et al., 2017; Onumah & Duho, 2019). Critics argue that IC assessments often overemphasise quantitative measures, neglecting qualitative aspects like cultural and institutional contexts (Kaufmann & Schneider, 2004; Marr & Chatzkel, 2004). The drive to quantify IC can also result in a short-term focus, where organisations prioritise immediate, measurable outcomes over long-term value creation (Edvinsson, 2002).
- Inconsistent IC reporting guidelines contribute to quality and comparability issues (Ahmed Haji, 2015; Ståhle & Ståhle, 2012).
- IC relevance varies across sectors and nations, necessitating context-specific adaptations (Bounfour, 2003; Reed et al., 2006; Mačerinskienė & Aleknavičiūtė, 2017). Adapting IC frameworks to the specific needs and circumstances of each context requires significant time, resources, and expertise (Käpylä et al., 2012).
- Translating IC assessments into effective policies is challenging due to the complexity of IC and the gap between theoretical frameworks and practical applications (Salonius & Lönnqvist, 2012; Ståhle & Bounfour, 2008). Resistance to adopting IC frameworks requires raising awareness about IC's significance (Petty & Guthrie, 2000; Sullivan, 2000).
- Specific models, such as the VAIC model and balanced scorecard, face criticism for their limited scope and oversimplification (Norreklit, 2000; Ståhle et al., 2011; Forte et al., 2019). Likewise, the Skandia Navigator has faced criticism for its complexity and the difficulty of implementing it in practice (Dumay, 2009). Other models like the technology broker model and the intellectus model also have limitations in evaluating synergies, modularity, adaptability, and dealing with complexity and heterogeneity (Brooking, 1998; Bueno et al., 2006). At the macro level, applying micro-level models and refining existing national IC measurement models is difficult due to the absence of standardised techniques and reliable data (Aleknavičiūtė & Mačerinskienė, 2015; Lin & Edvinsson, 2010; Užienė, 2014). Existing measurement and reporting models for national IC require further theoretical refinement to improve their accuracy and reliability (Labra & Paloma Sánchez, 2013; Radjenović & Krstić, 2017).
- Practical implementation of IC frameworks faces significant challenges. Chiucchi and Dumay (2015) highlight the difficulty of embedding IC practices in organisational routines, noting that IC initiatives often fail to gain traction beyond initial implementation.
- Guthrie et al. (2012) point out that many organisations struggle with the resource-intensive nature of comprehensive IC measurement and reporting.
- Mouritsen (2006) argues that the ambiguity in IC measurements can lead to manipulative practices, where organisations selectively report IC metrics to present a favourable image. These practical challenges raise questions about the real-world applicability and value of IC frameworks in diverse organisational contexts.

Addressing these critiques requires developing standardised definitions and taxonomies, implementing effective integration strategies, adopting context-specific approaches, and refining measurement models for accuracy and reliability (Andriessen, 2003; Bontis et al., 1999; Marr & Chatzkel, 2004; Pike & Roos, 2007; Roos et al., 2005; Sveiby, 2010).

7 Can Other Approaches Provide the Same Insights on the Micro, Meso, and Macro Levels

While the IC approach provides valuable insights, several other approaches offer overlapping, complementary, or alternative perspectives. The balanced scorecard (Epstein & Manzoni, 1997; Kaplan & Norton, 1992; Rafiq et al., 2020) emphasises financial and nonfinancial measures, but may not fully capture knowledge creation and application central to IC (Andriessen, 2004). Knowledge management frameworks, such as Nonaka and Takeuchi's SECI model, focus on knowledge processes but may not align IC resources with business objectives (Kianto et al., 2013; Nonaka & Takeuchi, 1995). The resource-based view (Barney, 1991) and dynamic capabilities framework (Teece et al., 1997) highlight internal resources and adaptability but lack specific guidance on measuring IC resources (Andriessen, 2004). National Innovation Systems (Freeman, 1987; Lundvall, 1992) offer macro-level insights but may not fully address structural and relational capital (Bontis, 2004a, b; Andriessen, 2004). Competence-based approaches, such as the aggregated indices randomisation method (AIRM), focus on evaluating human capital enabling development programs to enhance organisational performance (Strelnikova & Lembrikova, 2017) but do not capture the contributions of structural and relational capital (Andriessen, 2004). CSR and accountability frameworks like the Global Reporting Initiative focus on nonfinancial performance but may miss specific contributions of IC resources (Andriessen, 2004; Veltri & Bronzetti, 2014). Economic and mathematical models provide rigorous assessments but may not capture qualitative aspects like culture and relationships (Andriessen, 2004; Zaytsev et al., 2020). Other approaches such as Porter's Five Forces, PESTEL analysis, SWOT analysis, value chain analysis, the knowledge-based view, Organisational Learning Theory, Social Capital Theory, Complexity Theory, Institutional Theory, and Systems Thinking provide additional strategic insights (Porter, 1980; DiMaggio & Powell, 1983; Porter, 1985; Senge, 1990; Hill & Westbrook, 1997; Anderson, 1999; Johnson et al., 2008; Thelen et al., 2023). Integrating these alternative approaches with IC frameworks can enhance the understanding of intangible assets' role in performance and competitiveness at various levels.

Combining the resource-based view (RBV) with IC frameworks helps organisations identify and leverage unique intellectual resources for sustainable competitive advantages (Reed et al., 2006; Roos, 2019). Similarly, integrating dynamic capabilities with IC frameworks develops necessary skills and processes for effectively leveraging IC resources (Kianto et al., 2014). National Innovation Systems (NIS) integration provides a comprehensive understanding of IC resources in national competitiveness and development (Ståhle & Bounfour, 2008). Competence-based approaches combined with IC frameworks offer a holistic view of an organisation's IC resources (Andriessen, 2004).

8 The Unique Benefits of Applying the Intellectual Capital Lens on the Micro, Meso, and Macro Levels

At the micro level, the IC framework provides a holistic view of a firm's IC resources including the interdependencies and synergies between the different resources, essential for strategic decision-making and aligning these resources with organisational goals which traditional financial metrics may not fully be able to provide (Bontis, 2001; Bontis et al., 1999; Chen et al., 2005; Edvinsson & Malone, 1997; Marr & Roos, 2005; Roos et al., 2005; Sveiby, 1997). This is further facilitated by specific models to assist in optimising the deployment of IC, like the IC Navigator (Roos, 2019).

At the meso level, the IC lens facilitates knowledge sharing and innovation within and across industries, emphasising the importance of relational capital and providing tailored, sector-specific insights (Hussain et al., 2023; Nahapiet & Ghoshal, 1998; Reed et al., 2006; Roos, 2018; Roos et al., 2005; Нагорняк & Ханнуф, 2023). The application of the IC lens helps sectors integrate their IC resources into broader sustainability strategies (María Viedma Marti, 2001; Bielienkova et al., 2022; Гречко & Очеретяна, 2022).

At the macro level, the IC approach offers a comprehensive view of a nation's intangible assets, linking human capital development to economic outcomes and enabling policymakers to make data-driven decisions that foster sustainable economic growth and resilience (Afzal & Lawrey, 2012; Becker, 1964; Cojanu et al., 2010; Dženopoljac et al., 2022; Hanushek & Woessmann, 2008; Lin & Edvinsson, 2010; Lin & Edvinsson, 2013; Vo & Tran, 2024). Assessing and managing IC enables nations to create an environment that fosters innovation and technological advancements, thereby enhancing their global competitiveness (Käpylä et al., 2012; Salonius & Lönnqvist, 2012). The IC perspective also promotes cross-country comparisons and benchmarking, helping nations identify strengths and weaknesses and adopt best practices for economic and social progress (Dženopoljac et al., 2022; Januškaitė & Užienė, 2016; Lin & Edvinsson, 2010). Despite challenges in measuring and quantifying intellectual capital, the IC approach is valuable in understanding and developing the wealth and potential of organisations, industries, and nations (Kuzminykh et al., 2020; Michalczuk & Fiedorczuk, 2018).

While the IC perspective provides valuable insights, it is important to acknowledge its limitations. Measuring and quantifying IC resources at all levels remains a challenge, and there is a need for further research to refine and standardise methodologies (Michalczuk & Fiedorczuk, 2018). Additionally, the IC approach should be used in conjunction with other frameworks and indicators to provide a comprehensive understanding of development and well-being at the micro, meso, and macro levels (Kuzminykh et al., 2020).

9 Reflection on the Way Forward for Intellectual Capital on the Micro, Meso, and Macro Levels

The field of IC has made significant strides in both understanding and leveraging IC resources. However, both academic and practitioner domains face challenges and opportunities. Academically, IC is recognised for driving innovation and economic growth, using various measurement models (Sveiby, 1997; Edvinsson & Malone, 1997; Andriessen, 2004; Bontis, 2004a, b; Bounfour & Edvinsson, 2005; Vahanyan et al., 2019; Ali et al., 2023; Petrusova et al., 2024) as well as increased use of interdisciplinary research, integrating insights from economics, management, and other fields to enhance the insights generated by the IC lens (Bontis, 2004a, b; Rachmawati et al., 2024). Yet, there is no consensus on IC definitions, and challenges persist in measuring intellectual capital (Andriessen, 2004; Kaufmann & Schneider, 2004; Roos & Pike, 2007; Lin & Edvinsson, 2010; Titova, 2019; Ferreira et al., 2021;Jardon & Martinez-Cobas, 2021; Ali et al., 2023). There is also limited empirical evidence on the long-term impact of IC on organisational and economic performance (Albertini & Berger-Remy, 2019; Bontis, 2001; Bontis et al., 1999; Nguyen & Doan, 2020; Radonić et al., 2021).

Opportunities lie in refining and standardising measurement frameworks, addressing global challenges, and leveraging advanced technologies (Edvinsson, 2002; Labra & Paloma Sánchez, 2013; Mačerinskienė & Aleknavičiūtė, 2017; Popescu, 2020; Secundo et al., 2020; Gravili et al., 2021; Arshad et al., 2023; Li et al., 2023; Vo & Tran, 2023; Синегуб, 2023). Threats include resistance to IC frameworks and difficulty translating research into practice (Petty & Guthrie, 2000; Marr & Chatzkel, 2004; Salonius & Lönnqvist, 2012, Yao et al., 2019; Ali et al., 2023; Gross-Golacka et al., 2024) as well as potential oversimplification or misinterpretation of IC concepts in pursuit of quantification and comparability (Al-Alawi & Alghasra, 2024; Andriessen, 2004; Dumay, 2009).

In the practitioner domain, the strategic importance of IC was initially increasingly recognised, with growing adoption of management practices (Edvinsson & Malone, 1997; Sveiby, 1997; Bontis, 1998; Mouritsen et al., 2001; Roos et al., 2005), but this initial interest seems to have waned over the latter decade (Roos, 2019). Integrating IC into traditional financial reporting remains difficult, and stakeholder buy-in is limited (Petty & Guthrie, 2000; Andriessen, 2004; Roos et al., 2005; Dumay, 2016; Hakiki & Herlina, 2021; Kovács & Lippai-Makra, 2023). There are also resource constraints, particularly for small- and medium-sized enterprises, in implementing comprehensive IC management and reporting systems (Marzo & Scarpino, 2016). Opportunities include driving innovation and sustainability, developing sector-specific frameworks (Bontis, 2004a, b; Käpylä et al.,

2012; Kianto et al., 2017; Secundo et al., 2017; Mačerinskienė & Survilaitė, 2019; Iacuzzi & Pauluzzo, 2023; Martínez-Falcó et al., 2023). Further opportunities lie in collaborating with academic institutions and professional bodies to develop practical tools and guidelines for IC management (Bontis & Girardi, 2000; Secundo et al., 2017). Threats involve resistance within organisations and potential misuse of IC information (Petty & Guthrie, 2000; Dumay & Garanina, 2013; Dumay, 2016). Another threat is the difficulty in attributing organisational performance to specific IC components, leading to skepticism about the value of IC management (Andriessen, 2004; Mouritsen, 2006; O'Sullivan, 2009).

External events (financial crisis, COVID-19 pandemic, etc.) have underscored the importance of IC in navigating crises and building resilience (Holienka & Pilkov, 2014; Osadchy & Akhmetshin, 2015; Papíková & Papík, 2022). Organisations with strong IC foundations have demonstrated greater adaptability, innovation, and responsiveness in the face of unprecedented challenges (Ganawati et al., 2021; Rupeika-Apoga et al., 2022). The pandemic has also accelerated digital transformation, emphasising the need for organisations to effectively manage and integrate their digital capital with other IC components to thrive in the postpandemic world (Ganawati et al., 2021; Rupeika-Apoga et al., 2022).

The apparent decline in interest in IC over the past decade (Roos, 2019) can be attributed to several factors. Dumay and Garanina (2013) suggest that the difficulty in translating IC theory into practical, value-creating activities has led to disillusionment among practitioners. Additionally, the global financial crisis of 2008 shifted focus toward more tangible assets and short-term financial metrics (Abhayawansa et al., 2015). The rise of big data and analytics has also redirected attention from IC to more data-driven approaches to understanding organisational performance (Secundo et al., 2017). Understanding these trends is crucial for revitalising interest in IC and adapting the field to contemporary business challenges.

Future research in IC should address several key gaps. First, there is a need for more longitudinal studies to understand the long-term impact of IC management on organisational performance (Inkinen, 2015). Second, research should explore how IC frameworks can be adapted for different organisational sizes, industries, and cultural contexts (Kianto et al., 2014). Third, studies should investigate the interaction between IC and emerging technologies like artificial intelligence and blockchain (Albertini & Berger-Remy, 2019). Potential research questions include the following: How does the value and composition of IC change over an organisation's lifecycle? How can IC frameworks be effectively implemented in SMEs with limited resources? How do national culture and institutional environments influence the development and use of IC? How can IC measurement and management practices adapt to the challenges and opportunities presented by existing and emerging digital technologies?

Moving forward, refining and standardising IC measurement frameworks, exploring new approaches, and enhancing collaboration between academia and industry are essential. Addressing conceptual ambiguities and measurement challenges will help organisations better leverage IC for sustainable growth as will the provision of evidence that the management of IC resources generate the desired outcomes.

10 Discussion and Conclusion

The reflections from the literature demonstrate that applying the IC lens provides unique and valuable insights. At the firm level, the IC framework enables a holistic view of intellectual capital, aids in strategic management, provides measurement tools, and enhances overall organisational performance. At the industry level, the IC approach facilitates knowledge sharing, tailors insights to specific sectors, integrates with sustainability strategies, and optimises collective assets. Nationally, IC assessments capture knowledge assets, emphasise innovation and learning, link human capital to economic outcomes, enable data-driven policymaking, and allow for global benchmarking. While alternative approaches offer complementary perspectives, the IC lens uniquely provides a comprehensive understanding of all intangible asset classes and their interdependencies. Integrating IC with other relevant models and theories can further enrich the insights gained.

However, IC research and application face challenges, including conceptual ambiguity, measurement issues, data reliability, quantification bias, comparability limitations, and implementation difficulties. Overcoming stakeholder resistance and bridging the academic-practitioner divide are also key hurdles. Specific IC measurement models have faced scrutiny for their limitations. Macrolevel IC assessment is especially complex, lacking both standardisation and comprehensive data.

Despite the critiques, the potential of the IC approach cannot be overlooked. Researchers and practitioners must collaboratively refine IC frameworks, explore technological solutions, incorporate sustainability considerations, and develop accessible, actionable tools. External shocks have further underscored the importance of IC in building organisational and economic resilience. Future research should address the identified challenges while leveraging emerging opportunities.

To advance the field, researchers and practitioners must collaborate to refine IC definitions and taxonomies, develop robust and context-specific measurement tools, leverage technology, integrate sustainability considerations, and create actionable frameworks. Overcoming resistance and bridging the academic-practitioner gap are also crucial as is evidencing the beneficial outcome of putting IC lens generated insights to use.

References

Abhayawansa, S., Aleksanyan, M., & Bahtsevanoglou, J. (2015). The use of intellectual capital information by sell-side analysts in company valuation. *Accounting and Business Research, 45*(3), 279–306.

Adams, S., & Simnett, R. (2011). Integrated reporting: An opportunity for Australia's not-for-profit sector. *Australian Accounting Review, 21*(3), 292–301.

Afzal, M. N. I., & Lawrey, R. (2012). Investigating World Bank knowledge assessment methodology (KAM) using data envelopment analysis (DEA): A study in the ASEAN region. *Research Journal of Science & IT Management, 1*(12), 33–38.

Ahmed Haji, A. (2015). The role of audit committee attributes in intellectual capital disclosures: Evidence from Malaysia. *Managerial Auditing Journal, 30*(8/9), 756–784.

Al-Alawi, A. I., & Alghasra, A. Y. (2024). A systematic review investigating Cyberthreats and the preservation of intellectual capital in big data. In *2024 ASU international conference in emerging Technologies for Sustainability and Intelligent Systems (ICETSIS)* (pp. 6–11). IEEE.

Albertini, E., & Berger-Remy, F. (2019). Intellectual capital and financial performance: A meta-analysis and research agenda. *M@n@gement, 22*(2), 216–249.

Aleknavičiūtė, R., & Mačerinskienė, I. (2015). Comparative evaluation of national intellectual capital measurement models. *Business: Theory and Practice, 16*(1), 1–14.

Ali, B. O. (2023). The impact of the accounting disclosure of intellectual capital on increasing the value of companies. *Tikrit Journal of Administration and Economics Sciences, 19*(64 part 2), 702–719.

Ali, M. A., Hussin, N., Flayyih, H. H., Haddad, H., Al-Ramahi, N. M., Almubaydeen, T. H., Hussein, S. A., & Hasan Abunaila, A. S. (2023). A multidimensional view of intellectual capital and dynamic innovative performance. *Journal of Risk and Financial Management, 16*(3), 139.

Anderson, P. (1999). Perspective: Complexity theory and organization science. *Organization Science, 10*(3), 216–232.

Andreou, A. N., Green, A., & Stankosky, M. (2007). A framework of intangible valuation areas and antecedents. *Journal of Intellectual Capital, 8*(1), 52–75.

Andriessen, D. (2003). *Making sense of intellectual capital: Designing a method for the valuation of intangibles*. Routledge.

Andriessen, D. (2004). IC valuation and measurement: Classifying the state of the art. *Journal of Intellectual Capital, 5*(2), 230–242.

Arshad, M. Z., Arshad, D., Lamsali, H., Alshuaibi, A. S. I., Alshuaibi, M. S. I., Albashar, G., Shakoor, A., & Chuah, L. F. (2023). Strategic resources alignment for sustainability: The impact of innovation capability and intellectual capital on SME's performance. Moderating role of external environment. *Journal of Cleaner Production, 417*, 137884.

Baima, G., Forliano, C., Santoro, G., & Vrontis, D. (2021). Intellectual capital and business model: A systematic literature review to explore their linkages. *Journal of Intellectual Capital, 22*(3), 653–679.

Barney, J. (1991). Firm resources and sustained competitive advantage. *Journal of Management, 17*(1), 99–120.

Becker, G. (1964). *Human capital: A theoretical and empirical analysis, with special reference to education*. Columbia University Press.

Biedenbach, G., Hultén, P., & Tarnovskaya, V. (2019). B2B brand equity: Investigating the effects of human capital and relational trust. *Journal of Business & Industrial Marketing, 34*(1), 1–11.

Bielienkova, O. I., Loktionova, Y. F., Stetsenko, S. P., & Tytok, V. V. (2022). Інтелектуальний капітал як чинник інноваційного сталого розвитку. *Ways to Improve Construction Efficiency, 2*(50), 281–291.

Bolter, K., & Robey, J. (2020). Agglomeration economies: A literature review. In *Prepared for the fund for our economic future (FFEF)*. W.E. Upjohn Institute for Employment Research.

Bontis, N. (1998). Intellectual capital: An exploratory study that develops measures and models. *Management Decision, 36*(2), 63–76.

Bontis, N., Dragonetti, N. C., Jacobsen, K., & Roos, G. (1999). The knowledge toolbox: A review of the tools available to measure and manage intangible resources. *European management journal, 17*(4), 391–402

Bontis, N., & Girardi, J. (2000). Teaching knowledge management and intellectual capital lessons: an empirical examination of the TANGO simulation. *International Journal of Technology Management, 20*(5–8), 545–555.

Bontis, N. (2001). Assessing knowledge assets: A review of the models used to measure intellectual capital. *International Journal of Management Reviews, 3*(1), 41–60.

Bontis, N. (2004a). National intellectual capital index: A United Nations initiative for the Arab region. *Journal of Intellectual Capital, 5*(1), 13–39.

Bontis, N. (2004b). National intellectual capital: A contrasted analysis of Asia and Europe. *Journal of Intellectual Capital, 5*(1), 8–28.

Bontis, N., Dragonetti, N. C., Jacobsen, K., & Roos, G. (1999). The knowledge toolbox: A review of the tools available to measure and manage intangible resources. *European Management Journal, 17*(4), 391–402.

Bontis, N., Keow, W. C. C., & Richardson, S. (2000). Intellectual capital and business performance in Malaysian industries. *Journal of Intellectual Capital, 1*(1), 85–100.

Bounfour, A. (2002). *The management of intangibles: The organisation's most valuable assets*. Routledge.

Bounfour, A. (2003). The IC-dVAL approach. *Journal of Intellectual Capital, 4*(3), 396–413.

Bounfour, A., & Edvinsson, L. (2005). *Intellectual capital for communities: Nations, regions, and cities*. Butterworth-Heinemann.

Brooking, A. (1998). *Intellectual capital: Core asset for the third millennium*. International Thomson Business Press.

Bueno, E., Salmador, M. P., Rodríguez, Ó., & Martín De Castro, G. (2006). Internal logic of intellectual capital: A biological approach. *Journal of Intellectual Capital, 7*(3), 394–405.

Burgman, R. J., Roos, G., Ballow, J. J., & Thomas, R. J. (2005). No longer "out of sight, out of mind": Intellectual capital approach in AssetEconomics Inc. and Accenture LLP. *Journal of Intellectual Capital, 6*(4), 588–614.

Cabrita, M. D. R., & Bontis, N. (2008). Intellectual capital and business performance in the Portuguese banking industry. *International Journal of technology management, 43*(1-3), 212–237.

Calisir, F., Gumussoy, C. A., Bayraktaroğlu, A. E., & Deniz, E. (2010). Intellectual capital in the quoted Turkish ITC sector. *Journal of Intellectual Capital, 11*(4), 538–554.

Campbell, B. A., Kryscynski, D., & Olson, D. M. (2017). Bridging strategic human capital and employee entrepreneurship research: A labor market frictions approach. *Strategic Entrepreneurship Journal, 11*(3), 344–356.

Canning, D., & Pedroni, P. (2008). Infrastructure, long-run economic growth and causality tests for cointegrated panels. *The Manchester School, 76*(5), 504–527.

Cenciarelli, V. G., Greco, G., & Allegrini, M. (2018). Does intellectual capital help predict bankruptcy? *Journal of Intellectual Capital, 19*(2), 321–337.

Chen, D. H., & Dahlman, C. J. (2006). *The knowledge economy, the KAM methodology and World Bank operations* (World Bank Institute Working Paper, 37256).

Chen, M. C., Cheng, S. J., & Hwang, Y. (2005). An empirical investigation of the relationship between intellectual capital and firms' market value and financial performance. *Journal of Intellectual Capital, 6*(2), 159–176.

Chiucchi, M. S., & Dumay, J. (2015). Unlocking intellectual capital. *Journal of Intellectual Capital, 16*(2), 305–330.

Cojanu, S. F., Stroe, C., & Militaru, E. (2010). Competitiveness through knowledge–assessment of the European Union member states based on the knowledge assessment methodology (KAM) developed by the World Bank. *Annals of Spiru Haret University, Economic Series, 1*(4), 151–157.

Cooke, P., Uranga, M. G., & Etxebarria, G. (1997). Regional innovation systems: Institutional and organisational dimensions. *Research Policy, 26*(4–5), 475–491.

DiMaggio, P. J., & Powell, W. W. (1983). The iron cage revisited: Institutional isomorphism and collective rationality in organizational fields. *American Sociological Review, 48*(2), 147–160.

Dumay, J. C. (2009). Intellectual capital measurement: A critical approach. *Journal of Intellectual Capital, 10*(2), 190–210.

Dumay, J., & Garanina, T. (2013). Intellectual capital research: A critical examination of the third stage. *Journal of Intellectual Capital, 14*(1), 10–25.

Dumay, J. (2016). A critical reflection on the future of intellectual capital: From reporting to disclosure. *Journal of Intellectual capital, 17*(1), 168–184.

Dženopoljac, V., Georgievski, B., Cavagnetto, S., & Abidi, O. (2022). National intellectual capital: A comparative longitudinal study. *Ekonomika preduzeća, 70*(3–4), 147–160.

Edvinsson, L. (1997). Developing intellectual capital at Skandia. *Long Range Planning, 30*(3), 366–373.

Edvinsson, L. (2002). *Corporate longitude: What you need to know to navigate the knowledge economy*. Financial Times Prentice Hall.

Edvinsson, L., & Malone, M. S. (1997). *Intellectual capital: Realizing your company's true value by finding its hidden brainpower*. HarperBusiness.

Edvinsson, L., & Stenfelt, C. (1999). Intellectual capital of nations—For future wealth creation. *Journal of Human Resource Costing & Accounting, 4*(1), 21–33.

El Borsaly, A., Hassanein Abd-Elrahman, A. E., & Osman, S. (2023). The Impact of Intellectual capital on Organizational performance in Egyptian Mobile Telecommunications Sector. مجلة الدراسات مجلة الدراسات التجارية المعاصرة., 15(9), 765–791.

Endo, K., & Ikeda, S. (2022). How can developing countries achieve sustainable development: Implications from the inclusive wealth index of ASEAN countries. *International Journal of Sustainable Development & World Ecology, 29*(1), 50–59.

Epstein, M. J., & Manzoni, J. F. (1997). The balanced scorecard and tableau de bord: Translating strategy into action. *Strategic Finance, 79*(2), 28–36.

Evans, J. M., Brown, A., & Baker, G. R. (2015). Intellectual capital in the healthcare sector: A systematic review and critique of the literature. *BMC Health Services Research, 15*, 1–14.

Ferreira, J. J., Fernandes, C., & Veiga, P. (2021). Multilevel approaches to advancing the measurement of intellectual capital research field–what can we learn from the literature? *Journal of Intellectual Capital, 22*(6), 971–999.

Forte, W., Matonti, G., Nicolo, G., & Tucker, J. (2019). MtB versus VAIC in measuring intellectual capital: Empirical evidence from Italian listed companies. *African Journal of Business Management, 13*(17), 588–601.

Freeman, C. (1987). *Technology policy and economic performance: Lessons from Japan*. Pinter.

Freeman, T. (2002). Using performance indicators to improve health care quality in the public sector: A review of the literature. *Health Services Management Research, 15*(2), 126–137.

Ganawati, N., Soraya, D., & Yogiarta, I. M. (2021). The role of intellectual capital, organizational learning and digital transformation on the performance of SMEs in Denpasar, Bali-Indonesia. *International Journal of Science and Management Studies (IJSMS)*, 235–246.

García-Sánchez, I. M., & Noguera-Gámez, L. (2017). Integrated reporting and stakeholder engagement: The effect on information asymmetry. *Corporate Social Responsibility and Environmental Management, 24*(5), 395–413.

Gogan, M. L. (2014). An innovative model for measuring intellectual capital. *Procedia-Social and Behavioral Sciences, 124*, 194–199.

Gogan, L. M., & Draghici, A. (2013). A model to evaluate the intellectual capital. *Procedia Technology, 9*, 867–875.

Gorji, E., & Alipourian, M. (2011). The knowledge economy & the knowledge assessment methodology (the case study of Iran & some other countries). *Iranian Economic Review, 15*(29), 43–72.

Gravili, G., Manta, F., Cristofaro, C. L., Reina, R., & Toma, P. (2021). Value that matters: Intellectual capital and big data to assess performance in healthcare. An empirical analysis on the European context. *Journal of Intellectual Capital, 22*(2), 260–289.

Gross-Golacka, E., Brzozowska, A., Balcerzyk, R., & El Emary, I. M. (2024). Barriers to sustainable Management of Organizational Intellectual Capital. *Marketing and Management of Innovations, 15*(1), 252–263.
Guthrie, J., Ricceri, F., & Dumay, J. (2012). Reflections and projections: A decade of intellectual capital accounting research. *The British Accounting Review, 44*(2), 68–82.
Hakiki, R. A., & Herlina, E. (2021). The effect of intellectual capital investment, corporate governance, and barriers to entry on the intellectual capital performance of banking companies. *Journal of Economics, Business, & Accountancy Ventura, 24*(3), 458–468.
Hanushek, E. A., & Woessmann, L. (2008). The role of cognitive skills in economic development. *Journal of Economic Literature, 46*(3), 607–668.
Hashim, M. J., Osman, I., & Alhabshi, S. M. (2015). Effect of intellectual capital on organizational performance. *Procedia-Social and Behavioral Sciences, 211*, 207–214.
Hill, T., & Westbrook, R. (1997). SWOT analysis: It's time for a product recall. *Long Range Planning, 30*(1), 46–52.
Holienka, M., & Pilkov, A. (2014). Impact of intellectual capital and its components on firm performance before and after crisis. *Electronic Journal of Knowledge Management, 12*(4), 261–272.
Hussain, A., Nisar, Q. A., Khan, W., Niazi, U. I., & Malik, M. (2023). When and how big data analytics and work practices impact on financial performance: An intellectual capital perspective from banking industry. *Kybernetes*. https://doi.org/10.1108/K-11-2022-1623
Hussinki, H., Ritala, P., Vanhala, M., & Kianto, A. (2017). Intellectual capital, knowledge management practices and firm performance. *Journal of Intellectual Capital, 18*(4), 904–922.
Iacuzzi, S., & Pauluzzo, R. (2023). Looking for missing outcomes: Accounting for intellectual capital and value creation in ecosystems. *Journal of Management and Governance*, 1–33.
Inkinen, H. (2015). Review of empirical research on intellectual capital and firm performance. *Journal of Intellectual Capital, 16*(3), 518–565.
Januškaitė, V., & Užienė, L. (2016). Benchmarking in the national intellectual capital measurement: Is it the best available approach? *International Journal of Learning and Change, 8*(1), 64–79.
Jardon, C. M., & Martinez-Cobas, X. (2021). Measuring intellectual capital with financial data. *PLoS One, 16*(5), e0249989.
Johanson, U., Mårtensson, M., & Skoog, M. (2001). Measuring to understand intangible performance drivers. *European Accounting Review, 10*(3), 407–437.
Johnson, G., Scholes, K., & Whittington, R. (2008). *Exploring corporate strategy: Text and cases*. Pearson Education.
Kaplan, R. S., & Norton, D. P. (1992). The balanced scorecard: Measures that drive performance. *Harvard Business Review, 70*(1), 71–79.
Käpylä, J., Kujansivu, P., & Lönnqvist, A. (2012). National intellectual capital performance: A strategic approach. *Journal of Intellectual Capital, 13*(3), 343–362.
Kaufmann, L., & Schneider, Y. (2004). Intangibles: A synthesis of current research. *Journal of Intellectual Capital, 5*(3), 366–388.
Khalifa, M., & Khalid, P. (2015). Developing strategic health care key performance indicators: A case study on a tertiary care hospital. *Procedia Computer Science, 63*, 459–466.
Khan, A. M. (2018). An empirical study of the impact of intellectual capital on the financial performance of the Indian IT sector. *Корпоративные финансы, 12*(1), 7–19.
Kianto, A., Andreeva, T., & Pavlov, Y. (2013). The impact of intellectual capital management on company competitiveness and financial performance. *Knowledge Management Research & Practice, 11*(2), 112–122.
Kianto, A., Ritala, P., Spender, J. C., & Vanhala, M. (2014). The interaction of intellectual capital assets and knowledge management practices in organizational value creation. *Journal of Intellectual Capital, 15*(3), 362–375.
Kianto, A., Sáenz, J., & Aramburu, N. (2017). Knowledge-based human resource management practices, intellectual capital and innovation. *Journal of business research, 81*, 11–20.
Kizil, C., & Arslan, M. L. (2019). Measuring intellectual capital of Turkish banks listed on borsa Istanbul banking index (BIST XBANK) with the market value/book value method and

value added intellectual coefficient (VAIC) model. *Emerging Markets Journal (EMAJ), 9*(1), 101–116.

Kovács, Z. I., & Lippai-Makra, E. (2023). Intellectual capital disclosure and non-financial reporting–current issues related to policymaking. *PRO, 10*(3), 4.

Kuzminykh, N., Mashkina, D., & Roze, N. (2020). *International experience in managing intellectual capital of territories for innovative development*. Atlantis Press.

Labra, R., & Paloma Sánchez, M. (2013). National intellectual capital assessment models: A literature review. *Journal of Intellectual Capital, 14*(4), 582–607.

Lazuka, V. (2012). National intellectual capital: Concept and measurement. Lund University Publications.

Li, W., Bhutto, M. Y., Waris, I., & Hu, T. (2023). The nexus between environmental corporate social responsibility, green intellectual capital and green innovation towards business sustainability: An empirical analysis of Chinese automobile manufacturing firms. *International Journal of Environmental Research and Public Health, 20*(3), 1851.

Lin, C. Y.-Y., & Edvinsson, L. (2010). *National intellectual capital: A comparison of 40 countries*. Springer Science & Business Media.

Lin, C. Y.-Y., & Edvinsson, L. (2013). National intellectual capital in Israel and financial crisis impact. *International Journal of Knowledge-Based Development, 4*(3), 245–273.

Long Kweh, Q., Chuann Chan, Y., & Wei Kiong Ting, I. (2013). Measuring intellectual capital efficiency in the Malaysian software sector. *Journal of Intellectual Capital, 14*(2), 310–324.

Lu, W. M., Kweh, Q. L., & Huang, C. L. (2014). Intellectual capital and national innovation systems performance. *Knowledge-Based Systems, 71*, 201–210.

Lundvall, B. A. (1992). *National systems of innovation: Towards a theory of innovation and interactive learning*. Pinter.

Luis Hervas-Oliver, J., & Dalmau-Porta, J. I. (2007). Which IC components explain national IC stocks? *Journal of Intellectual Capital, 8*(3), 444–469.

Mačerinskienė, I., & Aleknavičiūtė, R. (2017). National intellectual capital influence on economic growth in the European Union countries. *Equilibrium: Quarterly Journal of Economics and Economic Policy, 12*(4).

Mačerinskienė, I., & Survilaitė, S. (2019). Company's intellectual capital impact on market value of Baltic countries listed enterprises. *Oeconomia Copernicana, 10*(2), 309–339.

Magliarditi, E., Siddiqi, A., & de Weck, O. (2019). Remote sensing for assessing natural capital in inclusive wealth of nations: Current capabilities and gaps. In *IGARSS 2019–2019 IEEE international geoscience and remote sensing symposium* (pp. 4411–4414). IEEE.

Malinowska-Olszowy, M. (2013). The choice of appropriate tools for measuring intellectual capital as a determinant of success with special emphasis on the textile and clothing market. *Autex Research Journal, 13*(4), 122–127.

Marco-Lajara, B., Zaragoza-Sáez, P. D., Martínez-Falcó, J., & Ruiz-Fernández, L. (2022). The effect of Green intellectual capital on Green performance in the Spanish wine industry: A structural equation modeling approach. *CompLex, 2022*, 6024077.

María Viedma Marti, J. (2001). ICBS–intellectual capital benchmarking system. *Journal of Intellectual Capital, 2*(2), 148–165.

Marr, B., & Chatzkel, J. (2004). Intellectual capital at the crossroads: Managing, measuring, and reporting of IC. *Journal of Intellectual Capital, 5*(2), 224–229.

Marr, B., & Roos, G. (2005). A strategy perspective on intellectual capital. In B. Marr (Ed.), *Perspectives on intellectual capital* (pp. 28–41). Elsevier Butterworth-Heinemann.

Martínez-Torres, M. R. (2006). A procedure to design a structural and measurement model of intellectual capital: An exploratory study. *Information & Management, 43*(5), 617–626.

Martínez-Falcó, J., Sánchez-García, E., Millan-Tudela, L. A., & Marco-Lajara, B. (2023). The role of green agriculture and green supply chain management in the green intellectual capital–sustainable performance relationship: A structural equation modeling analysis applied to the Spanish wine industry. *Agriculture, 13*(2), 425.

Martins Rodriguez, B., & Martí, J. M. V. (2006). The region's intellectual capital benchmarking system: Enabling economic growth through evaluation. *Journal of Knowledge Management, 10*(5), 41–54.

Maskell, P., & Malmberg, A. (1999). Localised learning and industrial competitiveness. *Cambridge Journal of Economics, 23*(2), 167–185.

Marzo, G., & Scarpino, E. (2016). Exploring intellectual capital management in SMEs: An in-depth Italian case study. *Journal of Intellectual capital, 17*(1), 27–51.

Michalczuk, G., & Fiedorczuk, J. (2018). National intellectual capital taxonomy. *Economics and Business, 32*(1), 89–101.

Mouritsen, J. (2006). Problematising intellectual capital research: Ostensive versus performative IC. *Accounting, Auditing & Accountability Journal, 19*(6), 820–841.

Mouritsen, J., Larsen, H. T., & Bukh, P. N. (2001). Valuing the future: Intellectual capital supplements at Skandia. *Accounting, Auditing & Accountability Journal, 14*(4), 399–422.

Nadeem, M., Dumay, J., & Massaro, M. (2017a). If you can measure it, you can manage it: A case of intellectual capital. *Accounting & Finance, 58*(1), 1–26.

Nadeem, M., Gan, C., & Nguyen, C. (2017b). Does intellectual capital efficiency improve firm performance in BRICS economies? A dynamic panel estimation. *Measuring Business Excellence, 21*(1), 65–85.

Nahapiet, J., & Ghoshal, S. (1998). Social capital, intellectual capital, and the organizational advantage. *Academy of Management Review, 23*(2), 242–266.

Navarro, J. L. A., Ruiz, V. R. L., & Peña, D. N. (2011). An alternative to measure national intellectual capital adapted from business level. *African Journal of Business Management, 5*(16), 6707–6716.

Nazari, J. A., & Herremans, I. M. (2007). Extended VAIC model: measuring intellectual capital components. *Journal of Intellectual Capital, 8*(4), 595–609.

Nedoluzhko, O. V. (2018). Management of intellectual capital development of an organization based on the system contradictions between its elements. *The Journal of Social Sciences Research*, 228–234.

Nerdrum, L., & Erikson, T. (2001). Intellectual capital: A human capital perspective. *Journal of Intellectual Capital, 2*(2), 127–135.

Nguyen, A. H., & Doan, D. T. (2020). The impact of intellectual capital on firm value: Empirical evidence from Vietnam. *International Journal of Financial Research, 11*(4), 74–85.

Nonaka, I., & Takeuchi, H. (1995). *The knowledge-creating company: How Japanese companies create the dynamics of innovation*. Oxford University Press.

Noordin, M. A., & Mohtar, S. (2013). An exploratory of the intangible assets: Methods of measuring intellectual capital. *International Journal of Humanities and Applied Sciences (IJHAS), 2*(2), 36–40.

Norreklit, H. (2000). The balance on the balanced scorecard a critical analysis of some of its assumptions. *Management Accounting Research, 11*(1), 65–88.

Onumah, J. M., & Duho, K. C. T. (2019). Intellectual capital: its impact on financial performance and financial stability of Ghanaian banks. Athens *Journal of Business and Economics, 5*(3), 243–268.

O'Connor, A., & Roos, G. (2018). Visualising intellectual capital transformations for strategic design of entrepreneurial business models. In S. Griffith, K. Carruthers, & M. Bliemel (Eds.), *Visual tools for developing cross-disciplinary collaboration, innovation and entrepreneurship capacity* (pp. 243–260). Common Ground Research Networks.

OECD. (1996). *The knowledge based economy*. OECD Publishing.

OECD. (2001). *The Well-being of nations: The role of human and social capital*. OECD Publishing.

Osadchy, E. A., & Akhmetshin, E. M. (2015). The intellectual capital importance and the role of organizations against the backdrop of a crisis: Innovation vector. *Social Sciences, 10*(6), 1013–1020.

O'Sullivan, K. (Ed.). (2009). *Strategic intellectual Capital Management in Multinational Organizations: Sustainability and successful implications*. IGI Global.

Pap, E., Petković, M., & Simićević, A. (2021). Measuring distribution of intellectual capital components contribution: French context. *The European Journal of Applied Economics, 18*(1), 1–14.
Papíková, L., & Papík, M. (2022). Intellectual capital and its impacts on SMEs profitability during COVID-19 pandemic. *Journal of Eastern European and Central Asian Research (JEECAR), 9*(3), 521–531.
Peppard, J., & Rylander, A. (2001). Using an intellectual capital perspective to design and implement a growth strategy: The case of APiON. *European Management Journal, 19*(5), 510–525.
Petrusova, I., Andrejovska, A., & Barski, R. (2024). The impact of intangible assets on market valuation: Evidence from EURO STOXX 50 companies. *Acta Tecnología- International Scientific Journal about Technologies, 10*(1), 31–35.
Petty, R., & Guthrie, J. (2000). Intellectual capital literature review: Measurement, reporting and management. *Journal of Intellectual Capital, 1*(2), 155–176.
Pike, S., & Roos, G. (2004). Mathematics and modern business management. *Journal of Intellectual Capital, 5*(2), 243–256.
Pike, S., & Roos, G. (2007). The validity of measurement frameworks: Measurement theory. In A. Neely (Ed.), *Business performance measurement: Unifying theory and integrating practice* (pp. 218–236). Cambridge University Press.
Pike, S., Fernström, L., & Roos, G. (2005). Intellectual capital: Management approach in ICS ltd. *Journal of Intellectual Capital, 6*(4), 489–509.
Pirozzi, M. G., & Ferulano, G. P. (2016). Intellectual capital and performance measurement in healthcare organizations: An integrated new model. *Journal of Intellectual Capital, 17*(2), 320–350.
Pomeda, J. R., Moreno, C. M., Rivera, C. M., & Martil, L. V. (2002, November). *Towards an intellectual capital report of Madrid: New insights and developments*. Paper presented at The Transparent Enterprise: The Value of Intangibles.
Popescu, C. R. G. (2020). Sustainability assessment: Does the OECD/G20 inclusive framework for BEPS (base erosion and profit shifting project) put an end to disputes over the recognition and measurement of intellectual capital? *Sustainability, 12*(23), 10004.
Porter, M. E. (1980). *Competitive strategy: Techniques for analyzing industries and competitors*. Free Press.
Porter, M. E. (1985). *Competitive advantage: Creating and sustaining superior performance*. Free Press.
Porter, M. E. (1998). Clusters and the new economics of competition. *Harvard Business Review, 76*(6), 77–90.
Pulić, A. (1998). Measuring the performance of intellectual potential in the knowledge economy. In *The 2nd World Congress on the Management of Intellectual Capital*.
Pulić, A. (2000). VAIC™–an accounting tool for IC management. *International Journal of Technology Management, 20*(5–8), 702–714.
Rachmawati, R., Novatiani, R. A., & Octavia, E. (2024). Emerging trends in intellectual capital research: A decade review. *Jurnal Ilmu Manajemen dan Bisnis, 15*(1), 68375.
Radjenović, T., & Krstić, B. (2017). *The microeconomic perspectives of intellectual capital measurement* (pp. 189–202). Facta Universitatis, Series: Economics and Organization.
Radonić, M., Milosavljević, M., & Knežević, S. (2021). Intangible assets as financial performance drivers of IT industry: Evidence from an emerging market. *E&M Economics and Management, 2*(1), 92–105.
Rafiq, M., Zhang, X., Yuan, J., Naz, S., & Maqbool, S. (2020). Impact of a balanced scorecard as a strategic management system tool to improve sustainable development: Measuring the mediation of organizational performance through PLS-smart. *Sustainability, 12*(4), 1365.
Rana, M. S., & Hossain, S. Z. (2023). Intellectual capital valuation of DSE-listed non-financial companies in Bangladesh. *Archives of Business Research, 11*(10), 129–144.
Reed, K. K., Lubatkin, M., & Srinivasan, N. (2006). Proposing and testing an intellectual capital-based view of the firm. *Journal of Management Studies, 43*(4), 867–893.

Richard, J., & Akhtar, M. (2017). Impact of strategic management on performance: Mediating role of intellectual capital. *Management, 6*(1), 1–9.

Roos, G. (2018). Resource deployment system implications of migrating the firm into a digital value creation paradigm. *Knowledge Management Research & Practice, 16*(3), 281–291.

Roos, G. (2019). Optimising resource deployment within the firm: Overcoming theoretical problems with a practical application. *Doctoral dissertation*, University of South Australia.

Roos, G., & Gromova, I. (2020). The English language school case. In D. Remenyi (Ed.), *6th knowledge management and intellectual capital excellence awards 2020: An anthology of case histories* (pp. 23–44). Academic Conferences International Limited.

Roos, G., & Pike, S. (2007, May 3–4). *Intellectual capital research: A personal view*. Paper presented at the IC-Congress. Inholland University of Professional Education.

Roos, G., & Roos, J. (1997). Measuring your company's intellectual performance. *Long Range Planning, 30*(3), 413–426.

Roos, J., Roos, G., Edvinsson, L., & Dragonetti, N. (1997). *Intellectual capital: Navigating in the new business landscape*. Macmillan Publications.

Roos, G., Pike, S., & Fernström, L. (2005). *Managing intellectual capital in practice*. Butterworth-Heinemann.

Rupeika-Apoga, R., Petrovska, K., & Bule, L. (2022). The effect of digital orientation and digital capability on digital transformation of SMEs during the COVID-19 pandemic. *Journal of Theoretical and Applied Electronic Commerce Research, 17*(2), 669–685.

Salonius, H., & Lönnqvist, A. (2012). Exploring the policy relevance of national intellectual capital information. *Journal of Intellectual Capital, 13*(3), 331–342.

Saxenian, A. (1994). *Regional advantage: Culture and competition in Silicon Valley and route 128*. Harvard University Press.

Secundo, G., Del Vecchio, P., Dumay, J., & Passiante, G. (2017). Intellectual capital in the age of big data: Establishing a research agenda. *Journal of Intellectual Capital, 18*(2), 242–261.

Secundo, G., Ndou, V., Del Vecchio, P., & De Pascale, G. (2020). Sustainable development, intellectual capital and technology policies: A structured literature review and future research agenda. *Technological Forecasting and Social Change, 153*, 119917.

Seleim, A., Ashour, A., & Bontis, N. (2004). Intellectual capital in Egyptian software firms. *The Learning Organization, 11*(4/5), 332–346.

Seleim, A., & Bontis, N. (2013). National intellectual capital and economic performance: Empirical evidence from developing countries. *Knowledge and Process Management, 20*(3), 131–140.

Senge, P. M. (1990). *The fifth discipline: The art and practice of the learning organization*. Doubleday/Currency.

Ståhle, P., & Bounfour, A. (2008). Understanding dynamics of intellectual capital of nations. *Journal of Intellectual Capital, 9*(2), 164–177.

Ståhle, P., Ståhle, S., & Aho, S. (2011). Value added intellectual coefficient (VAIC): A critical analysis. *Journal of Intellectual Capital, 12*(4), 531–551.

Ståhle, S., & Ståhle, P. (2012). Towards measures of national intellectual capital: An analysis of the CHS model. *Journal of Intellectual Capital, 16*(1), 27–39.

Ståhle, P., Ståhle, S., & Lin, C. Y. (2015). Intangibles and national economic wealth–a new perspective on how they are linked. *Journal of Intellectual capital, 16*(1), 20–57.

Strelnikova, L. A., & Lembrikova, M. M. (2017). Using economic and mathematical models and methods to assess the human capital of a company in the field of IT industry. *π-Economy, 10*(2), 88–97.

Subramaniam, M., & Youndt, M. A. (2005). The influence of intellectual capital on the types of innovative capabilities. *Academy of Management Journal, 48*(3), 450–463.

Sucena, A., Matos, F., & Nunes, A. (2024). Intellectual Capital in Construction SMEs: A systematic literature review. *Journal of Open Innovation: Technology, Market, and Complexity, 100276*.

Sullivan, P. H. (2000). *Value-driven intellectual capital: How to convert intangible corporate assets into market value*. John Wiley & Sons.

Sveiby, K. E. (1997). *The new organizational wealth: Managing & measuring knowledge-based assets*. Berrett-Koehler Publishers.

Sveiby, K. E. (2010). *Methods for measuring intangible assets.* https://www.sveiby.com/files/pdf/intangiblemethods.pdf

Teece, D. J., Pisano, G., & Shuen, A. (1997). Dynamic capabilities and strategic management. *Strategic Management Journal, 18*(7), 509–533.

Thelen, J., Sant Fruchtman, C., Bilal, M., Gabaake, K., Iqbal, S., Keakabetse, T., Kwamie, A., Mokalake, E., Mupara, L. M., Seitio-Kgokgwe, O., Zafar, S., & Cobos Muñoz, D. (2023). Development of the systems thinking for health actions framework: A literature review and a case study. *BMJ Global Health, 8*(3), e010191.

Titova, N. (2019). Intellectual capital: From definition to impact assessment. *Regional Formation & Development Studies, 27*(1), 79–87.

Tuunanen, T., Lumivalo, J., Vartiainen, T., Zhang, Y., & Myers, M. D. (2023). Micro-level mechanisms to support value co-creation for design of digital services. *Journal of Service Research, 10946705231173116.*

Umar, A., & Dandago, K. I. (2023). The knowledge economy: How intellectual capital drives financial performance of non-financial service firms in Nigeria. *FUDMA Journal of Accounting and Finance Research [FUJAFR], 1*(2), 113–122.

United Nations. (2015). *Transforming our world: The 2030 agenda for sustainable development. A/RES/70/1*. United Nations.

Užienė, L. (2014). Measurement of national intellectual capital: The benchmarking of the Baltic countries in the context of Europe. In *Proceedings of the European conference on intellectual capital* (pp. 283–292). Academic Conferences and Publishing International.

Vahanyan, G. A., Vahanyan, H., & Ghazaryan, M. (2019). Interactive innovative tool for early diagnosis of global pre-crisis processes (based on measurement and assessment of the virtual intellectual capital). *Journal of Intellectual Capital, 20*(2), 190–207.

Veltri, S., & Bronzetti, G. (2014). Intellectual capital reporting in the Italian nonprofit sector. An image-building or an accountability tool? *Advances in Public Interest Accounting*, 251–278.

Vitolla, F., Raimo, N., & Rubino, M. (2019). Intellectual capital disclosure and firm performance: An empirical analysis through integrated reporting. In *7th international OFEL conference on governance, management and entrepreneurship: Embracing diversity in Organisations* (pp. 245–255). Governance Research and Development Centre (CIRU).

Vitolla, F., Raimo, N., Marrone, A., & Rubino, M. (2020). The role of board of directors in intellectual capital disclosure after the advent of integrated reporting. *Corporate Social Responsibility and Environmental Management, 27*(5), 2188–2200.

Vo, D. H., & Tran, N. P. (2023). Measuring national intellectual capital and its effect on country's competitiveness. *Competitiveness Review: An International Business Journal, 33*(4), 820–839.

Vo, D. H., & Tran, N. P. (2024). Does national intellectual capital matter for economic growth in the Asia–Pacific economies? *Journal of Intellectual Capital.* https://doi.org/10.1108/JIC-09-2022-0184

Wang, M. (2011). Measuring intellectual capital and its effect on financial performance: Evidence from the capital market in Taiwan. *Frontiers of Business Research in China, 5*(2), 243–265.

Windle, A., Javanparast, S., Freeman, T., & Baum, F. (2023). Factors that influence evidence-informed meso-level regional primary health care planning: A qualitative examination and conceptual framework. *Health Research Policy and Systems, 21*(1), 99.

Xue, Q., Cheng, D., Li, Y., Guan, D., & Zhao, W. (2022). Sustainable development pathways for Chinese cities: An assessment of the advanced inclusive wealth index. *Earth's Future, 10*(9), e2022EF002695.

Yang, C. C., & Lin, C. Y. Y. (2009). Does intellectual capital mediate the relationship between HRM and organizational performance? Perspective of a healthcare industry in Taiwan. *The International Journal of Human Resource Management, 20*(9), 1965–1984.

Yao, H., Haris, M., Tariq, G., Javaid, H. M., & Khan, M. A. S. (2019). Intellectual capital, profitability, and productivity: Evidence from Pakistani financial institutions. *Sustainability, 11*(14), 3842.

Youndt, M. A., Subramaniam, M., & Snell, S. A. (2004). Intellectual capital profiles: An examination of investments and returns. *Journal of Management Studies, 41*(2), 335–361.

Zambon, S. (2002). *Accounting, intangible and intellectual capital: An overview of the issues and some considerations. PRISM project*. University of Ferrara.

Zaytsev, A., Rodionov, D., Dmitriev, N., & Ilchenko, S. (2020). Assessing intellectual capital from the perspective of its rental income performance. *International Journal of Technology, 11*(8), 1489–1498.

Zhang, M., Lettice, F., & Pawar, K. (2019). Effects of intellectual capital and university knowledge in indigenous innovation: Evidence from Indian SMEs. *Production Planning & Control, 30*(10–12), 799–812.

Zhang, Z., Wang, X., & Chun, D. (2022). The effect of knowledge sharing on ambidextrous innovation: Triadic intellectual capital as a mediator. *Journal of Open Innovation: Technology, Market, and Complexity, 8*(1), 25.

Гречко, А. В., & Очеретяна, О. В. (2022). Методи оцінки впливу інтелектуального капіталу на сталий розвиток підприємства. *Науково-виробничий журнал «Бізнес-навігатор», 69*, 76–80.

Нагорняк, Г., & Ханнуф, К. (2023). Особливості Викликів Та Можливостей Формування Інтелектуального Капіталу Вітчизняних Підприємств Машинобудівного Сектору України В.

Синєгуб, П. С. (2023). Економічний механізм управління інтелектуальним капіталом бізнес-спільноти в умовах дигіталізації [Докторська дисертація, Донецький національний університет імені Василя Стуса].

Building and Retaining Intellectual Capital Through Onboarding Activities

Eva Didion, Ute Ambrosius, Daniel Catala-Perez, and Maria Rosario Perello-Marin

Abstract Although adopting human resource management (HRM) practices has been shown to be positively related to intellectual capital, onboarding and organizational socialization have not been discussed as potential drivers of intellectual capital. The Socialization Resource Theory shows how personal, relational, and structural resources influence newcomer adjustment, which is linked with various outcomes like organizational commitment, intention to quit, turnover, and job performance. Therefore, the purpose of this chapter is to describe organizational socialization as an essential factor in building and retaining intellectual capital. During socialization, human capital can be developed through training, skill development, and newcomer learning. Successful newcomer adjustment helps to preserve intellectual capital because it decreases intention to quit and, thus, retains valuable and knowledgeable employees. Through organizational socialization, newcomers acquire relational resources that might enhance organizations' relational capital. Finally, a structured onboarding process can be an integral part of an organization's organizational capital that helps to codify knowledge. In essence, onboarding is instrumental in managing, developing, and leveraging the human capital that forms

---

E. Didion (✉)
Hochschule Ansbach - University of Applied Sciences, Faculty of Business and Management, Ansbach, Germany

Universitat Politècnica de València (UPV), Departamento de Organizacion de Empresas, Valencia, Spain
e-mail: eva.didion@hs-ansbach.de

U. Ambrosius
Hochschule Ansbach - University of Applied Sciences, Faculty of Business and Management, Ansbach, Germany
e-mail: ute.ambrosius@hs-ansbach.de

D. Catala-Perez · M. R. Perello-Marin
Universitat Politècnica de València (UPV), Departamento de Organizacion de Empresas, Valencia, Spain
e-mail: dacapre@ade.upv.es; rperell@upvnet.upv.es

F. Matos et al. (eds.), *Intellectual Capital in a Global Business Landscape*, Contributions to Management Science, https://doi.org/10.1007/978-3-031-86362-2_12

a significant part of intellectual capital. The novelty of this article is to connect intellectual capital and organizational socialization in a comprehensive model. The effective implementation of onboarding measures can enhance organizational performance, innovation, and long-term sustainability. The chapter also explores the potential benefits of virtual and digital onboarding in adapting practices to individual newcomer needs. The overarching focus is on human capital, digitization, and performance.

1 Introduction

Although research has demonstrated a positive correlation between the implementation of human resource management (HRM) practices and intellectual capital (Afshari & Hadian Nasab, 2021; Chen et al., 2020; Gupta, 2021; Sokolov & Zavyalova, 2021; Wang & Chen, 2013), the role of onboarding and organizational socialization as potential contributors to intellectual capital remains unexplored. By fostering human, social, and organizational capital, organizations can enhance their overall intellectual capital, which leads to a competitive advantage. Of its three most commonly examined components, namely, human, social, and organizational capital, so far only social capital has been addressed as an outcome of newcomer socialization (Fang et al., 2011; Korte & Lin, 2013; Lapointe & Vandenberghe, 2018). Organizational socialization focuses on the individual level, although its effects certainly impact the whole organization (Cooper-Thomas & Anderson, 2006).

Intellectual capital loss is often associated with turnover because human capital in employees leaves the company together with them, and relational and social capital are affected when employees drop out, and they take with them not only skills but also intangible assets of knowledge and social relationships (Hollenbeck & Jamieson, 2015; Subramaniam & Youndt, 2005). Turnover is costly, and investments that have been made in recruitment and training are lost when newcomers prematurely leave the organization (Kammeyer-Mueller & Wanberg, 2003). Research suggests that newcomer adjustment early in the socialization process can be instrumental in decreasing turnover intention while fostering organizational commitment, job satisfaction, engagement, and job performance (Bauer et al., 2007; Harris, 2023; Saks et al., 2007; Saks & Gruman, 2011). Finding ways to improve the socialization process should, therefore, be in the interest of the organizations that wish to retain intellectual capital by reducing turnover.

Moreover, organizational socialization and intellectual capital are both linked with organizational learning. Organizations learn at multiple levels through informal processes and formal systems. Socialization contributes to organizational learning in a two-way process between newcomers and organizational insiders (S. W. Kozlowski et al., 2009). It is surprising that, so far, the organizational socialization and intellectual capital concepts have not been put in context because this will provide insights for both knowledge fields and practitioners.

In this chapter, we intend to make two contributions. We first wish to draw attention to organizational socialization for remaining an overlooked factor to date in developing intellectual capital. As this is an unexplored knowledge field, we address the need for building new theoretic relationships by rigorously exploring the existing literature and deriving a conceptual model on building intellectual capital through onboarding measures. Our second intention is to provide practical insights into the management of organizational socialization and onboarding processes, particularly in the dynamic landscapes of virtual and remote working environments. Therefore, we review recent publications on remote work and virtual teams literature to find hints about how to ameliorate the onboarding experience in those contexts.

2 Literature Review

In this section, we first conceptualize intellectual capital by describing the four subcategories that are most commonly used in the intellectual capital literature: human capital, relational capital, social capital, and organizational capital (Inkinen, 2015). We also choose these categories because they cover areas that are relevant for learning processes during organizational socialization. For each subcategory, we aim to summarize findings on how these assets evolve and what role organizations and organizational agents play in this process. Then, we outline insights from research into organizational socialization that can help to explain how onboarding activities and socialization might influence intellectual capital building and retention. Therefore, we first introduce the organizational socialization and onboarding concepts and then show the effects of successful onboarding and organizational socialization.

Intellectual capital refers to a company's knowledge and knowing capability (Nahapiet & Ghoshal, 1998). The term intellectual capital can be defined as intangible assets of knowledge and social relationships that can be leveraged into value by the organization (Edvinsson & Sullivan, 1996; Kucharska, 2021). This concept was introduced as a means to measure these resources to be able to better manage them and to, thus, increase organizational competitiveness and productivity (Bornemann et al., 2021; Kucharska, 2021; J. Yang et al., 2015; Youndt et al., 2004). Intellectual capital is a multicomposite variable that normally comprises human capital, relational/social capital, and organizational/structural capital (Inkinen et al., 2017). It is important to note that these three subcategories are not necessarily independent (Matos et al., 2020). Although this categorization is helpful in understanding the phenomenon, when examining the development and use of human, relational, and organizational capital, dependences, interactions, and causal effects need to be considered (Matos et al., 2020; Youndt et al., 2004).

From the very beginning of research into intellectual capital, *human capital* has played a pivotal role and is commonly referred to as a component of intellectual capital (Edvinsson & Malone, 1997; Inkinen, 2015). It comprises the knowledge, abilities, and behaviors or attitudes of an organization's employees (Martín-de-Castro et al., 2011; Subramaniam & Youndt, 2005). It is owned and controlled by employees, who act as gatekeepers toward the organization for accessing and using those resources (Roos & Pike, 2018).

There are two ways that an organization can increase its human capital. First, human resource development measures, such as training programs or performance feedback, contribute to human capital building. Second, attracting talent from the labor market and selecting candidates with valuable skills and knowledge increase an organization's human capital (C.-C. Yang & Lin, 2009; Youndt et al., 2004). To maximize the benefits of investing in human capital, organizations also need to foster social capital development. This investment facilitates networking and knowledge sharing, which are needed to fully harness their employees' potential (Subramaniam & Youndt, 2005).

Besides human capital, we include *relational capital* within our framework because it is frequently used besides human capital to capture the assets that form intellectual capital. Relational capital is an expanded version of Edvinsson's and Malone's (1997) customer capital. It incorporates the resources that result from the company's external relationships with different agents on the market and in society, such as customers, suppliers, clients, partners, or representatives (Roos & Pike, 2018; Youndt & Snell, 2020). In most studies, relational capital refers to the relationships with individuals or organizations outside the company (Inkinen, 2015). It includes the relationships of organizational members who act on behalf of the organization and also the relationships that the organization directly has (Roos & Pike, 2018).

We also include *social capital* to our framework because it is the only component of intellectual capital that has been discussed in research into organizational socialization (Fang et al., 2011). It describes the value of the social structures and networks that facilitate access to social resources (Fang et al., 2011; Nahapiet & Ghoshal, 1998; Seibert et al., 2001), which explicitly include the relationships inside the organization. Zhou et al. (2022) discovered a U-shaped relation between newcomers' peer connections in their unit and role clarity, which was then related to job satisfaction, performance, and turnover. Onboarding programs that support these connections up to a moderate level seem to be most beneficial. Lapointe and Vandenberghe (2018) examined the positive relation between trust in the supervisor and newcomers' social capital development. Some conceptualizations further distinguish external and internal social capital. Most studies about intellectual capital use either relational or social capital as a third component of intellectual capital (Inkinen, 2015); for an exception, see Delgado-Verde et al. (2011). Within our framework, we include both concepts with relational capital to refer to the relationships with persons and organizations outside the organization and to social capital with the focus relationships within the organization.

Regarding the development of intellectual capital, there are some insights into how companies can build relational and social capital. The organizations investing in human resource management practices not only foster human capital building but also support an increase in social capital. Training programs can create opportunities to communicate and build relationships. Carefully selecting employees that fit in well might also contribute to social capital building within the organization (Youndt et al., 2004). Digital technologies influence organizations' external and internal relationships. Computer-mediated tools, such as social media, might foster building relational and social capital by offering new possibilities for exchanging ideas and collaborating (Paoloni & Lombardi, 2023). At the same time, chatbots and other artificial intelligence (AI) applications are replacing interactions between employees and customers. As a consequence, relational capital will diminish and be replaced with organizational capital elements (Paoloni & Lombardi, 2023).

Finally, *organizational capital* is the fourth component of intellectual capital that our framework includes. It embodies institutionalized knowledge and codified experience (Youndt et al., 2004). It comprises databases, routines, procedures, corporate culture, intellectual property, manuals, and programs (Inkinen, 2015; Roos & Pike, 2018; Subramaniam & Youndt, 2005). Some researchers use the structural capital term for this concept (Stewart, 2007). However, to fall in line with Youndt and Snell, we prefer the term organizational capital because the organization actually owns this capital, unlike the human capital owned by individual employees (Bontis, 1998; Stewart, 2007; Yang et al., 2015).

Kucharska (2021) showed that formal knowledge processes help to build structural capital, but are not effective in developing human and relational capital. In contrast, her study underlines the importance of tacit knowledge sharing to develop human and relational capital.

Intellectual capital does not grow and develop by itself but depends on managerial action. Youndt et al. (2004) revealed how the companies that invested in human resource management and information technology (IT) exhibit higher intellectual capital profiles. Intellectual capital can be increased by combining knowledge and experiences and exchanging knowledge. The latter can be done explicitly or through social interaction and coworking activities (Nahapiet & Ghoshal, 1998). Exchanging knowledge and building social relationships that facilitate knowledge exchange is the essence of what happens during the socialization of organizational newcomers. Therefore, we wish to shed light on the organizational socialization and onboarding concepts.

Organizational socialization refers to the process during which newcomers become integrated and effectively functioning insiders of the organization by acquiring the necessary behaviors, skills, and knowledge (Bauer & Erdogan, 2011; Van Maanen & Schein, 1979). It can be defined as a "learning and adjustment process that enables an individual to assume an organizational role that fits both organizational and individual needs" (Chao, 2012, p. 7). Newcomer adjustment is mostly defined by three key aspects: understanding one's role in terms of what tasks have to be done and how (role clarity); gaining proficiency in accomplishing one's tasks (task mastery); and being liked and trusted by colleagues (feeling of acceptance) (Bauer et al., 2021; Wanberg, 2012b).

The meta-analyses by Bauer et al. (2007) and Saks et al. (2007) provide evidence that newcomer adjustment is related positively to performance, job satisfaction, and commitment and negatively to turnover. There is a consensus in the literature about organizational socialization being linked with positive outcomes for both newcomers and organizations. Although research to date into organization socialization has emphasized the outcomes of newcomer adjustment, more research that examines the methods, content, timing and practices is needed (Batistič, 2018). In line with this, a growing number of organizational socialization scholars examine socialization resources as drivers for newcomer adjustment (Ellis et al., 2015; Harris et al., 2020, 2022; Saks & Gruman, 2018). We find this approach promising for examining the influence of onboarding measures on intellectual capital because, according to the Conservation of Resources Theory, resource gains lead to the accumulation of further resources and lack of resources may reinforce resources loss (Hobfoll, 2011; Hobfoll et al., 2018).

With practitioners, the *onboarding* term is widely used, whereas the organizational socialization term abounds in the academic literature. It refers to "all formal and informal practices, programs, and policies enacted or engaged in by an organization or its agents to facilitate newcomer adjustment" (Klein & Polin, 2012, p. 268). Whereas socialization is an ongoing process that occurs within a person, onboarding is the sum of all the measures set up by an organization or its agents (i.e., managers, coworkers, or mentors) for successfully socializing new employees (Klein et al., 2015). Onboarding is one factor among others, such as newcomer information seeking, that can influence organizational socialization (Wanberg, 2012a). As we aim to show how organizations can positively impact their intellectual capital building through onboarding measures, in the next paragraph, we wish to go through the onboarding and organizational socialization literature to summarize the current research state in this field.

3 Effective Onboarding Components

As we have shown that successful and timely organizational socialization is highly relevant for organizations to be competitive, they need to know how these processes work and how they can be successfully managed. Therefore, this section offers an overview of the state of the onboarding and organizational socialization literature by focusing on management implications.

Early organizational socialization research focused on socialization tactics based on a typology developed by Van Maanen and Schein (1979). Their six bipolar tactics were later categorized into institutionalized (collective, formal, sequential, fixed, serial, investiture) or individualized (individual, informal, random, variable, disjunctive, divestiture) by Jones (1986). Several studies have confirmed that institutional tactics are related to lower role ambiguity, role conflict, and turnover intentions (Saks et al., 2007) and to newcomer adjustment in role clarity terms (Bauer et al., 2007). Allen (2006) empirically showed that investiture socialization tactics are related to lower turnover via on-the-job embeddedness and serial tactics (the provision of experienced employees as role models) directly and negatively affect turnover. Structured and formalized socialization tactics are associated with newcomers engaging more in proactive behaviors and relationship building (Gruman et al., 2006; Klein & Heuser, 2008).

Socialization tactics research has been criticized for offering very little guidance on what organizations can do, except for possibly making the process more formal and structured (Saks & Gruman, 2012). The categories that the tactics offer focus on the structural side of socialization, but fail to inform about the content, the specific activities, and the context in which socialization takes place (Ellis et al., 2015; Saks & Gruman, 2012, 2018).

To react to these shortcomings, Klein and Heuser (2008) developed the Inform-Welcome-Guide framework. It offers a comprehensive classification of activities (i.e., tour of the company facilities, Q&A session with senior leader) that organizations can apply in these three categories, with the inform category further divided into communication, resources, and training. Although Klein et al. (2015) found that newcomers perceived most practices as helpful for their onboarding experience and that the number of practices correlated positively with adjustment, the concept remains vague and has no proper theoretical basis. Indeed, the different practices could be shaped quite differently in practice (Harris, 2023).

Newcomer proactivity is another important driver of newcomer socialization (Kammeyer-Mueller et al., 2011; Saks & Gruman, 2018). A recent meta-analysis by Zhao et al. (2022) reveals an overall positive relation between newcomer proactive behaviors and newcomer socialization. Although proactivity is seen as personal (Miller & Jablin, 1991), which might then be influenced by an organization only during selection, there is evidence for a more interactionist approach. The social environment at entry and continued support are related to newcomers' proactive behaviors (J. Kammeyer-Mueller et al., 2013; Zhao et al., 2022). Consequently, organizations should encourage insiders to support newcomers and to positively react to their proactivity. Furthermore, some types of proactive behaviors that prove effective should be supported and trained by the organization. Of the proactive behaviors that have proven effective in newcomer socialization, positive framing is the strongest predictor of socialization outcomes. Relationship building facilitates social integration, and sensemaking is associated with role clarity and task mastery (Zhao et al., 2022).

Based on the Job Demands-Resources Model (Bakker & Demerouti, 2007), Saks and Gruman (2012) developed the Socialization Resource Theory. It assumes that starting a new job is stressful, and providing newcomers with resources that help them to cope with these challenges is required for them to successfully adjust. They describe 17 socialization resources that are needed at different times of the socialization process, such as formal orientation, supervisor support, or training (Saks & Gruman, 2012). As Saks and Gruman concentrate on resources made available by the organization, Ellis (2015) propose three categories of newcomer resources: personal, relational, and structural resources. We use these three categories to integrate the newcomer proactivity perspective and insights from the Socialization Resource Theory for modeling antecedents of newcomer adjustment.

Organizational socialization has often been described as a learning process (Ashford et al., 2007; Chao, 2012) which poses the question of which content is learned during socialization? Several scales have been developed in recent decades to measure socialization content. Chao et al. (1994) distinguish six dimensions of socialization content: performance proficiency, language, people, politics, organizational goals and values, and history. Performance proficiency describes learning how to master the tasks required to do the job. The people dimension refers to establishing relationships with organizational members. Politics describes knowing the power structures and relationships within the organization. The language dimension includes knowing the technical knowledge used in the job, as well as acronyms, slang, and jargon. Learning organizational values and goals also includes formal and unspoken rules and principles and extends to the informal, tacit goals and values anchored in an organization's organizational culture. Finally, history refers to knowledge about organizations' past, stories, and backgrounds of important organizational representatives (Chao et al., 1994; Chao, 2012).

Another measure of socialization content developed by Morrison (1995) includes seven categories: technical information (how to perform the job), referent information (expectations and role requirements), social information (social norms and getting along), appraisal information (feedback), normative information (history, rituals and culture), organizational information (structures and policies), and political information (power structure).

Klein and Heuser (2008) further differentiated the scale developed by Chao et al. (1994) into 12 knowledge domains that should be measured at different organizational levels at distinct times during the socialization process.

By reacting on critique of those scales for high intercorrelations between the domains and content overlap with other constructs, the newcomer understanding and integration scale (NUIS) was devised by Cooper-Thomas et al. (2020). It aims to assess socialization content through the three domains of role, relationships, and organization. For effective newcomer adjustment, newcomers need to learn how to successfully perform their tasks and what is expected of the role they are taking on. The NUIS measures this role factor. Additionally, establishing effective workplace relationships can be measured to cover the second domain of socialization content. The third domain refers to the organization by assessing how well the newcomer is familiar with the organizational culture and context (Cooper-Thomas et al., 2020). A number of studies and the meta-analysis by Bauer et al. (2007) and Saks et al. (2007) provide evidence for the positive relation of newcomer adjustment with job satisfaction, organizational commitment, turnover, and performance (Bauer & Erdogan, 2011). The NUIS offers organizations a short questionnaire to measure socialization content, which is associated with well-being, engagement, job satisfaction, self-rated performance, and less intention to quit (Cooper-Thomas et al., 2020).

Finally, research that was conducted during the COVID-19 pandemic with enforced remote work regimes has concluded that onboarding newcomers in remote and virtual settings pose additional challenges for individuals and organizations (Rodeghero et al., 2021; Sani et al., 2022; Yarbrough & Ramos Salazar, 2023). Remote work persists after the pandemic: The Working from Home Around the Globe: 2023 Report (Aksoy et al., 2023) stated that in the 34 countries that formed part of the study, on average 8 percent of employees worked fully remote and 26 percent worked in a hybrid working arrangement. Therefore, organizations need to find a way how to socialize newcomers in these new working environments.

4 Building Intellectual Capital: A Conceptual Framework

In order to undermine our proposition that onboarding can contribute to intellectual capital development, we analyze the components of the socialization process and intellectual capital to develop a model that can serve as a conceptual framework by bridging organizational socialization and intellectual capital research (Ellis et al., 2015; Harris, 2023; Saks & Gruman, 2018). By building on the Socialization Resources Theory, Fig. 1 integrates and summarizes how socialization processes affect an organization's intellectual capital. By establishing a relation between organizational socialization and intellectual capital, we provide a theoretical model to gain insights into intellectual capital formation and retainment.

Our model of onboarding for building intellectual capital starts with socialization resources as antecedents of newcomer adjustment. Of all the resources included in socialization resources, our model includes three categories: personal, relational, and structural resources. We choose these three in line with Ellis (2015).

Personal resources are personal characteristics that help newcomers to adjust to their new role. Self-efficacy, proactive personality, extraversion, conscientiousness, pre-entry knowledge, and adaptability are examples of personal resources that influence newcomer adjustment (Ellis et al., 2015; Kammeyer-Mueller & Wanberg, 2003). Organizations can pay attention to these personal characteristics during recruitment and selection to choose the new employees who are more likely to possess resources that help them to adjust. As previously stated, recent publications on

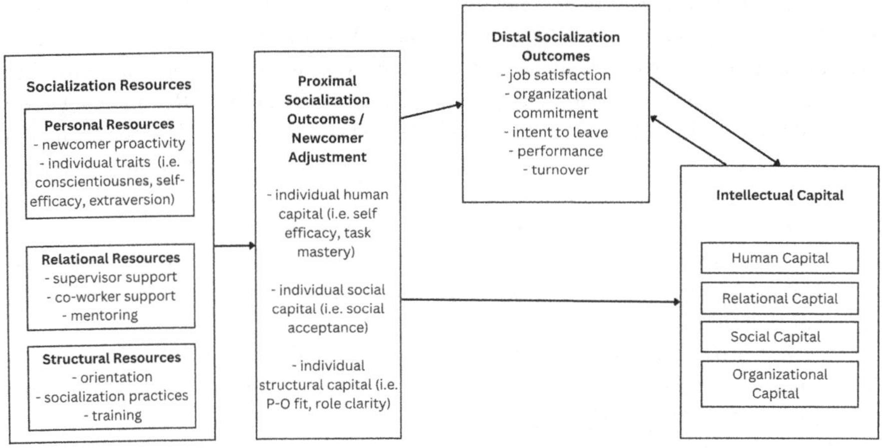

Fig. 1 Model of onboarding for building intellectual capital. (Source: the authors)

newcomer proactivity stress the fact that newcomer proactivity is not a stable individual trait, but can be influenced by socialization agents (Zhao et al., 2022).

Relational resources refer to socializing agents, such as coworkers, supervisors, and mentors. Supervisor support has been widely accepted as an important factor for successful socialization (Lee, 2022; Morrison, 2002; Ostroff & Kozlowski, 1993). Even though it is evident that organizations should offer training and development for supervisors to improve supervisor support, this has been neglected (Lee, 2022). Organizational socialization is a mutually reliant relational process between newcomers and organizational insiders. Support through building and maintaining relationships is provided when both recognize the relationship as being valuable and, thus, engage in reciprocation (Batistič & Kaše, 2022). Hence, coworkers play an important role in fostering newcomer adjustment by providing information, feedback, support, and acceptance (Ellis et al., 2015). Providing formal assistance by assigning a buddy or mentor has been found to facilitate newcomer adjustment (Allen et al., 1999; Korte, 2010; Ostroff & Kozlowski, 1993; Rollag et al., 2005). Organizations should provide possibilities for newcomers and insiders to develop and deepen relationships, such as social activities or events, and should encourage relationship building (Harris et al., 2020).

Structural resources encompass the features that organizations provide newcomers with for learning about their role and the organization, such as norms, structure, objectives, or culture (Harris, 2023). The resources identified by Saks and Gruman (2012) as work-related resources following orientation and formal orientation fall in this category. Examples of such are training, information, personal planning, or feedback. It still has to be examined how these different resources might interact or which bundles of resources may be particularly helpful for certain organizations or contexts (Saks & Gruman, 2018). For instance, formal orientation programs on behalf of the organization help newcomers to gain knowledge about goals/values and history and also positively influence relationship building (Klein & Weaver, 2000).

We assume that these three types of socialization resources relate to newcomer adjustment as a proximal socialization outcome. As previously mentioned, role clarity, self-efficiency, and social acceptance are common indicators of newcomer adjustment (Bauer et al., 2007). Following the Conservation of Resources Theory (Halbesleben et al., 2014; Hobfoll, 1989, 2011; Hobfoll et al., 2018), we argue that newcomers wish to protect, maintain, and acquire resources. Availability of socialization resources will promote the development of further resources (Harris, 2023; Saks & Gruman, 2018). Therefore, we view *proximal socialization* outcomes as resources or individual capital that newcomers acquire during the socialization process. The proximal outcomes that indicate newcomer resource development include personal, relational, and structural resources (Ellis et al., 2015).

The first proximal outcome consists of the personal resources that increase the newcomer's human capital. It refers to newcomers' learning outcomes, such as task mastery and self-efficacy (Ellis et al., 2015).

The second proximal outcome lies in the relational resources that encompass the social capital that newcomers build during socialization. It refers to the social relationships and network of social ties that newcomers build, the feeling of social acceptance and learning about social aspects in the organization (Ellis et al., 2015; Harris, 2023).

The third proximal outcome consists of newcomers' structural capital. It describes how well they fit in with the organization's structure and processes and comprises Person-Organization fit (P-O fit) and role clarity (Ellis et al., 2015).

Distal outcomes refer to the broader organizational consequences of newcomer adjustment. We include job attitudes and behaviors in our model, as widely acknowledged in the literature. Job attitudes, job satisfaction, organizational commitment, and intention to remain are among the most studied socialization outcomes (Bauer et al., 2007). Performance also relates to newcomer adjustment because the employees who are clear about expectations inherent to their role and those who can rely on good relationships with their coworkers can improve their performance (Bauer et al., 2007). Early unwanted turnover is linked with insufficient social acceptance, role confusion, or lack of confidence regarding their task and is an indicator of poor onboarding (Bauer & Erdogan, 2012). In their meta-analysis, Bauer et al. (2007) established that turnover was consistently related to newcomer adjustment and correlated with self-efficacy, role clarity, and social acceptance.

These interrelations should be considered potential drivers of intellectual capital. We argue that newcomer adjustment has direct and indirect effects on intellectual capital. In developing personal resources through the sociation process, newcomers can increase their individual human capital, which sums at an organizational level to increased human capital. The same applies to newcomers' social capital building, which increases an organization's social capital. Developing social capital also positively affects human capital by facilitating knowledge sharing among employees (Subramaniam & Youndt, 2005). As newcomers also build relationships with stakeholders outside the organization, similar effects on an organization's relational capital can be expected. Finally, how well newcomers are adjusted regarding their role, their perception of fit, and their alignment with structures and processes in the organization will impact an organization's organizational capital. Distal socialization outcomes also have a potential effect on intellectual capital. The most obvious factor related to intellectual capital is turnover because it directly prevents knowledge loss and impaired social and relational capital. Other distal outcomes, such as organizational commitment, job satisfaction, and job performance, also certainly have a positive effect on intellectual capital dimensions. The direction of the relation between distal socialization outcomes and intellectual capital may be bidirectional, with intellectual capital affecting job attitudes (Longo & Mura, 2011), as indicated by the reciprocal arrows in our model.

5 The Role of Technology and Virtual Work in Onboarding

The COVID-19 pandemic was a catalyst for digitization and remote work (Ameen et al., 2023). Nevertheless, mobile work is here to stay. Numbers obtained from the 2023 Working From Home Around the Globe Report (Aksoy et al., 2023) indicate that full-time employees from 34 countries work an average share of 0.9 days from home per week, with 26 percent working a hybrid working arrangement and 8 percent as fully remote employees. Therefore, it is important to mitigate the negative consequences of virtual organizational socialization and, at the same time, leverage the opportunities that it might also bring. When we wish to inform organizations about how to build intellectual capital through onboarding activities, adding the challenges and opportunities that digitization and virtual work imply is essential for capturing these new developments.

Research evidence indicates that organizational socialization is a social process that heavily depends on interactions between newcomers and insiders (Harris et al., 2022). It occurs through the observation and informal interactions with peers, supervisors, and coworkers (Reichers, 1987). According to Batistič and Kaše (2022), socialization is an interdependent relational process between organizational insiders that provides support for organizational newcomers. Korte (2010) identified how relationships with coworkers and supervisors, along with the quality of interactions, contribute the most to newcomer learning and socialization. Rollag et al. (2005) showed that the speed at which newcomers establish relationships with colleagues is the key factor in their successful adjustment and socialization.

Given the shift to remote work, occasions for newcomers to observe, meet, and interact with peers, supervisors, and coworkers have diminished and, thus, challenge successful newcomer socialization (Saks & Gruman, 2021). When working remotely, newcomers are deprived of actively witnessing coworkers and managers. So this way of learning about roles and tasks is limited (Woo et al., 2022). Asynchronous work and not seeing the availability of colleagues in virtual work environments make it harder to reach out to coworkers and regularly establish contact (Schinoff et al., 2020). Therefore, relationship building may suffer from virtual work. This is not only relevant for intraorganizational relationships, but also for relationships with suppliers, customers, and other stakeholders linked with a company's relational capital. A major hindrance in working remotely that could have been observed with the transition to remote work during the pandemic was lack of casual interactions, which take place automatically when people work at the same place. They also facilitate learning, knowledge sharing, relationship building, and well-being (Deepa et al., 2023).

Although research into virtual organizational socialization is scarce (Didion et al., 2022), there are recommendations for successfully socializing newcomers in virtual and hybrid work arrangements that can be derived from the literature on remote and computer-mediated work. Organizations have the means to facilitate informal communication. Contrary to the commonly accepted hypothesis that the need for relatedness is less satisfied among teleworkers than office workers, Brunelle and Fortin (2021) found the opposite to be true in a study they did in an IT company. They explained this unexpected outcome by two measures that were implemented. First, the company provided resources for organizing informal socialization opportunities, such as sports activities, during which teleworkers and office workers can physically meet. Second, an instant messaging system for quick and easy communication is available and might contribute to a feeling of connectedness. Advanced communication technologies (ACTs) allow effective communication when working remotely. However, these chances are taken only when users make the most of ACTs' interactivity, immediacy, schedulability, shareability, and cue communicability, which very much depend on the structural context, such as job characteristics (Fuchs & Reichel, 2023). Viererbl et al. (2022) identified five typical scenarios of informal communication in remote work environments: (1) pre- and postmeeting talk; (2) parallel chats; (3) follow-up communication; (4) informal talks; and (5) informal meetings. Whillans et al. (2021) distinguished task interactions, process interactions, and relationship interactions, which all need to be adapted to the virtual working environment because some of these interactions fall short, like huddle interactions (i.e., meeting in the hallway). Therefore, time for these should be scheduled. Onboarding in the office makes room for informal communication, but informal communication via information and communication systems also creates an emotional bond between remote employees (Lee, 2023). Therefore, remote newcomers should be encouraged to proactively use digital information sources. By providing rich information, this will have a positive influence on newcomer learning (Woo et al., 2022). Providing the necessary resources, and installing virtual onboarding practices that improve internal communication and facilitate building work relationships, is seen as helpful for retaining virtual newcomers (Yarbrough & Ramos Salazar, 2023). Additionally, regular one-on-one meetings might allow managers to quickly react in the difficulties that arise while integrating remote or hybrid newcomers and nurturing the relationship with newcomers (Russo et al., 2023).

Another strategy for dealing with virtual onboarding challenges is shift to agile. Agile working practices entail more networking and exchange among employees and, therefore, benefit newcomers who work remotely (Britto et al., 2018). Agile work mediates working-from-home success and companies that apply agile work can support employees through HRM actions (Heidt et al., 2022). So far, agile working practices have not been examined as tools for successful newcomer onboarding. Future research could analyze the effect that these methods might have in this regard.

Digital technology and virtual work do not only constrain organizational socialization but also create additional learning opportunities. The use of e-learning systems has proven beneficial for newcomers' organizational socialization and job adaptation (Chen, 2012). AI use might soon significantly reduce the time and costs of producing e-learning modules and facilitate more individualized solutions. Organizational support helps employees to successfully adapt to remote work (Ng et al., 2022). This can include the promotion of smart working practices that enhance remote work outcomes (Adekoya et al., 2022).

Not all employees react similarly to the shift to digitization and virtualization. Newcomers with more introvert personalities might feel more at ease in these environments thanks to less hostility in digital environments, and previous experience with remote work might also have an effect (Sani et al., 2022).

Trust is an essential factor for facilitating knowledge sharing among teleworkers. When trust is lacking, frequent face-to-face interactions lead to higher knowledge sharing. Once trust has been gained, face-to-face interactions are less critical for knowledge sharing (Golden & Raghuram, 2010). Regarding onboarding new employees, this means that before gaining trust, the facilitation of face-to-face interaction seems beneficial. Besides face-to-face interactions, using electronic tools can facilitate knowledge sharing when trust and commitment are minimum (Golden & Raghuram, 2010). As trust was an important factor for newcomer adjustment (Nifadkar et al., 2019) in forced remote work during the pandemic, a study found trust to be not only an important emotional resource but also a type of organizational support while perceived monitoring, such as micromanagement, was unfavorable for organizational support (H. Lee, 2021). To summarize, first research studies in the aftermath of the COVID-19 pandemic provided a mixed picture of the effect of remote work and digitization on organizational socialization. Organizations that successfully capitalize digital onboarding opportunities and, at the same time, set up measures to mitigate the hindrances of virtual and remote work will have a competitive advantage in attracting and retaining human capital.

6 Conclusion, Implications for Theory, and Future Research

In this chapter, we seek to integrate the literature about organizational socialization and intellectual capital to develop a framework that will hopefully stimulate and guide scholars in these fields and inspire future research. With our model of onboarding for building intellectual capital, we provide a framework that shows how supporting newcomers during their adjustment can contribute to an organization's human, relational, social, and organizational capital.

By reviewing the literature about organizational socialization and intellectual capital, we explored how successful newcomer adjustment through onboarding activities can contribute to intellectual capital building and retention. Bridging the knowledge fields of intellectual capital and organizational socialization research is novel and provides promising avenues for future research projects.

Additional research could aim to explore the causal influences and temporal dynamics of the relations between newcomer adjustment, proximal and distal socialization outcomes, and intellectual capital dimensions. Adding moderation variables could further enhance the model. Future research should also explore the potential of digital technology and AI for newcomer socialization to help newcomers to access knowledge, which is tailored to their individual needs. Technologies, such as virtual and augmented reality, might substitute face-to-face contacts better than videoconferencing tools and offer additional learning opportunities.

7 Implications for Practice

Onboarding is a multifaceted tool for building intellectual capital by facilitating knowledge transfer, skill development, cultural integration, and networking. Consequently, organizations that invest in effective onboarding processes will most likely observe a positive impact on their intellectual capital.

To implement impactful socialization processes, organizations should look at three types of socialization resources: personal, relational, and structural.

Personal resources can be addressed by looking for certain traits that have proven beneficial for successful newcomer adjustment and favorable during the recruitment process. Looking for proactive personalities should be complemented by training supervisors and coworkers how to encourage newcomer proactivity. Additionally, personal resources can be improved by providing training (Albrecht et al., 2015).

To provide relational socialization resources, assigning a mentor or buddy to newcomers is one measure that organizations can take. Additionally, organizations can provide possibilities for building and strengthening relationships between newcomers and organizational insiders. The importance of fostering relationships should be pointed out to newcomers, and they should be encouraged to seek opportunities for establishing social networks (Cooper-Thomas & Anderson, 2006). To compensate for lack of the casual interactions that naturally take place when coworkers are collocated, organizations with highly distributed and virtual workforces need to support informal communication through, for example, the provision of suitable communication platforms or by organizing onsite or virtual social events. Supervisor support is another relational resource that significantly impacts newcomer adjustment. Bauer et al. (2019) showed that servant leadership is especially beneficent during socialization for being able to compensate for low newcomer proactivity. When coworker support and perceived fairness by coworkers are poor, support and informational justice by supervisors are perceived by newcomers as a substitute (Nasr et al., 2019). Taken together, it is advisable for HR departments to include the topic of newcomer onboarding in their leadership development programs (Didion et al., 2024).

Finally, organizations can facilitate newcomer adjustment by providing structural resources during socialization. HR departments are increasingly concerned about designing onboarding programs for this purpose. Nevertheless, a recent survey held with German HR professionals revealed that the majority of companies have no centralized, structured onboarding process (Haufe, 2023). Those onboarding processes should transfer socialization content to newcomers by providing information, training, and feedback (Saks & Gruman, 2012). Klein et al. (2015) found that the onboarding practices that are required and formally offered are associated with increased socialization.

Taken together, managers and HR departments should increase their efforts to facilitate newcomer socialization through suitable onboarding measures to increase companies' intellectual capital. The shift to remote or hybrid work, which continues to be the new normal for many companies, calls for intensifying onboarding measures because observation and informal interactions are hampered. At the same time, digitization and AI use offer opportunities for improving the onboarding experience for organizational newcomers.

References

Adekoya, O., Adisa, T., & Aiyenitaju, O. (2022). Going forward: Remote working in the post-COVID-19 era. *Employee Relations, 44*(6), 1410–1427. https://doi.org/10.1108/ER-01-2021-0161

Afshari, L., & Hadian Nasab, A. (2021). Enhancing organizational learning capability through managing talent: Mediation effect of intellectual capital. *Human Resource Development International, 24*(1), 48–64. https://doi.org/10.1080/13678868.2020.1727239

Aksoy, C. G., Barrero, J. M., Bloom, N., Davis, S. J., Dolls, M., & Zarate, P. (2023). Working from Home Around the Globe: 2023 Report.

Albrecht, S. L., Bakker, A. B., Gruman, J. A., Macey, W. H., & Saks, A. M. (2015). Employee engagement, human resource management practices and competitive advantage: An integrated approach. *Journal of Organizational Effectiveness: People and Performance, 2*(1), 7–35. https://doi.org/10.1108/JOEPP-08-2014-0042

Allen, D. (2006). Do organizational socialization tactics influence newcomer embeddedness and turnover? In. *Journal of Management, 32*(2), 237–256. https://doi.org/10.1177/0149206305280103

Allen, T., McManus, S., & Russell, J. (1999). Newcomer socialization and stress: Formal peer relationships as a source of support. *Journal of Vocational Behavior, 54*(3), 453–470. https://doi.org/10.1006/jvbe.1998.1674

Ameen, N., Papagiannidis, S., Hosany, A. R. S., & Gentina, E. (2023). It's part of the "new normal": Does a global pandemic change employees' perception of teleworking? *Journal of Business Research, 164*. https://doi.org/10.1016/j.jbusres.2023.113956

Ashford, B. E., Sluss, D. M., & Saks, A. M. (2007). Socialization tactics, proactive behavior, and newcomer learning: Integrating socialization models. *Journal of Vocational Behavior, 70*(3), 447–462. https://doi.org/10.1016/j.jvb.2007.02.001

Bakker, A. B., & Demerouti, E. (2007). The Job Demands-Resources model: State of the art. *Journal of Managerial Psychology, 22*(3), 309–328. https://doi.org/10.1108/02683940710733115

Batistič, S. (2018). Looking beyond—Socialization tactics: The role of human resource systems in the socialization process. *Human Resource Management Review, 28*(2), 220–233. https://doi.org/10.1016/j.hrmr.2017.06.004

Batistič, S., & Kaše, R. (2022). Emergence and persistence of work relationships in early socialization: Contrasting interpersonal and organizational perspectives. *European Journal of Work and Organizational Psychology*. https://doi.org/10.1080/1359432X.2022.2050220

Bauer, T. N., Bodner, T., Erdogan, B., Truxillo, D. M., & Tucker, J. S. (2007). Newcomer adjustment during organizational socialization: A meta-analytic review of antecedents, outcomes, and methods. *Journal of Applied Psychology, 92*(3), 707–721. https://doi.org/10.1037/0021-9010.92.3.707

Bauer, T. N., & Erdogan, B. (2011). Organizational socialization: The effective onboarding of new employees. In S. Zedeck (Ed.), *APA handbook of industrial and organizational psychology, Vol 3: Maintaining, expanding, and contracting the organization* (pp. 51–64). American Psychological Association. https://doi.org/10.1037/12171-002

Bauer, T. N., & Erdogan, B. (2012). *Organizational socialization outcomes: Now and into the future*. Oxford University Press. https://doi.org/10.1093/oxfordhb/9780199763672.013.0006

Bauer, T. N., Erdogan, B., Caughlin, D., Ellis, A. M., & Kurkoski, J. (2021). Jump-starting the socialization experience: The longitudinal role of day 1 newcomer resources on adjustment. *Journal of Management, 47*(8), 2226–2261. https://doi.org/10.1177/0149206320962835

Bauer, T. N., Perrot, S., Liden, R. C., & Erdogan, B. (2019). Understanding the consequences of newcomer proactive behaviors: The moderating contextual role of servant leadership. *Journal of Vocational Behavior, 112*, 356–368. https://doi.org/10.1016/j.jvb.2019.05.001

Bontis, N. (1998). Intellectual capital: An exploratory study that develops measures and models. *Management Decision, 36*(2), 63–76.

Bornemann, M., Alwert, K., & Will, M. (2021). Lessons learned in intellectual capital management in Germany between 2000 and 2020 – History, applications, outlook. *Journal of Intellectual Capital, 22*(3), 560–586. https://doi.org/10.1108/JIC-03-2020-0085
Britto, R., Cruzes, D. S., Smite, D., & Sablis, A. (2018). Onboarding software developers and teams in three globally distributed legacy projects: A multi-case study. *Journal of Software: Evolution and Process, 30*(4), e1921. https://doi.org/10.1002/smr.1921
Brunelle, E., & Fortin, J.-A. (2021). Distance makes the heart grow fonder: An examination of teleworkers' and office workers' job satisfaction through the lens of self-determination theory. *SAGE Open, 11*(1). https://doi.org/10.1177/2158244020985516
Chao, G. T. (2012). Organizational socialization: Background, basics, and a blueprint for adjustment at work. In S. W. J. Kozlowski (Ed.), *The Oxford handbook of organizational psychology* (Vol. 1, 1st ed., pp. 579–614). Oxford University Press. https://doi.org/10.1093/oxfordhb/9780199928309.013.0018
Chao, G. T., O'Leary-Kelly, A. M., Wolf, S., Klein, H. J., & Gardner, P. D. (1994). Organizational socialization: Its content and consequences. *Journal of Applied Psychology, 79*(5), 730–743. https://doi.org/10.1037/0021-9010.79.5.730
Chen, H.-J. (2012). Clarifying the empirical connection of new entrants' e-learning systems use to their job adaptation and their use patterns under the collective-individual training environment. *Computers and Education, 58*(1), 321–337. https://doi.org/10.1016/j.compedu.2011.07.010
Chen, M. Y.-C., Lam, L. W., & Zhu, J. N. Y. (2020). Should companies invest in human resource development practices? The role of intellectual capital and organizational performance improvements. *Personnel Review, 50*(2), 460–477. https://doi.org/10.1108/PR-04-2019-0179
Cooper-Thomas, H. D., & Anderson, N. (2006). Organizational socialization: A new theoretical model and recommendations for future research and HRM practices in organizations. *Journal of Managerial Psychology, 21*(5), 492–516. https://doi.org/10.1108/02683940610673997
Cooper-Thomas, H. D., Stadler, M., Park, J. H., Chen, J., Au, A. K. C., Tan, K. W. T., Paterson, N. J., & Tansley, S. (2020). The newcomer understanding and integration scale: psychometric evidence across six samples. *Journal of Business and Psychology, 35*(4), 435–454. https://doi.org/10.1007/s10869-019-09636-9
Deepa, V., Baber, H., Shukla, B., Sujatha, R., & Khan, D. (2023). Does lack of social interaction act as a barrier to effectiveness in work from home? COVID-19 and gender. *Journal of Organizational Effectiveness, 10*(1), 94–111. https://doi.org/10.1108/JOEPP-11-2021-0311
Delgado-Verde, M., Emilio Navas-López, J., Cruz-González, J., & Amores-Salvadó, J. (2011). Radical innovation from relations-based knowledge: Empirical evidence in Spanish technology-intensive firms. *Journal of Knowledge Management, 15*(5), 722–737. https://doi.org/10.1108/13673271111174294
Didion, E., Ambrosius, U., Perello-Marín, M. R., & Catalá-Pérez, D. (2022). Virtual Organizational Socialization – a structured literature review and research agenda. *Proceedings - 4th International Conference Business Meets Technology 2022*. https://doi.org/10.4995/bmt2022.2022.15541
Didion, E., Perello-Marin, M. R., Catala-Perez, D., & Ambrosius, U. (2024). Mapping the organizational socialization and onboarding literature: A bibliometric analysis of the field. *Cogent Business & Management, 11*(1), 2337957. https://doi.org/10.1080/23311975.2024.2337957
Edvinsson, L., & Malone, M. S. (1997). *Intellectual capital: Realizing your company's true value by finding its hidden roots*. Harper Collin.
Edvinsson, L., & Sullivan, P. (1996). Developing a model for managing intellectual capital. *European Management Journal, 14*(4), 356–364. https://doi.org/10.1016/0263-2373(96)00022-9
Ellis, A. M., Bauer, T. N., Mansfield, L. R., Erdogan, B., Truxillo, D. M., & Simon, L. S. (2015). Navigating uncharted waters: Newcomer socialization through the lens of stress theory. *Journal of Management, 41*(1), 203–235. https://doi.org/10.1177/0149206314557525
Fang, R., Duffy, M. K., & Shaw, J. D. (2011). The organizational socialization process: Review and development of a social capital model. *Journal of Management, 37*(1), 127–152. https://doi.org/10.1177/0149206310384630

Fuchs, C., & Reichel, A. (2023). Effective communication for relational coordination in remote work: How job characteristics and HR practices shape user–technology interactions. *Human Resource Management*. https://doi.org/10.1002/hrm.22161

Golden, T. D., & Raghuram, S. (2010). Teleworker knowledge sharing and the role of altered relational and technological interactions. *Journal of Organizational Behavior, 31*(8), 1061–1085. https://doi.org/10.1002/job.652

Gruman, J. A., Saks, A. M., & Zweig, D. I. (2006). Organizational socialization tactics and newcomer proactive behaviors: An integrative study. *Journal of Vocational Behavior, 69*(1), 90–104. https://doi.org/10.1016/j.jvb.2006.03.001

Gupta, K. (2021). Impact of knowledge-based HRM practices on organizational performance: mediating effect of intellectual capital. *International Journal of Knowledge Management, 18*(1), 1–22. https://doi.org/10.4018/IJKM.290026

Halbesleben, J. R. B., Neveu, J.-P., Paustian-Underdahl, S. C., & Westman, M. (2014). Getting to the "COR": Understanding the role of resources in conservation of resources theory. *Journal of Management, 40*(5), 1334–1364. https://doi.org/10.1177/0149206314527130

Harris, L. (2023). The social side of socialization: Exploring how relationships shape newcomer learning and adjustment.

Harris, L., Cooper–Thomas, H., Smith, P., & Cheung, G. W. (2022). Influence of relational learning and job autonomy in associations between social capital resources and newcomer adjustment: A moderated mediation study. *Career Development International*. https://doi.org/10.1108/CDI-02-2022-0038

Harris, L., Cooper-Thomas, H., Smith, P., & Smollan, R. (2020). Reclaiming the social in socialization: A practice-based understanding of newcomer adjustment. In *Human resource development quarterly* (Vol. 31(2), pp. 193–211). https://doi.org/10.1002/hrdq.21384

Haufe. (2023). Zu wenig Strukturen beim Onboarding—Haufe Onboarding Umfrage 2023. https://www.myonboarding.de/studien?utm_source=direkt&utm_id=84834%2F04393689&akttyp=direkt&aktnr=84834&wnr=04393689

Heidt, L., Gauger, F., & Pfnur, A. (2022). Work from home success: Agile work characteristics and the mediating effect of supportive HRM. *Review of Managerial Science*. https://doi.org/10.1007/s11846-022-00545-5

Hobfoll, S. E. (1989). Conservation of resources: A new attempt at conceptualizing stress. *American Psychologist, 44*(3), 513–524. https://doi.org/10.1037/0003-066X.44.3.513

Hobfoll, S. E. (2011). Conservation of resource caravans and engaged settings: Conservation of resource caravans. *Journal of Occupational and Organizational Psychology, 84*(1), 116–122. https://doi.org/10.1111/j.2044-8325.2010.02016.x

Hobfoll, S. E., Halbesleben, J., Neveu, J.-P., & Westman, M. (2018). Conservation of resources in the organizational context: The reality of resources and their consequences. *Annual Review of Organizational Psychology and Organizational Behavior, 5*(1), 103–128. https://doi.org/10.1146/annurev-orgpsych-032117-104640

Hollenbeck, J. R., & Jamieson, B. B. (2015). Human capital, social capital, and social network analysis: Implications for strategic human resource management. *Academy of Management Perspectives, 29*(3), 370–385. https://doi.org/10.5465/amp.2014.0140

Inkinen, H. (2015). Review of empirical research on intellectual capital and firm performance. *Journal of Intellectual Capital, 16*(3), 518–565. https://doi.org/10.1108/JIC-01-2015-0002

Inkinen, H., Kianto, A., Vanhala, M., & Ritala, P. (2017). Structure of intellectual capital – an international comparison. *Accounting, Auditing & Accountability Journal, 30*(5), 1160–1183. https://doi.org/10.1108/AAAJ-11-2015-2291

Jones, G. R. (1986). Socialization tactics, self-efficacy, and newcomers' adjustments to organizations. *Academy of Management Journal, 29*(2), 262–279. https://doi.org/10.2307/256188

Kammeyer-Mueller, J. D., Livingston, B. A., & Liao, H. (2011). Perceived similarity, proactive adjustment, and organizational socialization. *Journal of Vocational Behavior, 78*(2), 225–236. https://doi.org/10.1016/j.jvb.2010.09.012

Kammeyer-Mueller, J. D., Wanberg, C. A., Rubenstein, A. L., & Song, Z. (2013). Support, undermining, and newcomer socialization: Fitting in during the first 90 days. *Academy of Management Journal, 56*(4), 1104–1124. https://doi.org/10.5465/amj.2010.0791

Kammeyer-Mueller, J. D., & Wanberg, C. R. (2003). Unwrapping the organizational entry process: Disentangling multiple antecedents and their pathways to adjustment. *Journal of Applied Psychology, 88*(5), 779–794. https://doi.org/10.1037/0021-9010.88.5.779
Klein, H. J., & Heuser, A. E. (2008). The learning of socialization content: A framework for researching orientating practices. In *Research in personnel and human resources management* (Vol. 27, pp. 279–336). https://doi.org/10.1016/S0742-7301(08)27007-6
Klein, H. J., & Polin, B. (2012). 14 Are organizations on board with best practices onboarding? *The Oxford handbook of organizational socialization*, 267.
Klein, H. J., Polin, B., & Leigh Sutton, K. (2015). Specific onboarding practices for the socialization of new employees: Onboarding practices. *International Journal of Selection and Assessment, 23*(3), 263–283. https://doi.org/10.1111/ijsa.12113
Klein, H. J., & Weaver, N. A. (2000). The effectiveness of an organizational-level orientation training program in the socialization of new hires. *Personnel Psychology, 53*(1), 47–66. https://doi.org/10.1111/j.1744-6570.2000.tb00193.x
Korte, R. (2010). First, get to know them': A relational view of organizational socialization. *Human Resource Development International, 13*(1), 27–43. https://doi.org/10.1080/13678861003588984
Korte, R., & Lin, S. (2013). Getting on board: Organizational socialization and the contribution of social capital. *Human Relations, 66*(3), 407–428. https://doi.org/10.1177/0018726712461927
Kozlowski, S. W., Chao, G. T., & Jensen, J. M. (2009). Building an infrastructure for organizational learning: A multilevel approach. In *Learning, training, and development in organizations* (pp. 363–403). Routledge.
Kucharska, W. (2021). Leadership, culture, intellectual capital and knowledge processes for organizational innovativeness across industries: The case of Poland. *Journal of Intellectual Capital, 22*(7), 121–141. https://doi.org/10.1108/JIC-02-2021-0047
Lapointe, É., & Vandenberghe, C. (2018). Trust in the supervisor and the development of employees' social capital during organizational entry: A conservation of resources approach. *The International Journal of Human Resource Management, 29*(17), 2503–2523. https://doi.org/10.1080/09585192.2016.1244097
Lee, A. S. (2022). A proposed research agenda concerning supervisor training for newcomer organizational socialization. *European Journal of Training and Development.* https://doi.org/10.1108/EJTD-06-2021-0082
Lee, H. (2021). Changes in workplace practices during the COVID-19 pandemic: The roles of emotion, psychological safety and organisation support. *Journal of Organizational Effectiveness, 8*(1), 97–128. https://doi.org/10.1108/JOEPP-06-2020-0104
Lee, Y. (2023). ICT use, internal communication satisfaction, and engagement of working-from-home employees: The moderating role of affiliative tendency. *Computers in Human Behavior, 138*. https://doi.org/10.1016/j.chb.2022.107472
Longo, M., & Mura, M. (2011). The effect of intellectual capital on employees' satisfaction and retention. *Information & Management, 48*(7), 278–287. https://doi.org/10.1016/j.im.2011.06.005
Martín-de-Castro, G., Delgado-Verde, M., López-Sáez, P., & Navas-López, J. E. (2011). Towards 'An Intellectual Capital-Based View of the Firm': Origins and nature. *Journal of Business Ethics, 98*(4), 649–662. https://doi.org/10.1007/s10551-010-0644-5
Matos, F., Vairinhos, V., & Godina, R. (2020). Reporting of intellectual capital management using a scoring model. *Sustainability, 12*(19), 8086. https://doi.org/10.3390/su12198086
Miller, V. D., & Jablin, F. M. (1991). Information seeking during organizational entry: Influences, tactics, and a model of the process. *The Academy of Management Review, 16*(1), 92. https://doi.org/10.2307/258608
Morrison, E. (2002). Newcomers' relationships: The role of social network ties during socialization. *Academy of Management Journal, 45*(6), 1149–1160. https://doi.org/10.2307/3069430
Morrison, E. W. (1995). Information usefulness and acquisition during organizational encounter. *Management Communication Quarterly, 9*(2), 131–155.

Nahapiet, J., & Ghoshal, S. (1998). Social capital, intellectual capital, and the organizational advantage. *The Academy of Management Review, 23*(2). https://doi.org/10.2307/259373

Nasr, M. I., El Akremi, A., & Coyle-Shapiro, J. A. M. (2019). Synergy or substitution? The interactive effects of insiders' fairness and support and organizational socialization tactics on newcomer role clarity and social integration. *Journal of Organizational Behavior, 40*(6), 758–778. https://doi.org/10.1002/job.2369

Ng, P. M. L., Lit, K. K., & Cheung, C. T. Y. (2022). Remote work as a new normal? The technology-organization-environment (TOE) context. *Technology in Society, 70*. https://doi.org/10.1016/j.techsoc.2022.102022

Nifadkar, S. S., Wu, W., & Gu, Q. (2019). Supervisors' work-related and nonwork information sharing: Integrating research on information sharing, information seeking, and trust using self-disclosure theory. *Personnel Psychology, 72*(2), 241–269. https://doi.org/10.1111/peps.12305

Ostroff, C., & Kozlowski, S. W. J. (1993). The role of mentoring in the information gathering processes of newcomers during early organizational socialization. *Journal of Vocational Behavior, 42*(2), 170–183. https://doi.org/10.1006/jvbe.1993.1012

Paoloni, P., & Lombardi, R. (Eds.). (2023). *When the crisis becomes an opportunity: The role of women in the post-covid organization*. Springer International Publishing. https://doi.org/10.1007/978-3-031-21932-0

Reichers, A. E. (1987). An interactionist perspective on newcomer socialization rates. *The Academy of Management Review, 12*(2). https://doi.org/10.2307/258535

Rodeghero, P., Zimmermann, T., Houck, B., & Ford, D. (2021). Please turn your cameras on: Remote onboarding of software developers during a pandemic. In *2021 IEEE/ACM 43rd International Conference on Software Engineering: Software Engineering in Practice (ICSE-SEIP)*, (pp. 41–50). https://doi.org/10.1109/ICSE-SEIP52600.2021.00013

Rollag, K., Parise, S., & Cross, R. (2005). Getting new hires up to speed quickly. *MIT Sloan Management Review, 46*(2).

Roos, G., & Pike, S. (2018). *Intellectual capital as a management tool: Essentials for leaders and managers* (1st ed.). Routledge. https://doi.org/10.4324/9780429448119

Russo, M., Morandin, G., & Manca, C. (2023). How can organizations improve virtual onboarding? Key learnings from the pandemic. In S. Bergum, P. Peters, & T. Vold (Eds.), *Virtual management and the new normal* (pp. 203–221). Springer International Publishing. https://doi.org/10.1007/978-3-031-06813-3_11

Saks, A. M., & Gruman, J. A. (2011). Getting newcomers engaged: The role of socialization tactics. *Journal of Managerial Psychology, 26*(5), 383–402. https://doi.org/10.1108/02683941111139001

Saks, A. M., & Gruman, J. A. (2012). Getting newcomers on board: A review of socialization practices and introduction to socialization resources theory. *The Oxford Handbook of Organizational Socialization*, 27–55.

Saks, A. M., & Gruman, J. A. (2018). Socialization resources theory and newcomers' work engagement: A new pathway to newcomer socialization. *Career Development International, 23*(1), 12–32. https://doi.org/10.1108/CDI-12-2016-0214

Saks, A. M., & Gruman, J. A. (2021). How do you socialize newcomers during a pandemic? *Industrial and Organizational Psychology, 14*(1–2), 217–220. https://doi.org/10.1017/iop.2021.44

Saks, A. M., Uggerslev, K. L., & Fassina, N. E. (2007). Socialization tactics and newcomer adjustment: A meta-analytic review and test of a model. *Journal of Vocational Behavior, 70*(3), 413–446. https://doi.org/10.1016/j.jvb.2006.12.004

Sani, K. F., Adisa, T. A., Adekoya, O. D., & Oruh, E. S. (2022). Digital onboarding and employee outcomes: Empirical evidence from the UK. *Management Decision*. https://doi.org/10.1108/MD-11-2021-1528

Schinoff, B. S., Ashforth, B. E., & Corley, K. G. (2020). Virtually (In)separable: The centrality of relational cadence in the formation of virtual multiplex relationships. *Academy of Management Journal, 63*(5), 1395–1424. https://doi.org/10.5465/amj.2018.0466

Seibert, S. E., Kraimer, M. L., & Liden, R. C. (2001). A social capital theory of career success. *Academy of Management Journal, 44*(2), 219–237. https://doi.org/10.2307/3069452

Sokolov, D., & Zavyalova, E. (2021). Human resource management systems and intellectual capital: Is the relationship universal in knowledge intensive firms? *International Journal of Manpower, 42*(4), 683–701. https://doi.org/10.1108/IJM-11-2018-0372

Stewart, T. A. (2007). *The wealth of knowledge: Intellectual capital and the twenty-first century organization*. Crown Currency.

Subramaniam, M., & Youndt, M. A. (2005). The influence of intellectual capital on the types of innovative capabilities. *Academy of Management Journal, 48*(3), 450–463. https://doi.org/10.5465/amj.2005.17407911

Van Maanen, J. E., & Schein, E. H. (1979). Toward a theory of organizational socialization. In B. M. Staw (Ed.), *Research in organizational behavior* (pp. 209–264). JAI Press.

Viererbl, B., Denner, N., & Koch, T. (2022). "You don't meet anybody when walking from the living room to the kitchen": Informal communication during remote work. *Journal of Communication Management, 26*(3), 331–348. https://doi.org/10.1108/JCOM-10-2021-0117

Wanberg, C. R. (2012a). Facilitating organizational socialization: An introduction. *The Oxford Handbook of Organizational Socialization, 360*.

Wanberg, C. R. (Ed.). (2012b). *The Oxford handbook of organizational socialization*. Oxford University Press. http://www.loc.gov/catdir/enhancements/fy1205/2011047728-b.html

Wang, D., & Chen, S. (2013). Does intellectual capital matter? High-performance work systems and bilateral innovative capabilities. *International Journal of Manpower, 34*(8), 861–879. https://doi.org/10.1108/IJM-07-2013-0167

Whillans, A., Perlow, L., & Turek, A. (2021). Experimenting during the shift to virtual team work: Learnings from how teams adapted their activities during the COVID-19 pandemic. *Information and Organization, 31*(1). https://doi.org/10.1016/j.infoorg.2021.100343

Woo, D., Endacott, C. G., & Myers, K. K. (2022). Navigating water cooler talks without the water cooler: Uncertainty and information seeking during remote socialization. *Management Communication Quarterly*. https://doi.org/10.1177/08933189221105916

Yang, C.-C., & Lin, C. Y.-Y. (2009). Does intellectual capital mediate the relationship between HRM and organizational performance? Perspective of a healthcare industry in Taiwan. *The International Journal of Human Resource Management, 20*(9), 1965–1984. https://doi.org/10.1080/09585190903142415

Yang, J., Brashear, T. G., & Asare, A. (2015). The value relevance of brand equity, intellectual capital and intellectual capital management capability. *Journal of Strategic Marketing, 23*(6), 543–559. https://doi.org/10.1080/0965254X.2014.1001863

Yarbrough, J. W., & Ramos Salazar, L. (2023). Virtual onboarding and socialization, an exploration of employee discussions and experiences. *Corporate Communications: An International Journal*. https://doi.org/10.1108/CCIJ-12-2022-0158

Youndt, M. A., & Snell, S. A. (2020). Human resource configurations, intellectual capital, and organizational performance. *Journal of Managerial Issues, 32*(1), 60–84.

Youndt, M. A., Subramaniam, M., & Snell, S. A. (2004). Intellectual capital profiles: An examination of investments and returns*. *Journal of Management Studies, 41*(2), 335–361. https://doi.org/10.1111/j.1467-6486.2004.00435.x

Zhao, T., Liu, J., Zawacki, A. M., Michel, J. S., & Li, H. (2022). The effects of newcomer proactive behaviours on socialization outcomes: A meta-analysis. *Journal of Occupational and Organizational Psychology, 00*, 1–32. https://doi.org/10.1111/joop.12407

Zhou, L., Park, J., Kammeyer-Mueller, J. D., Shah, P. P., & Campbell, E. M. (2022). Rookies connected: Interpersonal relationships among newcomers, newcomer adjustment processes, and socialization outcomes. *Journal of Applied Psychology, 107*(3), 370–388. https://doi.org/10.1037/apl0000894

Calculating Monetary Value for ESG Scores: A Case Study on GNO

Maria Weir and Philip Sugai

Abstract Sustainability reporting and current environmental, social, and governance (ESG) metrics have gained significant importance in assessing organizational performance beyond traditional financial metrics. However, quantifying sustainability and ESG scores in monetary terms remains a challenge. This paper explores how the value model, developed within Doshisha University in Kyoto, Japan, and Areopa's ten-step and four-leaf models, incorporating the 77 formulas and 927 added value-creating phenomena, can be combined to assign monetary values to ESG scores. Using GNO, a biologicals company as a case study, this paper demonstrates the practical application of the proposed framework to assign monetary value to ESG scores. The chapter also discusses the potential future research into how business models may affect ESG scoring and asset attribution.

1 Introduction

Environmental, social, and governance (ESG) metrics provide insights into a company's ethical impact and sustainability practices, which are increasingly important for investors, stakeholders, and regulatory bodies. Despite their importance, translating ESG scores into monetary values remains complex. The value model (Sugai et al., 2021) places emphasis on holistic value creation together with Areopa's ten-step and four-leaf models, offering structured approaches to intellectual capital (IC) valuation that go far beyond traditional assessments of value across stakeholder

M. Weir (✉)
Areopa Ltd and ARICC, Brussels, Belgium
e-mail: maria.weir@areopa.com

P. Sugai
Doshisha University's Graduate School of Business, Kyoto, Japan
e-mail: psugai@mail.doshisha.ac.jp

F. Matos et al. (eds.), *Intellectual Capital in a Global Business Landscape*, Contributions to Management Science, https://doi.org/10.1007/978-3-031-86362-2_13

networks. This paper proposes a synergistic framework combining these models to effectively monetize ESG scores, using GNO as an illustrative example.

2 ESG Metrics

2.1 *History of ESG*

Sustainability reporting originated in the 1970s, initially focusing on environmental issues in response to growing public awareness and activism around pollution and resource depletion by major corporations. For example, the establishment of the Environmental Protection Agency (EPA) in the United States in 1970 and subsequent environmental regulations that were developed underscored the need for companies to begin to disclose their actual environmental impacts (Bergmann, 2017). In the following decades, the scope of corporate responsibility broadened to include social and governance factors, driven by investors' increasing demands for transparency and accountability.

The 1990s marked a significant shift toward standardized ESG reporting with the advent of frameworks such as the Global Reporting Initiative (GRI), established in 1997 following the large public outcry related to the Exxon Valdez oil spill. The GRI provided the first comprehensive guidelines for sustainability reporting, outlining how companies should measure and report their environmental, social, and economic performance in a consistent manner (KPMG, 2020). This period also saw the emergence of socially responsible investing (SRI), which pressured companies to disclose ESG information to attract investment. It was at this time that the European Environment Agency (EEA) was established in 1990, which assesses the state of the environment, providing forecasts and identifying emerging environmental issues for European regulators.

The UN's launch of the Principles for Responsible Investment (PRI) in 2006 further cemented ESG disclosure as a critical component of corporate strategy, promoting responsible investment practices globally (UN PRI, n.d.).

In the past two decades, ESG reporting has evolved from a niche practice to a mainstream corporate responsibility. The introduction of the Task Force on Climate-related Financial Disclosures (TCFD) in 2015 and the EU's Non-Financial Reporting Directive (NFRD) in 2014 significantly advanced the quality and scope of ESG disclosures (TCFD, 2017; European Commission, 2021). In 2023, the EU's Corporate Sustainability Reporting Directive (CSRD) came into full force, requiring companies to honestly report their ESG impacts that are then assured by an independent outside third-party auditor. Similarly in the United States, the IFRS formalized its own global sustainability reporting standard, with the launch of its IFRS S1 and S2 reporting standards.

While this brief history may sound as if the sustainability standards reporting ecosystem is organizing around one or two global standards, in reality as of the writing of this chapter, there are hundreds of competing standards, frameworks, and models related to sustainability reporting, placing enormous pressure on companies to comply with different standards and frameworks across countries, being called an "alphabet soup" of sustainability reporting (Liang & Chan, 2022) with no comprehensive system in place to help companies measure, monitor, and strategically manage sustainability topics.

While there have been repeated calls for a standardized, comprehensive system to measure and manage sustainability topics (c.f. Gudmundsdottir & Sigurjonsson, 2024; Büyüközkan & Karabulut, 2018) for businesses, governments, and individuals, to date, no such model has yet emerged. In light of this, the value model has been developed in an effort to fill this gap.

2.2 The Value Model

Japan has a long history of integrating ethical approaches into capitalism, where multiple stakeholders are considered in the long-term strategic planning of a business. This tradition can be traced back to the teachings of Ishida Baigan (1685–1744), who promoted ethical business practices through his philosophy of Sekimon Shingaku. Building on this foundation, the Ohmi merchants in the seventeenth century became renowned for their "sanpo yoshi" principle, which asserts that a "good" business creates value for three stakeholders including (1) the seller, (2) the buyer, and (3) society. This integration of ethics and business with an emphasis on multistakeholder value creation is far different than the shareholder primacy view of business that has dominated the West, and its evolution in Japan offers a solid philosophical and practical foundation for modern-day multistakeholder value creation initiatives.

This centuries-old stakeholder-focused approach to capitalism aligns well with recent announcements from both the Business Roundtable (2019) and the World Economic Forum (Schwab, 2019) whose announcements of the "new" purpose of business that has shifted away from a shareholder primacy view to a multistakeholder one. Both of these organizations mandate that businesses must now create value not only for their shareholders but across seven key stakeholders including (1) the firm itself, (2) its shareholders or owners, (3) employees, (4) customers, (5) partners, (6) society, and (7) the planet. Yet, while both the Business Roundtable and the World Economic Forum share this new commitment to value creation across these stakeholders, the question remains as to how such value can be objectively, transparently, and consistently measured across a heterogeneous set of businesses in terms of their size, industry, or location. As outlined by Sugai et al. (2021, 2022, 2023), the value model was developed to provide such value measurement and management system which integrates both financial and nonfinancial performance indicators to assess an organization's overall value.

To do so, Sugai et al. (2021, 2022, 2023) have conducted four waves of consecutive research, in which they collected individual sustainability disclosure requirements (called impact measurements) from 45 of the world's top ESG and sustainability reporting frameworks ranging from global standards such as ISSB and EFRAG, to important frameworks such as GRI and GIIN-IRIS, to country-specific models such as the National TOM (UK), BRSR (India), and the Singapore Stock Exchange (Singapore). In total, these contributed more than 1,200 individual impact measurements to these four waves of research, and these were each classified into first 27 themes, then 81 underlying goals, and finally 168 precise subgoals with their related key performance indicators (KPIs).

Reclassification of these results using the Areopa's four-leaf model into first four forms of intellectual capital structural, human, strategic alliance, and customer and then quantifies these results using the Areopa's ten-step process, a way of analyzing and valuing intellectual assets using the rules of IAS 38 and Areopa's 77 proprietary formulas, which offers a dynamic and fundamentally different way to value the intellectual capital inherent within the relationships between a business and its key stakeholders.

2.3 *Areopa's Ten-Steps and Four-Leaf Models*

Areopa's ten-step model is designed to quantify intellectual capital by identifying and valuing intangible assets. This structured approach facilitates the conversion of nonfinancial metrics into monetary values, aligning with IAS 38 standards. Additionally, Areopa's four-leaf model categorizes intangible assets into human capital (HC), structural capital (SC), strategic alliance capital (SAC), and customer capital (CC), aiding in a more nuanced understanding and valuation of these assets. The ten-step model incorporates the 77 formulas for valuation and 927 added value-creating phenomena, providing a detailed framework for assessing and monetizing intangible assets. The importance of intangible assets in driving value and growth for organizations cannot be overstated. Effective management and valuation of these assets are crucial for transparency and investor confidence.

The remainder of this chapter outlines an approach for how this combined use of the value model with the Areopa's ten-step and four-leaf models to provide an entirely new approach to the valuation of sustainability practices and stakeholder value creation using a structured four-stage process as outlined below.

3 Methodology

This methodology presents a comprehensive framework aimed at transforming ESG initiatives into monetizable intangible assets. By integrating the value model and Areopa's ten-step and four-leaf models into a combined five-stage process, the methodology aligns ESG performance with financial value creation. It is grounded in both qualitative and quantitative approaches, supported by empirical testing through a detailed case study on GNO Inc.

Stage 1: ESG Scoring as a Foundation for Value Assessment
The initial stage involves assessing a company's ESG metrics using the value model, consolidating over 1,200 individual impact measurements. High-evidence artifacts, such as documented policies and sustainability frameworks, are evaluated and scored. This structured scoring system identifies and prioritizes key artifacts for further valuation.

Stage 2: Development of ESG Artifacts and Knowledge Assets
In this stage, the company consolidates its high-scoring ESG artifacts into a comprehensive repository of explicit knowledge. Artifacts are systematically compiled and managed within a specially assembled data room forming the foundation for future classification and valuation as per IAS 38 standards.

Stage 3: Reclassification Using the Areopa's Four-Leaf Model
The artifacts are reclassified into four categories of intellectual capital: human capital, structural capital, customer capital, and strategic alliance capital. The focus is on structural capital, emphasizing documented knowledge that aligns with IAS 38.

Stage 4: Inventory Compilation and Valuation Through the Areopa's Ten-Step Model
This stage applies the Areopa's ten-steps model for a systematic valuation of the identified intangible assets. The model uses Areopa's proprietary formulas, integrating 927 value-creating phenomena to ensure precise valuations. The values are then validated and incorporated into the organization's financial statements, enhancing transparency and compliance with IAS 38.

Areopa and the Value Center Combined Five-Stage Valuation Process
The Areopa value center employs a comprehensive five-stage process, designed to enhance transparency and reliability in valuing intellectual capital. The stages include the following:

1 Discovery and contextual analysis: identifies sources of intellectual capital in alignment with strategic goals
2 IC mapping and artifact identification: maps intangible assets using the Areopa's four-leaf model (Pyis, 2011), focusing on IAS 38 compliance
3 Valuation preparation: prepares data and artifacts for precise valuation using Areopa's formulas
4 Quantitative valuation and reporting: assigns monetary values and prepares detailed reports for financial statements
5 Strategic integration and monitoring: integrates valued assets into business strategy and ensures ongoing monitoring for market adaptation

Conclusion
The integration of the value model with Areopa's ten-step and four-leaf models and value center five-stage process offers a comprehensive framework for monetizing

ESG initiatives. This approach ensures compliance with international standards, enhances transparency, and provides a replicable model for future applications. The empirical application in GNO Inc. demonstrates the practical utility and robustness of this combined framework.

As described above, this methodology is grounded in a combination of qualitative and quantitative approaches, utilizing both theoretical models and empirical testing. The theoretical underpinning is provided by the value model, which categorizes and scores ESG performance, and the Areopa models, which provide frameworks for identifying, classifying, and valuing intangible assets. Empirical testing was conducted through a detailed case study on GNO Inc., allowing for a practical application of the proposed methodology and ensuring its validity.

3.1 *Stage 1: ESG Scoring as a Foundation for Value Assessment*

The initial stage involves systematically assessing a company's ESG metrics using the value model. This model consolidates over 1,200 individual impact measurements drawn from global standards and frameworks, such as GRI and GIIN-IRIS, organized into 27 themes, 81 goals, and 168 subgoals. The objective of this stage is to identify high-evidence artifacts—specific ESG initiatives or policies that demonstrate the organization's commitment to sustainability and governance.

A. ESG Evaluation
The company's environmental, social, and governance practices are assessed against the value model's metrics. Data is collected on key indicators, such as carbon emissions, diversity initiatives, and corporate governance structures.

B. Scoring and Prioritization
Each ESG artifact is scored based on its alignment with the value model's goals and themes. Artifacts with the highest scores are prioritized for further analysis.

3.2 *Stage 2: Development of ESG Artifacts and Knowledge Assets*

In this stage, the company consolidates its high-scoring ESG artifacts into a cohesive repository of explicit knowledge. Artifacts are defined as documented policies, sustainability frameworks, stakeholder engagement strategies, and proprietary research that reflect the organization's value-creating activities.

A. Artifact Compilation
The identified artifacts are compiled into a structured repository, ensuring that each artifact is explicitly documented.

B. Knowledge Asset Management
The company creates and manages a formal record of all artifacts, laying the groundwork for future reclassification and valuation.

3.3 Stage 3: Reclassification Using the Areopa's Four-Leaf Model

The third stage involves reclassifying the consolidated artifacts into intellectual capital categories using the Areopa's four-leaf model. This model divides intellectual capital into four key types: human capital, structural capital, customer capital, and strategic alliance capital. The focus is primarily on structural capital, as it encompasses explicit knowledge and documented processes that meet IAS 38 standards.

A. Categorization of Artifacts
Each artifact is categorized based on its nature and relevance to the organization's strategic goals. Artifacts that demonstrate documented policies and clear procedural value are classified as structural capital.

B. Verification for Compliance
Artifacts are verified to ensure they meet the recognition criteria outlined in IAS 38, particularly in terms of future economic benefits and reliable measurement.

3.4 Stage 4: Inventory Compilation and Valuation through the Areopa's Ten-Step Model

Following reclassification, the company applies the Areopa's ten-step model to manage and value its intangible assets systematically. This model provides a step-by-step approach to identifying, protecting, and quantifying the company's intellectual capital.

A. Identification and Protection
The company documents each identified asset, applying intellectual property safeguards to ensure its protection.

B. Valuation Using Areopa's Formulas
Each intangible asset is valued using Areopa's 77 proprietary formulas, which integrate 927 value-creating phenomena to ensure a precise valuation. This process aligns with IAS 38, which requires that recognized assets must be measured reliably.

3.5 Stage 5: Validation and Strategic Planning

A. Validation for Financial Reporting
The assets' values are validated to ensure compliance with IAS 38, allowing them to be reported in the company's financial statements. This is then combined with an action plan in the form of a management report to ensure company understand steps required to achieve future growth.

3.6 Application of the Methodology

This five-stage methodology adheres to international accounting and reporting standards, ensuring that intangible assets derived from ESG initiatives are reliably identified, valued, and protected. The integration of expert intervention with standardized processes further enhances the credibility and robustness of the framework. By linking the evaluation of ESG artifacts to financial reporting standards, the methodology provides a systematic way for organizations to monetize their sustainability efforts and enhance investor confidence.

With this methodology serving as our foundation, we next offer a detailed case analysis for how such an approach can be practically implemented, using the example of GNO.

4 Case Study: Integration of the Value Model and Areopa Models in GNO Inc.'s Intellectual Capital and Sustainability Performance

4.1 Case Example Overview

This research-based case study provides an in-depth analysis of GNO Inc.'s present and future value, focusing on its intellectual capital (IC) and sustainability performance through the lenses of environmental, social, and governance (ESG) issues. It examines the integration of the value model and the Areopa's four-leaf and ten-step models to support GNO's growth and sustainability initiatives. The study highlights the following key points:

- Present intellectual capital value: $8.9 million
- Future intellectual capital value: $236 million (estimated over the next 3 years)
- Future ESG analysis: graphs illustrating the company's performance and growth potential in sustainability practices, social impact, and governance mechanisms

4.2 Introduction and Research Rationale

GNO Inc. is an innovative company specializing in trade-secreted biologicals aimed at the home gardening retail market. These biologicals enable faster growth, higher plant nutrition, stronger plants, wide-ranging climate adaptability, and lower costs.

GNO's primary objective in participating in this research was to explore how growing their intangible assets and enhancing their ESG performance would increase their attractiveness to investors. Our analysis of GNO progressed as follows.

4.3 Stage 1: ESG Scoring as a Foundation for Value Assessment

A. ESG Evaluation

We began this case study by first assessing GNO's existing sustainability and ESG metrics through the lenses of the value model. To do so, we began by defining the specific ESG (environmental, social, and governance) metrics relevant to the organization's operations using a standard materiality lens. These metrics were first categorized into environmental, social, and governance dimensions, for example, metrics such as carbon footprint were categorized into the environmental category, while employee engagement was categorized into the social category and board diversity into the governance category.

B. Scoring and Prioritization

We then proceeded to map these ESG metrics to the value's 27 themes, 81 goals, and 168 subgoals following a standard three-tiered process.

Tier 1: Governance Practices

We then worked to collect data to understand the organization's governance practices related to the value model's 81 goals and score them accordingly. Scores of 1-point point were allocated for existing and enforced policies and 0 points for those that were missing.

In the case of GNO, they were able to achieve an overall policy score of 28 out of 81 possible points, or 35%. As shown in Fig. 1, they have many employee-related policies in place, with coverage of nearly all stakeholders except for shareholders.

Tier 2: Data Disclosure Quality

Then, we assessed GNO's performance against each of the 168 subgoals in the value model. To do so, we scored across each of the 168 subgoals using a 4-point scale ranging from 0 to 3 points based on the data's completeness and specificity. Zero point represents no data related to that specific subgoal; 1 point represents the existence of only qualitative data; 2 points represent quantitative data that has been disclosed, but does not allow for measurement against the stated subgoal (e.g., a

Company: GNO Inc. VALUE RESEARCH MODEL SCORE

POLICY SCORE	DISCLOSURE QUALITY SCORE	ABSOLUTE VALUE SCORE	RELATIVE VALUE SCORE
35%	5%	4%	78%

POLICY SCORE	OVERALL	Employee	Nature	Society	Firm	Customer	Partner	Shareholder
Company Score	28	14	5	1	3	2	3	0
Max Score	81	23	22	12	8	6	9	1

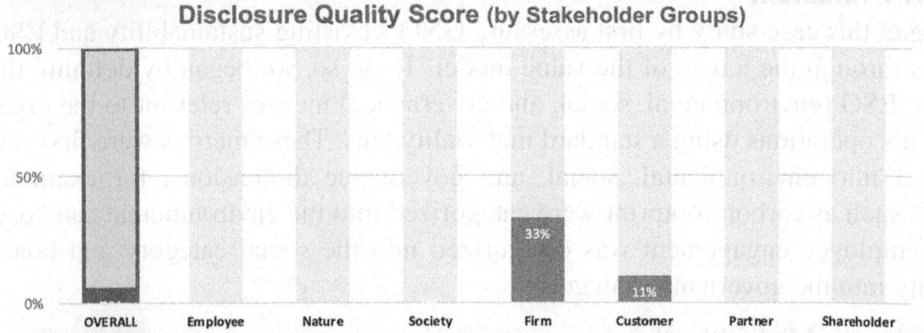

DISC QUALITY	OVERALL	Employee	Nature	Society	Firm	Customer	Partner	Shareholder
Company Score	27	0	0	0	21	6	0	0
Max Score	504	126	132	48	63	57	75	3

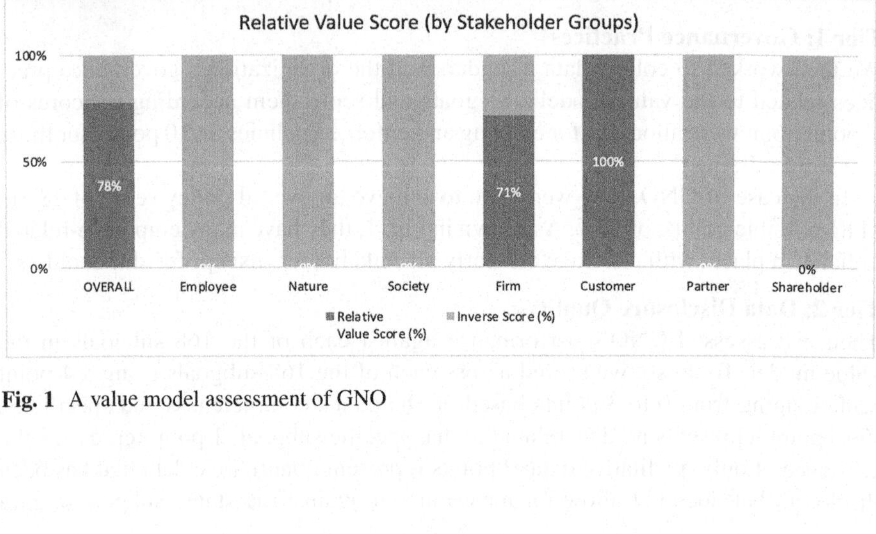

Fig. 1 A value model assessment of GNO

REL. VALUE SCORE	OVERALL	Employee	Nature	Society	Firm	Customer	Partner	Shareholder
Company Score	70	0	0	0	50	20	0	0
Max Rel Value Score	90	0	0	0	70	20	0	0

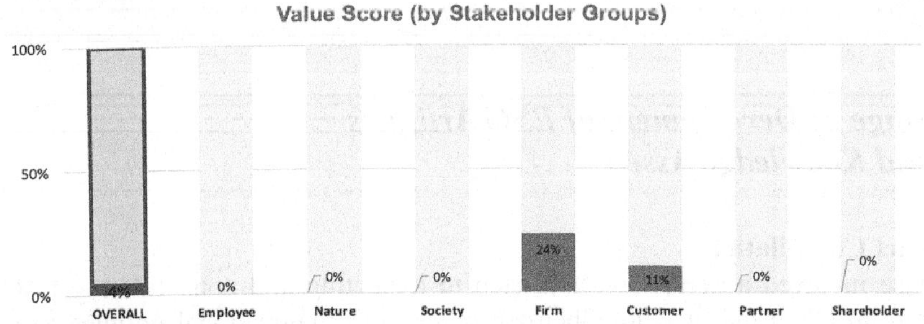

VALUE SCORE	OVERALL	Employee	Nature	Society	Firm	Customer	Partner	Shareholder
Company Score	70	0	0	0	50	20	0	0
Max Score	1680	420	440	160	210	190	250	10

Fig. 1 (continued)

disclosure of a percentage reduction in plastic waste without a benchmark for how much actual overall plastic waste has been created); and 3 points represent quantitative data that can be used to measure performance against that specific subgoal.

Scoring in this way ensures that value scoring which occurs in the next research tier has a zero base, such that a 0-point value score means that the organization has achieved 0% of the stated goal. Without a disclosure quality scoring, a 0-point score could also mean the absence of scoring data, which would confuse the subsequent valuation process.

As outlined in Fig. 1, GNO achieved a disclosure quality score of 5%, with 27 out of 504 possible points representing their disclosures related to both their own firm and customers, with all other stakeholders currently achieving 0 points.

Tier 3: Value Scoring

Only data points with a full 3 points in the disclosure quality step proceed to goal achievement scoring. Goals are scored on a 10-point scale based on their level of target achievement. For example, carbon emission reductions scored toward achieving 100% carbon neutrality.

Absolute value score: Within this scoring process, an overall value score is calculated by dividing the total points achieved by a company by the total possible points available across all 168 subgoals (1680 points) to arrive at their overall value score. Here, GNO achieved an absolute value score of 4% with only 70 out of 1680 possible points.

Relative value score: A relative value score is given by dividing the total points achieved by a company by the total possible points available only from 3-point disclosure subgoals. So for example, if a company has been found to disclose across only 100 out of the 168 subgoals at the 3-point level, then their total score from these 100 subgoals will be divided by 1000 which represents the total possible full score that is achievable.

In the case of GNO, of the nine subgoals that did have actionable value model data available, they achieved a total of 70 points, giving them a relative value score of 78%.

4.4 *Stage 2: Development of ESG Artifacts and Knowledge Assets*

A. Artifact Compilation
This phase involved a systematic approach to collecting and consolidating ESG artifacts from GNO Inc. A comprehensive review of organizational policies, sustainability initiatives, and proprietary research was conducted. The process engaged key personnel and covered business areas, such as human resources, research and development, and operations, to identify and document explicit knowledge assets, including training manuals, stakeholder engagement frameworks, and strategic alliance agreements. The artifacts were standardized in documentation format to ensure consistency, and a centralized digital repository was established for efficient management.

B. Knowledge Asset Management
A detailed record of each artifact was created, specifying its source, strategic relevance, and potential impact on GNO's ESG objectives. A robust version control system was implemented to monitor updates, enhancing the traceability of knowledge assets.

C. Protection and Safeguarding
These artifacts were then held in a secure data room so that future decisions on categorizations could be made easily by the project team.

D. Capacity Building
Workshops and training sessions were conducted to build capacity among GNO's management, emphasizing the significance of effective knowledge asset management for financial valuation and ESG reporting.

4.5 *Stage 3: Reclassification Using the Areopa's Four-Leaf Model*

E. Categorization of Artifacts
The artifacts were rigorously categorized using the Areopa's four-leaf model, which classifies intangible assets into human capital, structural capital, customer capital, and strategic alliance capital. Collaborative sessions with GNO's leadership team

facilitated the accurate classification of each artifact based on its primary function and strategic contribution. A classification matrix was developed, visually mapping the artifacts to GNO's long-term strategic objectives, aligning them with the organization's ESG framework.

F. Verification for Compliance
A thorough compliance review was performed to ensure that all categorized artifacts met the recognition criteria outlined in IAS 38, particularly focusing on the asset's ability to generate future economic benefits. An independent external auditor was engaged to validate the compliance of the artifacts, strengthening the credibility and robustness of the classification process. Discrepancies identified during the audit were addressed promptly, ensuring adherence to international reporting standards.

4.6 *Stage 4: Inventory Compilation and Valuation through the Areopa's Ten-Step Model*

G. Identification and Protection
An exhaustive inventory of GNO's intangible assets was compiled, with a focus on identifying key knowledge assets integral to the company's strategic goals. Protective measures, including intellectual property rights, nondisclosure agreements, and data security protocols, were implemented to safeguard these assets. This step ensured the legal and operational protection of proprietary knowledge, critical for sustaining long-term competitive advantage.

H. Valuation Using Areopa's Formulas
The valuation process employed Areopa's 77 proprietary formulas, integrating 927 value-creating phenomena to derive precise monetary estimates for each intangible asset. Workshops were conducted with GNO's finance and strategy teams to facilitate a thorough understanding of the valuation methodology.

Scenario analyses were performed to evaluate the sensitivity of asset valuations under varying market conditions, enhancing the reliability of the financial projections.

I. Validation for Financial Reporting
A comprehensive internal review was carried out to ensure that the valuation results adhered to the measurement criteria set by IAS 38. GNO's finance team collaborated with external auditors to validate the assigned values, integrating them into the company's financial statements in a manner consistent with international accounting standards. The validated results were documented in a detailed report, which was presented to stakeholders to demonstrate the financial impact of GNO's ESG initiatives and their contribution to the company's intellectual capital.

4.7 Present Value

Using the above approach, the present value of GNO's intellectual capital is estimated at $8.9 million. This includes the following (Fig. 2):

- Human capital (HC): $2,849,232
- Structural capital (SC): $4,269,512
- Strategic alliance capital (SAC): $1,781,256
- Customer capital (CC): $0

The total combined IC value is $8.9 million. Approximately 52% of this is tacit and must be seen as a risk, and 48% is documented assets (Fig. 3).

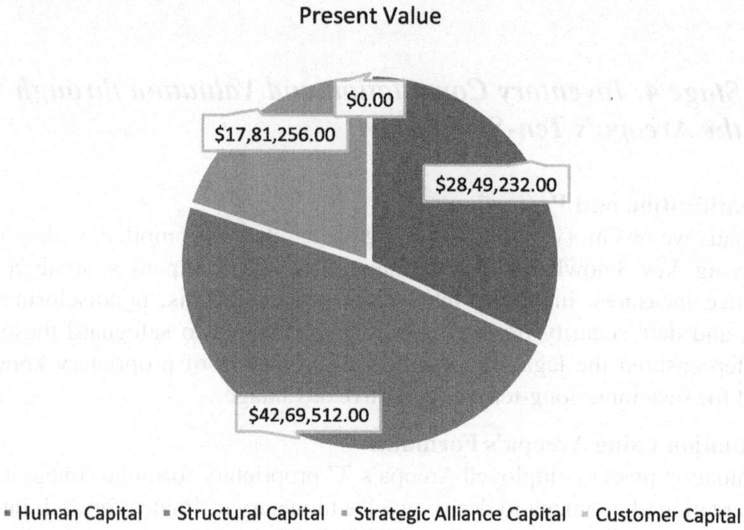

Fig. 2 The pie chart shows the estimated value of GNO inc against the four capitals as valued used the proprietary methodology of Areopa

Fig. 3 The pie chart shows the level of documented intangible assets (Explicit) vs the level of undocumented Intellectual Capital (Tacit)

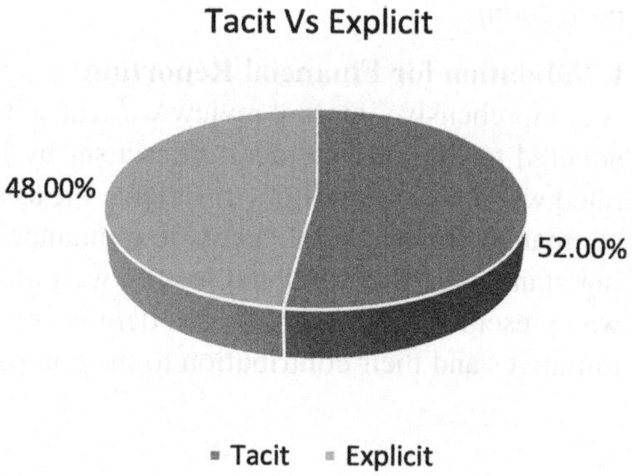

4.8 Future Value

The future value of GNO's intellectual capital is projected to reach $256 within the next 3 years, assuming the action plan is followed. This includes the following:

- Human capital (HC): $24,712,464
- Structural capital (SC): $147,076,688
- Strategic alliance capital (SAC): $65,889,248
- Customer capital (CC): $18,321,600

However, this again includes an amount of tacit knowledge. It must be noted that under IAS rules only IC is documented and creates future commercial value (the Areopa definition of structural capital can be placed on the balance sheet).

4.9 Valuation of Intangible Assets via IAS 38 and Areopa's Ten-Step Model

IAS 38 provides the framework for recognizing, measuring, and valuing intangible assets. The Areopa's ten-step model complements this by providing a structured approach to managing and valuing intellectual capital:

1. Identification: determine the intangible assets within the organization
2. Separation: distinguish these assets from other business components
3. Protection: implement measures to protect intellectual capital
4. Knowledge safeguarding: ensure key knowledge is retained and safeguarded
5. Management: manage these assets effectively
6. Control: maintain control over the assets to ensure they are used optimally
7. Ensuring future commercial value routes: identify and secure future commercial opportunities
8. Estimation of value: estimate the value of these intangible assets
9. Account: record these assets accurately in the financial statements
10. Audit: conduct regular audits to ensure compliance and accuracy

4.10 Stage 5: Strategic Integration and Ongoing Monitoring

Stage 5 focuses on the strategic integration of the valued intellectual capital assets into GNO Inc.'s business model and the implementation of an ongoing monitoring framework. This stage ensures that the intangible assets continue to generate value and adapt to changing market conditions, regulatory environments, and strategic objectives. The following actions were undertaken as part of this stage:

1. Integration into Business Strategy
GNO's management team collaborated with strategic consultants to incorporate the newly valued intangible assets into the company's overall business strategy. This involved aligning key assets, such as proprietary knowledge and stakeholder relationships, with GNO's strategic goals for market expansion and sustainability initiatives. Scenario planning workshops were conducted to explore how the identified assets could be leveraged to drive competitive advantage, particularly in emerging markets for biological products. The integration plan included actionable steps for utilizing the intellectual capital in product innovation, process optimization, and enhanced customer engagement.

2. Development of an Asset Utilization Framework
A comprehensive asset utilization framework was established to guide the effective deployment of GNO's intellectual capital. This framework provided detailed guidelines for integrating intangible assets into various operational processes, including R&D, marketing, and customer relationship management. Specific focus was placed on optimizing the use of human capital through training and upskilling initiatives, while structural capital assets were employed to streamline internal processes and enhance organizational efficiency.

3. Implementation of an Ongoing Monitoring System
To ensure the continuous value generation of the intellectual capital assets, an ongoing monitoring system was developed. This system used key performance indicators (KPIs) aligned with GNO's strategic objectives and IAS 38 compliance requirements. The monitoring process included regular assessments of asset performance, with metrics such as innovation output, employee productivity, and customer satisfaction levels. Quarterly reviews were implemented to provide updates on asset performance, allowing for timely adjustments and reallocation of resources as needed.

4. Stakeholder Communication and Reporting
An essential component of Stage 5 was the establishment of a clear communication strategy to report on the value and impact of GNO's intellectual capital assets to stakeholders. Detailed reports were prepared for investors, highlighting the financial contribution of the intangible assets to the company's overall growth and profitability. GNO's ESG performance improvements, driven by the strategic utilization of intellectual capital, were also documented and shared with relevant stakeholders to enhance transparency and build trust.

5. Continuous Improvement and Revaluation
Recognizing the dynamic nature of intangible assets, a process for continuous improvement and periodic revaluation was implemented. Annual revaluations of the intellectual capital assets were scheduled, incorporating updates based on changes in market conditions, regulatory standards, and business model adaptations. Feedback from stakeholders and performance data were used to refine the valuation process, ensuring that GNO's reported asset values remained accurate and reflective of their true economic potential.

5 Discussion

The integration of the value model and Areopa's ten-step and four-leaf models represents a significant advancement in the field of intellectual capital and ESG valuation. By combining these models, organizations can better monetize sustainability and ESG scores, providing a robust framework that links intangible asset valuation with financial reporting. This discussion explores the implications and benefits of this integration for the intellectual capital and ESG communities.

5.1 Enhancing Financial Reporting

Accurate and transparent financial reporting is crucial, especially for intangible assets. By integrating these models, organizations can effectively assign monetary values to their ESG performance and sustainability initiatives. Connecting Areopa's valuation method to IAS 38 ensures compliance with international accounting standards, enhancing the credibility and reliability of financial reports. This alignment is beneficial for investors, regulators, and other stakeholders who depend on these reports.

5.2 Strengthening Strategic Decision-Making

Strategic decision-making is greatly enhanced when organizations can quantify the financial impacts of their ESG and sustainability efforts. The value model, combined with Areopa's methodologies, provides a solid framework for achieving this. With monetized ESG and sustainability scores, companies can make informed decisions about strategic planning and resource allocation. This ensures that business models are aligned with market demands and stakeholder expectations, promoting long-term growth and competitiveness.

5.3 Improving Stakeholder Communication

Effective communication with stakeholders is essential for building trust and engagement. The integrated framework allows organizations to clearly convey the financial value of their sustainability and ESG initiatives. By demonstrating a commitment to sustainable and responsible business practices, companies can enhance their reputation and strengthen relationships with investors, customers, employees, and the community.

5.4 *Promoting Compliance and Standardization*

Linking the Areopa valuation method to IAS 38 not only ensures compliance with international accounting standards but also promotes a standardized approach to intangible asset valuation. This standardization is critical for ensuring consistency and comparability across organizations and industries, providing a reliable foundation for financial reporting and strategic decisions.

5.5 *Future Research Directions*

Future research can further refine this framework and explore its application across different industries. Each industry has unique characteristics and challenges, and customizing these models to fit specific contexts could enhance their effectiveness. Additionally, ongoing research should focus on developing new methodologies for integrating emerging ESG metrics and trends into the valuation process. These efforts will strengthen the connections between markets, business models, scenario planning, stakeholder engagement, policy, and IAS 38 evidence drivers.

5.6 *Promoting Sustainable and Ethical Business Practices*

The ultimate goal of combining the value model with Areopa's ten-step and four-leaf models is to promote sustainable and ethical business practices. By providing a clear financial incentive for ESG performance, this integrated approach encourages organizations to prioritize sustainability and social responsibility. This not only benefits the organization but also contributes positively to society and the environment.

5.7 *Emphasizing the Need for Future Business Model Adaptations*

In today's rapidly evolving market landscape, it is crucial for organizations to continuously review and adapt their business models. The integration of the value model and Areopa's methodologies offers a dynamic framework that can evolve with these changes. Anticipating future business model adaptations and incorporating them into the valuation processes ensures that organizations remain relevant and competitive, directly linking business models to market demands and stakeholder expectations.

5.8 Constantly Reviewing Future Scenarios

To stay ahead, companies must regularly review future scenarios and adjust their strategies accordingly. Market conditions, stakeholder expectations, and regulatory environments are continually evolving. These changes must be reflected in the organization's assumptions and strategic planning. By frequently updating future scenarios, organizations can proactively address potential risks and opportunities, ensuring long-term sustainability and growth. Scenario planning helps bridge the gap between current business models and future market conditions, aligning with stakeholder interests and regulatory requirements.

5.9 Centering Observations in Assumptions Testing

Placing market and stakeholder observations at the center of all assumptions tested by the integration of the value model and Areopa's methodologies is essential. Continuously validating and adjusting the models based on real-time data and feedback from the market and stakeholders ensures that valuation and strategic planning processes are grounded in current realities and can effectively guide decision-making. This process also aligns with IAS 38 evidence drivers, providing a robust foundation for financial reporting and strategic decisions.

5.10 Enhancing Stakeholder Engagement and Policy Integration

Effective stakeholder engagement is crucial for understanding and addressing the interests and concerns of various groups. Integrating feedback from stakeholders into the value model and Areopa's methodologies ensures that the organization's strategic direction aligns with stakeholder expectations. Additionally, aligning these methodologies with organizational policies and regulatory standards, such as IAS 38, enhances transparency and accountability in the valuation of intangible assets.

6 Final Thoughts

The integration of these models offers a comprehensive and adaptable framework for valuing intangible assets and ESG performance. By embracing future business model changes, continuously reviewing future scenarios, and centering observations in assumptions testing, organizations can enhance their strategic planning and drive sustainable growth. Future research will continue to refine and expand these methodologies, ensuring they remain effective across various industries and evolving market conditions. This holistic approach ensures that organizations are well prepared to meet the demands of the market, stakeholders, and regulatory bodies, ultimately fostering long-term success and sustainability.

7 Engaging the Community

We invite members of the intellectual capital and ESG communities to reflect on and contribute to the ongoing development of these models. How can we further refine these methodologies to address the specific needs of different industries? What additional metrics and trends should be incorporated to ensure these models remain relevant and effective? By engaging in this conversation, we can collectively advance the practice of valuing intangible assets and ESG performance, promoting more sustainable and ethical business practices worldwide.

Acknowledgments We would like to extend our thanks to Dhiyan Arini from the Value Research Center for her analysis of GNO using the value model framework and Simon Boulanger for his analysis using the Areopa models. We also thank GNO for all the participation in this research.

References

Bergmann, A. (2017). History of environmental reporting. In *Environmental management and reporting* (pp. 17–36). Springer. Retrieved from Springer.

Business Roundtable. (2019). *Business Roundtable Redefines the Purpose of a Corporation to Promote an Economy that Serves all Americans*. (Accessed February 1, 2023), [available at https://purpose.businessroundtable.org/]

Büyüközkan, G., & Karabulut, Y. (2018). Sustainability performance evaluation: Literature review and future directions. *Journal of Environmental Management, 217*, 253–267. https://doi.org/10.1016/j.jenvman.2018.03.064

European Commission. (2021). *Non-financial reporting*. Retrieved from European Commission

Gudmundsdottir, S., & Sigurjonsson, T. O. (2024). A need for standardized approaches to manage sustainability strategically. *Sustainability, 16*(6), 2319. https://doi.org/10.3390/su16062319

KPMG. (2020). *The time has come: The KPMG survey of sustainability reporting 2020*. Retrieved from KPMG.

Liang, H., & Chan, K. C. (2022). The alphabet soup in reporting and measuring ESG. *Asian Management Insights, 9*(2), 19–24. Retrieved from Singapore Management University.

Pyis, L. (2011). Intellectual capital accounting: How to measure the unmeasurable. In G. Turner (Ed.), *ECIC2011 Proceedings of the 3rd European Conference on Intellectual Capital* (pp. 1–15). Academic Conferences Limited.

Schwab, K. (2019). *Davos Manifesto 2020: The universal purpose of a company in the Fourth Industrial Revolution*. Retrieved October 13, 2024, from https://www.weforum.org/agenda/2019/12/davos-manifesto-2020-the-universal-purpose-ofa-company-in-the-fourth-industrial-revolution/

Sugai, P., Koizumi, R., Linnan, N., Phattanaprayoonvong, S., & Phetharn, J. (2022). *A value model for responsible business* (DBS Discussion Paper Series, DBS-21-01). Retrieved from Doshisha University.

Sugai, P., Phattanaprayoonvong, S., Phetharn, J., & Yamazaki, M. (2021). *Valuing value: A synthesis of global sustainability frameworks to establish objective and transparent goals to measure value for a firm, its shareholders, customers, employees, partners, society and the planet* (DBS Discussion Paper Series, DBS-21-01, 1-156). Retrieved from Doshisha University.

Sugai, P., Wai Khuen, W., & Arini, D. (2023). Impact and value measurement – A way forward. *DBS Discussion Paper Series, 23*(4), 1–64. Retrieved from Doshisha University.

Task Force on Climate-related Financial Disclosures (TCFD). (2017). *Final report: Recommendations of the Task Force on Climate-related Financial Disclosures*. Retrieved from TCFD.

UN PRI. (n.d.). *What are the Principles for Responsible Investment?* Retrieved from UN PRI.

Boosting Intellectual Capital-Powered Innovation with Human Resource Management Practices

Josune Sáenz, Aino Kianto, and Nekane Aramburu

Abstract In today's fast-paced environment, continuous renewal and innovation are crucial for an organization's performance and survival. We argue that renewal capital (RC) is a key component of intellectual capital (IC) in fostering innovation. RC refers to a firm's dynamic capability to update and renew its knowledge assets, making it a critical driver of innovation performance. Since it is the people within the organization who learn and innovate, human resource management (HRM) plays a significant role in empowering RC and fostering innovation. In this study, we develop a theoretical model to identify the HRM practices that are particularly essential for advancing RC as part of IC and, consequently, enhancing innovation performance. We test our theory using data collected from 180 Spanish companies, employing structural equation modeling based on partial least squares. Our empirical findings reveal that knowledge-based HRM practices—specifically, knowledge-based recruiting and selection, training and development, performance assessment, and compensation—are key antecedents of RC. Furthermore, RC plays a substantial role in promoting innovation. However, only training and development and, to a lesser extent performance assessment have a significant direct impact on innovation performance.

J. Sáenz (✉) · N. Aramburu
University of Deusto, Deusto Business School, San Sebastián, Spain
e-mail: josune.saenz@deusto.es; nekane.aramburu@deusto.es

A. Kianto
LUT University, LUT Business School, Lahti, Finland
e-mail: Aino.Kianto@lut.fi

F. Matos et al. (eds.), *Intellectual Capital in a Global Business Landscape*,
Contributions to Management Science, https://doi.org/10.1007/978-3-031-86362-2_14

1 Introduction

In today's rapidly changing environment, knowledge becomes obsolete more quickly than it did before. Therefore, it is imperative that firms engage in continuous organizational renewal and that workers constantly develop new competences (Lundvall & Nielsen, 2007). Recent literature on intellectual capital (IC) (e.g., Buenechea-Elberdin et al., 2017; Cabrilo et al., 2018; Cesaroni et al., 2015; Del Baldo et al., 2015; Hussinki et al., 2017; Inkinen et al., 2017; Kianto et al., 2010; Ritala et al., 2023; Zlatković, 2020) has conceptualized organizational learning and adaptation as renewal capital (RC).

RC encompasses organizational resources and capabilities related to the ability of the firm to renew what it knows and can do through knowledge-related activities (Hussinki et al., 2017), and it can be characterized as the actualized learning capability of the firm (Kianto et al., 2010). However, even though RC is argued to be "the new bottom line" of IC (Edvinsson, 2002) and is included even in the classical first generation of IC frameworks (see Kianto, 2008) such as the Skandia Navigator model (Edvinsson & Malone, 1997), the Intangible Assets Monitor (Sveiby, 1997), and IC-Index (Roos et al., 1998), previous research on its antecedents is very scarce (Zlatković, 2020).

RC is closely linked to human capital (HC) because it is people who perform the renewing activities, and organizational members are the media through which learning generally occurs (Argote & Miron-Spektor, 2011). Nevertheless, RC is both conceptually and empirically distinct from HC (Buenechea-Elberdin et al., 2017).

According to Takeuchi et al. (2003), there is agreement among researchers that organizational members are the critical learners. This perspective aligns with the "IC multiplier effect" as posited by Edvinsson (2002). In this effect, human capital is essential to leverage both relational capital (knowledge embedded in relationships) and structural capital (knowledge inherent in organizational structures). Essentially, individuals act as the driving force, determining the caliber of knowledge creation and organizational learning (OL). Put differently, organizations learn because individuals learn (Kim, 1993). Hence, human resource management (HRM) could play a substantial role in the promotion of organizational learning capability and innovation (Chen & Li, 2015). However, although some studies focus on the relationship between HRM and organizational learning capability (Jérez-Gómez et al., 2019), to the best of our knowledge, there are no previous studies addressing the relationship between HRM and renewal capital.

Moreover, although several studies have examined the relationship between HRM and innovation (e.g., Chen & Li, 2015; De Saá-Pérez & Díaz-Díaz, 2010; Haneda & Ito, 2018; Jiménez-Jiménez & Sanz-Valle, 2008; Shipton et al., 2005; Shipton et al., 2006), the knowledge-based perspective of HRM practices (Kang et al., 2012; Minbaeva, 2013; Minbaeva et al., 2009; Swart & Kinnie, 2013) has only recently been considered in empirical research (e.g., Evangelista et al., 2023; Gupta, 2022; Hussinki et al., 2018; Kianto et al., 2017) and, to the best of our knowledge, studies linking HRM, RC, and innovation together are nonexistent.

Additionally, the majority of studies have followed a systems or "bundle" approach (Seeck & Diehl, 2017) in which HRM practices are combined into coherent packages (Marchington & Grugulis, 2000) without identifying what specific practices within the package should be prioritized or deserve special attention (e.g., De Saá-Pérez & Díaz-Díaz, 2010; Jiménez-Jiménez & Sanz-Valle, 2008; Zhou et al., 2013). According to Chowhan (2016, p. 113), "a focus on systems has meant that clear prescriptions outlining what practices to use under particular strategies and contexts are not available to the practitioner."

Furthermore, Budhwar and Debrah (2001) as well as Budhwar and Khatri (2001) have highlighted how national factors—like culture, institutions, and evolving business landscapes—can influence HRM practices. Take Spain as an example. The proportion of involuntary temporary employment there is significantly above the European average: 12.8% in Spain compared to 4.3% for the European Union-27 (EUROSTAT, 2023). Moreover, the latest World Talent Ranking by the Institute for Management Development (IMD, 2023) indicates that employee training is not a top priority in Spain. The country ranks 40th out of 64, scoring just 5.69 out of 10 on the survey item that evaluates whether "employee training is a high priority in companies." Given this context, it is crucial to discern whether it is more beneficial to continually invest in training and developing current employees or to consistently replace those who no longer align with company needs via recruitment and selection. This is essentially the debate between pursuing a human capital development strategy versus a talent acquisition approach (Youndt & Snell, 2004).

Considering these gaps in current understanding, the aim of this paper is to analyze the influence of different knowledge-based HRM practices on RC and innovation in a set of Spanish manufacturing and service firms with more than 100 employees through a nonbundled approach, which allows for assessment of the degree of relevance of each practice—knowledge-based recruiting and selection, training and development, performance assessment, and compensation—on RC and innovation performance.

2 Theoretical Background and Hypothesis Development

2.1 Knowledge-Based Human Resource Management Practices

As RC and innovation involve primarily human processes, HRM practices have a substantial potential to impact a company's capability to learn and innovate. In line with Minbaeva et al. (2009), Minbaeva (2013), and Kianto et al. (2017), the authors assert that to enhance RC and innovation, managers should customize traditional HRM practices to advance knowledge creation and knowledge sharing in a firm. In this vein, knowledge-based HRM includes those HRM practices that are purposefully designed to enhance knowledge processes within an organization. Such practices are described below (Kianto et al., 2017):

- Knowledge-based recruiting and selection: According to De Winne and Sels (2010), recruiting and selection play a pivotal role in knowledge creation. This is because those responsible for recruiting and interviewing are making decisions about the knowledge that new hires bring into an organization. Specifically, "Hiring selectively for the right skills, aptitude, cultural fit, and attitude is paramount for work teams to successfully integrate diverse knowledge bases" (Malik et al., 2020, p. 526). The educational level of individuals helps to improve their understanding of what they know (Smith et al., 2005) and their receptivity to new ideas (Hambrick & Mason, 1984). Supporting this perspective, Subramaniam and Youndt (2005) showed that organizational innovation is dependent on the organization's knowledge base, which begins by recruiting talented people into the organization (Jiang et al., 2012). However, according to Lepak and Snell (2002), new employees should be selected based more on their potential than on their current knowledge, skills, and experience. Furthermore, as learning primarily happens through social interaction (e.g., Nonaka & Takeuchi, 1995), knowledge-based recruitment should consider a candidate's ability to collaborate. Therefore, knowledge-based recruitment involves a strong and explicit focus on choosing candidates with relevant knowledge and abilities for learning and networking.
- Knowledge-based training and development: As Robbins et al. (2010) pointed out, even the most skilled employees cannot retain their competency indefinitely. Skills can wane and become outdated, making continuous learning essential. Through the design and implementation of training and development activities, the organization bridges the gap between current and requisite knowledge and skills and thus contributes to knowledge creation (De Winne & Sels, 2010) and human capital development (Cabello-Medina et al., 2011). Investments in training also support knowledge sharing and integration (Malik et al., 2020). Furthermore, according to Mumford (2000), creative work requires progressive acquisition of skills and expertise (Jiang et al., 2012). More precisely, training could enhance employees' relevant knowledge and skills to increase creative thought processes and provide opportunities that enhance task domain expertise (Jiang et al., 2012; Lau & Ngo, 2004). Hence, knowledge-based training and development involve regularly developing the depth and breadth of employees' knowledge and expertise, personalizing training to fit specific needs and ensuring continuous employee development.
- Knowledge-based performance assessment: Performance evaluation is also a very significant mechanism for guiding employee behavior. To bolster knowledge-related processes, it is imperative to have pertinent performance criteria in place. Specifically, performance appraisals should prioritize development and constructive feedback (Lepak & Snell, 2002). Furthermore, evaluations centered on learning and personal growth can instill the confidence employees need to pursue more advanced learning opportunities (Jiang et al., 2012). In sum, knowledge-based performance assessment involves evaluating employees according to their

contributions to organizations' knowledge processes: knowledge sharing, creation, and application (e.g., Alavi & Leidner, 2001).

- Knowledge-based compensation: Following Shaw et al. (2005), compensation systems are considered especially relevant when an employer wants employees to acquire the valuable and unique competences necessary for the firm's operations (Cabello-Medina et al., 2011). Appropriate compensation systems help attract and retain more valuable employees and motivate them to develop the required competences (Cabello-Medina et al., 2011; Park et al., 2004). Several previous studies (e.g., Andreeva & Kianto, 2012; Chen & Huang, 2009; Kamhawi, 2012) demonstrated that incentive systems are important mechanisms for motivating employees to take the time needed to share knowledge and generate new ideas. As pointed out by Gubbins (2019, p. 179), "Incentives including recognition and rewards are often recommended as practices to facilitate knowledge sharing and help build a supportive knowledge-sharing culture." Both tangible (e.g., bonuses and one-off rewards) and intangible (e.g., status and recognition) incentives can be used to motivate employees to share, create, and apply knowledge (Andreeva & Kianto, 2012; Inkinen et al., 2015; Scarbrough, 2003). Knowledge-based compensation implies rewarding employees according to their contributions to the key knowledge processes of knowledge sharing, creation, and application.

2.2 *HRM and RC*

Knowledge-based HRM practices can promote the type of behavior that is needed for organizational renewal—i.e., the actualized learning capability of the firm (Kianto et al., 2010)—to occur. In this regard, Chan and Scott-Ladd (2004, p. 344) pointed out that human resource (HR) practitioners "have the important role of designing and facilitating a workplace that encourages experimentation, tolerance, and learning from mistakes, and rewarding staff fairly for their contributions." This approach fosters a knowledge sharing culture and continuous learning. Similarly, López-Cabrales et al. (2011) argued that HRM practices can be regarded as learning facilitators, because they play a significant role in orientating employees' behavior and promoting positive attitudes toward learning and renewal.

These authors analyzed whether HRM practices (selection, development, performance appraisals, and rewards) contributed to OL in a set of Spanish firms from most innovative sectors. They found that selection practices—based on personnel's potential to learn and share knowledge—competence-based appraisals and rewards led to positive and significant OL contributions, while development practices did not. These results differ slightly from those obtained in another survey carried out in Spain by Pérez-López et al. (2006), who found that, unlike contingent rewards or compensation practices, selective hiring, strategic training, and employee participation in decision-making positively affected OL. However, Jérez-Gómez et al. (2005) found that some compensation practices (skill-based pay and high wages) did exert a positive and significant influence on several OL dimensions. More recently, and following a systems approach, Hooi and Ngui (2014) showed that the application of human capital-enhancing HRM practices in Malaysian small and medium enterprises (SMEs) positively affected OL.

Based on the above findings (which, in general terms, highlight a positive connection between HRM and OL, which constitutes the main foundation of RC) and on the conceptualization of knowledge-based HRM practices outlined in the previous section, the following research hypothesis was formulated:

Hypothesis 1 Knowledge-based HRM practices—(a) recruiting and selection, (b) training and development, (c) performance assessment, and (d) compensation—are positively related to RC.

2.3 RC and Innovation

Innovation (i.e., the generation of value creating novelties in terms of products, services, processes, and strategies) is fundamentally a knowledge-related issue, as it hinges on the successful development and implementation of new ideas (Nonaka & Takeuchi, 1995; Tidd et al., 2005). Therefore, knowledge resources in an organization's reach—in other words, its intellectual capital (IC)—constitute an essential driver of innovation (e.g., Subramaniam & Youndt, 2005).

In this respect, RC, which represents the most dynamic facet of IC stocks (Kianto, 2007) is especially relevant because it encompasses the organization's resources to renew what it knows and can do (Kianto et al., 2010) through the processes of knowledge creation and learning (Inkinen et al., 2017). Thus, RC describes how well the organization can make use of its other IC elements to foster learning and development—and thereby innovation and long-term survival even in turbulent conditions (Bontis, 2004). Furthermore, as an organization with high RC can build on previous knowledge and acquire and generate new knowledge, it will also be able to develop new products, services, and inventive ideas on a continuous basis (Tseng & Goo, 2005).

In fact, several recent empirical studies demonstrate that RC significantly increases innovation performance in firms. Cabrilo et al. (2018) studied IC and innovation in Serbian companies and found that out of a variety of six different IC components, RC is the best predictor of overall innovation performance, followed by internal relational capital and structural capital. In the case of Spain, Buenechea-Elberdin et al. (2017) found that RC increases innovation performance in both high technology and low-technology firms and that RC is the only IC component that directly impacts innovation performance in firms operating in low-technology industries, fully mediating the impact of human capital and entrepreneurial capital on innovation. In addition, in a study addressing Italian firms, Cesaroni et al. (2015) found that RC is statistically related with firm performance in terms of ROA and ROI and argued that RC should be considered the new "bottom line" of IC. More recently, Ritala et al. (2023) analyzed the influence of RC on incremental and radical innovation, demonstrating that RC has a positive and significant impact on both types of innovation.

Hence, the following hypothesis was formulated:

Hypothesis 2 RC is positively related to innovation performance.

2.4 HRM and Innovation

Several studies have already demonstrated the direct influence of HRM practices on innovation. However, fewer studies have deeply examined how HRM practices affect innovation or have considered potential moderating or mediating variables in the HRM-innovation linkage (Seeck & Diehl, 2017). Regarding indirect effects (which constitute the focus of this research), several variables have been proposed to mediate the relationship between HRM and innovation. Some of them refer to different types of employee knowledge, capabilities, perceptions, attitudes, and behaviors that HRM practices could enhance and that are relevant for innovation to occur, whereas others refer to different dimensions of organizational climate and knowledge that could contribute to innovation.

Focusing on the organizational level, in their study of 332 firms in Hong Kong, Lau and Ngo (2004) found that organizational culture mediated the relationship between an innovation-oriented HR system (i.e., a system that emphasizes extensive training, performance-based reward, and team development) and the development of new products and services. Two years later, in a study of 136 high-tech US firms, Collins and Smith (2006) showed that commitment-based HRM practices affected innovation performance through their effects on different dimensions of social climate (trust, cooperation, and shared codes and language) and on knowledge exchange and combination. Following with knowledge as a mediating variable, Chen and Huang (2009) found that knowledge management capacity mediated the relationship between strategic HR practices and innovation performance in a set of 146 Taiwanese companies, while more recently, Kianto et al. (2017) showed that intellectual capital (i.e., the stock of an organization's knowledge resources: human capital, structural capital, and relational capital) mediated the relationship between knowledge-based HRM practices and innovation performance.

Moreover, several studies focus on the mediating role of OL capability in the relationship between HRM practices and innovation. In this vein, Chen and Li (2015) found that OL capability acts as an intermediate between flexible HRM and organizational innovation performance, and Jérez-Gómez et al. (2019) verified that OL capability mediated the relationship between high-performance HR practices and firm's innovation in a sample of 85 Spanish companies in the chemical industry.

Considering that RC "represents how well the organization can utilize its human, structural and relational capital in order to foster continuous learning, innovation and development, and to sustain its competitiveness even in changing conditions" (Kianto et al., 2010, p. 309), and given that RC is the only mediating variable considered in this study (according to Hypothesis 1, knowledge-based HRM practices

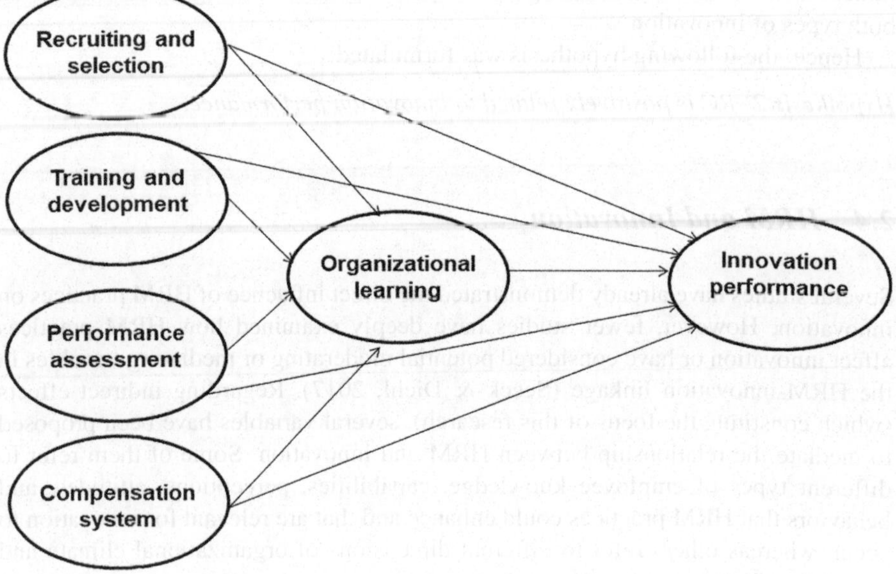

Fig. 1 Research model analyzed in Tables 1 and 2

are positively related to RC, whereas according to Hypothesis 2, RC positively affects innovation), the extensive list of mediators in the HRM-innovation relationship mentioned above shows that RC should be considered as a partial mediator in the HRM-innovation relationship. In other words, according to previous empirical findings, HRM practices could have additional positive effects on other innovation-conducive variables beyond those exerted on RC. Therefore, the following hypothesis was formulated:

Hypothesis 3 RC partially mediates the relationship between knowledge-based HRM practices—(a) recruiting and selection, (b) training and development, (c) performance assessment, and (d) compensation—and innovation.

Figure 1 summarizes the research model.

3 Research Methods

3.1 Sample and Data Collection

In the present survey, the target population was composed of Spanish companies with at least 100 employees. To identify such companies, the Sistema de Análisis de Balances Ibéricos (SABI) database, which contains financial information about Spanish and Portuguese firms, was utilized. A total of 1289 companies satisfying the established criteria were identified. Of these, only 700 were contacted due to budget constraints and an effort was made to preserve the industry and size proportions in the population. A questionnaire was administered to these firms via phone interviews (see Table 1, item wording column), although some companies preferred to receive and respond to the questionnaire by email. Of the 700 firms contacted, 180 completed the survey, representing a response rate of 25.71%. Most of the

Table 1 Measurement model evaluation

Constructs and measures	Item wording	Mean	Std. dev.	VIF	Weight	p-val.	Loading	p-val.
Recruiting and selection Mode "B" composite	Please rate from 1 to 5 (1 = strongly disagree; 5 = strongly agree) your degree of agreement or disagreement with the following statements							
REC1	When recruiting, we pay special attention to relevant expertise	3.989	0.901	1.136	**0.455**	**0.036**	0.711	0.000
REC2	When recruiting, we pay special attention to learning and development ability	4.183	0.799	1.467	**0.406**	**0.046**	0.791	0.000
REC3	When recruiting, we evaluate the candidates' ability to collaborate and work in various networks	3.911	0.935	1.432	**0.448**	**0.036**	0.794	0.000
Training and development Mode "B" composite	Please rate from 1 to 5 (1 = strongly disagree; 5 = strongly agree) your degree of agreement or disagreement with the following statements							
TD1	We offer our employees opportunities to deepen and expand their expertise	3.956	0.862	2.505	0.270	0.099	0.765	0.000
TD2	We offer training that provides employees with up-to-date knowledge	4.089	0.884	2.804	0.197	0.170	0.811	0.000
TD3	Our employees have an opportunity to develop their competence through training tailored to their specific needs	3.627	1.056	2.091	0.015	0.469	0.726	0.000

(continued)

Table 1 (continued)

Constructs and measures	Item wording	Mean	Std. dev.	VIF	Weight	p-val.	Loading	p-val.
TD4	Competence development needs of employees are discussed with them regularly	3.411	1.053	1.938	**0.669**	**0.000**	0.932	0.000
Performance assessment Mode "B" composite	Please rate from 1 to 5 (1 = strongly disagree; 5 = strongly agree) your degree of agreement or disagreement with the following statements							
PA1	The sharing of knowledge is one of our criteria for work performance assessment	3.328	1.102	1.770	**0.348**	**0.023**	0.830	0.000
PA2	The creation of new knowledge is one of our criteria for work performance assessment	3.483	1.001	2.160	**0.631**	**0.000**	0.949	0.000
PA3	The ability to apply knowledge acquired from others is one of our criteria for work performance assessment	3.836	0.975	1.865	0.149	0.190	0.756	0.000
Compensation Mode "B" composite	Please rate from 1 to 5 (1 = strongly disagree; 5 = strongly agree) your degree of agreement or disagreement with the following statements							
COMP1	Our company rewards employees for sharing knowledge	2.765	1.134	2.297	**0.549**	**0.023**	0.938	0.000
COMP2	Our company rewards employees for creating new knowledge	3.150	1.176	2.908	0.397	0.095	0.907	0.000
COMP3	Our company rewards employees for applying knowledge	3.439	1.141	2.690	0.150	0.282	0.834	0.000

(continued)

Table 1 (continued)

Constructs and measures	Item wording	Mean	Std. dev.	VIF	Weight	p-val.	Loading	p-val.
Renewal capital Mode "B" composite	Please rate from 1 to 5 (1 = strongly disagree; 5 = strongly agree) your degree of agreement or disagreement with the following statements							
RC1	Our company has acquired a great deal of new and important knowledge	3.450	0.896	1.927	**0.532**	**0.000**	0.886	0.000
RC2	Our employees have acquired a great deal of skills and abilities	3.492	0.801	1.896	0.070	0.289	0.718	0.000
RC3	The operations of our company can be described as creative and inventive	3.383	0.996	1.644	**0.541**	**0.000**	0.885	0.000
Innovation performance Mode "B" composite	Compared to its competitors, how successfully has your company managed to create innovations in the following areas during the past year? (1 = much worse; 5 = much better)							
IP1	Products and services for customers	3.469	0.883	1.594	**0.322**	**0.049**	0.778	0.000
IP2	Production methods and processes	3.460	0.848	1.866	0.259	0.173	0.801	0.000
IP3	Management practices	3.399	0.781	1.705	**0.357**	**0.028**	0.807	0.000
IP4	Marketing practices	3.136	1.008	1.692	0.181	0.180	0.719	0.000
IP5	Business models	3.277	0.869	1.644	0.176	0.176	0.702	0.000
Size (control)	Natural logarithm of the number of employees	334	541	N.A.	N.A.	N.A.	N.A.	N.A.
Industry (control)	Manufacturing firm = 1; service firm = 0	48%	0.500	N.A.	N.A.	N.A.	N.A.	N.A.
R&D intensity (control)	Proportion of R&D staff of all employees	11%	0.168	N.A.	N.A.	N.A.	N.A.	N.A.

Note: Numbers in bold show significant weights

respondents held positions such as HR director or manager (67%), other director or manager (18%), expert or clerical work (11%), or managing director (4%), and all of them indicated their expertise and key position regarding the topics under study.

The sample size obtained is sufficiently large for a statistical study using a partial least squares (PLS) structural equation modeling (SEM) approach. According to the square root method suggested by Kock and Hadaya (2018) for sample calculation (which evaluates the likelihood that the ratio of a path coefficient to its standard error will surpass the critical value of a test statistic at a specific significance level), and following recommendations by Hair et al. (2022), the minimum sample size suggested for cases where the smallest significant path coefficient is projected to be between 0.31 and 0.4 (as is true for our research) is 39. Thus, our final sample of 180 companies is well above the minimum threshold.

3.2 *Common Method Bias*

As data regarding dependent and independent variables were obtained using a single method (i.e., a questionnaire answered by a key informant from each company), there was a risk of common method bias (Podsakoff et al., 2003). To assess the extent of method variance in our dataset, a full collinearity test developed specifically for PLS-SEM was conducted. According to Kock (2015), if a full collinearity test reveals that all variance inflation factors (VIFs) from this test are 3.3 or below, the model can be considered free of common method bias. In our study, the highest recorded VIF was 2.201. As a result, concerns related to common method variance were ruled out from the research.

3.3 *Measures*

The research model encompasses six latent variables: four of them pertain to knowledge-based HRM practices (recruitment and selection, training and development, performance assessment, and compensation). The remaining two are associated with RC and innovation performance. Each of the independent, mediating, and dependent variables was conceptualized as a combination of different elements, which defined the conceptual variable they represented. In other words, the variables "emerge" from the indicators rather than being caused by them, as articulated by Hair et al. (2022). Thus, indicators do not necessarily correlate.

Setting out from HRM practices, the specific indicators used for the four scales were already reported in Kianto et al. (2017). Knowledge-based recruiting and selection are characterized by three core attributes to be considered during the hiring process: relevant expertise, the capacity for continuous learning and development, and the aptitude for collaboration within diverse networks. While a specific company might prioritize one, two, or all three of these attributes (i.e., such attributes need not necessarily be correlated), emphasizing all three is what truly defines a knowledge-based recruiting and selection process. Performance assessment and compensation are delineated by three indicators tied to distinct knowledge processes that companies might prioritize when evaluating and compensating their staff: knowledge sharing, knowledge creation, and knowledge application. While a particular company might emphasize just one of these knowledge processes, a combination of two, or all three, giving weight to all three leads to a truly knowledge-based approach to performance assessment and compensation. Regarding training and development, the chosen indicators span various aspects: regular conversation with employees about competence development needs, providing avenues for employees to expand and refine their expertise, the topicality of training content, and how tailored this content is to specific needs. Again, while individual companies might emphasize these aspects in diverse ways, engaging in all of them culminates in a more robust talent development system.

For RC, drawing on research by Hughes and Morgan (2007), Kianto et al. (2010), and García-Morales et al. (2006, 2007), it is posited that a company's ability to renew itself stems from a mix of individual learning, company-wide learning, and creative and inventive processes. Additionally, based on Weerawardena (2003), innovation performance was categorized into various forms of innovation: product/service innovation, process innovation, and innovations in management practices, marketing practices, and business models. Once more, excelling in one specific type of innovation does not automatically indicate proficiency in others.

For variables that are emergent, as is the case in this research, a composite measurement model applies (Henseler, 2017). In composite measurement, scores for latent variables are derived from linear combinations of their indicators. There are two approaches to determine the weights of indicators in these combinations: mode "A" and mode "B." In mode "A," weights are determined based on simple correlations, whereas in mode "B," they are derived from multiple regression. The decision between these modes hinges on the collinearity level of the indicators for a given construct. High collinearity could pose challenges in estimating indicator weights for mode "B" composites. In such cases, mode "A" might be more suitable (Henseler, 2017; Rigdon, 2016). Since our study did not encounter collinearity issues (as will be discussed in the measurement model evaluation section), we opted for mode "B." This choice lets us evaluate the relative significance of each indicator in maximizing the variance explained in the mediating and dependent variables.

To control possible confounding effects, additional relevant variables were included, such as company size, the degree of commitment to renewing the company's knowledge base (measured in terms of R&D intensity; Lane & Lubatkin, 1998), and industry. Table 1 shows all the constructs and measures that were used, including the mean and standard deviation of each item.

3.4 Statistical Analysis

We analyzed the proposed research model using SEM based on PLS through the SmartPLS 3.3.5 software (Ringle et al., 2015). Our choice to use this method stems from the "emergent" nature of the variables being studied. Unlike covariance-based SEM that uses a common factor approach, PLS-based SEM solely relies on composites (Rigdon, 2016). The PLS-based SEM process consists of two main phases: (1) evaluating the measurement model and (2) appraising the structural model. Following this sequence ensures that the measurements of the constructs are valid and reliable before making inferences about the relationships between these constructs (Barclay et al., 1995).

4 Research Findings

4.1 Measurement Model Evaluation

In composite measurement, traditional evaluation methods—intended to validate that chosen indicators stem from a singular underlying phenomenon—are not applicable. Instead, the concepts are derived by combining the elements present in their definitions. Therefore, the assessment of the measurement model should ensure that these indicators truly reflect the core of the conceptual variables, a principle referred to as "conceptual fidelity" (Rigdon, 2012). For HRM practices, the indicators detailed under the "Research Methods" heading, and listed in Table 1, align closely with the definitions and justifications given for each type of knowledge-based HRM practice in the "Theoretical Background and Hypothesis Development" section. As for RC, the selected indicators are consistent with the concept's definition presented in the "Introduction." Finally, the indicators that define innovation performance reflect the categories addressed for a long time in national innovation surveys.

After ensuring conceptual fidelity, collinearity among indicators should be assessed. Collinearity can pose challenges in estimating indicators' weights (Rigdon, 2016). Ideally, VIF values should be at or below 3 (Hair et al., 2022). As demonstrated in Table 1, all indicators' VIF values are well under this threshold. Consequently, mode "B" estimation was retained.

Finally, the significance and relevance of indicators' weights need to be evaluated (Hair et al., 2022). Indicators' weights indicate the relative importance of each item in maximizing the explained variance of the dependent variables. We tested the significance levels using a one-tailed 5,000 subsample bias-corrected and accelerated (BCA) bootstrap, as outlined by Hair et al. (2022). The results are presented in Table 1. Given that the loadings for nonsignificant indicators are still statistically relevant, we opted to retain all the indicators in the model. This decision is based on their absolute contributions (i.e., loadings) being statistically significant. Additionally, retaining all indicators ensures alignment with conceptual definitions. Detailed comments regarding indicators' weights will be provided in the next section once the overall role of each independent and mediating variable is clarified.

4.2 Structural Model Evaluation

Once the measurement model's quality was confirmed, we tested the strength of the established relationships between the constructs using the same one-tailed 5000 subsample BCA bootstrap, as recommended by Hair et al. (2022). Findings are reported in Table 2.

However, before conducting the BCA bootstrap, a collinearity test was executed. This test aimed to rule out any potential bias in path coefficients due to critical levels of collinearity among the predictor constructs (Hair et al., 2022). As in the

Table 2 Structural model evaluation

	Effects	St. dev.	t statistics	p-values
Direct relationships regarding renewal capital (R^2 = 40.2%)				
Size	0.091	0.057	1.618	0.053
Industry	**−0.121**	**0.062**	**1.958**	**0.025**
R&D intensity	0.018	0.057	0.320	0.374
Recruiting and selection	**0.195**	**0.074**	**2.634**	**0.004**
Training and development	**0.193**	**0.077**	**2.521**	**0.006**
Performance assessment	**0.288**	**0.083**	**3.476**	**0.000**
Compensation	**0.139**	**0.077**	**1.807**	**0.035**
Direct relationships regarding innovation performance (R^2 = 33.5%)				
Size	−0.040	0.089	0.452	0.326
Industry	0.022	0.106	0.204	0.419
R&D intensity	0.033	0.097	0.338	0.368
Recruiting and selection	−0.027	0.094	0.293	0.385
Training and development	**0.209**	**0.089**	**2.335**	**0.010**
Performance assessment	0.040	0.108	0.368	0.356
Compensation	−0.002	0.098	0.025	0.490
Renewal capital	**0.429**	**0.095**	**4.493**	**0.000**
Indirect relationships between knowledge-based HRM practices and innovation perf. via RC				
Indirect relationship regarding recruiting and selection	**0.084**	**0.038**	**2.172**	**0.015**
Total degree of association between recruiting and selection and innovation performance (direct + indirect)	0.056	0.088	0.637	0.262
Indirect relationship regarding training and development	**0.083**	**0.039**	**2.106**	**0.018**
Total degree of association between training and development and innovation performance (direct + indirect)	**0.292**	**0.085**	**3.423**	**0.000**
Indirect relationship regarding performance assessment	**0.123**	**0.045**	**2.719**	**0.003**
Total degree of association between performance assessment and innovation performance (direct + indirect)	0.163	0.109	1.504	0.066
Indirect relationship regarding compensation	**0.060**	**0.035**	**1.691**	**0.045**
Total degree of association between compensation and innovation performance (direct + indirect)	0.057	0.102	0.564	0.286

Note: Numbers in bold show significant effects

assessment of composite measurement models, VIF values should be lower than 3. In our case, the highest value obtained was 2.201. Therefore, collinearity in the structural model was not a problem in this research.

As we can see in Table 2, all knowledge-based HRM practices have a positive and significant relationship with RC, with performance assessment emerging as the most influential. Furthermore, RC is positively and strongly related to innovation performance. Therefore, Hypotheses 1 and 2 are supported.

However, training and development is the only knowledge-based HRM practice directly and significantly related to innovation performance. Given that the indirect relationships between other knowledge-based HRM practices and innovation performance through RC are positive and significant (as seen in Table 2), this suggests that RC fully mediates the relationship between (1) knowledge-based recruiting and selection and innovation performance, (2) knowledge-based performance assessment and innovation performance, and (3) knowledge-based compensation and innovation performance. Therefore, these knowledge-based HRM practices enhance innovation performance to the extent that they promote organizational renewal. For training and development, however, partial mediation applies. Consequently, Hypothesis 3b is supported, while Hypotheses 3a, 3c, and 3d are not.

As far as total effects of knowledge-based HRM practices on innovation performance are concerned, Table 2 reveals that training and development is the predominant component. Performance assessment follows behind, with its total effect bordering on statistical significance. In contrast, the total effects of both recruiting and selection and compensation are notably low.

In evaluating the relative importance of different elements within mode "B" composites, the indicator weights provided in Table 1 offer relevant insights. For the knowledge-based recruiting and selection composite, the relative importance of its indicators is almost uniform. However, when looking at training and development, the indicator emphasizing regular discussions about employees' competence development needs stands out as the most significant. In performance assessment, the focus on both knowledge sharing and knowledge creation emerges as statistically relevant, but the emphasis on knowledge application does not. As for the compensation composite, the concentration on knowledge sharing is pivotal, though the focus on knowledge creation also approaches significance. For RC, it is noteworthy that while employee learning is not statistically significant, both company-wide learning and the creativity and inventiveness of operations are. This suggests that individual learning holds significance only when it culminates in organizational learning.

Regarding predictive power (refer to Table 2), the variance explained amounted to 40.2% for RC and 33.5% for innovation performance. Additionally, to assess the models' out-of-sample predictive relevance, we conducted a Stone-Geisser test using blindfolding, as suggested by Hair et al. (2022). Sufficient predictive relevance is indicated when the cross-validated redundancy (Q2) of endogenous constructs exceeds zero. In this study, this criterion was met, with values of 0.245 for RC and 0.167 for innovation performance.

5 Discussion

5.1 Theoretical Contributions

While the findings concerning the relationships between training and development, RC, and innovation, as well as between performance assessment, RC, and innovation, were as expected, the reasons for the extremely low total effects of recruiting and selection and compensation on innovation were not immediately apparent. One explanation for this might be related to the potential negative interactions or substitutive effects among the different HRM practices.

Traditionally, HRM practices are viewed as mutually reinforcing bundles (e.g., Bowen & Ostroff, 2004; Boxall et al., 2011). Yet, recent discussions suggest the possibility of substitutive effects. In other words, certain practices might offset others, indicating that not all are necessary or even beneficial for achieving a specific outcome. There could also be negative trade-offs where one practice reduces the effectiveness of another (Andreeva et al., 2017; Ennen & Richter, 2010; Minbaeva et al., 2009). These substitution effects might further elucidate why RC fully mediates the relationship between HRM practices (with the exception of training and development) and innovation, even when other mediating variables have been identified in literature.

In terms of recruiting and selection, their very small influence on innovation performance can be explained by referencing the idea of Youndt and Snell (2004) that there are two alternative forms of human capital-enhancing HRM configurations: acquisition and developmental. The key feature of the acquisition HRM strategy is selective staffing practices, while the developmental HRM configuration is essentially based on training and educating the staff. These HRM strategies function as alternatives for building human capital by either buying or making it. While Youndt and Snell (2004) examined the impact of these strategies on organizations' financial performance, as mediated by human capital, and Soo et al. (2017) examined their impact on innovation, as mediated by absorptive capacity, our study extends these findings by demonstrating their role in RC-mediated innovation performance.

While recruiting and selection may be a viable means for increasing RC, according to our results, they only slightly augment resultant innovation performance. This finding demonstrates that, even if hiring new employees brings new knowledge to the organization, the new recruits may need time to develop the firm-specific expertise that will enable them to participate in developing value generating renewals (i.e., innovations) for the organization. Thus, it may be that recruitment should be coupled with work orientation and other means to adequately socialize the newcomers into the organization. This is understandable, since innovating does not take place in a vacuum, but is typically a team activity where intraorganizational interactions and context-specific knowledge are essential (Jiang & Chen, 2018; Van Knippenberg, 2017).

Overall, our findings point against the common view that a set of well-aligned HRM practices leads to mutually reinforcing benefits (e.g., Bowen & Ostroff, 2004). In contrast, it seems that high innovation performance can be achieved by investing in only a couple of HRM practices, instead of opting for the full set of complimentary practices across all HRM activities.

Our findings also showed a significant and positive relationship between RC and innovation performance. Thereby, this paper strengthens the existing evidence that innovation performance hinges on RC and that RC is a key facet of intellectual capital for boosting innovation (Buenechea-Elberdin et al., 2017; Cabrilo et al., 2018; Cabrilo & Dahms, 2020; Ritala et al., 2023). Going beyond current knowledge, while prior studies have considered associations between RC and innovation (see the above references) and HRM and innovation (e.g., Adla et al., 2020; De Saá-Pérez & Díaz-Díaz, 2010; Haneda & Ito, 2018; Jiang et al., 2012; Jiménez-Jiménez & Sanz-Valle, 2008; Lau & Ngo, 2004; Shipton et al., 2005, 2006; Zhou et al., 2013), this study brings new knowledge by examining how HRM impacts RC and demonstrating how RC mediates the relationship between HRM and innovation.

Finally, considering that a knowledge-based approach to HRM is a relatively understudied but emerging topic, this study moves beyond identifying the role of knowledge in HRM to understanding key HRM practices from a knowledge perspective and demonstrating their essential role in affording learning benefits and innovation performance for organizations. The present study, thereby, significantly contributes to building the novel knowledge-based approach to HRM and extends the arguments of López-Cabrales et al. (2011), Minbaeva et al. (2009), and Minbaeva (2013) by demonstrating the role of explicitly knowledge-based HRM practices on RC and innovation.

5.2 *Practical Implications*

From a practical perspective, our study highlights the paramount relevance of investing in employees' training and development to support RC and subsequent innovation, instead of mainly relying on talent acquisition (Youndt & Snell, 2004). As pointed out in the "Introduction" section, this is a very important message for Spanish managers, given the apparently low relevance awarded to human capital development in Spanish firms and the strong reliance on temporary work in Spain as opposed to other countries (IMD, 2023).

Related to the above implication, Christiansen (2000) found that the most innovative firms experienced very low turnover. Several reasons seem to support this; beyond the technical skills that employees leaving a company take with themselves, their accumulated knowledge of the company is even harder to replace. According to Christiansen, each person in the firm is an important part of the company's information and knowledge network and, if he or she leaves, a node in the network would be lost. Moreover, the person leaving the company takes his or her fluency in the company's common language: "A newly hired person may have the same technical skills, but he will not necessarily be able to communicate as easily with others in the company. [S]he will not know the company's experience. [S]he will not know the examples which work and which motivate people. [S]he will not know the values that underlie people's behavior" (Christiansen, 2000, p. 147).

One reason that may deter companies from investing in training and development may be related to past difficulties with ensuring transfer of learning back to the workplace (Torrington et al., 2014). Some useful guidelines for ensuring such a transfer can be inferred from a previous study by Nielsen (2009), who observed that collaborative activities upon their return to the workplace helped trainees transfer their course-based learning to the organization. Moreover, in a study by Longenecker and Ariss (2002), it was found that developing goals or plans for implementing new skills was very useful, as well as reviewing materials immediately after the training program, being actively involved in the learning itself, making a report to peers or superiors on what was learned, reviewing material and development plans with one's mentor or manager, and including development goals in performance reviews.

This stresses the relevance of knowledge-based performance appraisals, as has also been revealed by our study. According to Lublin (1994), few activities are more unpleasant for a manager than providing performance feedback to employees (Robbins et al., 2010). In the case of Spain, this difficulty may be increased due to the relatively collectivist nature of Spanish society compared to other Western European countries (The Hofstede Centre, 2018). According to Hofstede et al. (2010), in collectivist societies, personal relationships prevail over the task, and managers frequently feel very uncomfortable when they have to discuss performance appraisals openly with subordinates, as this could affect harmony in the workplace and may be felt by subordinates as an affront to their reputations (Hofstede et al., 2010; Sáenz et al., 2017). One solution to this would be to train managers to conduct constructive feedback sessions (Robbins et al., 2010). Specifically, the performance review should be designed more as a counselling activity than a judgement process. This can be accomplished by allowing the review to evolve out of the employee's self-evaluation (Robbins et al., 2010).

5.3 *Limitations and Future Research*

This paper provides evidence on the role of knowledge-based HRM practices as drivers of RC and innovation performance in organizations. However, the findings are subject to several limitations. First, the data in this study was collected from a cross-industrial sample of Spanish organizations. As there is evidence that HRM practices and mechanisms used for managing knowledge differ between national contexts (e.g., Fey et al., 2004; Hussinki et al., 2017; Magnier-Watanabe & Senoo, 2010), future studies could include a cross-cultural design to further explore generalizability of the linkages discovered in this research. Second, as the hypothesized linkages in this study were of a causal nature, ideally, the data used for testing them would have been longitudinal. However, in this paper, we had to utilize cross-sectional data. Given this, future research could adopt a longitudinal design, if possible. Third, data for this study was collected from only one managerial respondent per organization and thus may not represent the views of all organizational actors concerning the key study variables. Involving a wider group of respondents within an organization to discover a more general perception concerning its HRM practices, RC and innovation could be a viable route for future studies. Alternatively, utilizing data from other sources for RC and innovation performance may be advisable. Nevertheless, the Kock test carried out revealed that common method bias was not a likely concern in this study.

5.4 Conclusion

This study examined how knowledge-based HRM practices impact innovation performance through supporting RC as a key facet of intellectual capital. Our empirical findings demonstrate the relevance of knowledge-based HRM practices as predictors of innovation performance and the role of RC as a mediating factor between HRM and innovation. Overall, the results extend existing understanding of the interrelationships between HRM, intellectual capital, and innovation in organizations and thereby contribute to the knowledge-based view of the firm as well as to discussions on intellectual capital, strategic HRM, and innovation management.

References

Adla, L., Gallego-Roquelaure, V., & Calamel, L. (2020). Human resource management and innovation in SMEs. *Personnel Review, 49*(8), 1519–1535.

Alavi, M., & Leidner, D. E. (2001). Review: Knowledge management and knowledge management systems: Conceptual foundations and research issues. *MIS Quarterly, 25*(1), 107–136.

Andreeva, T., & Kianto, A. (2012). Does knowledge management really matter? Linking knowledge management practices, competitiveness and economic performance. *Journal of Knowledge Management, 16*(4), 617–636.

Andreeva, T., Vanhala, M., Sergeeva, A., Ritala, P., & Kianto, A. (2017). When the fit between HR practices backfires: Exploring the interaction effects between rewards for and appraisal of knowledge behaviours on innovation. *Human Resource Management Journal, 27*(2), 209–227.

Argote, L., & Miron-Spektor, E. (2011). Organizational learning: From experience to knowledge. *Organization Science, 22*(5), 1123–1137.

Barclay, D., Higgins, C., & Thompson, R. (1995). The partial least squares (PLS) approach to causal modeling: Personal computer adoption and use as an illustration. *Technology Studies, 2*(2), 285–309.

Bontis, N. (2004). National intellectual capital index: A United Nations initiative for the Arab region. *Journal of Intellectual Capital, 5*(1), 13–39.

Bowen, D. E., & Ostroff, C. (2004). Understanding HRM–firm performance linkages: The role of the 'strength' of the HRM system. *Academy of Management Review, 29*(2), 203–221.

Boxall, P., Ang, S. H., & Bartram, T. (2011). Analysing the 'black box' of HRM: Uncovering HR goals, mediators, and outcomes in a standardized service environment. *Journal of Management Studies, 48*(7), 1504–1532.

Budhwar, P. S., & Debrah, Y. (2001). Rethinking comparative and cross-national human resource management research. *The International Journal of Human Resource Management, 12*(3), 497–515.

Budhwar, P. S., & Khatri, N. (2001). HRM in context: Applicability of HRM models in India. *International Journal of Cross-Cultural Management, 1*(3), 333–356.

Buenechea-Elberdin, M., Sáenz, J., & Kianto, A. (2017). Exploring the role of human capital, renewal capital and entrepreneurial capital in innovation performance in high-tech and low-tech firms. *Knowledge Management Research and Practice, 15*(3), 369–379.

Cabello-Medina, C., López-Cabrales, A., & Valle-Cabrera. (2011). Leveraging the innovative performance of human capital through HRM and social capital in Spanish firms. *The International Journal of Human Resource Management, 22*(4), 807–828.

Cabrilo, S., & Dahms, S. (2020). The role of multidimensional intellectual capital and organizational learning practices in innovation performance. *European Management Review, 17*, 835–855.

Cabrilo, S., Kianto, A., & Milic, B. (2018). The effect of IC components on innovation performance in Serbian companies. *VINE Journal of Information and Knowledge Management Systems, 48*(3), 448–466.

Cesaroni, F. M., Del Baldo, M., Demartini, P., & Paoloni, P. (2015). Entrepreneurial, renewal and trust capital of Italian firms: Insights from an empirical study. *International Journal of Management, Knowledge and Learning, 4*(1), 69–89.

Chan, C. C. A., & Scott-Ladd, B. (2004). Organizational learning: Some considerations for human resource practitioners. *Asia Pacific Journal of Human Resources, 42*(3), 336–347.

Chen, C. J., & Huang, J. W. (2009). Strategic human resource practices and innovation performance: The mediating role of knowledge management capacity. *Journal of Business Research, 62*(1), 104–114.

Chen, J., & Li, W. (2015). The relationship between flexible human resource management and enterprise innovation performance: A study from organizational learning capability perspective. In *16th International Conference on Informatics and Semiotics in Organisations (ICISO), March, Toulouse, France* (pp. 204–213).

Chowhan, J. (2016). Unpacking the black box: Understanding the relationship between strategy, HRM practices, innovation and organizational performance. *Human Resource Management Journal, 26*(2), 112–133.

Christiansen, J. A. (2000). *Building the innovative organization: Management systems that encourage innovation*. Macmillan Press Ltd..

Collins, C. J., & Smith, K. G. (2006). Knowledge exchange and combination: The role of human resource practices in the performance of high-technology firms. *Academy of Management Journal, 49*(3), 544–560.

De Saá-Pérez, P., & Díaz-Díaz, N. L. (2010). Human resource management and innovation in Canary Islands: An ultra-peripheral region of the European Union. *The International Journal of Human Resource Management, 21*(10), 1649–1666.

De Winne, S., & Sels, L. (2010). Interrelationships between human capital, HRM and innovation in Belgian start-ups aiming at an innovation strategy. *The International Journal of Human Resource Management, 21*(11), 1863–1883.

Del Baldo, M., Cesaroni, F. M., Demartini, P., & Paoloni, P. (2015). Entrepreneurial and renewal capital of Finnish and Italian firms: Insights from an empirical study. In *Managing Intellectual Capital and Innovation for Sustainable and Inclusive Society: Managing Intellectual Capital and Innovation. Proceedings of the MakeLearn and TIIM Joint International Conference 2*. ToKnowPress.

Edvinsson, L. (2002). *Corporate longitude: What you need to know to navigate the knowledge economy*. Pearson Education.

Edvinsson, L., & Malone, M. S. (1997). *Intellectual capital: Realizing your company's true value by finding its hidden brainpower*. HarperCollins Publishers Inc..
Ennen, E., & Richter, A. (2010). The whole is more than the sum of its parts—or is it? A review of the empirical literature on complementarities in organizations. *Journal of Management, 36*(1), 207–233.
EUROSTAT, European Commission. (2023, September). *Involuntary temporary employment*. Retrieved from https://ec.europa.eu/eurostat/databrowser/view/tesem190/default/table?lang=en
Evangelista, P., Kianto, A., Hussinki, H., Vanhala, M., & Nisula, A. M. (2023). Knowledge-based human resource management, logistics capability, and organizational performance in small Finnish logistics service providers. *Logistics, 7*(12), 1–21.
Fey, C. F., Pavlovskaya, A., & Tang, J. (2004). Does one shoe fit everyone? A comparison of human resource management in China, Russia, and Finland. *Organization Dynamics, 33*(1), 79–97.
García-Morales, V. J., Llorens-Montes, F. J., & Verdú-Jover, A. J. (2006). Antecedents and consequences of organizational innovation and organizational learning in entrepreneurship. *Industrial Management and Data Systems, 106*(1), 21–42.
García-Morales, V. J., Llorens-Montes, F. J., & Verdú-Jover, A. J. (2007). Influence of personal mastery on organizational performance through organizational learning and innovation in large firms and SMEs. *Technovation, 27*(9), 547–568.
Gubbins, C. (2019). Knowledge and organizational learning and its management through HR practices: A critical perspective. In D. G. Collings, G. T. Wood, & L. T. Szamosi (Eds.), *Human resource management: A critical approach* (2nd ed., pp. 171–193). Routledge.
Gupta, K. (2022). Impact of knowledge-based HRM practices on organizational performance: Mediating effect of intellectual capital. *International Journal of Knowledge Management, 18*(1), 1–22.
Hair, J. F., Hult, G. T. M., Ringle, C. M., & Sarstedt, M. (2022). *A primer on partial least squares structural equation modeling (PLS-SEM)* (3rd ed.). Sage.
Hambrick, D. C., & Mason, P. A. (1984). Upper echelons: The organization as a reflection of its top managers. *Academy of Management Review, 9*(2), 193–206.
Haneda, S., & Ito, K. (2018). Organizational and human resource management and innovation: Which management practices are linked to product and/or process innovation? *Research Policy, 47*, 194–208.
Henseler, J. (2017). Bridging design and behavioral research with variance-based structural equation modeling. *Journal of Advertising, 46*(1), 178–192.
Hofstede, G., Hofstede, G. J., & Minkov, M. (2010). *Cultures and organizations: Software of the minds* (3rd ed.). McGraw-Hill.
Hooi, L. W., & Ngui, K. S. (2014). Enhancing organizational performance of Malaysian SMEs: The role of HRM and organizational learning capability. *International Journal of Manpower, 35*(7), 973–995.
Hughes, M., & Morgan, R. E. (2007). Deconstructing the relationship between entrepreneurial orientation and business performance at the embryonic stage of firm growth. *Industrial Marketing Management, 36*(5), 651–661.
Hussinki, H., Kianto, A., & Adibe, P. (2018). Best knowledge-based human resource management practices: Findings from Finnish firms. In *Proceedings of the 19th European Conference on Knowledge Management* (Vol. 2, pp. 342–350). Academic Conferences International Limited.
Hussinki, H., Kianto, A., Vanhala, M., & Ritala, P. (2017). Assessing the universality of knowledge management practices. *Journal of Knowledge Management, 21*(6), 1596–1621.
IMD World Competitiveness Centre. (2023). *IMD World Talent Ranking 2023*. IMD: Institute for Management Development.
Inkinen, H., Kianto, A., & Vanhala, M. (2015). Knowledge management practices and innovation performance in Finland. *Baltic Journal of Management, 10*(4), 432–455.
Inkinen, H., Kianto, A., Vanhala, M., & Ritala, P. (2017). Structure of intellectual capital–an international comparison. *Accounting, Auditing and Accountability Journal, 30*(5), 1160–1183.

Jérez-Gómez, P., Céspedes-Lorente, J., & Pérez-Valls, M. (2019). Do high-performance human resource practices work? The mediating role of organizational learning capability. *Journal of Management & Organization, 25*(2), 189–210.

Jérez-Gómez, P., Céspedes-Lorente, J. J., & Valle-Cabrera, R. (2005). Organizational learning and compensation strategies: Evidence from the Spanish chemical industry. *Human Resource Management, 44*(3), 279–299.

Jiang, J., Wang, S., & Zhao, S. (2012). Does HRM facilitate employee creativity and organizational innovation? A study of Chinese firms. *The International Journal of Human Resource Management, 23*(19), 4025–4047.

Jiang, Y., & Chen, C. C. (2018). Integrating knowledge activities for team innovation: Effects of transformational leadership. *Journal of Management, 44*(5), 1819–1847.

Jiménez-Jiménez, D., & Sanz-Valle, R. (2008). Could HRM support organizational innovation? *The International Journal of Human Resource Management, 19*(7), 1208–1221.

Kamhawi, E. M. (2012). Knowledge management fishbone: A standard framework of organizational enablers. *Journal of Knowledge Management, 16*(5), 808–828.

Kang, S. C., Snell, S., & Swart, J. (2012). Options-based HRM, intellectual capital, and exploratory and exploitative learning in law firms' practice groups. *Human Resource Management, 51*(4), 461–485.

Kianto, A. (2007). What do we really mean by the dynamic dimension of intellectual capital? *International Journal of Learning and Intellectual Capital, 4*(4), 342–356.

Kianto, A. (2008). Assessing organisational renewal capability. *International Journal of Innovation and Regional Development, 1*(2), 115–129.

Kianto, A., Hurmelinna-Laukkanen, P., & Ritala, P. (2010). Intellectual capital in service- and product-oriented companies. *Journal of Intellectual Capital, 11*(3), 305–325.

Kianto, A., Sáenz, J., & Aramburu, N. (2017). Knowledge-based human resource management practices, intellectual capital and innovation. *Journal of Business Research, 81*, 11–20.

Kim, D. H. (1993). The link between individual and organizational learning. *Sloan Management Review, 35*(1), 37–50.

Kock, N. (2015). Common method bias in PLS-SEM: A full collinearity assessment approach. *International Journal of e-Collaboration, 11*(4), 1–10.

Kock, N., & Hadaya, P. (2018). Minimum sample size estimation in PLS-SEM: The inverse square root and gamma-exponential methods. *Information Systems Journal, 28*(1), 227–261.

Lane, P. J., & Lubatkin, M. (1998). Relative absorptive capacity and interorganizational learning. *Strategic Management Journal, 19*(5), 461–477.

Lau, C. M., & Ngo, H. Y. (2004). The HR system, organizational culture and product innovation. *International Business Review, 13*(6), 685–703.

Lepak, D. P., & Snell, S. A. (2002). Examining the human resource architecture: The relationships among human capital, employment and human resource configuration. *Journal of Management, 28*(4), 517–543.

Longenecker, C., & Ariss, S. (2002). Creating competitive advantage through effective management education. *Personnel Review, 21*(9), 640–654.

López-Cabrales, A., Real, J. C., & Valle-Cabrera, R. (2011). Relationships between human resource management practices and organizational learning capability. *Personnel Review, 40*(3), 344–363.

Lublin, J. S. (1994, October 3). It's shape-up time for performance reviews. *The Wall Street Journal*, B1.

Lundvall, B. Å., & Nielsen, P. (2007). Knowledge management and innovation performance. *International Journal of Manpower, 28*(3-4), 207–223.

Magnier-Watanabe, R., & Senoo, D. (2010). Shaping knowledge management: Organization and national culture. *Journal of Knowledge Management, 14*(2), 214–227.

Malik, A., Froese, F. J., & Sharma, P. (2020). Role of HRM in knowledge integration: Towards a conceptual framework. *Journal of Business Research, 109*, 524–535.

Marchington, M., & Grugulis, I. (2000). 'Best practice' human resource management: Perfect opportunity or dangerous illusion? *The International Journal of Human Resource Management, 11*(6), 1104–1126.
Minbaeva, D. (2013). Strategic HRM in building micro-foundations of organizational knowledge-based performance. *Human Resource Management Review, 23*(4), 378–390.
Minbaeva, D., Foss, N. J., & Snell, S. (2009). Bringing the knowledge perspective into HRM. *Human Resource Management, 48*(4), 477–483.
Mumford, M. D. (2000). Managing creative people: Strategies and tactics for innovation. *Human Resource Management Review, 10*(3), 313–351.
Nielsen, K. (2009). A collaborative perspective on learning transfer. *Journal of Workplace Learning, 21*(1), 58–70.
Nonaka, I., & Takeuchi, H. (1995). *The knowledge-creating company*. Oxford University Press.
Park, H. J., Gardner, T. M., & Wright, P. M. (2004). HR practices or HR capabilities: Which matters? Insights from the Asia Pacific region. *Asia Pacific Journal of Human Resources, 42*(3), 260–273.
Pérez-López, S., Montes-Peón, J. M., & Vázquez-Ordás, C. J. (2006). Human resource management as a determining factor in organizational learning. *Management Learning, 37*(2), 215–239.
Podsakoff, N. P., Podsakoff, P. M., MacKenzie, S. B., & Lee, J. (2003). Common method biases in behavioral research: A critical review of the literature and recommended remedies. *Journal of Applied Psychology, 88*(5), 879–903.
Rigdon, E. E. (2012). Rethinking partial least squares path modeling: In praise of simple methods. *Long Range Planning, 45*(5-6), 341–358.
Rigdon, E. E. (2016). Choosing PLS path modeling as analytical method in European management research: A realist perspective. *European Management Journal, 34*(6), 598–605.
Ringle, C. M., Wende, S., & Becker, J.-M. (2015). *SmartPLS 3*. SmartPLS GmbH.
Ritala, P., Kianto, A., Vanhala, M., & Hussinki, H. (2023). To protect or not to protect? Renewal capital, knowledge protection and innovation performance. *Journal of Knowledge Management, 27*(11), 1–24.
Robbins, S. P., Judge, T. A., & Campbell, T. T. (2010). *Organizational behaviour*. Pearson Education.
Roos, J., Roos, G., Dragonetti, N. C., & Edvinsson, L. (1998). *Intellectual capital: Navigating in the new business landscape*. New York University Press.
Sáenz, J., Aramburu, N., Buenechea, M., Vanhala, M., & Ritala, P. (2017). How much does firm-specific intellectual capital vary? Cross-industry and cross-national comparison. *European Journal of International Management, 11*(2), 129–152.
Scarbrough, H. (2003). Knowledge management, HRM, and the innovation process. *International Journal of Manpower, 24*(5), 501–516.
Seeck, F., & Diehl, M. R. (2017). A literature review on HRM and innovation—taking stock and future directions. *The International Journal of Human Resource Management, 28*(6), 913–944.
Shaw, J., Gupta, N., Mitra, A., & Ledford, G. (2005). Success and survival of skill-based pay plans. *Journal of Management, 31*(1), 28–49.
Shipton, H., Fay, D., West, M., Patterson, M., & Birdi, K. (2005). Managing people to promote innovation. *Creativity and Innovation Management, 14*(2), 118–128.
Shipton, H., West, M. A., Dawson, J., Birdi, K., & Patterson, M. (2006). HRM as a predictor of innovation. *Human Resource Management Journal, 16*(1), 3–27.
Smith, K. G., Collins, C. J., & Clark, K. D. (2005). Existing knowledge, knowledge creation capability and the rate of new product introduction in high-technology firms. *Academy of Management Journal, 48*(2), 346–357.
Soo, C., Tian, A. W., Teo, S. T., & Cordery, J. (2017). Intellectual capital–enhancing HR, absorptive capacity, and innovation. *Human Resource Management, 56*(3), 431–454.
Subramaniam, M., & Youndt, M. A. (2005). The influence of intellectual capital on the types of innovative capabilities. *Academy of Management Journal, 48*(3), 450–463.

Sveiby, K. E. (1997). The intangible assets monitor. *Journal of Human Resource Costing and Accounting, 2*(1), 73–97.

Swart, J., & Kinnie, N. (2013). Managing multi-dimensional knowledge assets: HR configurations in professional service firms. *Human Resource Management Journal, 23*(2), 160–170.

Takeuchi, N., Wakabayashi, M., & Chen, Z. (2003). The strategic HRM configuration for competitive advantage: Evidence from Japanese firms in China and Taiwan. *Asia Pacific Journal of Management, 20*(4), 447–480.

The Hofstede Centre. (2018, February 27). Retrieved from https://www.hofstede-insights.com/product/compare-countries/

Tidd, J., Bessant, J., & Pavitt, K. (2005). *Managing innovation integrating technological, market and organizational change*. John Wiley and Sons Ltd..

Torrington, D., Hall, L., Taylor, S., & Atkinson, C. (2014). *Human resource management* (9th ed.). Pearson Education Ltd..

Tseng, C. Y., & Goo, Y. J. J. (2005). Intellectual capital and corporate value in an emerging economy: Empirical study of Taiwanese manufacturers. *R&D Management, 35*(2), 187–201.

Van Knippenberg, D. (2017). Team innovation. *Annual Review of Organizational Psychology and Organizational Behavior, 4*, 211–233.

Weerawardena, J. (2003). Exploring the role of market learning capability in competitive strategy. *European Journal of Marketing, 37*(3-4), 407–429.

Youndt, M. A., & Snell, S. A. (2004). Human resource configurations, intellectual capital, and organizational performance. *Journal of Managerial Issues, 16*(3), 337–360.

Zhou, J., Hong, Y., & Liu, J. (2013). Internal commitment or external collaboration? The impact of human resource management systems on firm innovation and performance. *Human Resource Management, 52*(2), 263–288.

Zlatković, M. (2020). Knowledge tacitness and renewal capital. *Dynamic Relationships Management Journal, 9*(1), 23–38.

The manufacturer's authorised representative in the EU is Springer Nature Customer Service Centre GmbH, Europaplatz 3, 69115 Heidelberg, Germany. If you have any concerns regarding our products, please contact ProductSafety@springernature.com

Printed and bound by CPI Group (UK) Ltd, Croydon, CR0 4YY
30/09/2026
02225570-0010